Continued on next page

THE BEACON
HANDBOOK

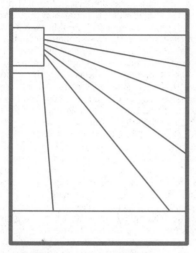

THE BEACON HANDBOOK SECOND EDITION

INSTRUCTOR'S EDITION

ROBERT PERRIN
Indiana State University

Houghton Mifflin Company   **Boston**
Dallas   Geneva, Illinois   Palo Alto   Princeton, New Jersey

Contents

Contents

vii

Contents

Contents

Contents

Mechanics 412

Contents

Preface

The primary goal of *The Beacon Handbook* is to offer students clear, succinct, accessible explanations of the basic issues of grammar, usage, punctuation, and mechanics within the larger context of writing to communicate meaning. Although this goal did not change between the first and second editions, the means used to achieve it changed substantially; revisions have been made at every level of the text — from the forms of expression to the format of information to the design of the pages.

Recognizing that although a handbook must be complete and accurate to be useful, it must be accessible to be used, *The Beacon Handbook* includes several features designed to enhance both content and accessibility.

Accessibility

Three Colors for Visual Emphasis. The three colors used in *The Beacon Handbook* add interest and appeal while drawing pedagogically useful distinctions among text elements.

- Precept numbering, heading within sections, and "Connections" and "Making Connections."

- Word-processing advice and exercises related to or available on computer.

- "Quick References," tables, notes on exceptions and special cases, example labels, and exercises.

"Quick Reference." A "Quick Reference," placed near the beginning of each chapter, abstracts and presents succinctly the most important information in that chapter. "Quick References" can be used to preview or review chapters as well as drawn on for quick answers to students' pressing questions.

Clear Explanations. Students are introduced to grammatical terms and principles through definitions and explanations couched in everyday language. Sample sentences, many accompanied by specific parenthetical explanations, illustrate discussions.

Tables and Other Graphic Displays. Numerous tables, charts, lists, and checklists, emphasized by the use of red, present information clearly and concisely. Checklists are especially useful for students working independently.

"Connections" and "Making Connections." "Connections" and "Making Connections" are designed to encourage students to think about and extend their roles as active writers by reminding them that the conventions of English are not a collection of tired rules employed by pedants but vital tools in the effort to communicate effectively and by encouraging them to consider how the text's concepts affect their writing or thinking about writing.

Thematic Exercises. Each exercise, whether in sentence or paragraph format, treats a single topic, allowing students to apply newly learned information and skills within a realistic, coherent context of written expression.

Word Processing. Because of their versatility and ease of use as a tool for learning and writing, computers have introduced new possibilities for exploration and control of writing by writers at every level of experience. *The Beacon Handbook* offers specific, practical information and advice for using a word processor to make writing easier. Word-processing advice, clearly marked with the symbol ▨ , is incorporated into the text where it is most directly helpful, either within text discussions or in separate sections. Some advice, particular to a specific problem, will benefit only a few students; other advice will be of use to all students with access to a word processor; but even students without word processors may find it useful to adapt to paper some of the techniques described for the screen. Exercises marked with the computer symbol are available in ASCII files.

Content

The Writing Process. *The Beacon Handbook* emphasizes the writing process — the discovery of meaning, expression, and form through planning, drafting, and revising — providing thorough grounding in writing the essay and the research paper, two formats typical in college writing.

Critical Thinking and Writing. Chapter 5, "Critical Thinking and Writing," leads students through some of the basic concepts underlying critical thinking and writing skills, emphasizing the importance to communication, whether spoken, read, or written, of logical sequences of ideas, clearly and correctly articulated assertions, and apt and adequate supporting evidence.

Professional Samples. Paragraph-length samples from respected writers such as Henry Thoreau, E. B. White, Martin Luther King, Jr., and Joan Didion provide students with interesting reading as well as effective, varied models.

Samples of Full-length Papers. *The Beacon Handbook* includes a full-length model of each of the three types of paper discussed in detail: the essay, the argument, and the research paper. "The Composing Process" follows Jacob, a student writing on film adaptations of novels, through his planning, drafting, and revising to his final paper. "Critical Thinking and Writing" contains Norman Ornstein's essay "You Get What You Pay For,"[1] annotated to show use of logical strategies. The research process and final paper of Michele, a student writer, illustrate "Research"; the paper, on intelligence testing, is annotated to show Michele's rhetorical, stylistic, and technical choices.

The Research Paper. *The Beacon Handbook* describes and illustrates the entire research process, beginning with the selection and evaluation of potential topics and sources and ending with

1. Norman Ornstein, "You Get What You Pay For," *Newsweek* 16 Jan. 1989: 10.

preparation of the final copy. Through the model of one student's research and paper, students see the relation among all stages and the bearing of each on the final paper. Coverage of proper documentation forms includes both the Modern Language Association of America[2] style and, in an appendix, American Psychological Association[3] style.

Instructional Supplements

The Beacon Workbook, by Cynthia L. Frazer, Old Dominion University. A collection of 180 supplemental exercises accompanied by an instructor's manual with answers to all exercises.

Instructor's Edition of _The Beacon Handbook._ The student edition of the text, with bound-in instructor's manual.

Instructor's Support Package. An assortment of more than 350 reproducible teaching items available as photocopy masters and in computerized form as ASCII files.

Transparency Package. Eighty-two two-color transparencies of charts, lists, and sample student writing from the text.

Correction Charts. A brief version of the handbook table of contents, with correction symbols and abbreviations, available as a unique self-standing chart and as a wall poster.

Diagnostic Tests. Three fourteen-page tests available as photocopying masters in the Instructor's Support Package or in computerized form for Apple II[®] and IBM[®] computers.

Beacon Exercises and Review. A grammar and review program of nearly three hundred exercises available in computerized form for IBM[®] and Macintosh[®] computers.

2. Joseph Gibaldi and Walter S. Achtert, *MLA Handbook for Writers of Research Papers,* 3rd ed. (New York: MLA, 1988).
3. *Publication Manual of the American Psychological Association,* 3rd ed. (Washington: APA, 1983).

Beacon Editing Exercises. Sixty-five thematic exercises available in computerized form as ASCII files.

Also of interest to those using computers is *Fine Lines* by William H. Koon and Peter L. Royston, a writing-process software program available for IBM® computers.

ACKNOWLEDGMENTS

The second edition of *The Beacon Handbook* has been thought about, planned, written, evaluated, rewritten, reevaluated, rewritten again, edited, and finally presented in its final form. My work during these stages has been made infinitely easier and more productive because of the excellent staff at Houghton Mifflin. No author could expect better help than I received. The staff at Houghton Mifflin also made it possible for me to receive important evaluation and advice from a number of teachers who reviewed the manuscript:

Brenda Ameter, Indiana State University
Ted Atkinson, Edinboro University of Pennsylvania
Linda Bannister, Loyola Marymount University, CA
Larry Beason, Eastern Washington University
Josephine Bloomfield, University of California, Davis
Judith L. Burken, Kellogg Community College, MI
Joan Bush, The University of Michigan-Dearborn
Patsy Callahan, Central Washington University, WA
Janet Carr, Northeastern University, MA
Janice U. Clayton, San Antonio College, TX
Catherine Cox, University of Florida
Tahita Fulkerson, Tarrant County Junior College, TX
Douglas R. Garrison, College of the Desert, CA
Clark Germann, Front Range Community College, CO
Peter Gingiss, University of Houston
César A. González-T, San Diego Mesa College, CA
Norma Cruz-Gonzales, San Antonio College, TX
Patricia H. Graves, Georgia State University

William H. Green, Chattahoochee Valley State College, AL
Huey S. Guagliardo, Louisiana State University
Gary M. Heba, Purdue University, IN
Peggy Jolly, University of Alabama
Howard Jones, Allan Hancock College, CA
Linda Julian, Furman University, SC
Frederica Kaven, Ithaca College, NY
Elizabeth Keating, San Diego City College, CA
Edward Klonoski, University of Hartford, CT
Leonard Lizak, California University of Pennsylvania, CA
Helen Lojek, Boise State University, ID
Irma Luna, San Antonio College, TX
Joanne H. McCarthy, Tacoma Community College, WA
Douglas J. McMillan, East Carolina University, NC
Alice C. McWaters, Rose State College, OK
Gary Myers, Mercyhurst College, PA
Gwen Neary, Santa Rosa Junior College, CA
Gretchen Niva, Western Kentucky University
Kim H. Noling, Hartwick College, NY
Katherine Parrish, Southeast Missouri State University
William Peirce, Prince George's Community College
Karen Propp, University of Lowell, MA
Marie Saunders, Central State University, Edmond,OK
Joel Super, University of Illinois at Urbana-Champaign
John W. Taylor, South Dakota State University
Sally Taylor, Brigham Young University
Susanna Tracy, Cerritos College, CA
Robert S. Utterback, Owens Technical College, OH
John O. White, California State University, Fullerton
Jane Yarbrough, University of Wisconsin Center-Mariette
James Zoller, Houghton College, NY

In addition I would like to acknowledge several people who offered help with specific sections of the book. Raymond Dolle, Indiana State University, provided useful suggestions for improving Appendix D, Business Writing. My students have also offered useful comments on the effectiveness of explanations and exercises. In particular, I would like to thank Michele Newton for allowing me to use her preliminary research work and her research paper as the basis for much of the discussion in the research unit.

As always, I wish to thank Judy, Chris, and Jenny for their patience, encouragement, and support.

R.P.

To the Student

The Beacon Handbook combines a brief introduction to writing with a complete yet compact reference to the conventions of standard English, the expected means for communication in college and the work place. Parts 1 and 7 cover the process of writing essays and research papers, respectively; parts 2, 3, 4, 5, and 6 describe and illustrate the conventions of English grammar, usage, punctuation, and mechanics.

Designed to be used efficiently, *The Beacon Handbook* organizes information in a consistent format. After reviewing *The Beacon Handbook's* organization and learning to use its features, you will see that you can easily find the information you need, even when you are not sure what information you are looking for. And after you have found what you are looking for, *The Beacon Handbook's* features also help you to understand clearly and apply effectively the principles of good writing.

Finding Information

Organization. The seven parts of *The Beacon Handbook* are divided into thirty-four chapters, each treating a specific aspect of composition or English grammar and usage. Each chapter is divided into precepts (rules to guide your work), coded with the chapter number and a letter of the alphabet; up to three levels of headings may subdivide precept sections. Look, for example, at Chapter 15, "Fragments": the first precept, coded 15a, reads "Revise fragments that are phrases." Two headings at the same level, "Fragments Lacking Subjects" and "Fragments Lacking Verbs," subdivide the discussion. For an example of subdivisions at more than one level, see precept 22d.

Note that precept numbers appear in the top outside corner of each page. These work like the guide words at the tops of dictionary pages; the precept number at the top of the left page indicates the first precept on that page, and the precept number at the top of the right page indicates the last precept on that page. See pages 208–209.

Guides to the Organization. The endpapers, the heavy pages used to join the book cover to the text pages, contain a brief outline of the book and a list of correction symbols similar to those your instructor will use to comment on your papers, with cross references to relevant text sections.

The table of contents provides a complete outline of the text. See pages v–xv.

Two indexes, one to word-processing information (see pages 673–75) and a general index (see pages 676–708), provide detailed, alphabetical listings of the text's contents.

"Quick References." "Quick References," located near the beginning of each chapter and set off by red boxes, list in a clear, brief, accessible format the most crucial information in the chapter. See pages 80 and 462.

Color Coding. Color coding in *The Beacon Handbook* distinguishes text features. Blue ■ highlights organizational features: precept numbering, headings within sections, "Connections," and "Making Connections" (see pages 80–81 and page 104). Green ■ marks computer applications and exercises (see pages 215 and 311). Red ■ emphasizes especially useful or important features: "Quick References," tables, checklists, special notes, example labels, and exercises (see pages 297–98, 305, and 309).

Appendixes and Glossaries. The appendixes and glossaries provide useful information in accessible locations and formats. Four appendixes are included: Appendix A, on preparing typed and handwritten manuscripts (see pages 595–99); Appendix B, on the basic features of the American Psychological Association documentary style (see pages 600–17); Appendix C, on writing essay examinations (see pages 618–23); and Appendix D, on the basic forms of business letters and resumes (see pages 624–34).

Two glossaries are included: the Glossary of Usage explains troublesome or often-confused words and provides examples of correct usage (see pages 635–52); and the Glossary of Grammatical Terms defines grammatical terms used in the book and provides an example of each (see pages 653–72).

Using Information

Examples, Tables, and Special Notes. Throughout the text, examples, tables, and special notes augment definitions and explanations. Use them to assure your understanding of and as convenient references to chapter concepts and information.

Examples, set off with extra space and distinguished by typeface and labels, illustrate the principle under discussion. Explanation of examples may follow in parentheses, when needed, to point out the pros and cons of specific choices. See pages 222 and 434 for samples.

Tables, charts, and lists, set off by boxes and emphasized using red, present crucial information succinctly in an easily located, readable format. See pages 147, 261, and 450–58.

Special notes, marked with the symbol **》》》   《《《** , describe exceptions to rules or offer hints for applying specific principles in your writing. See pages 302 and 357.

"Connections" and "Making Connections." Each part of the book and some chapters begin with a brief essay labeled "Connections." These essays explore the relation between that text section and writing, bringing into focus the interdependence between every choice of expression you make, no matter how mechanical it might seem, and achieving communication and meaning. See pages 349 and 356.

A section called "Making Connections" appears at the end of each chapter and provides activities and questions that will help you to think about how the chapter's concepts affect your writing or your thinking about writing, which will in turn help you to improve your writing. See page 79.

Computer Notes, Boxes, and Exercises. Advice for using a word processor to improve your writing appears in computer notes within discussions (see page 10) or separate computer boxes (see pages 43–44); both are marked with the symbol ▣ and the color green. Choose among the strategies suggested according to your needs as a writer or the nature of a particular project. Try all of the strategies; by playing with the computer you will find your own best strategies and style of working.

You will notice that some of the exercises in *The Beacon Handbook* are marked with the green disk symbol. This means that those exercises may be available on disk from your instructor or in your writing lab. If so, you can complete the exercises using your word-processing program, which will enable you to correct, revise, and rewrite freely, without retyping. If the disk version is not available or you do not have access to a word processor, you can, of course, still complete the computer exercises as you would any of the others, by recopying them.

Whether you are using *The Beacon Handbook* as a text, with chapters assigned by your instructor, or as a reference, using it as necessary when you are writing for any of your courses or for your own reasons, a preliminary review of its features and information will give you increasing control of your writing.

R.P.

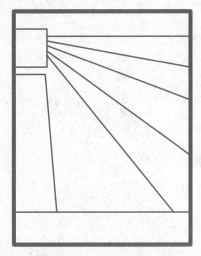

THE **BEACON**
HANDBOOK

THE COMPOSING PROCESS

C · O · N · N · E · C · T · I · O · N · S

Most writers move from idea to final paper by working through the stages of planning, drafting, and revising. Not all writers use the same sequence of stages, however, and not all writers use the same sequence for everything they write. Writers may become so intrigued by a sudden thought that they put aside any plan and wrestle their inspiration into polished form; alternatively, they may return to earlier stages of idea generation and research when a promising line of thought fails to support their main idea. Thus, writers alter the nature or order of stages to suit their methods of working and the requirements and discoveries of their writing projects.

As you learn how to think as a writer and how to transfer your thoughts effectively to paper, you, too, will find different techniques and combinations of techniques that work well for you. At each stage of the writing process, you will need to evaluate your work frequently, sometimes returning to earlier stages to modify it slightly or substantially or, in some cases, to completely change its focus. Almost all writers do this, no matter how long they have been writing; some writers especially value this aspect of the composing process as an opportunity to fully control what they say and how they say it. This book is intended to help you feel that way, too.

1 Planning

Before sitting down at a desk or computer to write, most writers make plans. Whether those plans are formulated in the mind or on paper, writers begin to focus on particular subjects and make choices about ways of exploring them. Writers typically vary their planning strategies with each project as they respond to its individual requirements and challenges. This chapter explores some common and consistently helpful planning strategies.

Quick Reference

Planning strategies encourage exploration and discovery. Use the following approaches to think about your subject:

> *Be open-minded about potential subjects.*

> *Do not select a specific topic until you have explored the general subject from a variety of perspectives.*

> *Develop topics that interest you. Your enthusiasm will come through in your writing and will engage your readers.*

> *After determining your topic, clearly state the main idea in a working thesis statement that expresses the appropriate tone and any necessary qualifications.*

| 1a | To begin, select a general subject. |

Because the most effective writing develops from a writer's inter-

Note: The exercises in Chapters 1, 2, and 3 will take you from idea to final paper. Keep the work from each exercise to use in later exercises.

est in or commitment to a subject, select a general subject that appeals to you as you begin to plan your paper.   **》》》** *Often in academic and professional writing, circumstances or other people will determine your subject. In these cases, start with the strategies described in section 1b.* **《《《**

When beginning to select a subject, do not limit your thinking. Instead, keep an open mind and consider various general subjects, such as the following, before selecting one.

Regular activities. Think of your routine activities: working, studying, listening to music, shopping, watching television, eating, exercising, reading. Any of these routines can yield interesting topics if thoughtfully explored.

General reading. Thoughts about, associations with, and responses to your general (non-course-related) reading in books, magazines, and newspapers can lead to interesting subjects.

Special interests. Do you see every foreign film that comes to local theaters or every television documentary on ecology? Can you write computer programs to track baseball statistics or compile a club newsletter? Such special interests make good subjects because the more you know about a subject, the more you will have to write about it.

People you know. The appearance, personality, behavior, and beliefs of the people you know can provide interesting subjects. Consider anyone you know — a newspaper vendor, your landlord, a professor — not just close friends and family.

Places you have visited. Have you been to Spain, Montreal, or the Grand Canyon? What about a relative's farm or business, your city's police station, or the weight room at the local gym? Both familiar and unfamiliar places, explored in detail and without preconceptions, make interesting subjects.

Unusual experiences. If you have had experiences that most others have not had, you have the beginning of a good subject. Exploring these experiences on paper may lead you to insights both you and others will appreciate.

Problems people face. Personal, social, economic, and political problems demand attention. Serious problems to which you have given or would like to give serious thought can be provocative subjects.

Changes in your life. Think about significant changes in your life: going to college, getting a job, adjusting to the aging or death of a parent. Exploring the feelings and thoughts you had during and after these changes may provide a rewarding subject.

Likes and dislikes. Consider things you find appealing or unappealing: the network news, mystery novels, reunions, jazz. Consider especially the underlying attitudes and values that your preferences reveal, and be willing to discuss them openly.

Strong opinions. What strong opinions do you hold on important matters like censorship, U.S. immigration policy, or nuclear disarmament? Consider writing about the opinion that usually starts the liveliest discussions with relatives or friends.

Social, political, and cultural events. Local, national, and international issues and events can be fascinating to write about, whether the topic is the politics of the Olympics, the collapse of a local bridge, or the latest Broadway musical hit. Consider especially events that you have followed closely.

Academic courses. The information, insights, and associations that you have absorbed in academic courses make productive subjects to explore in writing. Remember that not everyone learns the same things, even in the same courses.

EXERCISE 1.1 ❯ General subjects

For each of the twelve general subjects presented above, list at least two potential subjects for a paper, a total of twenty-four.

| 1b | ❯ | **Develop ideas through planning.** |

Most writers do not move directly from selecting a general subject to writing a paper or an article. Rather, they take time to explore a general subject, to select and develop a manageably narrow topic by focusing on one aspect of the subject, to consider their knowledge of and opinion about the topic, and to explore alternative ways to develop ideas related to the topic. This multifaceted approach to planning leads to better writing by encouraging writers to think, make choices, reconsider emphases, and arrange ideas.

Planning strategies provide opportunities to think about a subject and explore ideas. When you have the freedom to select first your own subject and then your narrowed topic, these strategies will help you to decide what to write about. When you work from an assigned general subject or narrow topic, these strategies will help you to discover ways to clarify and develop your ideas about it. Sometimes completing one activity will be enough; sometimes you will need to try several.

Planning Strategies

Freewriting	Looping
Journal writing	Clustering
Journalists' questions	Brainstorming

Freewriting

Freewriting means writing spontaneously for brief, sustained periods of ten or fifteen minutes. Freewriting can be *unfocused* if

Basics for composing on the word processor

Writers experienced in using word processors follow the steps below to avoid losing or misplacing their work.

Save your work frequently. Every fifteen to twenty minutes and whenever you leave your computer, however briefly, use the "save" command to ensure that your work will be stored in the computer's memory.

At the end of every writing session, print a paper copy, known as a *hard copy,* of your work. If the electronic version is lost, you will still have your work, and a hard copy will be useful when your reread and revise.

At the end of every writing session, make a backup disk copy of your work. Store your disks carefully to avoid damage from liquids, dust, heat, magnetism, and so on.

Provide distinctive, easily recognizable names for each file, clearly indicating the project and its stage of development. When you revise, copy and rename the file before working on it.

Arrange the stages of your projects into logical directories and subdirectories that can be easily located. Regularly print hard copies of your directories so that you can locate material at a glance even when you are not at your computer.

Identify your work by placing its directory and file name at the bottom of the last page. You will then easily be able to locate the electronic file corresponding to any hard copy.

Date drafts of your projects so that you can determine the most recent version.

you are searching for a subject, or it can be *focused* if you know the subject but are deciding how to approach it. Freewriting generally uses full, linked sentences, but because it does not require any other formal constraints, it gives you an opportunity to relax and write down ideas that might not otherwise occur to you.

To begin, think briefly about your subject and then start writing about it. (If you do not have a subject, simply begin writing down whatever comes to mind.) Write quickly. Do not worry about grammar or mechanics, neatness or form. Avoid any urge to revise your sentences or to worry about logical connections among ideas. Write down all your thoughts; write until you can think of nothing else to say.

Consider this freewriting sample, which helped Jacob, a student writer, to identify a general subject for a paper assigned in his English class:

Yesterday Todd and I went to The Video Station to get a tape. We headed straight to the "action/adventure" section and picked out something that would be fun to see — relaxing, not demanding. As we walked back to the counter to pay for the tape, I got sidetracked in the "classics" section. I looked at the display boxes: <u>Great Expectations</u>, The Grapes of Wrath, <u>To Kill a Mockingbird</u>, <u>Romeo and Juliet</u>, and lots of others. Todd came to get me. "Gimme a break, Jay," he said. "We don't want any of those." I agreed at the time, but that action/adventure film turned out to be a bust — repetitive, chaotic, unbelievable, <u>boring</u> — and I got to thinking about those classics — good films that have been around awhile. Lots were based on novels and plays that I'd read — some in lit. class, some on my own — and I'd seen quite a few of the films. Sometimes the book was best, but sometimes the film was. I mentioned to Todd that the next time we got a tape I wanted to get one of those. "Ah, Jay," he moaned, "that'd be like being in class on the weekend." I thought to myself that it might be, but that wasn't so bad. I want <u>real</u> entertainment when I punch the "play" button on the VCR — and <u>maybe</u> something more.

Notice that Jacob's word choices are sometimes colloquial and vague, his sentences sometimes informal, and his ideas only loosely linked. But his ideas are flowing, and he is getting them down on paper.

To avoid mulling over the right word or revising a sentence until it is perfect — tendencies that interfere with the quickness and spontaneity that freewriting requires — turn off your computer screen or dim it so that words cannot be read. Then simply type, free from the urge to pause or tinker. You will be surprised by how much writing you will do, and you can revise or correct the text later if you wish.

Journal Writing

Keeping a journal means recording your thoughts and observations regularly, for your own use, usually in a notebook kept for the purpose. Like freewriting, journal writing gives writers a chance to record ideas for later evaluation; journal writing, however, more often focuses on and systematically develops a specific topic or event. Reflective by definition, journal writing offers you the chance to explore privately and in detail thoughts and feelings about people, actions, events, ideas — in short, anyone or anything of interest or concern. Writers who regularly keep a journal find that it leads to ideas, insights, and further observations that they would not otherwise have had.

To make the best use of this strategy, try to write in your journal every day. You might try carrying your notebook with you, writing briefly or at length whenever a thought occurs to you or an event or comment interests you. Or you might try writing in your journal by appointment, choosing a convenient time such as first thing in the morning or just before dinner. Whenever and wherever you write in your journal, give it a long trial, perhaps a month, of making regular entries. Journal writing may seem awkward at first, but it is likely to become easy and pleasurable as you find your own best method of working.

Jacob wrote systematically in his journal about one aspect of his freewriting:

> *Reading a novel or play and seeing a film adaptation do not produce similar responses in me — and they should not because the forms are different. Yet each experience can be rewarding. I can remember times when I was thrilled with a book and unimpressed by the film and vice versa. But why? I find some novels — especially long, complicated ones like <u>Great Expectations</u> — more enjoyable to read because I can move slowly through the story, reread sections to pick out details I might have missed, and concentrate on the details that place the story in its context. A film adaptation, even a very long one, must move quickly to include even the most basic elements of the plot, and except on video, viewers cannot go back to "spot check" a missed detail. Yet I must admit that films can do some things that novels can't. For example, I can't imagine (as Dickens' first readers could) what London streets looked like in Pip's day, but the film can <u>show</u> me. The challenge of adapting a novel for film must be enormous, and for the viewer, understanding and appreciating both forms is a big challenge as well.*

Jacob's journal entry, though not fully focused or developed, draws connections more clearly than did his freewriting as he explores the facets of film adaptation that interest him most.

Journalists' Questions

For decades, journalists have used a reliable set of questions — *who, what, when, where, how,* and *why* — to explore their subjects and to uncover the specific, detailed information that their readers want to know. By using these questions as prompts and refining them to suit your needs, you can pinpoint various aspects of your subject, finding pertinent and interesting connections and information that you didn't know you knew.

Jacob specifically modified the journalists' questions to extend his exploration of his subject, producing these notes:

Literary Works and Film Adaptations

Who sees films and reads novels? Lots of people: students, certainly, but others, too; Todd; my parents; people who read the book first and see the film second; people who see the film and then read the book.

What kinds of works are effectively adapted? Both classic and popular works: novels and plays; Romeo and Juliet, To Kill a Mockingbird, Sophie's Choice, A Streetcar Named Desire, Amadeus.

When do people become aware of adaptations? People see films of famous works during school; later in life, too, when they go out to a theater or watch TV.

Where do people see film adaptations? At school, at movie theaters, and at home on the TV, especially on cable channels, and on VCRs.

How are books modified? Plots are shortened, simplified; characterization is altered; themes are modified; visual images are emphasized; settings are changed.

Why are the changes necessary? Production costs; need for clear narrative pattern; time restrictions; mass distribution; visual nature of film; producer or director's interpretation.

Some of Jacob's questions yield more ideas than others. *What, how,* and *why* provided particularly specific and useful responses. The questions most useful for a given subject will vary, though any might provide useful details or lead to an interesting, focused topic.

Looping

Looping helps you to move from a general subject to a narrow topic through a series of progressively more specific freewritings.

To loop, begin with a general subject and freewrite for five to ten minutes. Then circle one element or detail and freewrite again, focusing on it. Repeat the process as often as necessary until you decide on a specific, restricted topic within your original, general subject.

Jacob's looping produced this series of brief paragraphs:

Freewriting

The nature of a literary work often changes in a film adaptation. Sometimes plots get simplified or secondary plots get dropped altogether. Sometimes directors alter characterizations to produce roles to suit specific actors or to make the characters more acceptable to a general audience. Sometimes even the locale or time period is changed, creating a different context.

Loop 1

Characterizations often change in film adaptations. Directors and actors may "soften" a pivotal negative character to make him or her more appealing to a mass audience. Sometimes a character that was well rounded (having both positive and negative qualities) in a novel or play becomes wholly positive. Sometimes secondary characters may disappear completely.

Loop 2

In film adaptations done in the 1940s and 1950s, negative characters tended to be "cleaned up." For instance, in the film version of the play A Streetcar Named Desire, Stanley is loud and verbally abusive but not as physically violent as he is in the original version. His behavior is so repugnant in the play that Stella leaves at the end; in the film version produced for American distribution, he is not so despicable, and Stella stays.

13

Notice the pattern in Jacob's looping: he writes first on a general subject, then on a specific topic, and finally on a specific example. Looping frequently, though not always, follows this sequence, allowing a writer to explore a subject and perhaps to select a topic and method of development.

The dimmed-screen approach described on page 10 works well with looping. Complete the first freewriting with the screen dimmed. Then turn the brightness up, read what you've typed, and select an aspect for further exploration. Turn the brightness down again and freewrite on your new topic. Repeat the process as often as is useful.

Clustering

Clustering, because it combines verbal with visual prompts, can lead to more flexible, nonlinear planning that emphasizes associations among rather than hierarchies of ideas. This free-form approach encourages some writers to pursue looser, more creative exploration of their subjects.

Begin a cluster with a circled key word or phrase in the center of a sheet of paper. Associating ideas freely, add lines radiating from the central idea leading to circled words or phrases that describe, define, or explain it. These ideas in turn will prompt further associations that branch from them. Continue adding ideas and connections as they occur to you. Evaluate your finished cluster. Use another color ink or pencil to trace the most interesting development and to cross out ones that did not work. Look for self-contained satellite clusters that move beyond the original idea. Consider whether portions of your cluster correspond to portions of the paper you are planning, thus indicating an organization. Finally, consider clustering around a new idea suggested by your first cluster.

Jacob, for example, began his clustering with the word *classics,* which he had used repeatedly in his other planning, and produced the cluster shown on page 15.

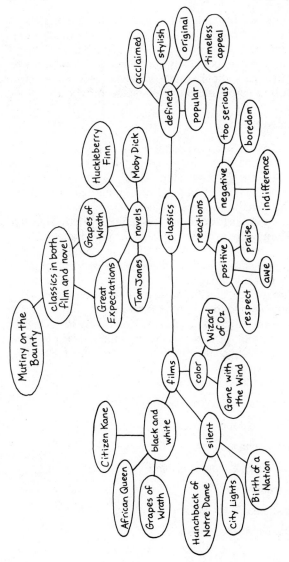

Analyzing his cluster, Jacob concluded that the branches "novels" and "films," by producing more specific and varied examples, illuminated *classics* and each other intriguingly.

Clustering may not always produce ideas that you will be able to use in a paper, but because of its flexible, nonlinear form, it can lead you to surprising discoveries and provocative associations.

Brainstorming

Use **brainstorming** to produce a list of everything you can think of that is related to your subject. A brainstorming list generally comprises freely associated ideas expressed in words and phrases. It may be developed by an individual writer or by a group working together on one project.

Begin a brainstorming list by thinking briefly about your subject. Then write without pausing, using single words or short phrases, until you run out of ideas. Brainstorming should be done rapidly and spontaneously, so do not pause to evaluate, analyze, or arrange your ideas.

Although lists are the most commonly used format for brainstorming, some writers prefer other, more graphic formats. They may organize their ideas into trees, showing ideas branching out of one another, or into clusters, in which ideas radiate from and circle around the main idea. Use any format that is comfortable for you and that encourages the lively generation of ideas.

Jacob's brainstorming produced this list:

Film Adaptations of Literature

classic and popular works

directors change plot

actors change characterization

larger audience

from mental to visual form

Romeo and Juliet

The Wizard of Oz

Frankenstein

Moby Dick

To Kill a Mockingbird

Sophie's Choice

viewers' reactions

subplots eliminated

settings changed

Todd

personal interpretation

public version

good film / weak book

good book / weak film

Jacob's long and varied list shows that he looked at his subject from many angles. The list reveals some connections among ideas but shows no formal arrangement.

To use a brainstorming list, arrange items in groups unified by a common idea or theme. Do not let your original list limit your thinking while grouping ideas. Drop items that do not fit your groups, repeat items in several groups if appropriate, and add new items whenever you think of them.

Grouping Ideas

Classify by topics.

Identify examples.

Arrange chronologically.

Compare or contrast.

Classify by Topics

Items from your list will generally suggest logical classes or categories into which to subdivide your subject. Group items from your list into the appropriate categories. Sometimes an item from your list will be a comprehensive category that in turn suggests additional items. At this point in planning, categories need not be logically related.

Items from Jacob's list suggested many categories, two of which are shown here:

Specific works

Romeo and Juliet

The Wizard of Oz

Frankenstein

To Kill a Mockingbird

Sophie's Choice

Kinds of changes

directors change plot

actors change characterization

mental to visual form

subplots eliminated

setting changed

Identify Examples

Specific examples make writing livelier than do abstract discussions. Use examples drawn from your brainstorming list to focus your topic, adding details as you think of them.

Jacob mentions several films in his brainstorming list. Discussing them could unify his ideas or stimulate new ones. Here is a sample:

Frankenstein

a classic work

directors changed plot

actors changed characterization

themes eliminated

seldom-read novel — quite good

often-seen film — entertaining but not good

Arrange Chronologically

Many subjects suggest a chronological, historical, or narrative pattern in which a series of events or the stages in a single event are recounted in sequence.

Jacob's subject, for example, could be developed chronologically:

1920s and 1930s

early reliance of filmmakers on literary sources and models

some successful adaptations of traditional narratives

emphasis on epic events

All Quiet on the Western Front

Gone with the Wind

1940s and 1950s

refinements in filmmaking led to more subtle adaptations

successful adaptations of psychological novels

emphasis on character, personal narratives

All the King's Men

Hamlet

On the Waterfront

1960s and 1970s

new techniques split traditional from innovative films

continued attempts

adaptations often remakes of classic films

themes, issues of central importance

Elmer Gantry

To Kill a Mockingbird

Dr. Zhivago

Compare or Contrast

Often, similarities or differences among items on your brainstorming list will suggest logical groupings. Comparing similar items or contrasting dissimilar ones may lead to an interesting perspective on, or to new items relevant to, your subject. Parallel lists, as in the following example, may be used to explore these relations. Revise your original entries, as necessary, to emphasize the points of comparison or contrast.

Books	**Adaptations**
complicated plots	*simplified plots*
many characters	*reduced number of characters*
unique themes	*mainstream themes*

mental images	*visual images*
(vary with reader)	*(specified by director)*
extended experience	*restricted experience*
(time)	*(time)*
reader's interpretation	*director's or producer's interpretation*

EXERCISE 1.2 ❱ *Planning strategies*

Using several of the general subjects you listed in Exercise 1.1, try each of the planning strategies: freewriting, journal writing, journalists' questions, looping, clustering, and brainstorming-grouping.

| 1c | ❭ | **Select a specific topic for your paper.** |

Having explored your general subject and discovered the aspects of it that interest you most, you should now work toward identifying a specific, narrowed topic.

To begin, review your planning materials. Then use these questions to decide on an effective topic:

Which topic seems most original? Look for interesting ideas, unusual connections, or unique observations.

Which topic interests you most? Notice recurrent ideas, repeated phrases, or often-used examples.

About which topic are you most informed? Notice your use of examples, specific details, facts, and names.

Which topic is the most useful? Look for problems to solve or contradictions to explore.

Which topic can you cover best in the space allowed for your paper? Consider a simple issue for a short paper but a complex issue for a long paper.

Finally, state your chosen topic in a sentence.

Reviewing his planning using the questions listed above, Jacob discovered several distinct patterns. Specific examples, appearing in different planning contexts, suggested that Jacob had extensive knowledge of and a keen interest in novels and their film adaptations. Jacob also saw that he had many ideas and opinions about the pros and cons of adaptation. On the basis of these discoveries, Jacob chose to contrast novels and their film adaptations, omitting references to plays. He would thus be able to use his experience, knowledge, and ideas to write a focused paper.

EXERCISE 1.3 ❯ *A specific topic*

Review your planning materials and select a specific topic. Then write a brief paragraph describing how you arrived at your selection. Describe your review of your planning materials; comment on how you selected ideas and rejected others; and end the paragraph by stating your topic in a sentence.

| 1d | **Identify your role, your readers, and your purpose.** |

As you narrow your topic and develop and arrange the ideas of the paper, consider in detail the context for your writing — your role, your readers, and your purpose.

Your Role as a Writer

Consider your perspective on your topic. If you are writing about horse racing, are you writing from your experience as a spectator or as a jockey? Do you own a racehorse or oppose horse racing? What knowledge of and attitude toward the sport does each of these positions involve? Defining your individual perspective on your topic — whether you are writing as an authority, an unbiased observer, or a probing nonspecialist — will help you to make choices of content and presentation.

Jacob enjoys both original literary works and their film versions and can write without bias on their relative merits. His familiarity with a number of novels and their screen adaptations allows him to choose appropriate examples and discuss them in detail. He can write open-mindedly and with a broad perspective.

Your Readers

Consider carefully the expectations, concerns, and knowledge of your audience. To do this, first identify your readers by answering these questions:

What are the probable age, educational level, and experience of your audience?

What information, concerns, and interests do your readers probably share?

What choices of tone and language will best communicate with your audience?

For example, twenty-year-olds and forty-year-olds have different experiences and concerns, so they are likely to know and be interested in different examples. Jacob might discuss Greta Garbo in *Anna Karenina* for an older audience and Meryl Streep in *Out of Africa* for a younger one. Similarly, appropriate tone and language can vary with audience; one audience might understand and enjoy reading current slang, while another might be confused by it. Differences in education and information require differences in the amount of detail offered in explanations. An informed audience may realize at once that *The Wizard of Oz* was a popular children's book by L. Frank Baum long before it was a movie starring Judy Garland; an uninformed audience might not.

 Dim the screen on your computer and freewrite for five minutes about your audience. Using specific details, describe your audience as completely as possible — age, education, opinions, activities, favorite television shows — as if you were writing quickly to a friend. When you have finished, turn the brightness up, read what you have written, and introduce italic or boldface codes to highlight the most revealing details about your readers.

Jacob decided that the audience for his paper — his teacher and college classmates — ranged in age from seventeen to forty-five, though most fell between seventeen and twenty-two. Seeing films based on books was a common experience for this group, but to avoid lengthy descriptions, he decided to concentrate on well-known films. Jacob thought the novels would be less familiar, however, and would require fairly detailed descriptions. Finally, concluding that he had a serious point to make on an academic topic, he decided that his readers would expect a serious tone and somewhat formal language.

Your Purpose

Your purpose for writing is never simply to fulfill a course requirement. Any time you write with careful attention to your thoughts, information, and audience, an organizing purpose will emerge.

Most writing has one of four general purposes: expressive, referential, persuasive, or argumentative. Writing for college courses may serve any of these purposes. In **expressive writing,** writers express their individuality by sharing experiences, opinions, perceptions, and feelings. Expressive papers explore the writer's perspective. **Literary writing,** not covered in this book, is a form of expressive writing in which writers share perceptions and insights using artistic forms such as the short story, poem, novel, or play. In **referential writing,** writers share information and ideas, often gathered through systematic research. A writer's focus in a referential paper is on the topic and often on specialists' views, which must be carefully documented. (For a discussion of documentation, see section 32g.) In **persuasive writing,** writers present information and opinions intended to alter readers' views or perceptions. A persuasive paper relies on evidence to convince readers to rethink the topic; some research (properly documented) may be required. Finally, in **argumentative writing,** writers present their opinions on arguable topics, topics on which there are many possible viewpoints, supporting their positions using ideas, information, experience, and insights. A writer's focus in an argumentative paper is on the issues.

Begin thinking about your specific purpose by deciding which general purposes suit your needs. In most writing, the general purposes overlap. Most persuasive writing is also expressive, and referential writing is often persuasive. As you develop a paper and make choices about structure, content, and style, you will discover how purposes blend naturally.

Jacob, for example, decided that his paper would be primarily referential because it would be based on a nonjudgmental assessment of the nature of film adaptations of novels and on facts such as copyright and film release dates. The paper would have an expressive element as well, for it would reveal his taste and perspective. Jacob was unsure whether he would develop a persuasive element in his paper.

EXERCISE 1.4 ❯ *Role, readers, and purpose*

Make a list that characterizes your role, readers, and purpose for the paper you have been planning. Consider how the results of this analysis will influence further planning and drafting.

Example

   Role: a lover of both books and film adaptations; someone familiar with many pairs of works.

   Readers: teacher and classmates; ages 17–45; most have seen film adaptations; some have read the corresponding original works; many may be unaware of what occurs in adaptation.

   Purpose: to write a referential paper but express my views.

| 1e | Write a working thesis statement. |

After narrowing your topic and characterizing your role, readers, and purpose, you should be able to formulate a **working thesis statement** — a brief statement of your topic and your opinion on it — to guide your draft. Later in the writing process you will want to refine your working thesis into a **final thesis** — generally a single sentence near the end of the introductory paragraph — that will guide readers in reading your paper.

   In finished paragraphs and even in papers, writers sometimes omit their thesis statements. The writer builds meaning implicitly through examples, details, or description, leaving it to the reader to formulate the meaning explicitly. Such works are said to have an **implied thesis.** This method generally works best for very personal descriptive or narrative papers. For most writing, a thesis statement helps both the writer and the reader understand the organization and follow the development of ideas. And even writers who, in their finished papers, rely on an implied thesis may have used a working thesis statement to help focus their thinking during planning, drafting, and revising. (See pages 84 – 85 for an example of a paragraph that has no thesis statement.)

   After a thoughtful review of your planning materials, moving from your topic to a working thesis statement should be a simple step. A review of your planning materials, concentrating on recurrent or especially fully developed ideas, may help you to pinpoint your opinion about your topic. From your analysis of your role, your readers, and your purpose, you know the general approach you want to take. Now consider how best to achieve that approach. Ask yourself what you want your readers to know or think about your topic and try to express the answer in a single sentence.

An effective thesis statement has three essential characteristics and may have three optional characteristics:

Essential

Identify a specific, narrow topic.

Present a clear opinion on, not merely facts about, the topic.

Establish a tone appropriate to the topic, purpose, and audience.

Optional

Qualify the topic as necessary, pointing out significant opposing opinions.

Clarify important points, indicating the organizational pattern.

Take account of readers' probable knowledge of the topic.

Carefully planned and written working thesis statements help writers to control their material by suggesting a focus for their thinking and a structure for their writing. In the final paper, a good thesis statement will prevent confusion by clarifying for readers the paper's central idea. Ineffective thesis statements like these do not help the writer or readers:

Attics are places to store belongings.   (This topic lacks an opinion; it merely states a fact.)

Cats make weird pets. (This narrowed topic contains an opinion, but it is imprecise, is stated too informally, and fails to qualify its criticism for readers who like cats.)

Liquor advertisements glamorize the drinking that leads to thousands of highway deaths each year. (The topic and opinion are clear, but this thesis statement ignores the variables in a controversial issue.)

First drafts of thesis statements are often as vague and incomplete as these. Careful writers, however, revise weak thesis statements by using the guidelines listed on page 27 and, often, by doing some additional planning. The weak thesis statements shown above were rewritten to produce these improved versions:

Attics are great places to store useless belongings. (The inclusion of *great* and *useless* defines the writer's opinion and establishes a humorous tone.)

Cats make unusually independent pets. (*Independent* is more precise and therefore clearer than *weird*. The change in wording creates the formal tone appropriate to a college paper.)

Although some advertisements now include warnings not to drink and drive, most continue to glamorize the drinking that leads to thousands of highway deaths each year. (This thesis statement still expresses a strongly held opinion, but the introductory qualification and the inclusion of *most* help make it more judicious than the original version.)

Here are Jacob's attempts to write an effective thesis statement:

First attempt
Film adaptations vary considerably from the original novels they are based on.

(The topic is vague, and the sentence presents a fact, not an opinion.)

Second attempt
Film adaptations distort the original novels they are based on but create workable equivalents to the originals.

(The topic is clearer and an opinion is stated, but the thesis statement is still imprecise and ineffectively worded.)

Third attempt

Although film adaptations of novels may seem to distort original works, the adaptations often create worthy counterparts to the origi-nals.

(The topic is more explicit, and placing the qualification first creates emphasis at the end.)

When writing working thesis statements, use to your advantage the computer's capability to copy easily. Type a first attempt at a thesis statement. Then copy it several spaces below (use the "block" and "copy" commands). Leaving the original version in place, analyze and revise the copy. Copy the second version and revise it to produce the third, and so on. Keeping all versions will allow you to reexamine your choices of wording and tone without substantial retyping or a clutter of markings. You may want to return to earlier versions to reclaim discarded phrases or words.

EXERCISE 1.5 ❯ Thesis statements

Briefly evaluate each of the following thesis statements. Note the strengths and weaknesses of each. Revise any ineffective thesis statements by narrowing and focusing the topic, changing the tone, or adding an opinion or any necessary qualifications.

1. Some critics maintain that the *Iliad* and the *Odyssey* are the founda-tion works on which all subsequent literature in the Western tradi-tion are based.

2. The 1988 Winter Olympics were held in Calgary.

3. Contrary to commonly held opinion, anti-Communist hysteria in the United States predated the rabid speeches and accusations made by Senator Joseph R. McCarthy in the early 1950s.

4. Even though a lot of people will disagree, I think that prayer is okay in public schools.

5. By encouraging managers in some U.S. corporations to play with a matchbox, some string, and a candle, cognitive psychologists are passing on important lessons in creative problem solving.

6. The United States government should retaliate quickly against terrorism.

7. Achieving competency in a foreign language is among the highest rewards of education.

8. Women should not always be awarded custody of children in divorce settlements.

EXERCISE 1.6 ❯ *Thesis statements*

Write a thesis statement about your topic. Revise it as often as necessary to achieve a clear statement of the topic, your opinion on it, and any necessary qualifications. Consider carefully your role, your readers, and your purpose, and establish an appropriate tone.

Planning on the word processor

After you have tried a number of the planning strategies in this chapter, start a file in which you record the guiding questions or categories of those that work best for you. For example, record the following:

the list of ways to think of topics (pages 5–6)

the questions used to narrow topics (pages 21–22)

the categories for classifying information (pages 17–21)

the questions journalists use to anticipate their readers' questions (pages 11–12)

the key concepts and questions useful for analyzing your role, audience, and purpose (pages 22–25)

the categories for evaluating your thesis (pages 26–29)

Include any additional comments, questions, or strategies that you have developed on your own. Separate each strategy with a page break and mark it with a key word as a heading so that you can use the "search" function to find quickly the material you need.

When planning a piece of writing, call up your file of planning strategies into a window or second screen and use its contents as prompts for varying your approach to your topic. Or "block" and "copy" a specific set of planning prompts to a separate file devoted to your topic and expand them with relevant notes — examples, facts, questions, possible sources, and so on.

As you continue to write, you will develop new strategies and modify old ones. Update your planning file from time to time to take advantage of your increasing experience.

MAKING   C O N N E C T I O N S

Individual writers approach writing in individual ways. They find that some approaches work better than others or suit different projects. After completing the exercises in this chapter, consider the questions that follow. They may help you to understand why some approaches worked for you and some did not. You might want to discuss your answers with a classmate to get another writer's perspective.

- How did you select subjects for writing? How did you find the subject you liked best and took farthest, to the point of composing a thesis statement about it? How did you find the subject you liked least and did least with?

- Describe the planning strategies that you used for two or three of the subjects you explored most fully. Which strategies generated the most ideas? Which strategies produced the idea or group of ideas that led you to your topic? What strategies did not produce any useful ideas or even any ideas at all? Use your favorite planning strategy to explore briefly why the best strategy was best and why the worst was worst.

- What steps did you use in selecting your specific topic? Describe the advantages of choosing your own topic and the advantages of working on assigned topics. What are the disadvantages of each?

- Which was the easiest to categorize: your role, your readers, or your purpose? Why? Which was most difficult to categorize? Why?

- How did you compose your thesis statement? Did you ask yourself questions, review your planning, reconsider your purpose and audience, or choose another method? How did you revise your thesis statement? What additional planning did you need to do?

2 | Drafting

Even during early stages of planning, most writers begin to think about ways to express their ideas. They think about structural patterns for the entire paper, but also about paragraph patterns, sentences, phrases, or even word choices. No matter what form or how long their planning takes, writers must at some point stop planning and sit down at a desk or keyboard to begin work on a rough draft.

Quick Reference

Drafting is an opportunity for you to experiment with ways to express your ideas, knowing that you can revise the work later. As you draft your paper, keep these principles in mind:

> ❯ *Use the broad organizational pattern that emerges most naturally from your planning.*

> ❯ *Use outlining to help you achieve a logical structure for your ideas, but do not let the outline dictate your draft. Revise the outline when necessary.*

> ❯ *Use drafting to get ideas on paper in a reasonably coherent form without pausing too much over the exact expression or striving for technical correctness.*

> ❯ *Experiment with various techniques for introducing a paper that interests readers and concluding a paper that satisfies them.*

Writing a rough draft is a rehearsal, an opportunity to explore possibilities for the arrangement and expression of ideas. In the drafting stage, writers organize ideas from their planning materials and explore ways to express them in sentences, paragraphs, and ultimately a complete, though not yet final, paper. Drafting a paper is rarely a neat and easy matter of writing up available notes, however. Writers must be flexible and open to new ideas that occur as they write, filling gaps and making new connections. Drafting begins the process of transferring ideas into sentences.

2a	**Organize your materials and continue to seek new ideas.**

Examine the materials you wrote during planning. Look for emerging patterns among ideas and for ideas that seem especially important or that illustrate your thesis especially well. Your planning materials generally will suggest a natural pattern for organizing your paper. Some common organizational arrangements are **chronological, spatial,** and **topical.**

Chronological Arrangement

Chronological arrangement presents information in sequence, explaining what happened first, second, third, and so on. Personal narratives, such as a description of your first day at a new job, and narratives of events, such as a political debate, make good use of a chronological arrangement.

Spatial Arrangement

Spatial arrangement recreates the physical features of a subject. For instance, a writer might describe a town by "leading" readers from a residential area in the north to a commercial or industrial area in the south. Spatial arrangement has limited application; but when physical features are important, it can convey insights more effectively than any other arrangement.

Topical Arrangement

Topical arrangement, a pattern often used in writing arguments, organizes supporting ideas to present the thesis with the greatest possible emphasis. Topical arrangement can follow a number of patterns according to your purpose — from most important point to least important, for instance, or from simplest to most complex. Sometimes a mixed pattern works best. For example, present your second most important point first, interesting readers with strong material, and then sandwich in lesser points to fill out the discussion; use your most important point last, thus closing with especially convincing evidence.

Other Methods of Arrangement

The organizational patterns used to arrange the ideas in paragraphs can also be used to organize full-length papers. Your planning materials, for example, may suggest one of these common patterns: analogy, cause and effect, process, classification, and definition. Jacob's planning materials reveal an emerging comparison and contrast pattern. The principles discussed in Chapter 4, "Paragraphs," can be expanded so that you use full paragraphs to develop each of your ideas within the overall organizational pattern.

EXERCISE 2.1 ❯ *Organizing materials*

Review your thesis and planning materials from Chapter 1 and experiment with each of the organizational patterns described above. (For more information on alternate patterns, see section 4d.) Choose one pattern and then organize your planning materials according to the arrangement suggested by the pattern.

2b ⟩ **Outline your paper.**

Having selected a pattern of arrangement, prepare an **outline,** a
structural plan using headings and subdivisions to clarify the main
features of your paper and the interrelationships among them.
Some writers create loosely structured, informal outlines; other
writers prefer to create highly systematic, formal outlines. Many
writers use both kinds, benefiting at different stages of their writing from the simplicity and freedom of informal outlines and the
clarity and completeness of formal outlines. In the earliest stages
of drafting — when writers are deciding what should come first,
second, third, and so on — informal outlines seem to work best.
At later stages, writers often use formal outlining to analyze their
work for consistency, completeness, and logic. Experiment to discover when and what form of outlining works best for
you. **》》》** *When classroom work or other specialized writing requires
you to produce a formal outline, follow the procedures discussed on
pages 38–39.* **《《《** Remember, informal and formal outlines are
plans, not descriptions of what you must do. Sometimes plans do
not work because they are flawed or incomplete. If your plan is
not working, do not frustrate yourself by trying to make it work.
Instead, decide why it does not work and make appropriate
changes.

Informal Outlines

Informal outlines, intended for the *writer's* use only, may be
simple lists marked with numbers, arrows, dots, dashes, or any
other convenient symbol to indicate relative importance among
ideas. Because they are not systematically composed, arranged,
and labeled, informal outlines can be completed more easily and
quickly than formal outlines. And because they seem less final,
writers feel freer to modify them.

Below is Jacob's brief, informal outline.

Plots

⟶ *Novels: complicated situations*

⟶ *Films: simplified situations*

Characterization

⟶ *Novels: variety of relationships*

⟶ *Films: smaller number of relationships*

Theme

⟶ *Novels: multiple themes*

⟶ *Films: primary theme*

Because they make it possible to move items easily without retyping, word-processing programs are ideal tools for informal outlining. Prepare and then print a first version of your informal outline. Evaluate the outline, marking the printed copy with changes. Use the "block" and "move" functions on your computer to execute the changes, and then print a clean version of the outline. A clean printed version of your informal outline is easier to work from than one with scribbled changes.

EXERCISE 2.2 ❯ Informal outlining

Compose an informal outline that arranges the large elements from your planning materials. Add missing details and examples as you continue to draft your paper.

Formal Outlines

When an outline is intended for *readers,* **formal outlines** are
used because they adhere to a commonly accepted and understood system. Writers often develop an informal outline and then,
as ideas and explanations take shape, a formal outline.

Note the following conventions of formal outlines:

Indicate *major topics* with upper-case roman numerals (*I, II,
III*). Each of these entries represents one or more whole paragraphs.

Indicate *subdivisions* of topics with upper-case letters (*A, B, C*).
Each of these generally represents a cluster of sentences within
a paragraph.

Indicate *clarifications* of subdivisions (examples, supporting
facts, and so on) with arabic numbers (*1, 2, 3*). Each of these
generally represents a sentence.

Indicate *details* in sentences with lower-case letters (*a, b, c*).

In addition, the following conventions are also observed:

Use parallel forms throughout. Use phrases and words in a
topic outline and full sentences in a **sentence outline.** An
outline may use topic sentences for major topics and phrases in
subdivisions of topics (a **mixed outline**) but should do so consistently.

Include only one idea in each entry. Subdivide entries that contain more than one idea.

Include at least two entries at each sublevel.

Indicate the inclusion of introductions and conclusions, but do
not outline their content.

Align headings of the same level at the same margin.

Many word-processing programs offer easy-to-use outlining features. These generally position automatically the roman numeral, capital letter, and other division indicators and correctly align the text that you supply for each level. If your word processor has these features, learn to use them. They will save you time and effort.

The formal outline below organizes Jacob's materials. It is a mixed outline, using sentences at the roman numeral, or paragraph, level and phrases for the topics within paragraphs.

INTRODUCTION

Thesis statement: Although film adaptations of novels may seem to distort original works, the adaptations often create worthy counterparts to the originals.

   I. Although plots are simplified for films, films retain the primary focus of the original work.

      A. Huckleberry Finn (Mark Twain): 1885

         1. Forty-three chapters, over three hundred pages

         2. Hundreds of episodes included

      B. Huckleberry Finn (Joseph Mankiewicz film, with Mickey Rooney): 1939

         1. Eighty-eight minutes

         2. Focuses on five primary episodes

  II. Films selectively develop characters, necessarily omitting some details from the novels.

      A. Out of Africa and Shadows on the Grass (Isak Dinesen): 1938 and 1960, respectively

        1. Character of first-person narrator introduced through description of life around her

        2. Character developed through cumulative effect of many episodes

   B. Out of Africa (Sidney Pollack film, with Meryl Streep): 1986

        1. Character revealed through narrative voice-overs

        2. Exploration limited to five selected episodes

III. Because of their nature, films often highlight a crucial theme rather than including the multiple themes found in novels.

   A. The Grapes of Wrath (John Steinbeck): 1939

        1. Thirty chapters, over six hundred pages

        2. Interwoven fiction and essays on social problems

        3. Multiple themes

   B. The Grapes of Wrath (Darryl Zanuck film, with Henry Fonda): 1940

        1. 129 minutes

        2. Three-part narrative

        3. Three major themes retained

CONCLUSION

Use the computer to revise your informal outline into a formal outline. Insert roman numerals and upper-case letters to mark major divisions and then move elements to align them correctly. Insert arabic numerals and lower-case letters, plus additional clarifying materials, to show the degree of detail that your paper will include. Use the word processor's abilities to insert and reformat without retyping existing materials.

EXERCISE 2.3 **❯**   *Formal outlining*

Using your informal outline from Exercise 2.2 as a starting point, complete a formal outline, providing necessary elaboration. Create either a mixed outline or a sentence outline, labeling it appropriately. Double-check your work against the guidelines for outlining given on page 38.

| 2c | ❯ | **Write a rough draft of your paper.** |

The **rough draft** is the first full-length, written form of a paper. It is usually very messy and unfocused. Some parts develop clearly and smoothly from your planning materials, but others develop only after three or four tries. That pattern is typical because writing a rough draft is a shifting process that requires thinking, planning, writing, rethinking, rewriting, replanning, and rewriting again.

Every rough draft has different requirements, varying from paper to paper even for the same writer. Most writers begin their rough drafts by working on the body paragraphs, postponing work on opening and closing paragraphs. They do, however, write with their thesis statements clearly in mind. These additional general strategies are helpful for most writers:

Gather all your materials together. Your work can proceed with relatively few interruptions if all your planning materials and writing supplies are nearby.

Work from your outline. Write one paragraph at a time, in any order, postponing work on troublesome sections until you have gained momentum.

Remember the purpose of your paper. As you write, concentrate on arranging and developing only the ideas presented in your outline or closely related ideas that occur to you.

Use only ideas and details that support your thesis statement. Resist any tendency to drift from your point or to provide interesting but extraneous details.

Remember your readers' needs. Include all information and explanations that readers will need to understand your discussion.

Do not worry about technical matters. Concentrate on getting your ideas down on paper. You can attend to punctuation, mechanics, spelling, and neatness later.

Rethink and modify troublesome sections. If your outline is not working, if an example seems weak or the order of the paragraphs no longer seems logical, change it.

Reread sections as you write. Rereading earlier sections as you write will help you to maintain a reasonably consistent tone.

Write alternative versions of troublesome sections. When you come to a problematic section, write multiple versions of it and then choose the one that works best.

Periodically give yourself a break from writing. Interrupting your writing too often creates problems with consistency of style or tone, but occasionally getting away from it will help you to maintain a fresh perspective and attain objectivity.

Drafting on the word processor

Composing at the computer can be fluid and productive. With the help of the "add," "delete," "move," and "reformat" features in your word-processing program, you will be able to generate a rough draft with relative ease, knowing that you can make both small and large changes without substantial retyping. Using a word processor now will enable you to do the following easily later:

Move words, phrases, sentences, and paragraphs.

Check spelling.

Check format and spacing.

Count the number of words.

Complete "search" and "replace" procedures to change words and phrases.

Begin by copying your outline to a new file, renaming it, and proceeding to compose and type sentences that explain and expand its divisions. Set the line spacing at double-space for good readability; later, when you are ready to print your draft, set the line spacing at triple-space to provide extra room for making changes during revision.

Draft freely, without worrying about missing details, exact wording, or technical correctness. Devise your own system of symbols or key words to mark places in the draft to which you would like to return. Keep your system simple and use it consistently so that it becomes part of your drafting technique and does not interfere with it. The following are helpful strategies:

Use symbols unlikely to appear in your writing (such as *, #, >, +, or ~) or double end punctuation marks. You might

Drafting on the word processor (cont.)

use + to mark places needing development or additional details, !! to mark places needing examples, or ?? to mark places at which you are unsure of your information or opinions.

Use brackets or boldface to include alternate word choices or versions of sentences or longer passages.

Use abbreviations or distinctive symbols in place of frequently used long phrases or difficult to spell words and names.

Symbols, abbreviations, and key words can be located using the "search" function. Make your changes and then delete the symbol and unwanted material, or use the "replace" feature to substitute the full form for any abbreviated form.

Until you have completed your final draft, use the "move" function to save material you are tempted to delete. Alternate versions, digressions, examples, and so on, can be moved to the end of the draft, where they will be available for review and possible retrieval. Insert a page break and a heading, such as "Scrap" or "Discard," and hold this material separate from your draft but convenient to it.

For many writers, the process of drafting creates a flood of ideas, not all of them relevant to the project at hand. If that is the case for you, use the capabilities of your word processor to capture these ideas before they escape you. Open a second file in a window or second screen or use your program's "notepad" feature to record ideas, images, questions, reminders, and so on for future use.

Remember to give your draft a clear, logical, recognizable file name; note the date at the beginning of the draft and the name at the end.

EXERCISE 2.4 ❯ *Rough draft*

Write a rough draft of your paper, using the guidelines given above. Work from your outline to ensure that your ideas are supported by adequate detail.

| 2d | ❯ | **Plan your title and introductory and concluding paragraphs.** |

The title and the beginning and ending paragraphs of a paper are important because first and final impressions are important. The best time to plan and write these special parts of a paper varies from one paper to the next. They can be developed, written, and rewritten at any time during your planning, drafting, or revising.

Titles

A good **title** is at once descriptive, letting readers know what the paper is about, and imaginative, sparking readers' interest. To achieve these ends, try one or more of these strategies:

Use words or phrases that explicitly identify your topic. Search your draft for expressions that are clear and brief.

Play with language. Consider variations of well-known expressions. Use **alliteration** (repetition of the initial sounds of words) or **assonance** (repetition of internal vowel sounds of words).

Consider two-part titles, the first part imaginative, the second part descriptive. Separate the two parts with a colon.

Match the tone of the title to the tone of the paper. Use serious titles for serious papers, ironic titles for ironic papers, factual titles for factual papers, and so on.

Keep an open mind as you write titles; write as many as you can and select the one that best clarifies your topic for your readers and piques their interest.

Jacob began his search for an effective title by describing his topic in a phrase: "Novels and their film adaptations." Although the phrase labeled his paper clearly, it would not create any special interest among readers. He tried playing with language and considered "A Moving Picture Can Be Worth a Thousand Words" (a variation of a well-known proverb) and "First There Was Fiction, Then There Was Film" (an experiment with alliteration and assonance). Jacob also tried combining his descriptive title with a phrase from his paper to create a two-part title: "From Page to Screen: Novels and Their Film Adaptations." He eventually chose his combined title.

Introductions

The **introduction** to a paper creates interest and clarifies your subject and your opinion for your readers. Depending on the length of the paper, an introduction may be one or several paragraphs long.

Writers generally prepare drafts of alternate introductions, keeping these general goals in mind:

Adjust the length of the introduction to the length of the writing. A brief paper needs a proportionately brief introduction.

Match the tone of the introduction to the tone of the paper. A casual, personal paper needs an informal introduction, whereas a serious, academic paper requires a formal introduction.

The introduction must draw readers into the discussion. It must create interest, suggest the direction the paper will take, and indicate the paper's development.

Although writers use many types of introduction, most openings begin with one or more of the following general strategies and end by presenting a specific thesis statement.

general strategy

specific thesis statement

Below are descriptions of ten of the most commonly used strategies for introductions, with examples.

Allusion

Refer to a work of art, music, literature, film, and so on, or to a mythical, religious, or historical person or event.

> Pity-and-terror, the classically prescribed emotional response to tragic representation, was narrowly restricted to drama by the ancient authorities. In my view, tragedy has a wider reference by far, and pity-and-terror is aroused in me by works of art immeasurably less grand than those which unfold the cosmic undoings of Oedipus and Agamemnon, Antigone, Medea, and the women of Troy. The standard Civil War memorial, for example, is artistically banal by almost any criterion, and yet I am subject to pity-and-terror whenever I reflect upon the dense ironies it embodies. — Arthur C. Danto, "Gettysburg"

Analogy

Make a comparison that is interesting, helpful, and relevant to the topic.

Were it announced tomorrow that anyone who fancied it might, without risk of reprisals or recriminations, stand at a fourth-storey window, dangle out of it a length of string with a meal (labelled "Free") on the end, wait till a chance passer-by took a bite and then, having entangled his cheek or gullet on a hook hidden in the food, haul him up to the fourth floor and there batter him to death with a knobkerry, I do not think there would be many takers. — Brigid Brophy, "The Rights of Animals"

Anecdote

Begin with a short description of a relevant incident.

One summer day in 1923 I was taken with two small cousins by trolley westward over the Queensborough Bridge. We were making an excursion to a matinee at Roxy's. To our left as we clanged across the great web of the bridge I had my first full view of Manhattan, the buildings in their dreamy altitudes piling up down the island around the tallest of all, the Woolworth tower. A heat haze enriched light and shadow on the distant masses. Here and there small plumes of vapor appeared. As the vista slowly shifted, I felt the wonder expected of me as a visiting twelve-year-old from the Midwest. The city already belonged to myth, standing like Asgard beyond the East River water, more of the sky than of the earth. I felt, even so, some formless question stirring at the edge of my mind as to what sense of life that skyline honored or expressed. There was as yet nothing like it in the world. — Robert Fitzgerald. "When the Cockroach Stood by the Mickle Wood"

Definition

Define a term central to your topic. Avoid defining terms already understood, unless such a definition serves a special purpose.

One of the most interesting and characteristic features of democracy is, of course, the difficulty of defining it. And this difficulty has been compounded in the United States, where we have been giving new meanings to almost everything. It is, therefore, especially easy for anyone to say that democracy in America has failed.

"Democracy," according to political scientists, usually describes a form of government by the people, either directly or through their elected representatives. But I prefer to describe a democratic society as one which is governed by a spirit of equality and dominated by the desire to equalize, to give everything to everybody. In the United States the characteristic wealth and skills and know-how and optimism of our country have dominated this quest. — Daniel J. Boorstin, "Technology and Democracy"

Description

Use a description of a scene, person, or event to establish context or mood for your topic.

A single knoll rises out of the plain in Oklahoma, north and west of the Wichita Range. For my people, the Kiowas, it is an old landmark; and they gave it the name Rainy Mountain. The hardest weather in the world is there. Winter brings blizzards, hot tornadic winds arise in the spring, and in summer the prairie is an anvil's edge. The grass turns brittle and brown, and it cracks beneath your feet. There are green belts along the rivers and creeks, linear groves of hickory and pecan, willow and witch hazel. At a distance in July or August the steaming foliage seems almost to writhe in fire. Great green and yellow grass-hoppers are everywhere in the tall grass, popping up like corn to sting the flesh, and tortoises crawl about on the red earth, going nowhere in the plenty of time. Loneliness is an aspect of the land. All things in the plain are isolate; there is no confusion of objects in the eye, but *one* hill or *one* tree or *one* man. To look upon that landscape in the early morning, with the sun at your back, is to lose the sense of proportion. Your imagination comes to life, and this, you think, is where Creation was begun. — N. Scott Momaday, "The Way to Rainy Mountain"

Facts and Figures

Begin with specific, interesting, useful information or statistics.

Molokai lies just twenty-six miles from Oahu across the Kaiwi Channel, but the two islands are worlds apart in terms of mood, style and pace. While Honolulu wrestles with traffic, pollution and all the other problems of urbanization, Molokai is relishing its peaceful, rural existence. It has no freeways, stoplights, movie theatres, bowling alleys, elevators, nightclubs, shopping centers, supermarket chains or fast-food outlets. None of its buildings stands more than three stories high. Newcomers may regard Molokai as being unsophisticated, perhaps even backward, but those who know it best recognize the magic in its simplicity. — Cheryl Chee Tsutsumi, "Molokai: One of the Last Hawaiian Outposts"

New Discussion of an Old Subject

Explain why a topic that may be "old hat" is worth examining again.

That the world is mad has been the judgment of self-denominated sane philosophers from the Greeks to the present day. It is not a discovery of our own age that both the public and private lives of human beings are dominated by folly and stupidity. Philosophers pressing the point have brought such charges not against human nature only — that is, the world of human relations — but against that larger universe in which the world of human relations is set. As far back as the Book of Job and probably much further back, for there must have been at least gruntingly articulate Jobs in prehistory, it is not only men who have been declared mad: by any standards of rationality the universe itself has been called irrational, pointless, meaningless, with incidental, unintended overtones of cruelty and injustice.

With the provincialism of each generation, ours imagines that the causes of cynicism and despair are new in our time. There have, of course, been modern improvements and refinements of stupidity and folly. No previous generation has been by way of organizing itself with insane efficiency for blowing the whole race to smithereens. It does not take a particularly logical mind at the present moment to discover that the world is quite mad, though a great many critics apparently think that the cruel absurdity of technical efficiency combined with moral bankruptcy is a discovery that it took great wit on their part to turn up. — Irwin Edman, "A Reasonable Life in a Mad World"

Question

Use a question or a series of questions to provoke readers to think about your subject.

> Motherhood is in trouble, and it ought to be. A rude question is long overdue: Who needs it? The answer used to be (1) society and (2) women. But now, with the impending horrors of overpopulation, society desperately *doesn't* need it. And women don't need it either. Thanks to the Motherhood Myth — the idea that having babies is something that all normal women instinctively want and need and will enjoy doing — they just *think* they do. — Betty Rollin, "Motherhood: Who Needs It?"

Quotation

Use what someone else has said or written in a poem, short story, book, article, or interview.

> "We began to sail up the narrow strait lamenting," narrates Odysseus. "For on the one hand lay Scylla, with twelve feet all dangling down; and six necks exceeding long, and on each a hideous head, and therein three rows of teeth set thick and close, full of black death. And on the other mighty Charybdis sucked down the salt sea water. As often as she belched it forth, like a cauldron on a great fire she would seethe up through all her troubled deeps." Odysseus managed to swerve around Charybdis, but Scylla grabbed six of his finest men and devoured them in his sight — "the most pitiful thing mine eyes have seen of all my travail in searching out the paths of the sea."
>
> False lures and dangers often come in pairs in our legends and metaphors — consider the frying pan and the fire, or the devil and the deep blue sea. Prescriptions for avoidance either emphasize a dogged steadiness — the straight and narrow of Christian evangelists — or an averaging between unpleasant alternatives — the golden mean of Aristotle. The idea of steering a course between undesirable extremes

emerges as a central prescription for a sensible life. — Stephen Jay Gould, "Darwin's Middle Road"

Startling Statement

Use an arresting statement to get readers' attention and arouse their interest.

Young people should have the right to control and direct their own learning, that is, to decide what they want to learn, and when, where, how, how much, how fast, and with what help they want to learn it. To be still more specific, I want them to have the right to decide if, when, how much, and by whom they want to be *taught* and the right to decide whether they want to learn in a school and if so which one and for how much of the time.

No human right, except the right to life itself, is more fundamental than this. A person's freedom of learning is part of his freedom of thought, even more basic than his freedom of speech. — John Holt, "The Right to Control One's Own Learning"

> **!** Write sample introductions at the computer, where you can easily copy and revise them. Decide on a number of strategies and quickly type out a draft of each, incorporating your thesis statement by using the "block" and "copy" commands to save typing time. Then print copies. Rereading the draft introductions in printed form is easy and gives you a clear sense of their length. Decide which introduction seems most effective, and move it to the beginning of the draft of your paper. You can always move it again and try another. Save all versions until you have completed your final draft; they may provide you with good ideas later.

Jacob considered a number of introductions for his paper, trying to find one that would interest his readers as well as clarify his topic:

Anecdote
   Tell about Todd and me at the video store.

Facts and figures
   Discuss details of making of The Birth of a Nation, the first major film adaptation of a novel.

Allusion
   Discuss the wide variety of books adapted into film: The Scarlet Letter, Of Human Bondage, Gone with the Wind, Great Expectations, and so on.

Jacob considered the anecdote but decided that its personal, informal tone did not match his purpose for the paper, which was to be informative. The facts about *The Birth of a Nation,* though interesting, if arranged as an anecdote, might not clearly relate to his thesis. A list of allusions might seem superficial. Jacob decided to combine facts and figures with allusions to create interest, connect with readers' experiences, and suggest the wide range of his topic.

EXERCISE 2.5   ❱   *Title and introductory paragraphs*

Write several titles for your paper and select the most effective one. Then write two draft versions of the introduction, using the guidelines given above. Make sure that your strategies both create interest and clearly and appropriately introduce your topic.

Conclusions

A **conclusion** reemphasizes the writer's point and provides an opportunity to create a desired final impression. Most conclusions begin with a brief but specific summary and then use a concluding strategy to present a general observation.

Some introductory strategies — such as allusion, analogy, anecdote, description, and quotation — can also be useful concluding strategies. The following strategies are particularly appropriate for conclusions.

Challenge

Ask readers to reconsider and change their behavior or ideas or to consider new behavior and ideas.

> These arguments give me reason to think that in setting out the finds from the Phylakopi Sanctuary in sometimes almost exhaustive detail we are not presenting the trivial minutiae of something that might better be relegated to an unregarded data archive. One can readily sense that there still remain possibilities within these data, as yet unexploited by us, for much broader and more illuminating interpretations. These will be difficult to develop effectively until we have the materials from other Aegean sanctuaries available to us with a comparable degree of detail. When we do, I believe that we shall begin to see our way of tackling more effectively some of the really big questions concerning the early development of Aegean life and culture. — Colin Renfrew, *The Archaeology of Cult*

Framing Pattern

Frame your essay by modifying some central words, phrases, or images used in the introduction to reflect the progress in thought made in the paper. When appropriate, the introductory strategy may be repeated as the concluding strategy, intensifying the framing effect, as in the following example using description. (The corresponding introduction appears on page 49.)

> The next morning I awoke at dawn and went out on the dirt road to Rainy Mountain. It was already hot, and the grasshoppers began to fill the air. Still, it was early in the morning, and the birds sang out of the shadows. The long yellow grass on the mountain shone in the bright light, and a scissortail hied above the land. There, where it ought to be, at the end of a long and legendary way, was my grandmother's grave. Here and there on the dark stones were ancestral names. Looking back once, I saw the mountain and came away. — N. Scott Momaday, "The Way to Rainy Mountain"

Summary

Summarize, restate, or evaluate the major points you presented in your paper. This strategy must be used carefully and thoughtfully to avoid becoming mere repetition.

> True as it is that the essential function of art for a class destined to change the world is not that of *making magic* but of *enlightening* and *stimulating action,* it is equally true that a magical residue in art cannot be entirely eliminated, for without that minute residue of its original nature, art ceases to be art.
>
> In all the forms of its development, in dignity and fun, persuasion and exaggeration, sense and nonsense, fantasy and reality, art always has a little to do with magic.
>
> Art is necessary in order that man should be able to recognize and change the world. But art is also necessary by virtue of the magic inherent in it. — Ernst Fischer, "The Function of Art"

Visualization of the Future

Predict what the nature or condition of your topic will be like in the near or distant future. Be realistic.

> Ultimately a new breed of pioneer will colonize space, just as last century's pioneers settled the western frontier of this country. Once the rockets are flying, the labs are orbiting, and the external tanks are

converted into habitable environments, workers who can't find jobs
on Earth will relocate to space, where industry will be as rich and mul-
tifarious as industry on Earth. "The next billionaires will be made in
space," says Amroc's Koopman. "The skies are paved with gold."
— Beth Karlin, "Starship Enterprise"

Work at the keyboard to produce a draft of your conclusion.
Work quickly, emphasizing important connections among
ideas in the body paragraphs. Remember that you will be
able to revise your work later.

Jacob, though aware that his plans might change as he wrote his
paper, considered several conclusion strategies:

*Use a quotation from E. D. Hirsch stating that people sometimes
know about novels they have not read from seeing film adaptations.*

*Challenge readers to read a novel whose film adaptation they have
seen (or to see the film version of a novel they have read) and then to
compare the two experiences.*

*As in introduction, allude to specific films, varying the list, and suggest
that readers take the opportunity to read the corresponding novels.*

Jacob ultimately decided to combine quotation and challenge.

EXERCISE 2.6 ❯ *Concluding paragraphs*

*Write two draft versions of your conclusion. Make sure that your strat-
egies are closely connected to the tone and topic of your paper.*

MAKING   C O N N E C T I O N S

All writers handle drafting a paper differently. Increase your awareness of *your* patterns for writing so that you can expand, refine, or alter them to be more effective or flexible. Consider the drafting methods you used to complete the exercises in this chapter and to create some recent papers, and then answer the following questions.

- Describe your approach to organizing materials. How and why did you choose your structural pattern? What other patterns might you have used?

- Describe and compare the usefulness of informal and formal outlining. Be specific about the benefits and drawbacks of each for your draft.

- Describe your work with titles and introductory and concluding paragraphs. Which strategies did you try? How did you plan and compose them? Which strategies did you use in your completed draft?

3   Revising

Few writers produce a clear, consistent, complete, and correct piece of writing with their first draft — and few expect to. Rather, writers work knowing that they will have the chance to go back to their drafts and reread and revise them. **Revision,** which means "to see again," provides an opportunity for writers to rethink, reorganize, rephrase, refine, and redirect their work. It allows writers to polish their work, preparing it for readers by putting it into the best possible form.

Quick Reference

Revising is much more than proofreading and correcting technical errors. It is a rich opportunity to refine, clarify, and, if necessary, reconceive the paper, from its large to its small features.

> *Evaluate your content critically and delete or replace anything that does not effectively support your main idea.*

> *Improve the style of your paper by reworking sentences to make them varied, emphatic, and clear.*

> *Eliminate technical errors. These interfere with easy reading and draw attention away from your ideas.*

> *Use peer review for an unbiased response to your specific questions and an assessment of the strengths and weaknesses of the paper as a whole.*

> *Prepare the final copy of your paper, making any additional changes necessary and following accepted guidelines for manuscript preparation.*

Experienced writers often revise by rereading their writing and making simultaneous changes in content, sentence structure, word choice, punctuation, and mechanics; such single-stage reworking is often called a **global revision.** When you have sufficient experience with writing, you too will be able to make global revisions. For now, it will be easier for you to revise in the three stages described in this chapter: **content revision, style revision,** and **technical revision.**

A Revision Sequence

Set aside the rough draft.

Reread the draft.

Revise content.

Revise style.

Revise technical errors.

Consult a peer editor.

Make final changes.

Prepare a final copy to submit.

 Set aside your rough draft for as long as possible.

After finishing your draft, take a break from your writing. At this point in the process, many writers are tired or even frustrated, and most cannot see their own work clearly. Absorbed in thinking about their topics, they sometimes assume that their drafts are clearer or more complete than they really are. Knowing this, most writers interrupt their work to relax briefly and to gain or regain objectivity about their drafts before they begin revision.

To begin your revision with objectivity, set your rough draft aside for as long as possible. Several days would be best, but if that is not possible, then stop working on the paper for at least several hours. Telephone a friend, listen to music, take a walk, or study for another course. Do *anything* that will rest and refresh your mind for writing and allow you to look at your work critically and with detachment.

3b	Revise the content of your paper.

When you return to your paper, examine its content for clarity, coherence, and completeness. To guide your revision, consider the following questions:

Are the title and the introductory strategy interesting, clear, and appropriate in tone?

Does the thesis statement clearly present the topic and your opinion about it?

Do the topics of the paragraphs support the thesis statement? Are they clearly stated?

Are the topics presented in a clear, emphatic order?

Are the paragraphs adequately developed? Is there enough detail? Are there enough examples? Does information in each paragraph relate to the thesis statement?

Are the summary and concluding strategy effective?

When you have many content revisions, do more than one revised draft.

Word processing and content revision

Revising papers written on a word processor can be relatively easy. Two basic approaches to computer revision are possible; the choice between them depends on how comfortable you feel working at the keyboard. Each is presented below.

"Hard-Copy" Revision

Working from a printed copy of the rough draft is best for writers who have limited experience with word processors or who are uncomfortable with computers.

Triple-space the draft; leave extra-wide margins.

"Hard-copy" revision allows you to evaluate several pages simultaneously, making it a good method for evaluating and correcting organizational and other large-scale problems.

Once you produce revision notes and rewritten portions of the draft, transfer them to the computer file, first making a back-up copy of the original and giving it a different file name. This transfer stage makes "hard-copy" revision somewhat slower than "on-screen" revision.

"Hard-copy" revision works best for complex or extensive revisions, such as remedying problems with logical coherence and transitions.

Advice: Avoid the urge to "respect" a printed version just because it looks finished; it may still require major reworking.

Word processing and content revision (cont.)

"On-Screen" Revision

"On-screen" revision works best for writers familiar and comfortable with computers and word-processing programs.

Keep a back-up copy of the original draft, giving it a different file name.

Work one screen at a time, evaluating each phrase, sentence, and paragraph and typing changes as you think of them.

Working "on screen" can be quicker than working on a "hard copy."

"On-screen" revision works best for simple revisions: additions, deletions, and limited rearranging of material.

Use whichever approach best matches your needs and experience with computers. Remember that each approach will help you to incorporate content revisions without completely retyping or rewriting the paper.

Figure 1 shows the content revisions that Jacob made in the rough draft of his first body paragraph: (1) he clarified several sentences; (2) he added important information about the film that he had inadvertently omitted; (3) he deleted an example that he had mistakenly thought was in the film; and (4) he added a sentence explicitly connecting the example to his thesis statement.

Figure 1

and selectively

Because of time limits films necessarally omit parts of a novel to fit

to 3

a 2 hour format. The filmmaker must choose the primary elements of

The Adventures of Huckleberry Finn (1885)

the plot to include. A good example is Twain's ~~Huck Finn~~. It is 43

chapters, it is 300+ pages, and it includes many episodes. Such a

in full form

long work could not be brought to the screen, so the 1939 film ver-

produced by J. Mankiewicz and starring Mickey Rooney

sion includes portions of Twains work, the the most important plot

the trip down the Mississippi river,

elements in abbreviated form. Huck and Jim's escape, the Duke

and Daulphin

episode, ~~the Sarah Mary Williams episode,~~ and the Grangerferd

feud are brought from the page to the screen, showing the the

most important of Huck's adventures, even though many secondary
seens are left out. Elements of novels must be cut. Most often filmakers
keep the important elements to capture the spirit of the original novel.

EXERCISE 3.1 ❯ *Content revision*

*Reread your draft and respond to the questions on page 60. Unless
you can answer each question with an unequivocal* yes, *revise your
draft until the content is clear, coherent, and complete.*

3c	❯	**Revise the style of your paper.**

Achieving clear, adequately developed content is the first step in
revision. The second step is achieving a clear and compelling presentation of that content.

Word processing and style revision

Style revision can be effectively done on the computer because you can add to, delete from, and combine or separate your sentences without completely retyping the text. Some specific guidelines follow:

Check sentence length. Have your word-processing program locate periods (most will end sentences) using the "search" commands. As the program executes the search, notice the approximate number of lines the cursor skips. If it is pausing frequently within lines or on every line, some sentences are probably too short. If the cursor often skips three or more lines, some sentences may be too long.

Check for repeated expressions. Use the "search" commands to locate words that you suspect you use too often. Especially look for slang, jargon, and technical terms, intensifiers like *very,* and proper names, all of which can be distracting if overused. Then change some of them.

Check for passive constructions. Search for forms of the verb *to be,* the auxiliary forms used to create passive sentences. When the search finds one of these verbs, reread the sentence, check for passive voice, and rephrase the sentence if necessary.

When you have developed strong content in your paper, refine the style, using these questions as a guide:

Do the lengths and types of sentences vary?

Do sentences clearly and concisely express their meaning?

Are word choices vivid, accurate, and appropriate?

Do most sentences use the active voice?

Do transitions adequately relate ideas?

To get a sense of how your paper flows, read it aloud, with or without an audience, noting where word choices are awkward or where phrases are difficult to follow. Your hesitations while reading orally will help you pinpoint areas that require reworking.

After revising the content of his paper, Jacob considered the effectiveness of its style. He decided to make a number of major and minor changes: (1) he altered his word choices throughout the paragraph, making them more vivid; (2) he added transitions; and (3) he combined some short, choppy sentences to improve the flow of the paragraph. Jacob's content revisions are shown in Figure 2.

Figure 2

constraints adaptations must distill
Because of time ~~limits~~ films ~~necessarally and selectively omit parts~~
, as a result, select
~~of~~ a novel to fit a 2 to 3 hour format. The filmmaker must ~~choose the~~
For example, Mark
primary elements of the plot to include. ~~A good example is~~ Twain's
a lengthy novel of presented in
The Adventures of Huckleberry Finn (1885). ~~It is~~ 43 chapters, ~~it is~~
approximately 300 pages. Its would make it impossible to
~~300+ pages, and it includes~~ many episodes. ~~Such a long work~~
bring the novel to film in its Consequently,
~~could not be brought in~~ full form ~~to the screen, so~~ the 1939 film
Joseph
version produced by ~~J.~~ Mankiewicz and starring Mickey Rooney
only the most pivatal presenting an abbreviated
includes portions of Twains work, ~~the the most important plot ele-~~
version of the novel.
~~ments in abbreviated form.~~ Huck and Jim's escape, the trip down

the Mississippi river, the Duke and Daulphin episode, and the

Grangerferd feud are ~~brought~~ *transposed* from the page to the screen, ~~show-ing~~ *presenting only* the the most important of Huck's adventures, ~~even though many secondary seens are left out.~~ Elements of novels must be cut. ~~Most often~~ filmakers ~~keep the important~~ *typically retain core* elements *of the plot* to capture the spirit of the original novel.

○ *Although*
like Huckleberry Finn

EXERCISE 3.2 ❯ *Style revision*

Revise the style of your paper by answering the questions on pages 64–65.

| 3d | **Eliminate technical errors and inconsistencies.** |

Technical revision focuses on grammar, punctuation, mechanics, spelling, and manuscript form. After eliminating major problems with content and style, consider the technical revisions that will make your paper correct and precise.

Ask yourself the following general questions and also watch for technical errors that you know you make frequently.

Are all words correctly spelled? (When in doubt, always look up the correct spelling in your dictionary.)

Are any necessary words omitted? Are any words unnecessarily repeated?

Is punctuation accurate? (See "Punctuation," starting on page 348.)

Are elements of mechanics properly used? (See "Mechanics," starting on page 412.)

Are all sentences complete?

Word processing and technical revision

Use word-processing capabilities to help you check for potential problems and make some technical revisions.

Check spelling. A spelling program (a standard feature of many word-processing programs) will search your manuscript for words not found in its dictionary. When the spelling program highlights a word that is suspect, consider the word carefully. It may be spelled incorrectly, or it may be a technical term or a proper name not found in the program's dictionary. Look up suspect words in a standard college dictionary. Spelling programs will also highlight words typed twice in succession.

▶▶▶ *Remember that spelling checkers will not highlight a misspelled word that happens to be another word correctly spelled (for example,* hale *instead of* half *) nor a correctly spelled word used in the wrong context (for example,* their *instead of* there *). Always carefully proofread the spelling of your papers.* **◀◀◀**

Check for specialized punctuation. Because some marks of punctuation — semicolons, colons, dashes, and parentheses — must be used with special care, use the "search" commands to locate them in your manuscript; then double-check their use. For example, search for colons and then check to see that they are preceded by full sentences.

Check pronoun usage. Use the "search" commands to find uses of pronouns (*he, she, they,* and others). Note whether each pronoun has a clear and correct antecedent (the word it refers to), and correct any unclear or inaccurate references.

Do nouns and pronouns and subjects and verbs agree in number and gender as appropriate?

Are all pronoun antecedents clear?

Are all modifiers logically positioned?

Make technical revisions slowly and carefully, giving particular attention to the kinds of errors that you have made in the past. If you are uncertain whether you have made an error, look up the applicable rule in this book.

After making his content and style revisions, Jacob made his technical revisions: (1) he corrected spelling errors; (2) he inserted necessary italics; (3) he corrected his use of numbers; (4) he eliminated words inadvertently repeated; (5) he corrected his punctuation. Jacob's style revisions are shown in Figure 3.

Figure 3

Because of time constraints, film adaptations must distill a novel to fit a ~~2 to 3 hour~~ two-to-three-hour format. ~~The filmaker~~ Filmmakers must, as a result, select primary elements of the plot to include. For example, Mark Twain's ~~The Adventures of Huckleberry Finn~~ *The Adventures of Huckleberry Finn* (1885) is a lengthy novel of ~~43~~ forty-three chapters, presented in approximately ~~300~~ three hundred pages. Its many episodes would make it impossible to bring the novel to film in its full form. Consequently, the 1939 film version, produced by Joseph Mankiewicz and starring Mickey Rooney, includes only the most ~~pivatal~~ pivotal portions of ~~Twains~~ Twain's work, presenting an abbreviated version of the novel. Huck and Jim's escape, the trip down the Mis-

River   Dauphin   Grangerford
sissippi ~~river~~, the Duke and ~~Daulphin~~ episode, and the ~~Granger~~-
                                                               ; the film presents
~~ferd~~ feud are transposed from the page to the screen ~~, presenting~~

only the most important of Huck's adventures. Although elements
                    Huckleberry Finn   filmmakers
of novels like ~~Huckleberry Finn~~ must be cut, ~~filmmakers~~ typically

retain core elements of the plot to capture the spirit of the original

novel.

EXERCISE 3.3 ❭ *Technical revision*

*Return to your paper and examine it for technical errors, revising to
eliminate them as you work. Work slowly and carefully, using Parts 4,
5, and 6 of this handbook to review rules of grammar, punctuation, and
mechanics.*

| 3e | ❭ | **Use peer editing to help you revise.** |

 A peer editor, often another student in the course for which you
are writing, will read your paper and evaluate its content, style,
and technical correctness. In many composition classes, sessions
are set aside for peer reviews; but when they are not (or for other
courses), ask another writer to read and respond to your paper — not to rework it for you but to point out anything incomplete, unclear, inconsistent, or incorrect.

 If your instructor does not provide specific guidance for peer
editing, consider these basic approaches:

 Find a peer editor with writing experience and standards that
are similar to yours. Ideally, your peer editor should be from

your class because then you and he or she are likely to share similar expectations about audience, purpose, and requirements for the paper.

Ask a peer editor specific questions, focusing on issues of particular importance to you. If, for instance, you are concerned about the organization of your paper, ask for an assessment of the order of the information or paragraphs. If you have difficulties with subject-verb agreement, ask the peer editor to check agreement. Don't simply ask for an editor to read and praise the paper, for such an undirected review will not help you to revise. Rather, ask for specific comments matched to your needs and expect criticism as well as praise.

Ask the peer editor to point out problems but to refrain from altering your paper. A good peer editor would note, for instance, that your introductory strategy does not reflect the tone or purpose of your paper but would leave it to you to reconsider and revise the strategy — if you agreed with his or her assessment. Don't expect the editor to rewrite your paper for you.

Consider carefully the comments and queries of your peer editor, but also trust your own judgment. Notes about confusing, incomplete, or incorrect passages will always require attention. But on matters of judgment or personal taste — specific word choices, titles, and so on — consider your editor's notations carefully but remember that the paper is *yours*. Make no subjective changes that do not seem right and necessary to you.

Peer editing will not substitute for your own careful evaluation and revision of your paper, and it will not eliminate all problems. It will elicit useful responses to your work before you prepare the final copy.

EXERCISE 3.4 ❯ *Peer editing*

Prepare for peer editing by listing four to six features that you would like an editor to check. They may relate to any aspect of the content, style, or technical correctness of your paper. Using your list of specific concerns and the following list of editing questions, ask a peer editor to evaluate your revised paper.

Introduction

Do the title and introductory strategy create interest? Are they appropriate?

Is the thesis statement appropriately positioned? Does it express a clear topic and opinion? Does it include any necessary qualifications and clarifications?

Body paragraphs

Is the order of the paragraphs appropriate? Would another arrangement work better?

Does the topic of each paragraph clearly relate to the thesis statement? Are topics developed sufficiently?

Are transitions smoothly made between sentences within paragraphs and between paragraphs?

Conclusion

Does the conclusion effectively draw together and summarize the paper?

Is the concluding strategy appropriate?

Style

Are the sentences varied, coherent, forceful, and smooth?

Are the word choices vivid, accurate, and appropriate?

Technical matters

Are the sentences grammatical?

Is the usage standard?

Are punctuation and mechanics correct?

Word processing and personal revision guidelines

Use the guidelines for revising content, style, and technical matters on pages 60, 64–65, and 66–68 as the basis for a personal file of revision guidelines. Type the questions listed, or as many of them as you regularly find useful in your college writing, into a separate file. Add to the file reminders about frequent or recurring problems in your drafts and useful suggestions for improving your writing made by peer editors and teachers. Add a list of words you most frequently misspell. Print a copy of the file to use when reviewing drafts, or use it on-screen, in a second screen or a window, as a personal revision checklist.

| 3f | **Prepare a final copy of your paper.** |

Most papers should be not handwritten but neatly and cleanly typewritten or printed on a computer printer, following the general manuscript guidelines that appear in Appendix A, "Manuscript Form." Your instructor will let you know of any specific requirements for preparing a final manuscript.

EXERCISE 3.5 ❯ *A final copy*

Prepare the final copy of your paper. Work carefully, proofreading each page before you remove it from the typewriter. As a safeguard, photocopy the final manuscript. Submit the original typed copy of your paper — on time.

Word processing and preparing a final manuscript

If you have been working on the computer, preparing the final copy will be easy.

Make final changes. Having made most of your substantive changes during content, style, and technical revision, in all probability you will need to make only small changes — for example, final adjustments in word choice.

Insert paging codes. For your final copy, include your name and the page number in the upper right corner of each page. Using the program's "menu," usually with the designation *heads* or *running heads,* insert the codes to print name and page number. One code will then run throughout the paper, and paging will be done automatically.

Print a draft-quality copy for yourself. Using the draft mode, prepare a copy of the final paper to keep for yourself. Double-check to make sure that the manuscript format is accurate; if it is not, make necessary changes.

Print a high-quality copy to submit. Use a letter-quality printer, if possible, to produce a manuscript that looks typed. If one is not available, use the correspondence-quality mode of the available printer.

Jacob Westgard   Westgard 1

English 105

Ms. Chiu

7 January 1990

From the Page to the Screen:

Novels and Their Film Adaptations

In 1915, just two decades after the first film was shown publicly, The Birth of a Nation premiered in New York. This major work by D. W. Griffith is a landmark film for a number of reasons, not the least of which is that it was the first full-length film adaptation of a novel, Thomas Dixon's The Clansman. In the decades which followed, other adaptations of novels--The Hunchback of Notre Dame, The Phantom of the Opera, The Scarlet Letter, Anna Karenina, and Mutiny on the Bounty, to name but a few--introduced works of literature to viewing audiences. The legacy of adaptations continues to our times, although some critics skeptically note that these are "Hollywood" versions, bastardizations of the novels that inspired them. But such films deserve our attention. Although film adaptations of novels may seem to distort original works, the adaptations often create worthy counterparts to the originals.

Because of time constraints, film adaptations must distill a novel to fit a two-to-three-hour format. Filmmakers must, as a result, select primary elements of the plot to include. For example, Mark Twain's The Adventures of Huckleberry Finn (1885) is a lengthy novel of forty-three chapters, presented in approximately three hundred pages. Its many episodes would make it impossible to bring the novel to film in its full form. Consequently, the 1939 film version, produced by Joseph Mankiewicz and starring Mickey Rooney, includes only the most pivotal portions of Twain's work, presenting an abbreviated version of the novel. Huck and Jim's escape, the trip down the Mississippi River, the Duke and Dauphin episode, and the Grangerford feud are transposed from the page to the screen; the film presents only the most important of Huck's adventures. Although elements of novels like Huckleberry Finn must be cut, filmmakers typically retain core elements of the plot to capture the spirit of the original novel.

Filmmakers also elliptically develop characters to create the essence of their novelistic counterparts. In Isak Dinesen's essay-novels Out of Africa (1938) and Shadows on the Grass (1960), the character Karen Blixen emerges through her descriptions of other characters and

incidents. It is a cumulative characterization, not one
described--for the character Karen Blixen is a self-
portrait. In the 1985 film Out of Africa, produced by
Sidney Pollack, Meryl Streep creates the crucial impressions of Karen Blixen in several important ways. She
narrates the opening and several key portions of the
film, helping to recreate the emotional distance Dinesen
established in her work. And a few wisely selected
episodes from the novels show Blixen's stoicism, independence, and temerity: her marriage of convenience, her
response to contracting syphilis from her husband, her
schooling of the Kikuyu children, her openly taking a
lover. These episodes become visual symbols representing
the character of Karen Blixen and capture the spirit of
the novels. All complexities of characterization are not
and cannot be included in Out of Africa and in other
adaptations, but because of similar selective portrayals,
films can offer representative and satisfying characterizations.

Because films must compress their messages into
restricted time frames, filmmakers must also reduce the
thematic complexities of novels when they are adapted for
the screen. When filmmakers select central themes to
concentrate upon, omitting minor ones, something of the

intricacy of the novel is lost, of course, but the major emphasis remains. John Steinbeck's <u>The Grapes of Wrath</u> (1939), for example, contains thirty chapters covering over six hundred pages. In a work so long, myriad themes emerge that could not possibly be treated in a two-to-three-hour film. Yet in the 1940 film adaptation, produced by Darryl Zanuck and starring Henry Fonda, the most powerful themes--humanity's powerlessness against nature, people's exploitation of other people, and the tantalizing nature of socialist reform--all come through. Secondary themes from the sweeping novel do not make their way to the screen, but the most important ones do. Filmmakers like Zanuck cannot hope to imbue their films with the multiple themes found in many novels, but through careful selection they reduce the number of themes and concentrate upon giving them the dramatic, visual impact that films can offer.

Novels and films are distinct genres, each with its strengths and appeals. Film adaptations--though necessarily simpler in terms of plot, character, and theme than the novels on which they are based--do represent the complexities of the printed works. E. D. Hirsch has noted, "The American conception of Sherlock Holmes has been formed more by the acting of Basil Rathbone than by

the writing of Conan Doyle. Judy Garland and Bert Lahr
have fixed our conception of The Wizard of Oz more vividly than Frank Baum" (147). What we must remember is
that reading novels and seeing film adaptations do not
have to be mutually exclusive activities. Instead, there
is insight to be gained and enjoyment to be found in
examining the ways that filmmakers take a novel from the
page to the screen.

Work Cited

Hirsch, E. D. Cultural Literacy: What Every American
    Needs to Know. Boston: Houghton, 1987.

MAKING C O N N E C T I O N S

Of the three stages of the writing process, revising may be the one most often overlooked or avoided. Yet it is crucial to achieving coherent, expressive content and style and eliminating technical errors. Revising is not easy, nor should it be a passive, unreflecting acceptance of changes suggested by a peer editor. Revising is worthwhile; some of the best writers consider their best writing to be due more to careful, thoughtful revising than to any other factor.

Think about your experience with revision, using your work on the exercises in this chapter as an example. By examining this experience, you can learn more about what effective techniques to keep using and what ineffective techniques to abandon. Improving your ability to revise may do more that anything else to improve your skill as a writer.

- How much time do you allow for revision? What do you do to gain or regain objectivity about your work?

- What strategies do you use to assess the completeness and effectiveness of the content of your paper? How do you revise content?

- Describe the style you usually use for college papers. How do you assess the appropriateness of this style for particular assignments? How do you revise your drafts to ensure that your style is consistent?

- Consider your strengths and weaknesses in grammar, punctuation, and spelling. How do you use your strengths? How do you compensate for and accommodate your weaknesses?

- What has revision taught you about your subject? What has it taught you about yourself as a writer?

4 Paragraphs

Paragraphs focus on single facets of a subject. A single paragraph describes or explains one idea; as part of a series of paragraphs in a paper, a single paragraph develops one aspect of the paper's thesis. Paragraph length varies with the writer's purpose, the nature of the material in the paragraph, and the function of the paragraph. To present ideas effectively, all paragraphs, short or long, must be unified, coherent, complete, and developed.

Quick Reference

Paragraphs, the building blocks of papers, must be focused, structured, and developed.

> *Write paragraphs that develop single ideas, using topic sentences, when appropriate, to clarify your focus for readers.*

> *Use the stylistic techniques of transition and repetition to link ideas within and between paragraphs.*

> *Use varied methods of paragraph development, selecting patterns appropriate to the ideas that you generated during planning.*

4a Develop unified paragraphs.

A **unified paragraph** includes information pertinent to the main idea and excludes information that is not pertinent. Often a topic

---

Note: Many of the exercises in this chapter will take you through the steps of writing paragraphs. Keep the work from each exercise to use in later exercises.

C • O • N • N • E • C • T • I • O • N • S

Each paragraph in a paper must have internal unity, coherence, organization, and purpose but must also adhere to the paper's overall thesis and purpose, contributing to the meaning of the paper as a whole. By varying paragraph strategies throughout a paper — for example, by interweaving paragraphs developed through facts with those developed through narration or description — writers control emphasis and pacing, two important means of engaging and maintaining readers' interest.

Whatever the development pattern of individual paragraphs, all paragraphs together contribute to the development pattern of the entire paper. Any of the paragraph patterns discussed in this chapter can be used to develop entire papers or segments of papers. For example, the student paper at the end of Chapter 3 builds (through paragraphs of description, facts, examples, and so on) a comparison and contrast pattern.

sentence states the main idea explicitly and indicates by its phrasing the pattern of development that the paragraph follows.

Lack of unity is a common problem in early drafts. You can avoid blurring the focus of a paragraph by keeping the following points in mind.

Focus on One Topic

A unified paragraph develops one main idea only; it does not include information that is loosely related to the main idea or that constitutes an additional main idea. The following paragraph is not unified because it describes two museums (two topics) without establishing a connection between them.

The Metropolitan Museum of Art in New York City is an impressive example of nineteenth-century architecture. Made of stone with massive columns and elaborately carved scrollwork, it is institutional architecture of the sort we expect in public buildings. Farther up Fifth Avenue, the Guggenheim Museum of Modern Art is built of reinforced concrete. This museum forms a spatial helix, a continuous spiral that expands as it rises; each level is marked by a narrow band of windows. Its design is severe and unusual.

Without any suggestion that the museums are being contrasted, the writer creates an unnecessary shift in topic as the discussion moves from one museum to the other. The writer could add a topic sentence to show the relationship between the Guggenheim and the Metropolitan Museum of Art or treat each museum in a separate, focused paragraph.

The Metropolitan Museum of Art in New York City is a typical example of nineteenth-century public architecture. Made of stone, with massive columns, tall casement windows, and an elaborately carved entablature, it is institutional architecture that conveys the dignity we expect in great public museum buildings. It is reminiscent of the Louvre in Paris, the British Museum in London, and the National Gallery in Washington. Familiar yet impressive, it suggests a grand purpose.

Farther up Fifth Avenue, the Guggenheim Museum of Modern Art offers a contrasting, twentieth-century view of museum architecture. Built of reinforced concrete in the form of a spatial helix, a continuous spiral that expands as it rises, it is adorned only by a continuous band of simple windows. In 1937, when it was designed by Frank Lloyd Wright, the building's severity made it seem very modern, very alien, and austere rather than august. Yet it changed the way Americans perceived institutional architecture, and we now find similar designs in a range of public buildings from libraries to high schools.

Include Relevant Details Only

In trying to be specific, writers sometimes include a number of interesting details, some of which are marginally related or irrelevant to the topic. Unrelated information takes a paragraph in too many directions and destroys unity, as in this paragraph:

(1) Hurricanes are cyclones that develop in the tropical waters of the Atlantic Ocean. (2) Forming large circles or ovals, they have winds of 75 miles per hour or more and can measure 500 miles across. (3) Years ago, hurricanes were named after women — Irene, Sarah, Becky, for example — but now they are also named after men. (4) They usually form hundreds of miles from land and then move slowly to the northwest at about 10 miles per hour. (5) For reasons unknown, they pick up speed rapidly when they reach the twenty-fifth parallel. (6) That means, in very practical terms, that they reach peak speed and destructive power by the time they hit North American coastlines. (7) Hurricanes that form in the Pacific Ocean are commonly called typhoons.

Here, all the material relates to hurricanes, but some of it only loosely. Sentences 1, 2, 4, 5, and 6 are factual descriptions of how the storms form and move. Sentences 3 and 7 include interesting but only marginally relevant information. The unity of the paragraph would be improved by omitting the unrelated material, which might fit into another paragraph.

Use Topic Sentences

A **topic sentence** presents a paragraph's main idea and indicates the writer's opinion about it. As succinct statements of the writer's idea and intended development of that idea, topic sentences unify the paragraphs in which they appear. In long papers, the topic sentences of all body paragraphs, taken together, constitute the ideas and major illustrations that support the paper's thesis.

A topic sentence at the beginning of a paragraph works like a map, providing an overview that guides readers through the writing. A topic sentence at the end of a paragraph summarizes its ideas. Sometimes, especially in descriptive paragraphs, a topic sentence is unnecessary; readers will be able to infer the writer's point from the paragraph as a whole. Writers sometimes feel that including a topic sentence in every paragraph makes writing mechanical and predictable. If you decide to omit a topic sentence from one of your paragraphs, remember that its absence may be confusing to your readers, who may not fully understand or may misinterpret your point.

Topic sentence at the beginning

Euphemisms thus serve as verbal placebos; they are particularly frequent when the ill-timed provocation could expose one to instant retaliation. Sports figures are always careful to speak with respect, even admiration, of their upcoming opponents, however inept. Precautionary and placatory euphemisms include variations on the theme, "They're a much better team than their record shows," and that minimal, thread-bare uncompliment, "They never give up." Everywhere except in politics (where it's accepted practice to toot one's own horn as loudly as possible), false modesty is useful protection against overconfidence on one's own part and provocation of the opponent. — Robert M. Adams, "Soft Soap and the Nitty-Gritty"

Topic sentence at the end

When we think of providing substance, we are perhaps tempted first to find some way of filling students' minds with a goodly store of general ideas, available on demand. This temptation is not necessarily a bad one. After all, if we think of adult writers who interest us, most of them have such a store; they have read and thought about man's major problems, and they have opinions and arguments ready at hand about how men ought to live, how society ought to be run, how literature ought to be written. Edmund Wilson, for example, one of the most consistently interesting men alive, seems to have an inexhaustible flow of reasoned opinions on any subject that comes before him. **Obviously our students are not going to interest us until they too have some ideas.** — Wayne C. Booth, "Boring from Within"

No topic sentence

Whenever I had nothing better to do in San Salvador I would walk up in the leafy stillness of the San Benito and Escalón districts, where the hush at midday is broken only by the occasional crackle of a walkie-talkie, the click of metal moving on a weapon. I recall a day in San Benito when I opened my bag to check an address, and heard the clicking of metal on metal all up and down the street. On the whole no one walks up here, and pools of blossoms lie undisturbed on the side-

walks. Most of the houses in San Benito are more recent than those in
Escalón, less idiosyncratic and probably smarter, but the most striking
architectural features in both districts are not the houses but their
walls, walls built upon walls, walls stripped of the copa de oro and
bougainvillea, walls that reflect successive generations of violence: the
original stone, the additional five or six or ten feet of brick, and finally
the barbed wire, sometimes concertina, sometimes electrified; walls
with watch towers, gun ports, closed-circuit television cameras, walls
now reaching twenty and thirty feet. — Joan Didion, "Salvador"

Use the computer's capabilities to block and move materials
to reposition your topic sentences, experimenting with
different ways to create emphasis. Print copies of different
versions and read and evaluate them, noting their relative
effectiveness. Choose the version that best suits your
purpose and tone to use in your draft.

EXERCISE 4.1 〉 *Topic sentences*

*The following paragraph lacks unity because it has a poor topic
sentence. Revise the topic sentence to give the paragraph a
clearer focus and then strike out any irrelevant material.*

In the early days of television, children in major roles were represented as middle class and stereotypically good looking and childlike.
Timmy, the boy on *Lassie,* had well-cut blond hair, sparkling eyes, a
straight-toothed smile. He even had dimples. He was naive in a way children were only when portrayed in early television. He ignored warnings,
got into trouble, was rescued by his dog, and learned a new lesson each
week — and the lesson always had to do with following adults' rules.
Timmy, in an idealized way, always learned to like adult rules. Nobody
on today's programs is like that. Certainly Kevin, the cute boy on *The
Wonder Years,* isn't so attuned to adult expectations. Like Timmy, Kevin
is adorable, has a good haircut, wears nice clothes, and has a winning
smile. But unlike Timmy, Kevin doesn't learn simple and positive lessons
about adult rules. In fact, Kevin often learns to accept the stupidity but
inevitability of adult rules with a wry and cynical maturity beyond his
years. He and Timmy may both be adorable, but Kevin shows that televi-

sion's portrayals of children have become more realistic in at least one way.

EXERCISE 4.2 ❯ *Topic sentences*

Using four of the subjects listed below, write topic sentences. Make sure that your topic sentences clearly identify the subject and indicate how you will discuss it.

Example

Subject: lawyers
Topic sentence: Lawyers sometimes act more as legal interpreters than as advocates.

1. Book censorship
2. Sibling rivalry
3. Nationalized medical insurance
4. The Olympic Games
5. Religious prejudice
6. Standardized achievement tests
7. National parks
8. Political debates
9. Holiday celebrations
10. Water conservation

4b ❯ **Create coherent paragraphs.**

To allow readers to proceed smoothly through paragraphs, writers must make the necessary effort to think clearly, to be thorough, and to explain ideas and the connections between ideas. When sentences fit together well, the paragraph is coherent and readers are able to concentrate on what the writer is saying. The strategies used to achieve coherence are *transition* and *repetition*.

Transitional Words and Phrases

Transition is movement from one facet of a subject to another. Transitional words and phrases facilitate these shifts in focus. The English language is rich in such words and phrases. Coordinating conjunctions (*and, but,* and others), subordinating conjunctions (*although, since,* and others), and correlative conjunctions (*either . . . or, not only . . . but also,* and others) are the most commonly used transitional words and phrases. Use transitional words and phrases to establish relationships within sentences, between paragraphs, or among the parts of a paper. The following lists indicate some of the relationships you can establish by using transitional words and phrases and give examples of words and phrases that produce each relationship.

Addition

also	furthermore
and	in addition
besides	moreover
equally	next
further	too

Similarity

also	moreover
likewise	similarly

Difference

but	in contrast
however	nevertheless

Difference (cont.)

on the contrary	yet
on the other hand	

Examples

for example	specifically
for instance	to illustrate
in fact	

Restatements or summaries

finally	in summary
in brief	on the whole
in conclusion	that is
in other words	therefore
in short	to sum up

Result

accordingly	so
as a result	therefore
consequently	thereupon
for this reason	thus

Chronology

after	earlier
afterward	finally
before	first
during	immediately

Chronology   *(cont.)*

in the meantime	soon
later	still
meanwhile	then
next	third
second	when
simultaneously	while

Location

above	opposite
below	there
beyond	to the left
farther	to the right
here	under
nearby	

The following paragraph makes use of a number of transitional words and phrases, each marked with italics, to emphasize the relationships among ideas.

In recent years, some doctors have begun diagnosing allergies by combining blood droplets with different allergens to determine a sensitivity. [Allergy specialist] Lieberman warns, *however,* that this method is less accurate, more expensive and takes longer to get answers than skin testing. *Generally,* doctors recommend the blood test when it might be dangerous to use the allergen directly on the skin — as might be the case in someone hypersensitive to bee venom, *for example* — *or* if a skin disease *such as* eczema makes it difficult to see the results of a skin test. — Cynthia Green, "Sneezy and Grumpy? See Doc"

Repeat Words and Phrases

Selective **repetition** of words and phrases can make writing unified and effective. To avoid monotony, use variations of key words or phrases, synonyms (words with the same meaning), and pronouns to create variety as you create unity. The following paragraph uses all three.

> *Laughter* is surely one of humanity's greatest gifts, for the ability to *laugh* — to appreciate the pleasure or *absurdity* in daily activities — allows people, young and old alike, to keep problems in perspective. Children are natural *laughers*. In situations, both appropriate and inappropriate, the *chuckles, giggles,* and outright *peals of laughter* of children can emphasize their innocence, their joyful ignorance of the problems of the world. *Levity* among adults is, unfortunately, far less common, but *it* is equally welcome. How fortunate are the adults who can react to potentially frustrating situations — a collapsed tent, a split seam in a pair of pants, a surprise guest — and see the sheer *absurdity* of their attempts to maintain absolute control. *Laughter* expresses pleasure, eases tension, and lifts the spirit. *It* is a gift we should all share more often.

Repeat Sentence Structures

The repetition of sentence structures creates unity within a paragraph by presenting similar ideas in similar ways. If you strive for variety in most sentences, then selectively repeated patterns will stand out. The following excerpt from a lengthy paragraph uses repeated sentence structures (all italicized) to focus attention on similar activities.

> But though I was initially disappointed at being categorized as an extremist, as I continued to think about the matter I gradually gained a measure of satisfaction from the label. *Was not Jesus an extremist for love:* "Love your enemies, bless them that curse you, do good to them that hate you, and pray for them which despitefully use you, and persecute you." *Was not Amos an extremist for justice:* "Let justice roll down like waters and righteousness like an ever-flowing stream." *Was*

not Paul an extremist for the Christian gospel: "I bear in my body the marks of the Lord Jesus." *Was not Martin Luther an extremist:* "Here I stand; I cannot do otherwise, so help me God." *And John Bunyan:* "I will stay in jail to the end of my days before I make a butchery of my conscience." *And Abraham Lincoln:* "This nation cannot survive half slave and half free." *And Thomas Jefferson:* "We hold these truths to be self-evident, that all men are created equal . . . " So the question is not whether we will be extremists, but what kind of extremists we will be. — Martin Luther King, Jr., "Letter from Birmingham Jail"

Use the word processor to add transitions to your paragraphs. The program will automatically reformat your paragraphs without retyping. Copy your paragraphs and experiment freely with repeating words, phrases, and sentence structures. You can always return to your original version or try another. Print out your paragraphs and mark the transitional words and phrases, as in the example on page 89, to check for consistency of pronoun and other references and for excessive repetition.

EXERCISE 4.3 ❯ *Transitions and repeated sentence elements*

Notice the use of transitional words and phrases and repetition in the following paragraphs, and comment on the purpose and effectiveness of each use.

One great difficulty in getting straightforward answers is that so many of the diseases in question have unpredictable courses, and some of them have a substantial tendency toward spontaneous remission. In rheumatoid arthritis, for instance, when such widely disparate therapeutic measures as copper bracelets, a move to Arizona, diets low in sugar or salt or meat or whatever, and even an inspirational book have been accepted by patients as useful, the trouble in evaluation is that approximately 35 percent of patients with this diagnosis are bound to recover no matter what they do. But if you actually have rheumatoid arthritis or, for that matter, schizophrenia, and then get over it, or if you are a doctor and observe this happen, it is hard to be persuaded that it wasn't *something* you did that was responsible. Hence you need very large numbers of patients and lots of time, and a cool head.

  Magic is back again, and in full force. Laetrile cures cancer, acupuncture is useful for deafness and low-back pain, vitamins are good for anything, and meditation, yoga, dancing, biofeedback, and shouting one another down in crowded rooms over weekends are specifics for the human condition. Running, a good thing to be doing for its own sake, has acquired the medicinal value formerly attributed to rare herbs from Indonesia. — Lewis Thomas, "On Magic in Medicine"

EXERCISE 4.4 ❱ *Transitions and repeated sentence elements*

Revise one of your paragraphs to make effective use of transitional words and phrases and repeated words, phrases, and sentence structures.

4c	**Write complete paragraphs.**

Paragraphs vary in length. Short paragraphs can be emphatic and useful for presenting simple ideas, but too many in succession may seem choppy and leave ideas undeveloped. Long paragraphs are useful for presenting complex ideas, but too many in succession may seem tiring and the ideas too concentrated. The best general rule about paragraph length is to make paragraphs long enough to explain ideas fully and to serve their purpose in a paper — and no longer. Look at the following paragraphs, which vary considerably in length.

Brief paragraph

  The drama begins to unfold with the arrival of the corpse at the mortuary. — Jessica Mitford, "Behind the Formaldehyde Curtain"   (This one-sentence paragraph creates an emphatic transition to a lengthy technical discussion of embalming procedures used by morticians.)

Moderate paragraph

Thus one can conclude that Chicano literature is, in essence, decidedly optimistic, even when it is set in what appears to be a hostile environment. Similarly, the Chicano self-image now emerging is a positive one, the antithesis of caricatures born of Anglo writers. Chicano writers are trying to paint a truer and more representative picture of themselves and their circumstances, of their present and past, while at the same time they are calling for conflict, action. But most important, Chicano writers are recording their own history, a history that never before has been written. — Luis Leal and Pepe Barron, "Chicano Literature: An Overview"   (This moderate-length paragraph uses four sentences to assess current attitudes among Chicano writers. It summarizes points already made and, through emphatic expression, creates interest in material to follow.)

Long paragraph

Poor Columbus! He is a minor character now, a walk-on in the middle of American history. Even those books that have not replaced his picture with a Mayan temple or an Iroquois mask do not credit him with discovering America — even for the Europeans. The Vikings, they say, preceded him to the New World, and after that the Europeans, having lost or forgotten their maps, simply neglected to cross the ocean again for five hundred years. Columbus is far from being the only personage to have suffered from time and revision. Captain John Smith, Daniel Boone, and Wild Bill Hickok — the great self-promoters of American history — have all but disappeared, taking with them a good deal of the romance of the American frontier. General Custer has given way to Chief Crazy Horse; General Eisenhower no longer liberates Europe single-handed; and indeed, most generals, even to Washington and Lee, have faded away, as old soldiers do, giving place to social reformers such as William Lloyd Garrison and Jacob Riis. A number of black Americans have risen to prominence: not only George Washington Carver but Frederick Douglass and Martin Luther King, Jr. W. E. B. Du Bois now invariably accompanies Booker T. Washington. In addition, there is a mystery man called Crispus Attucks, a fugitive slave about whom nothing seems to be known for certain except that he was a victim of the Boston Massacre and thus became one of the first casualties of the American Revolution. Thaddeus Stevens has been reconstructed — his character changed, as it were, from black to white, from cruel and vindictive to persistent and sincere. As for Teddy Roosevelt, he now champions the issue of conservation instead of charging up San Juan Hill. No single President really stands out as a hero, but all Presidents — except certain unmentionables in the second half of the nineteenth century — seem to have done as well as could be expected, given difficult circumstances — Frances FitzGerald, "Rewriting American History" (In this lengthy paragraph near the beginning of her essay, FitzGerald uses a series of examples to establish the scope of the essay.)

A complete paragraph presents the writer's ideas clearly, along with enough supporting detail to satisfy readers. Although supporting detail will vary from paragraph to paragraph, depending on purpose and length, complete paragraphs are usually developed through the use of specific examples, facts, and description, as described in section 4d.

EXERCISE 4.5 ❭ *Complete paragraphs*

Use one topic sentence from Exercise 4.2 to construct a paragraph that elaborates on your central idea.

EXERCISE 4.6 ❭ *Complete paragraphs*

Use the topic sentence that follows and the accompanying examples (or others of your choosing) to construct a paragraph that is complete enough to satisfy a reader's expectations.

Topic sentence

In recent years, presidents' wives have provided a useful focus on national issues.

Examples

Eleanor Roosevelt: supporter of minority and women's rights and international cooperation. Jacqueline Kennedy: supporter of historical preservation and the fine arts. Lady Bird Johnson: supporter of environmental protection, forestation, and parks preservation. Betty Ford: supporter of substance-abuse programs and the arts. Nancy Reagan: supporter of substance-abuse programs and foster-child programs. Barbara Bush: supporter of substance-abuse programs and literacy programs.

| 4d | Vary the organization and development of paragraphs. |

Organize Paragraphs in Alternative Ways

Deductive Structure

A **deductive paragraph** begins with a topic sentence and continues with supporting descriptions, examples, and facts. Writers use this structure frequently because it offers a sure way to make their meaning clear. This paragraph has a deductive structure:

The champions of applied science arose among the middle class. Scientific American ("The Advocate of Industry & Enterprise") was founded by a religious cultist named Rufus Porter in 1845, but it was sold the next year to a group of businessmen. The new owners linked it to a patent preparation service, aimed it at "Every Manufacturer, Mechanic, Inventor and Artisan," and spent the rest of the century gleefully promoting inventions, saluting technological progress and largely ignoring pure research. — Bob Coleman, "Science Writing: Too Good To Be True?"

Inductive Structure

The inverse of the deductive paragraph, an **inductive paragraph** begins with descriptions, examples, and facts and ends with the topic sentence. This structure builds suspense, heightens interest, and emphasizes details over generalization. Despite these advantages, the inductive structure should be used selectively to avoid dulling its effect or frustrating readers by asking them too often to wait for the main idea. This paragraph has an inductive structure:

On that particular day [4 September 1893] Beatrix Potter decided to write a letter, which was to become famous. It was to five-year-old Noel Moore, the youngest son of her ex-governess Annie Moore, a delicate boy who was often ill and who found great comfort in the generously illustrated letters that arrived regularly from 'Yours affectionately, Beatrix Potter'. This particular letter began: 'My dear Noel, I don't know what to write to you, so I shall tell you a story about four little rabbits whose names were Flopsy, Mopsy, Cottontail and Peter. They lived with their mother in a sand bank under the root of a big fir tree...' The letter continued with the whole of the now famous story of Peter Rabbit. — Judy Taylor, "The Tale of Beatrix Potter"

EXERCISE 4.7 ❱ *Deductive and inductive structure*

Using two of the topic sentences you wrote for Exercise 4.2, write one deductive and one inductive paragraph. Underline the topic sentence in each and number the details in the margin of the paper. Be ready to explain why you chose the paragraph structure you did for developing each topic sentence.

Develop Your Paragraphs

Purpose

Let purpose determine the development of your paragraphs. Although it is possible first to select an appropriate pattern of development and then to fit information to the pattern, the result is often awkward or mechanical. A better strategy is to complete some planning activities, decide on a general purpose and thesis for the whole paper, outline the information, and then write the first draft, letting the patterns of the paragraphs develop naturally. In this way, each paragraph extends and strengthens a paper's purpose.

For example, in her brief essay "In Bed," Joan Didion narrates her history of ignoring, fighting, and finally learning to live with migraine headaches. In the course of eight paragraphs, Didion vividly describes and provides facts on the effects, course, and treatment of this illness; she narrates her own experience from childhood; and, ultimately, she persuades readers that such afflictions can be beneficial when they remind us of the beauty and serenity of life.

Descriptions

All writing benefits from apt and vivid details that evoke the five senses. In your writing, search for words that describe your subject's sights (*mauve* wallpaper, *glistening* chrome), sounds (*faint* tapping, *shrill* laughter), touch (*satiny* varnish, *leathery* skin), tastes (*salty* crackers, *sour* apples), and smells (*fishy* smell, *lavender* scent). Be specific, and try for both originality and accuracy.

> To new arrivals in London, it seemed pitch black out of doors, too, but not, by 1943, to Londoners. People had become conscious again of the phases of the moon, the light from the stars. They had regained their country eyes. The darkness was full of noises, the echo of footsteps, of people talking, the cries for taxis. Sound itself seemed amplified and dependable in the half-blindness of the street. The smell was of dust, of damp plaster in the air, and of the formaldehyde scent of the smoke from the dirty coal that lodged in the yellow fog. The stained sandbags, the rust, the dull, peeling paint, damp that made great dark lines down the walls, made London seem like a long-neglected, leaky attic.
> — Mary Lee Settle, "London — 1944"

Examples

One of the most effective methods for developing a paragraph is through the use of specific, appropriate examples. Be precise; name names. Don't write "a comedy program"; write "*Cheers.*" Don't write "a school on the west coast"; write "Stanford." To be convincing, examples need to be precise, but also representative. Do not use extremely positive or negative examples that will seem to readers exceptional rather than typical. Often, presenting a single extended example will best show readers how you reached your conclusion. One useful way to present examples fully is to answer the journalists' questions: *who, what, when, where, how,* and *why*.

> Gold also remains an integral part of social and religious customs in many nations. From Morocco through the Middle East and on to India the status of a bride is still judged by the amount of gold in her dowry. The typical Saudi Arabian adornment for women includes 12 bangles for each wrist, a belt, a necklace, earrings and ring, all in 21-karat gold. This endowment may weigh over a kilo (32.5 troy ounces). Many Saudi brides are also decked out with *duru,* a lace-like embroidery of gold chains interwoven with small coins that often weighs two or three kilos (the gold worth over $70,000) that draped the bride from her neck to her knees like a cascade of armor. The normal American wedding ring containing four or five grams of 14-karat gold hardly bears comparison. — Timothy Green, "All That Glitters"

Facts

Using facts and technical and statistical information effectively demonstrates how and why you reached your conclusion. Be as specific as possible. Don't write that a car costs "a lot"; write "$54,000." Don't write that tuition has "increased dramatically" in the last decade; write "26 percent." If you use facts that you have gathered yourself, simply incorporate them in your writing. If your facts come from research, be sure to include full documentation (see pages 536–42 for guidelines).

> In 1955 state psychiatric hospitals had 559,000 patients. Today there are about 130,000, a decline of 75 percent. Now, the incidence of severe mental illness has not changed. (Schizophrenia, for example, afflicts about one percent of the population.) Nor have drugs and modern treatment yielded a cure rate of 75 percent. Many of the 75 percent discharged from the state hospitals have simply been abandoned. They have become an army of grate-dwellers. — Charles Krauthammer, "How to Save the Homeless Mentally Ill"

Comparison and Contrast

Comparison and contrast bring together two subjects in order to analyze their respective similarities and differences. Use this technique to explain the unfamiliar in terms of the familiar or use it to explore the features or qualities of your subjects. Your topic sentence should offer a clear synthesis of the compared or contrasted elements.

Comparison and contrast paragraphs can be structured in two ways: whole-to-whole and part-to-part. **Whole-to-whole,** or divided, **development** fully discusses first one subject and then the other. The topic sentence of a paragraph with this pattern generally emphasizes the two subjects, subordinating features or qualities.

> In the waning years of the nineteenth century, two remarkable women, exact contemporaries living at opposite ends of the immense American diversity, dissented from the cultural shibboleths and popular taste of their time in the way they wrote about the life they knew best. Kate Chopin (1851–1904) was consciously defiant of the decencies and sexual prudery of the late 1890s, and sought to uncover the sensuality and discontent of women which the stultifying conventions of the age refused to acknowledge. Sarah Orne Jewett (1849–1909) preferred to look back rather than forward to the emancipated future envisioned by Mrs. Chopin; her sensibility and values were deeply anchored in the past of a rural New England that was rapidly disappearing in her lifetime, but she, too, shunned the idealized versions of actuality which a culture dedicated to gentility demanded of its literature. — Pearl K. Bell, "Kate Chopin and Sarah Orne Jewett"

The second pattern for comparison and contrast, **part-to-part,** or alternating, **development** provides a point-by-point, alternating comparison between two subjects. The topic sentences generally emphasize qualities, features, or, as in the next example, the specific consequences following from the topic.

> Ethically, most Americans are simultaneously egalitarians and capitalists. This set of beliefs leads to an alarming chain reaction. A new and

expensive treatment is developed. Since, as capitalists, Americans believe that individuals should be allowed to spend their money on
whatever they wish, the wealthy are allowed to buy the treatment privately. People who cannot afford the treatment start to demand it. Being egalitarians, Americans do not have the political ability to say "no"
to any person dying from a treatable disease, and so ways are found to
pay for the treatment through private or public health insurance. As
egalitarians, we feel we have to provide the treatment to everyone or
deny it to everyone; as capitalists, we cannot deny it to those who can
afford it. But since resources are limited, we cannot afford to give it to
everyone. — Lester C. Thurow, "The Ethical Costs of Health Care"

Extended Analogy

An analogy illuminates a subject by pointing to an unexpected
connection between dissimilar things. This quality of the unexpected can make writing vivid, but be sure to select or construct
analogies in which the connections are reasonable and clear. The
following example contains three analogies.

All guardians of the language resemble a little the village idiot in the
shtetl of Frampol who was given the job of standing at the village gates
in wait for the coming of the Messiah. The pay is not high, he was told,
but he didn't have to worry about running out of work. The guardians
of the language need similarly never worry about running out of work.
Like Heraclitus's famous river — "Upon those who step into the same
river different and ever different waters flow down" — the river of language continues to flow along, never remaining the same, changing
every foot of the way. Heraclitus spoke of his river being in perpetual
flux but never of its muddying, whereas in the river of language flux
frequently does issue in mud, garbage, and other detritus. To change
classical references, the task of the guardian of the language can be
likened to cleaning out the Augean stables with the horses still in them.
This, for reasons needing no explanation, is not everybody's idea of a
good time. — Joseph Epstein, "What's the Usage?"

Cause and Effect

Analyzing an event or condition often involves asking why it happened or how it came to be — that is, inquiring into its known or

likely causes. Remember that a single cause may have multiple effects, and a single effect multiple causes. Remember, too, that a cause and effect relationship is not established by mere association. It is not necessary to document the relation in your paragraph, but if you are speculating, make that clear to your readers.

> Nonetheless, in 1917 fishermen and fox farmers convinced the Alaska Territorial Legislature that the eagles' appetite for salmon and small mammals should reduce them to varmint status. A bounty was posted — $1 per pair of talons, later raised to $2. By the time experts realized that foul play had been exaggerated, 128,000 eagles had been shot. The Bald Eagle Protection Act of 1940 made killing an eagle a federal offense. — Jessica Maxwell, "The Eagles Have Landed"

Process Analysis

To describe how something is done or made or how something happens, you need to describe accurately and completely the series of steps involved. A paragraph describing a process can be organized *spatially,* as when a writer describes the spreading consequences of the destruction of a rain forest by beginning with the cutting of one tree, or *chronologically,* as in this example.

> A homemade *sorbetto* [Italian sorbet] uses a sugar syrup, which is one part sugar and one part water boiled together for five minutes and then cooled. Two parts fruit puree or juice are added to the syrup, and the mixture is frozen. You can freeze the mixture in an ice-cream maker, which continuously beats air into it as it freezes, but you're almost as well off putting it into an ice tray with the dividers removed or into a cake pan, and transferring it to a chilled bowl to beat it twice — after it turns to slush and before it freezes completely. The whole freezing process takes between three and five hours. After the *sorbetto* is frozen hard, you should put it in the refrigerator for an hour or so to temper it before serving. — Corby Kummer, "Summer Ices"

Classification

A large subject can be examined by dividing it into its parts or subgroups. You must establish meaningful, consistent criteria for your division, supplying readers with the information they need to distinguish among the classes. Subgroups should not overlap.

> For present purposes, it will be useful to distinguish four degrees of poverty: *destitution,* which is lack of income sufficient to assure physical survival and to prevent suffering from hunger, exposure, or remediable or preventable illness; *want,* which is a lack of enough income to support "essential welfare" (as distinguished from comfort and convenience); *hardship,* which is lack of enough to prevent acute, persistent discomfort or inconvenience; and *relative deprivation,* which is lack of enough to prevent one from feeling poor by comparison with others. — Edward C. Banfield, "Several Kinds of Poverty"

Definition

Definitions clarify your thinking and your writing, explaining terms and concepts to your readers. A formal definition, such as those in dictionaries, places the subject in a class and then distinguishes it from other items in the same class.

> Some dunes, enormous, dwarf a three-story house. Lying between them are the *wadis, old water courses dry most of the year.* — Russell Fraser, "Wadi-Bashing in Arabia Deserta"

An informal or extended definition may describe the subject, provide examples of it, or compare or contrast it with some other thing. The following paragraph contains examples of both types of definition.

> Gardeners have long squabbled over what wildflowers are. Purists insist that they are native plants that grew before the arrival of the Europeans. Others include naturalized plants in the classification — those introduced from other parts of the world that reproduce freely in their nonnative habitat. Opinion these days favors the definition that includes both native and naturalized plants. Weeds, incidentally, are just wildflowers that grow when they are not wanted. Noxious weeds are plants that the authorities have determined threaten human health or agricultural practices. Some common attractive weeds are Queen Anne's lace (*Daucus carota*), chicory (*Cichorium intybus*) and even

oxeye daisy (*Chrysanthemum leucanthemum*). — Eva Hoepfner, "Wildflower Meadows"

EXERCISE 4.8 ❭ *Paragraph development*

Write a paragraph using one of the following methods of development. Use one of the topics provided, or select one of your own.

Description: an incident of prejudice, a scene showing family support, a situation in which trust was crucial, a depiction of a smoothly run business

Examples: the need for urban planning, the importance of energy conservation, the practical value of hobbies, the growing dependence on computers

Facts: high costs of education, everyday uses of mathematics, basic equipment necessary for cooking, questionable recruitment procedures in college athletics

Comparison and contrast: seeing a horror film on television and at a theater, celebrations in different cultures, two specialized magazines, your language patterns with close friends and with parents

Analogy: preparing for a date and for a religious ritual, political ads and soft-drink ads, a college campus and a city, marriage and a corporate merger

Cause and effect: a death in the family, the farming crisis in the United States, a major industry closing in your city, personal financial difficulties

Process: preparing a speech, analyzing a work of literature, buying a stereo, applying for college

Definition: music videos, patriotism, a good parent-child relationship, luck

Classification: types of museums, kinds of cartoon strips, types of radio stations, kinds of football fans

MAKING C O N N E C T I O N S

Using paragraphs comes so naturally to most writers that they never think about it. Thinking about your reactions to paragraph patterns in your writing and in the writing of others, however, can be useful.

- Discover your own paragraph patterns. Look at two or three papers that you have written recently for any class. Is your average paragraph long or short? Do you use both inductive and deductive paragraphs? Do you use some of the development patterns described on pages 96–103 frequently and others rarely or never? Use this information to vary your paragraphs in the next paper you write.

- Consider paragraph patterns in your reading. During the next week, as you read textbooks, other books, magazines, or newspapers, make note of the various paragraph patterns that you encounter. How do paragraphs vary in length, method of development, and use of topic sentences from one type of material to the next? Which source has the most readable and appropriate paragraphing? Apply the information you gather in your next paper to increase the effectiveness and variety of your paragraphs.

5   Critical Thinking and Writing

Human beings from a very young age continually think. Consciously or unconsciously, through every waking hour, we reflect, respond, react, infer, deduce, and intuit. Remembering and anticipating are further examples of ways we think about and try to understand our world. Trying to communicate that understanding to others, however, requires critical thinking skills.

All purposeful verbal communication — whether speaking, listening, reading, or writing — requires critical thinking, an active, focused engagement with the topic. When people speak or write, they first synthesize ideas and experiences and then communicate their insights or observations to others. Conversely, when people listen or read, they actively seek to comprehend the insights and observations of others, thus completing the speaker's or writer's intended communication.

Quick Reference

By thinking critically when you read and write, you will improve your understanding of others' writing and their understanding of yours.

⟩ *Think critically, actively focusing on the topic and its development.*

⟩ *Support different kinds of assertions with the appropriate kinds of evidence.*

⟩ *Evaluate discussions to determine whether supporting evidence is adequate.*

⟩ *Recognize patterns of fallacious reasoning. Challenge them in what you read and avoid them in what you write.*

Some people possess an apparently innate ability to think critically, to sort through information, to respond to experiences, and to articulate ideas with clarity and precision. Others gain these skills by studying and practicing the techniques of critical thinking and writing. The systematic study and practice of critical thinking and writing, whatever a person's innate ability, improves all forms of communication by fostering substantive, precise, and thorough analysis, expression, and response.

This chapter explores the techniques of critical thinking as they apply to both reading and writing.

 Think critically, actively focusing on the topic and its development.

Critical thinking involves active, focused, systematic engagement with the topic. The method and intensity of applying critical thinking skills varies with the topic and with the reader's and writer's purpose.

Critical thinking, required in most college work, involves systematic, objective, and rigorous scrutiny and evaluation of ideas — both in what you read and in what you write. When you read a paper, article, report, or book that argues a position, think about it critically, actively examining and evaluating its purpose, assumptions, evidence, and development. Ultimately, you must decide whether it has succeeded in establishing the validity of its position.

To work as a writer, you must use your critical thinking skills to clarify and support your own purposes, assumptions, evidence, and development. Your general goal in thinking critically when you write is to make certain that you demonstrate the validity of your position.

Critical thinking, then, can be used as you read, to deconstruct someone's thought processes, and as you write, to construct a presentation that will effectively convey your ideas.

In thinking critically, readers and writers use three patterns of reasoning: inductive, deductive, and warrant-based reasoning. These methods organize ideas and evidence in different ways that reflect differences in the type of evidence, in the writer's emphasis, and in the source of the main idea.

Inductive Reasoning

Writers use **induction** when they first compile a set of specific observations (examples, facts, testimony, and so on) and then, on the basis of the interpretation of those observations, derive a conclusion or generalization. The validity of inductive reasoning depends on both the representativeness of the observations and the accuracy of the interpretation.

Consider, for example, this circumstance. You discover through discussions that ten students in your writing class are on scholarships. You learn through conversations that many of your friends in other classes also have student loans and grants. You read a newspaper article that notes that college expenses have risen beyond the means of many parents. On the basis of these observations, you reasonably conclude by induction that many students at your college receive financial aid.

Deductive Reasoning

Writers use **deduction** when they reason from a general, accepted premise to a specific, related conclusion. In deductive reasoning, the writer provides support for or extends the original generalization using additional information (sometimes called a *minor premise*). The validity of a deductive pattern depends on the validity of the original premise and of the reasoning used to reach the conclusion.

A traditional form of the deductive argument is the **syllogism,** which consists of a *major premise,* a broad conclusion or generalization; a *minor premise,* a statement related to but more specific than the major premise; and a *conclusion,* the logical consequence of the major premise in light of the minor premise.

Major premise

Gasoline prices increase when OPEC raises its per-barrel price of crude oil.

Minor premise

OPEC has raised the price of crude oil.

Conclusion

Gasoline prices will rise.

Warrant-based Reasoning

Warrant-based reasoning is a process somewhat like the writing process. Beginning with an idea expressed as a thesis or an assertion, the writer accumulates necessary supporting evidence through research or other forms of planning. The writer's values and perspective emerge most clearly in the underlying warrant, the sometimes unstated or implicit connection that the writer makes between the assertion and the evidence. Although the writer's reasoning must be sound, it will not have the inevitability of deductive or inductive reasoning. Thus, in order for the writer to convince readers of the validity of the assertion, the evidence offered must be convincing and complete.

Assertion

Mr. Lidstrom will be an effective district attorney.

Evidence

Mr. Lidstrom has worked for ten years as an assistant district attorney.

Warrant

Ten years as assistant district attorney has provided Mr. Lidstrom with the range of experiences and the contacts and credibility he needs to do his new job well.

This kind of argument cannot be conducted according to deductive or inductive reasoning because there is an inevitable subjective element in deciding what makes a good district attorney. One writer's position is that length of service, rather than education or a particular kind of experience, such as prosecuting crime bosses or drug dealers, will help Lidstrom do a good job. Depending on the audience and the issue, the writer may want to offer more, and more varied, evidence. **》》》** *Be sure to think through your implicit warrants. An invalid warrant, even if unstated, can lead to invalid conclusions.*

Because college admissions tests are administered nationwide, they are an effective measure of student potential.   (The implicit warrant is that widely used tests are effective. Because this notion is questionable, the conclusion is questionable as well.) **《《《**

EXERCISE 5.1 》 *Patterns of critical thinking*

Complete the following arguments; then, using the guidelines given above, compose an inductive, a deductive, and a warrant-based argument.

Inductive argument

Evidence

_____

_____

Conclusion

College students contribute to and are responsible members of society and should be treated accordingly.

Deductive argument

Major premise

Children require good nutrition in order to concentrate and learn in school.

Minor premise

Schools have a responsibility and public mandate to ensure that students concentrate and learn.

Conclusion

_____

_____

Warrant-based argument

Assertion

Capital punishment is immoral and should be illegal.

Evidence

Executions do not deter others from similar crimes and encourage barbaric public displays in a carnival atmosphere.

Warrant

_____

_____

EXERCISE 5.2 ❱ *Warrants*

Identify the warrants, both implicit and explicit, in the following paragraph.

Low wages and lack of job security create frustration, however. This leads to a 40 percent turnover rate among congressional staffers.

There is something to be said for new blood, but not when a complete transfusion is taking place about every two years. The result is not only a less efficient staff but in the long run a less effective Congress. Without experienced staff, there is no institutional memory — those who will recall what happened on an issue four years before. Without them, in fact, Congress becomes more vulnerable to criticism even from the people it most benefits. — Jonathan Yates, "'Reality' on Capitol Hill"

| 5b | **Analyze purpose, audience, and content.** |

To read and write effectively, you must analyze the roles of purpose, audience, and content in ensuring communication. See section 1d for more information on audience and purpose.

Evaluate Purpose

To think critically about a piece of writing — one that you are reading or one that you are writing — you must evaluate its general purpose. Different kinds of writing require different kinds of development. The following four types apply to both spoken and written communication.

Purposes of Writing

In **expressive writing,** writers share perceptions and experiences, generally those gathered from personal observations. Personal essays and letters, poetry, and fiction are examples of expressive writing.

In **referential writing,** writers share information and ideas, generally those gathered through systematic research. Reports, research papers, memoranda, and informational articles in newspapers and magazines are examples of referential writing.

In **persuasive writing,** writers present information and observations with the specific intent of convincing readers to alter their perceptions or to take action. Letters to newspaper editors, requests, petitions, arguments in law courts, and advertisements are examples of persuasive writing.

In **argumentative writing,** writers present ideas, information, experiences, and insights to articulate an opinion about an arguable topic. The writer's goal is to state an opinion and to illuminate the topic. Debates, political and other speeches and articles, newspaper editorials, articles and essays of criticism and analysis are examples of argumentative writing.

Recognizing the different purposes that expressive, referential, persuasive, and argumentative writing serve will help you to test the validity of a paper's assumptions and presentation. For instance, a single apt, well-written example may effectively illustrate a point in an expressive paper but be inadequate support to convince readers in a persuasive paper on the same topic. The different reasons for writing establish different expectations for development.

Understanding an Audience

Effective writing always accommodates itself to the needs of its readers. Persuasive and argumentative writing, however, must do so even more thoroughly and systematically than other kinds of writing.

As a critical reader and writer, you can examine and evaluate the needs of a reading audience and assess how effectively the writing meets those needs.

Questions about Readers

- How much will they already know about the topic?
- How skeptical might they be about the assertion?
- What preconceptions or misconceptions might they have?

- What kinds of evidence will they require?

- What kinds of objections will they raise?

- What needs will they bring to the reading?

Because your position will be arguable, consider how your opposition will think about the topic. In a simulated debate, consider how your opposition might refute your claims. Similarly, how might you refute theirs? Consider ways you might reconcile these opposing views. A consideration of opposing views, especially in written form, will prepare you to write a balanced, knowledgeable paper.

For instance, you might freewrite to explore the opposition's objections to your views and then highlight the primary objections with a marker for consideration and incorporation in your paper. Or use two columns, listing your most important evidence on the left and an opponent's response on the right.

It is not always possible to accommodate all potential readers — their diversity is too great — but thoughtful writers who expect to have critical readers in their audience try to anticipate their needs and expectations.

Use the word processor to generate and organize thoughts about your audience. ■ Use freewriting to describe your audience. Turn off or dim your computer monitor and freewrite about your audience, using the questions listed above as guidelines. Assess your audience fairly, respecting opposing views. Record your thoughts quickly. ■ Organize your thoughts about your audience. Using the audience description you have generated, group ideas and assess your audience's general needs. ■ Brainstorm for objections to your position. If your topic is controversial, some members of your audience will disagree with your assertion. Use the computer to construct a brainstorming list of objections; then supply the counterarguments.

Summarize General Content

Reading is an active process of decoding written symbols (words) to reveal a writer's meaning or content. As a reader, you must first decide what is being said before you can evaluate its effectiveness or validity. The simplest technique for articulating a writer's content is to summarize it, in your head or on paper.

A **summary** is a brief, objective restatement in your own words of the central idea presented in a short written work or in a portion of a longer work. For brief texts of only a few paragraphs, a summary may be a single sentence; for longer texts, a complete summary may be several sentences or a paragraph.

Strategies for Writing Summaries

- Look for the writer's thesis statement or topic sentence. It will present the most direct, comprehensive statement of the central idea.

- Read the text carefully and then put it aside; do not look at the text while writing your summary.

- Select and restate the central idea(s) only.

- Omit details, explanations, examples, and clarifications.

- Express the text's main idea(s) in your own words, not in the writer's.

- Name the author or source explicitly in the summary, and provide a page citation.

Learning to write a summary takes practice, but the skill is valuable for your reading and your writing. Expect to revise a summary several times to make it brief, accurate, objective, and complete.

To demonstrate how summaries work, first read the following passage from an article in the *State Department Bulletin* on international trade competition and trade deficits:

What are the sources of competitive pressure on U.S. industry? Some competitive pressures result, in the normal course of events in a dynamic world economy, from shifting patterns of comparative advantage. As countries develop and mature they move into new lines of production and exports. The accumulation of capital, new technologies, and product innovations abroad may make nations internationally competitive in a new product line, and their exports can put pressure on existing producers elsewhere. While we may wish to protect ourselves from disruptive import surges, it is in our longrun interest to adjust to these changing conditions by either increasing our own competitiveness in these product lines or moving resources into other areas where our comparative advantage resides. While such adjustment is painful for the affected industries in the short run, the process is the mechanism through which the benefits of economic advance in one country are shared internationally. Certain U.S. industries are finding this adjustment very difficult and painful, but we should not confuse their plight with the problem of the overall trade deficit. — Elinor G. Constable, "International Competition, Trade Deficits, and National Policy"

A clear, concise, and complete summary of Constable's paragraph requires several drafts:

First attempt

    Trade competition arises for a number of reasons.   (Though concise, this summary is too simplistic.)

Second attempt

    Trade competition arises as foreign countries develop their technologies and enter world markets.   (Although this summary is clearer than the first, it presents only part of Constable's point. It needs further elaboration.)

Third attempt

    When trade competition arises because foreign countries develop their technologies and enter world markets, American companies must improve their own technologies or shift to other areas of trade. (This summary presents the major points of Constable's paragraph.)

Fourth attempt

Elinor G. Constable, in "International Competition, Trade Deficits, and National Policy," notes that when trade competition arises because foreign countries develop their technologies and enter world markets, American companies must either improve their own technologies or shift to other areas of trade (60).   (Citing the author, title, and page number completes the summary.)

>>> When including a summary as part of a paper, include a full citation of the source on your works cited page. **<<<**

Use a word processor to help you create and revise a clear and concise summary. ■ Draft the summary. Working at the keyboard, type out the first version of your summary. ■ Refine the summary. Use the add and delete capabilities of a word processor to incorporate overlooked central ideas and to eliminate extraneous details. ■ Add clarifying information. Incorporate the author, title, and page number of the original work.

EXERCISE 5.3 ❯ Summaries

Write a summary of each of the following paragraphs.

A.   The tropical rain forest north of Manaus, like that in many other parts of the Amazon basin, is being clear-cut from the edge inward. It is being lifted up from the ground entire like a carpet rolled off a bare floor, leaving behind vast stretches of cattle range and cropland that need artificial fertilization to sustain even marginal productivity for more than two or three years. A rain forest in Brazil differs fundamentally from a deciduous woodland in Pennsylvania or Germany in the way its key resources are distributed. A much greater fraction of organic matter is bound up in the tissues of the standing trees, so that the leaf litter and humus are only a few inches deep. When the forest is felled and burned, the hard equato-

rial downpours quickly wash away the thin blanket of top soil.
— Edward O. Wilson, "The Superorganism"

B.   When we look back in time and study old cultures and people, we
are impressed that death has always been distasteful to man and will
probably always be. From a psychiatrist's point of view this is very understandable and can perhaps be best explained by our basic knowledge
that, in our unconscious, death is never possible in regard to ourselves. It
is inconceivable for our unconscious to imagine an actual ending of our
own life here on earth, and if this life of ours has to end, the ending is
always attributed to a malicious intervention from the outside by someone else. In simple terms, in our unconscious mind we can only be killed;
it is inconceivable to die of a natural cause or of old age. Therefore death
in itself is associated with a bad act, a frightening happening, something
that in itself calls for retribution and punishment.   — Elisabeth
Kübler-Ross, "On the Fear of Death"

C.   In social organizations which embody a strong class system, such
as military units and large business concerns, there are many territorial
rules, often unspoken, which interfere with the official hierarchy.
High-status individuals, such as officers or managers, could in theory enter any of the regions occupied by the lower levels in the peck order, but
they limit this power in a striking way. An officer seldom enters a ser-
geant's mess or a barrack room unless it's for a formal inspection. He re-
spects those regions as alien territories even though he has the power to
go there by virtue of his dominant role. And in businesses, part of the
appeal of unions, over and above their obvious functions, is that with
their officials, headquarters, and meetings they add a sense of territorial
power for the staff workers. It is almost as if each military organization
and business concern consists of two warring tribes: the officers versus
the other ranks, and management versus the workers. Each has its special
home base within the system, and the territorial defense pattern thrusts
itself into what, on the surface, is a pure social hierarchy. Negotiations
between managements and unions are tribal battles fought out over the
neutral ground of a boardroom table, and are as much concerned with
territorial display as they are with resolving problems of wages and conditions. Indeed, if one side gives in too quickly and accepts the other's
demands, the victors feel strangely cheated and deeply suspicious that it
may be a trick. What they are missing is the protracted sequence of ritual

and counter-ritual that keeps alive their group territorial identity.
— Desmond Morris, "Territorial Behavior"

| 5c | **Evaluate assertions.** |

Assertions positively state ideas or information. Critical thinkers, whether in writing or when responding to reading, require appropriate, clearly expressed assertions.

Every written work contains many assertions. The most important assertion is the thesis statement, but that controlling idea will be supported by a number of other assertions, notably the topic sentences in supporting paragraphs. Assertions can take three forms, each requiring different substantiation and development.

Assertions

Facts

Assertions of fact state verifiable, objective information. Facts need not necessarily be verified in your paper, though facts not considered common knowledge must be documented (see section 31g).

Facts generally cannot provide, but only support, a thesis, since they are not themselves arguable. The assertion, for instance, that *The Phantom of the Opera* (1917) was the first colorized film may support a thesis about technical innovations in early films, but it cannot be the thesis of a developed paper. Facts, because they can be verified by referring to a reliable reference, cannot be the basis of formal arguments. Once a fact is verified, there is no debate.

Beliefs

Assertions of belief express nonverifiable, subjective ideas. Beliefs may be used to support a thesis, but they cannot be the basis for a thesis because they are not arguable. Someone might assert, for example, that Tchaikovsky's symphonies are overrated, but such an assertion is based on aesthetic taste rather than on objective evidence that can be substantiated. Other sources of belief are religious faith, cultural and social environment, and prejudice. Assertions of belief, appropriately used and strongly and knowledgeably expressed, can produce writing that persuades readers to agree.

Opinion

Assertions of opinion state conclusions that are logically inferred from facts. To assert, as Constable does (page 115), that tariffs harm rather than help a nation's economy is an assertion of an opinion formed after consideration of the data. Opinions can provide a thesis because they are arguable; writers reach different judgments even when they consider the same information because they approach facts, examples, testimony, and so on from their individual perspectives.

Supporting Assertions

The ability to recognize different kinds of assertions will prove helpful in your critical reading — and especially in researching. Assertions based on facts are often illustrated and verified by useful, detailed technical information. Assertions based on belief or opinion are almost always substantiated with extended explanations, facts, statistics, examples, and expert testimony — providing fully developed discussions of the topic. Knowing that assertions signal such development will help you to think critically and respond appropriately as you read, evaluate, and use materials. In your own writing, consider whether you have used assertions effectively and appropriately and supported them where necessary to enhance your credibility and communication with your readers.

EXERCISE 5.4 ❯ *Assertions*

Identify the following assertions, all from George F. Will's essay "Grandmother Was Right," as assertions of fact, belief, or opinion. Then describe the kind of verification you would expect to find for each one.

1. Americans do have a heightened interest in health, thanks in part to Dr. Kenneth H. Cooper.

2. Cooper's clinic has conducted 100,000 physical examinations, generating an invaluable data base for the study of preventative and rehabilitative behavior.

3. There is something sick about some contemporary thinking about health.

4. The modern refusal to accept material and social limits has enabled mankind to live better, materially and morally, than premodern peasants.

5. Many values of modernity conflict with another value, grace in the face of the fact of death.

| 5d | ❯ | **Evaluate evidence.** |

Evidence, material used to support an assertion, must be pertinent, verifiable, and reliable. Useful for assertions based on both beliefs and opinions, evidence can be classified as facts and statistics, examples, and expert testimony.

Facts and Statistics

A **fact** is objectively verifiable information; **statistics** are mathematical data. Familiar examples of facts and statistics include dates, percentages, and quantities. It is a verifiable fact that 58,135 American soldiers died in the Vietnam War. It is a verifiable statistic that roughly 65 percent of those killed were in the U.S. Army.

Facts and statistics, when relevant and accurate, are effective tools with which to support formal arguments. **>>>** *When facts are not common knowledge, they must be fully documented. See section 31g for a full discussion.* **<<<**

Examples

Examples are individual cases illustrating assertions of belief or opinion. Examples drawn from personal experience are considered **primary evidence** and are usually incorporated in expressive and persuasive papers. Examples drawn from other people's writing are considered **secondary evidence** and are most often used in referential, persuasive, and argumentative papers. To be effective, examples must be relevant, representative, and complete.

Relevant Examples

Relevant examples clearly illustrate the topic at hand. In supporting a paper asserting that film censorship today is ineffective, D. W. Griffith's *Intolerance* (1918) would not be a relevant example because the issues it raised — by its depiction of adultery, for example — are less controversial today than they were when the picture was made and are unlikely to be censored. The use of a more recent example, such as Martin Scorsese's *The Last Temptation of Christ* (1988), would allow a writer to discuss current censorship issues.

Representative Examples

Representative examples are neither extremely positive nor extremely negative. Extreme examples are exceptions, and thoughtful readers are likely to find them unconvincing. In a paper on the negative effects of state lotteries on family finances, for instance, a five-million-dollar winner would not be representative, nor would a person who spent the family's food money on lottery tickets. Representing extremes, neither example would convincingly support the assertion.

Complete Examples

Complete examples allow readers to see how the examples work as evidence. Incorporating responses to the journalists' questions (*who, what, when, where, how,* and *why*) is one useful way to guarantee completeness. Adding a summary can further clarify important connections.

Expert Testimony

Expert testimony in an argument, like expert testimony in court trials, is a statement of opinion or a judgment made by an expert or authority in a field. To support an assertion about sexual discrimination in government hiring, a specialist in labor practices or a statistician working with government hiring data could speak authoritatively. A feminist critic of literature would not have necessary expertise, even though he or she might have an informed opinion on discriminatory hiring practices.

Appeals

Critical thinking and writing involve more than assessing the reasoning in a paper. Writers use **appeals** to reach and convince their audiences, and critical readers learn to identify them. The three kinds of appeals are **logical, ethical,** and **emotional**.

Logical Appeals

Logical appeals emphasize the topic, stressing the central issues and supplying necessary evidence. The following paragraph uses a logical appeal, offering facts and statistics to support its position that chemical poisoning is gradually decreasing.

> It took the social activism of the 1960s and early 1970s to bring about controls. The Lead-based Paint Poisoning Prevention Act banned the manufacture and sale of leaded paint and directed the Department of Housing and Urban Development (HUD) to develop a strategy for re-

moving old paint from old housing. In the mid-1970s the Food and Drug Administration (FDA) pressured the food industry to remove lead solder from the seams of baby-food and baby-formula cans. According to the EPA, more than 161,000 metric tons of lead tainted the air in 1975. In an effort to lower this atmospheric pollution the agency ordered oil companies to start phasing out lead additives in gasoline beginning in 1977. By 1984 the count had fallen by 75 percent, to 39,000 metric tons. Each year since, the levels have continued to fall. — Michael Weisskopf, "Lead Astray: The Poisoning of America"

Ethical Appeals

Ethical appeals emphasize the writer, stressing his or her trustworthiness, honesty, clarity, and directness. Note that the ethical appeal refers not to the ethicalness of the writer's position but to the way in which the position is described. The writer of the following paragraph uses an ethical appeal by establishing his knowledge of and fairness to opposing views and by carefully qualifying his statements.

In the great debate over legalizing recreational drugs, the least convincing assertion of the pro-legalizers is that drug use might not even increase as a result. I can state for certain that drug use would increase. I don't use drugs now. If they were legal, I would use them. Or, rather, if marijuana were legal, I would use it occasionally instead of the legal drug I now use regularly, alcohol. To be sure, increased respect for the law is not the only reason so many middle-class, middle-age people have abandoned marijuana: you're also no longer so carefree about where your mind might take you on automatic pilot, especially in public. But society's official disapproval is a substantial deterrent. Without it, many of us would sneak the odd toke or two. — Michael Kinsley, "Glass Houses and Getting Stoned"

Emotional Appeals

Emotional appeals emphasize readers, stressing their needs, desires, hopes, and expectations. The following paragraph makes emotional appeals to readers' sympathy and self-interest.

Obviously the decisions that must be made when an elderly patient faces a medical crisis are difficult ones for everyone — patient, loved ones, doctors, hospitals and health-care personnel alike. When a satisfying, although perhaps restricted, life is possible if treatment is successful, the decisions are easy: You do everything you can. But when someone has had a medical crisis and is in failing health with little hope of recovery; when all the painful, costly, possibly degrading though heroic measures may gain no more than a few extra days or weeks or, maybe, months for a patient who is probably miserable and often unconscious, the decisions are more difficult and individuals may vary widely in their preferences — if, indeed, they are given a choice. — Roy Hoopes, "Turning Out the Light"

》》》 *Use emotional appeals cautiously. Although some highly charged topics require acknowledgment of their emotional aspect, and almost any topic may have an emotional aspect to those most intimately involved with it, readers may react with suspicion if the emotional appeal seems inappropriate or overdone.* **《《《**

EXERCISE 5.5 **》** *Evidence*

Identify the kinds of evidence used in the following paragraphs. Discuss why this evidence is effective and consider alternative ways to support the assertions in the paragraphs.

Spurred by a scientific consensus that significant greenhouse-effect warming will occur in the early decades of the next century, delegates from 46 countries at a Conference on the Changing Atmosphere held in Toronto have called for an urgent action plan. The conferees, who included scientists and policymakers (but no senior U.S. Government official), recommended that governments initially reduce emissions of carbon dioxide — thought to play a major role in greenhouse warming — by 20 percent before the year 2005.

Some workers maintain that greenhouse warming, which results when trace gases prevent infrared radiation from the earth's surface from escaping to space, has already set in; indeed, a scientist at the National Aeronautics and Space Administration (NASA) is searching for a greenhouse "fingerprint" in existing data. The four warmest years in a century of instrumental records have fallen within the 1980's, and the first five months of 1988 were the hottest five-month period ever recorded.

One climate analyst, James E. Hansen of NASA's Goddard Institute for Space Studies, told a Senate subcommittee in Washington just before the Toronto conference that the recent warming could be ascribed "with a high degree of confidence" to the greenhouse effect. At Toronto the delegates kept an open mind about whether the greenhouse effect has contributed to the warmth of the 1980's. They agreed, however, that past emissions of greenhouse gases make significant warming inevitable. Indeed the most recent computer models predict that accumulating trace gases will harm the lower atmosphere sooner than expected.

Carbon dioxide, which is increasing by .4 percent each year because of combustion of fossil fuels and the destruction of tropical forests, accounts for half of the predicted warming. Other greenhouse gases include methane, which is increasing at an even faster rate, and the synthetic refrigerants and solvents called chlorofluorocarbons (CFC's).

The consensus view was that a global warming of between three and nine degrees Fahrenheit is likely to occur by the middle of the next century if emissions are not curtailed. It is impossible to say what the climatic consequence for particular regions would be — the current U.S. drought, for example, cannot necessarily be blamed on the greenhouse effect. Nevertheless, some studies suggest that continental interiors will become dryer as greenhouse warming occurs. The sea level is expected to rise by at least 30 centimeters over the next 50 to 100 years. — Tim Beardsley, "Winds of Change"

| 5e | **Avoid logical fallacies.** |

Logical fallacies are errors in thinking and writing that result from faulty logic. The ability to identify logical fallacies will help you in two ways. First, you will be able to evaluate the accuracy of presentation in the materials you read. Second, you will be able to avoid logical fallacies in your own writing.

Hasty Generalization

A **hasty generalization** is a conclusion based on too little evidence. This fallacy suggests that a writer has reached a conclusion too quickly, without thoroughly investigating an issue, and seems to assume that readers will not challenge his or her assumptions.

Be especially careful not to generalize on the basis of a single example. That is the fault in the following example and the most common cause of hasty generalizations.

> The Bedderman Street Housing Project cost hundreds of thousands of dollars and is now a shambles. Federally subsidized housing is a waste of taxpayers' money.   (One failed housing project is not enough evidence to support the assertion that the whole system of subsidized housing has failed. A larger sampling is necessary to justify such a sweeping claim.)

Oversimplification

Oversimplification ignores the complexities, variations, and exceptions relevant to an issue.

> The influx of foreign cars almost destroyed the American automobile industry   (Imported cars caused some problems for the industry, but so did high prices, overly large cars with poor designs, dated technology, poor gas mileage, and other factors.)

Carefully consider exceptions before you reach a conclusion, and include in your writing the necessary qualifications.

Either/Or

The **either/or fallacy** suggests that only two choices exist when, in fact, there are more than two. This type of thinking is not only illogical (because multiple alternatives are almost always available) but also unfair (because ignoring complexities and choices distorts a discussion).

For the sake of learning, we must maintain the firmest kind of discipline, including corporal punishment, in our public schools, or we can expect chaos, disorder, and the disintegration of education as we know it.   (The two alternatives presented are extremes: firm discipline resulting in order versus relaxed discipline resulting in chaos. The statement at once ignores moderate methods of maintaining discipline and asserts that without firm discipline the worst will happen. It is highly manipulative.)

Begging the Question

Begging the question is a type of circular reasoning used to slant an issue. When writers beg the question, they include in their writing an idea that requires proof, but they offer no proof. Instead, they present the idea as if it were a fact or a foregone conclusion needing no support or explanation. Writers who beg the question undercut their credibility by implying knowledge that they do not demonstrate.

Since Senator Hillard is a pawn of major corporations, we can expect him to support their interests instead of ours.   (The writer provides no evidence that Hillard is controlled by corporations. The statement attempts to mislead readers by asserting that an affiliation exists rather than proving that it does.)

Sometimes begging the question is done very subtly, through word choice.

The antiwar demonstrators of the 1970s should be remembered as the cowards that they were.   (The writer uses the word *cowards* to define the group without making any attempt to prove the implicit warrant that protesting is cowardly.)

Association

Fallacies of association suggest that ideas or actions are acceptable or unacceptable because of the people who are associated with them. Such a fallacy ignores that ideas or actions should be evaluated on their own merits.

> The hijackers were Lebanese, so obviously the Lebanese people support terrorism. (This assertion links all people in Lebanon with a small group of terrorists. Such reasoning ignores that terrorists often act on their own or in groups and do not necessarily represent a country's people.)

Non Sequitur

Non sequitur is a Latin expression meaning "it does not follow." A non sequitur is a conclusion that is not the logical result of the premises or evidence that precedes it.

> Japanese children spend forty percent more time in the classroom than, and outperform, American children. American parents should take more interest in their children's schooling. (Both statements may be true, but the writer does not establish any logical connection between them.)

Bandwagon

The **bandwagon** fallacy suggests that if a majority of people express a belief or take an action that everyone should think or do the same. Such arguments give the weight of truth or inevitability to the judgments of the majority, which may not be justified and which may, in fact, be only a passing fashion or fascination.

> Over 70 percent of Americans favor tariffs on imports from Japan, and you should, too. (The argument falsely implies that the force of public opinion alone should sway undecided opinion. Such arguments are often bolstered by statistics from studies or surveys, but the use of numbers alone does not sufficiently support the writer's position. The advisability of tariffs should be decided on the basis of their effect on national and international interests, not on possibly uninformed or self-interested and emotional opinions.)

Red Herring

A **red herring** is an irrelevant issue introduced into an argument to draw attention from the central issue.

> This School Board should not vote to spend money for education in art and music when so many of our children fail to read at their grade levels. (Deplorable as the children's poor preparation in reading may be, it has no bearing on the quality or benefit to students of arts education programs.)

Post Hoc, Ergo Propter Hoc

Post hoc, ergo propter hoc is a Latin expression meaning "after this, therefore because of this." Post hoc reasoning asserts a cause and effect relationship between two actions even though one action simply preceded the other.

> Since Charles Braddock became mayor, housing prices have risen in our town. Clearly, Braddock's administration has been bad for prospective homeowners. (Although prices rose after Braddock became mayor, there is no necessary connection between the events.)

A cause must come before an effect, but not everything that occurs first is a cause of what follows. To avoid post hoc reasoning, take time to establish that the effects you note can be clearly and systematically linked to the causes you identify.

Ad Hominem

Ad hominem is a Latin expression meaning "to the man." Ad hominem reasoning occurs when writers attack the people involved with an issue rather than the issue itself. By shifting the focus from the idea to people, writers fail to address the real issues.

> Universities should not grant honorary degrees. After all, Walter Hale, who received a degree from Lawrence Institute, is supposedly linked

to organized crime.   (The main issue should not be Hale but rather honorary degrees. The mention of Hale inappropriately sidetracks the discussion and fails to make any case against the degrees themselves.)

False Analogy

A **false analogy** is a comparison that is not based on relevant points of similarity. For an analogy to be logical, the subjects must be similar in several important, not superficial, ways.

If eighteen-year-olds are old enough to get married, vote, and serve in the military, they are old enough to drink alcohol.   (This analogy falsely suggests that activities performed when under complete control have a bearing on an activity that often results in lack of control. The comparison is based on strained similarities.)

EXERCISE 5.6 ❯ *Logical fallacies*

Identify and explain the logical fallacies in the following sentences. Rewrite the sentences to qualify the statements and avoid the fallacies.

1. Ernest Hemingway's novels should not be regarded so highly. After all, he was clearly sexist.

2. Many Nobel Prize winners in science used animals in their experiments, so using animals in research must be acceptable.

3. I saw a woman at the grocery store use food stamps to buy steaks, artichokes, and hand-packed ice cream. Food stamps allow the unemployed to eat very well.

4. If secondary schools require four years of English, writing skills will no doubt improve.

5. If business people can deduct expenses for lunches, then factory workers should have the same privilege.

6. To reduce the trade deficit, all we need to do is increase taxes.

7. Unless we imprison industrial spies, all our technological secrets will end up in the hands of the Russians.

8. Atlanta is the home of both the Turner Broadcasting System and the Braves. It is a great place to raise a family.

9. If an actress lives long enough, she is sure to win an Academy Award.

10. Since smoking marijuana is immoral, we should punish anyone caught using it.

| 5f | **A sample argument.** |

The following article appeared in the "My Turn" section of *Newsweek* magazine, 16 January 1989. Numbered annotations listed on pages 134–36 identify important features and strategies.

You Get What You Pay For
by Norman Ornstein

1. There are few things that unite Americans more than the antipathy we feel toward government officials when pay raises come up.

2. We may divide over aid to the Nicaraguan contras, the Strategic Defense Initiative and nuclear power, but we join together powerfully when a blue-ribbon commission proposes increasing the pay of lawmakers, government executives and judges. Talk-radio telephone lines haven't stopped lighting up since the Quadrennial Commission on Executive, Legislative and Judicial Salaries issued its recommendations in December [1988], including raising congressional pay

3. from its current $89,500 to $135,000. (Pay of judges and top federal executives, tied to congressional salaries, would go up correspondingly.)

I suppose it should be heartening to find at least one policy area that brings Americans together. It would be — if they weren't wrong 4. about it. I live in Washington; while I'm not a part of government, I interact daily with congressmen, federal executives and judges and their counterparts in the private sector. My conclusion: in govern- 5. ment, as in any other area, you get what you pay for. Without a sizeable salary increase (combined, sensibly, with the elimination of honorariums for speeches called for by the commission), we will end up with fewer and fewer competent and experienced lawmakers and judges — and more and more millionaires, charlatans and ideologues.

6.   This argument does not play well, to put it delicately, with critics of a pay raise. To Pat Buchanan, now living comfortably after his government service on a half million dollars a year as a commentator, and to bachelor Ralph Nader, who has no kids to put through college and believes that everyone ought to live like Mother Teresa, $89,500 a year is enough for anybody to live on. To the assembly-line worker trying to get by on $25,000 in Wichita, the notion of needing more than $100,000 is nothing short of absurd.

It does no good to note that exactly the same arguments have been put forth by outraged citizens for 200 years, since our legislature tried to go from $6 per day to $7 a day. Whatever the size of the increase, raising the pay of public officials touches a deep and sensitive cultural nerve in our citizenry — one that reinforces our suspicions about venal and selfish politicians robbing the rest of us for their own personal gain, and that goes against our predispositions for "citizen-politicians" who labor for the public interest without regard to their own concerns.

For centuries, Congress has struggled with the dilemma of voting on its own compensation, along with that of presidents, Supreme Court judges and other federal officials. To justify its pay and to blunt the charge that lawmakers are unfairly feathering their nests,

7. Congress and the president created the blue-ribbon commission that meets every four years to examine the state of federal pay. But the firestorm over government pay increases turns out to have little to do with who proposes them.

It also has little to do with the amount of increase. Nevertheless, this year a raise from $89,500 to $135,000 has made it nearly impossible to even discuss with voters the reasons behind the increase. Most Americans get COLA's, raises or promotions every year or two, but federal pay is adjusted only every few years. In 1970 congressional pay went up from $30,000 to $42,500 (incidentally, provoking the same outraged reaction as now). In the years since, private-sector white-collar pay has gone up more than 200 percent and blue-collar pay almost as much. Social-security recipients have seen their sti-

8. pends go up 232 percent. The consumer price index has risen 219 percent. Congressional pay, however, has gone up 109.6 percent — barely more than half of the cost of living and half the increase in the private sector.

The numbers, though, are not nearly as important as the basic reality of the cost of living in Washington, and the realities of balancing an existence as a public official and a family breadwinner. A

9. reasonable, four-bedroom house in a decent but not posh neighborhood in Wichita probably would run around $100,000. Try to find something comparable in Washington or a close-in suburb for under $300,000. Add to that the astronomical costs of everything from food to insurance, and living a decent middle-class life in Washington simply doesn't compare in cost to the same lifestyle in Cleveland or Seattle, much less Wichita.

We all have crushing burdens, and for many of us, who work two jobs or have to leave children in costly childcare, using our tax dollars to cushion the burden for public servants, with all their perks and status, is too much to bear. But if we could get past the emotion, we would see the grim bottom line: the rewards for public officials have rarely been lower, the drawbacks higher. Increasingly, we are having difficulty finding top-flight people to run for Congress, to work on medical research or to serve as judges. Do we really want the satisfaction of slapping down congressmen, if it means, as

10. Anthony Fauci, head of the federal government's AIDS program, told the commission, that he cannot recruit a single senior researcher to try to find a cure for the disease because of poor federal pay and benefits? Who do we really want running our defenses or overseeing $1.2 trillion in federal spending each year?

11.   The fact is that to deal with the unbelievably complex and challenging problems facing us as a nation, we need to attract good people to government at all levels, and we need to keep many of them long enough to provide some maturity and some institutional memory. To do that, we need not pay what investment bankers or Wall Street lawyers make — but we do need to pay enough that government employees can live reasonable middle-class existences, comparable to top professionals at least in non-profit areas like higher education and the foundations. That is what the Quad Commission has recommended. If we reject it, we'll continue to play with fire, hoping we can get a better government than we are willing to pay for.

Annotations

1.   Ornstein's introductory paragraph is deductive, leading with a topic sentence that clearly states the premise and following with illustrative details.

2.   By using *we,* Ornstein skillfully makes an emotional appeal in order to establish a bond with his readers.

3.   Ornstein ends the first paragraph by specifying the salaries at issue. Throughout the essay, Ornstein skillfully uses facts to help make his point.

4.   In the second paragraph, Ornstein states that he is a resident of Washington and has daily contact with politicians.

Establishing this firsthand knowledge of politics constitutes an ethical appeal.

5. The second paragraph ends with Ornstein's thesis, which contains an implicit warrant. What Ornstein leaves unstated are his beliefs and opinions that (1) good people require good salaries, (2) we do not pay our political leaders good salaries, and (3) good salaries attract good people to politics. The use of an implicit warrant allows Ornstein to proceed with his discussion without immediately alienating readers who might disagree with him.

6. Ornstein uses an emotional appeal in the third paragraph. He cites opponents of salary increases but carefully chooses his words to make their objections seem untenable, and he creates a hypothetical worker in Wichita with whom he hopes readers will identify.

7. The fifth paragraph is inductive, leading readers through historical details to Ornstein's point that objections to pay raises arise no matter who proposes them.

8. Facts and statistics, salaries and percentages, create a specific context. Salaries alone, however, would not illustrate Ornstein's point, since they are higher than those earned by many average citizens. The use of percentages, as a result, becomes crucial to his argument.

9. Ornstein uses a four-bedroom home as an example, noting that comparable homes in Wichita and Washington would cost radically different amounts.

10. In an extended analogy (poor salaries in science have the same results as poor salaries in politics), Ornstein incorporates expert testimony from Anthony Fauci. Although testimony from an expert in political science might have

seemed a more logical choice, the conditions Fauci describes clearly apply to politics as well as to medical research.

11.   Ornstein closes his essay with a paragraph that explicitly states the warrant of his argument. Each sentence (and sometimes each clause) presents a premise that, if accepted, leads directly to the next. To conclude his essay and effectively underscore his thesis, Ornstein's position and reasoning must be very clear, and the use of explicitly stated warrants achieves that end.

MAKING   C O N N E C T I O N S

Critical thinking is central to all academic work, both reading and writing. Consider ways in which principles of critical thinking improve your writing.

- Note that thesis statements are assertions. The thesis statements that you have used in almost all of your writing are assertions. Examine your papers to see whether you have written assertions of fact, belief, or opinion. In what kinds of papers have you used each type of assertion? Which kind of assertion has helped you write the most effective papers?

- Examine your evidence. What types of evidence do you use most often? How well does the evidence support your assertions? What are the strengths of your evidence? What are the problems, and how can you eliminate them?

- Reconsider your readers as critical thinkers. How does this change the way you would revise your previous papers? Why would readers' critical expectations alter the way you would present your ideas?

- Return to earlier papers to look for logical fallacies. How could you have avoided them? How can you now eliminate them? Rewrite two or three paragraphs to eliminate their logical fallacies.

EFFECTIVE SENTENCES

C·O·N·N·E·C·T·I·O·N·S

Some writers have an intuitive sense of sentence structure and construct graceful, clear, and complete sentences without knowing how they did it. They are very lucky. Most writers approach sentence skills more systematically — they have to — and learn ways to discuss and improve their work.

Understanding sentences and sentence elements *is* fundamental to effective writing and revision. To communicate their ideas effectively, writers need to understand the parts of speech and parts of sentences and how they work to achieve precise meaning. To maintain readers' interest, writers vary sentence structure and employ various means of emphasis and parallelism, always maintaining the grammatical correctness that is their means to effective communication. The clarity and completeness of their ideas depend on the clarity and completeness of their sentences and paragraphs.

The goal of this section is to help you to learn and practice these skills and to acquire the technical language to analyze your sentences. Using that knowledge and language, you will be better able to evaluate and revise your writing to reach your readers.

6 Understanding Parts of Speech

Sentences consist of words used in specific ways according to their parts of speech. Words combined into phrases, clauses, and sentences create meaning.

This chapter explores parts of speech so that you will be able to use each of them flexibly and precisely to compose effective sentences.

Quick Reference

Learning about the parts of speech is a means to an end: technical knowledge of sentence elements allows you to analyze and improve your sentences.

❭ *Use the most specific nouns that suit the meaning of your sentence.*

❭ *Use only pronouns that have clear antecedents.*

❭ *Use verbs whose tenses create the time distinctions you intend.*

❭ *Use coordinating conjunctions to join equivalent elements; use subordinating conjunctions to join subordinate and independent clauses; use correlative conjunctions in pairs.*

English has eight parts of speech: **nouns, pronouns, verbs, adjectives, adverbs, conjunctions, prepositions,** and **interjections.** Learning to identify parts of speech in sentences is not an end in itself but a means to understanding how words work together in sentences. Knowing this, you can analyze your writing, identifying and eliminating grammatical inconsistencies and building sentences that express your exact meaning.

When analyzing the parts of speech in a sentence, note carefully how the words function. Remember that the same word can be used in different ways in different sentences. In the following sentences, *stain* appears as a noun, a verb, and an adjective.

Noun
> The oriental carpet in the foyer had a large *stain* in the center, the result of an accident long since forgotten.

Verb
> Grape juice will *stain* skin, fabric, wood, and almost anything else it touches.

Adjective
> Many common substances — such as milk, baking soda, and vinegar — are effective *stain* removers.

6a ▷ Nouns

A **noun** names a person, place, thing, idea, quality, or condition and can be proper, common, collective, abstract, or concrete.

Proper Nouns

Proper nouns name specific people, places, and things: *Julia Child, Stockholm, Corvette.* They are always capitalized.

> *Roger* lost his *Minolta X700* while vacationing in *Spain.*

Common Nouns

Common nouns name people, places, and things by general type: *chef, city, sports car.* They are not capitalized.

> My *friend* lost his thirty-five-millimeter *camera* while vacationing in a foreign *country.*

Collective Nouns

Collective nouns name groups of people or things; although each group includes two or more members, it is usually considered *one* group: *team, class, group, audience.*

The *congregation* at St. Mary's has raised four thousand dollars for the *hungry* in Africa.

Abstract Nouns

Abstract nouns name ideas, qualities, and conditions: *freedom, honesty, shyness.*

Concrete Nouns

Concrete nouns name things or qualities perceptible by the senses: *chair, salt, warmth, noise.*

6b	>	**Pronouns**

Pronouns substitute for nouns. Generally, a pronoun refers to a previously stated noun, called an **antecedent.**

The movers dropped the desk while carrying *it* up the stairs. *They* immediately filled out a damage report, *which* required John's signature. (*It, they,* and *which* are the pronouns; *desk, movers,* and *report* are the antecedents.)

Pronouns are classified as **personal, possessive, reflexive, interrogative, demonstrative, indefinite,** and **relative,** depending on their function in a sentence.

Personal Pronouns

Personal pronouns substitute for nouns that name people or things. The form of the pronoun depends on the gender and number of the antecedent and whether the pronoun is a subject or an object (see pages 179 and 183–84).

Subject		Object	
Singular	*Plural*	*Singular*	*Plural*
I	we	me	us
you	you	you	you
he		him	
she	they	her	them
it		it	

The archer was distracted by noisy people in the crowd, so *she* delayed the shot until the referee had quieted *them*.   (*She* and *them* are the pronouns; *archer* and *people* are the antecedents.)

Possessive Pronouns

Possessive pronouns show ownership.

Singular	*Plural*
my, mine	our, ours
your, yours	your, yours
his, his	
her, hers	their, theirs
its, its	

Use the first form, often called a **pronoun-adjective,** with a noun; use the second form if the pronoun stands alone in place of a noun.

Matt, *your* solution is more idealistic than *mine.*   (*Your,* a pronoun-adjective, modifies the noun *solution; mine* stands alone but also implies reference to the same antecedent, *solution.*)

》》》 *Do not confuse* its, *the possessive pronoun, with* it's, *the contraction for* it is. **《《《**

Reflexive Pronouns

Reflexive pronouns show that someone or something in the sentence is acting for or on itself; if used to show emphasis, they are sometimes called **intensive pronouns.**

Singular	*Plural*
myself	ourselves
yourself	yourselves
himself	
herself	themselves
itself	

Self-related action
The state senators voted *themselves* a raise for the third time in a decade.   (*Themselves* shows that the senators raised their own wages.)

Emphasis

Although his friends offered to help paint the apartment, Russell preferred to do it himself.   (*Himself* emphasizes that Russell wanted no help.)

Reflexive pronouns require antecedents within the same sentence and, as a result, should not be used as subjects.

Faulty

Joan and *myself* renovated the cabin.   (*Myself* cannot function as the subject of the sentence.)

Correct

Joan and *I* renovated the cabin *ourselves*.   (*I* is a suitable subject pronoun; *ourselves*, with *Joan and I* as the antecedents, is correctly used to show emphasis.)

Interrogative Pronouns

Interrogative pronouns are used to ask questions.

Subject	*Object*
who	whom
whoever	whomever
Other interrogative pronouns	
what	whose
which	

Who won the Nobel Peace Prize this year?

To *whom* should I send the application?

Which musical had the longer Broadway run, *Evita* or *Cats?*

Demonstrative Pronouns

Demonstrative pronouns are used alone to substitute for specific nouns.

Singular	*Plural*
this	these
that	those

Used with nouns, these four words function as **demonstrative adjectives.** If the antecedent of the demonstrative pronoun is unclear, use the demonstrative adjective with the noun.

Confusing

> Vonin hesitated before speaking. That helped her to control her emotions.   (Did *that* refer to hesitating or speaking or both?)

Clear

> Vonin hesitated before speaking. That pause helped her to control her emotions.

Indefinite Pronouns

Indefinite pronouns, pronouns without specific antecedents, serve as general subjects or objects in sentences. When using an indefinite pronoun as a subject, remember that some are singular and some are plural and choose the verb that agrees with the indefinite pronoun you are using.

Common Indefinite Pronouns		
Singular		
another	either	nobody
any	everybody	no one
anybody	everyone	one
anyone	everything	somebody
each	neither	someone
Plural		
all	few	several
both	many	some

When used alone, these words are pronouns. Some of these words — *someone's* passport, *anybody's* guess, *several* women — can also modify nouns and thus serve as pronoun-adjectives.

Someone is sure to discover that the dates in the chart are inaccurate. (Singular pronoun is the subject of the sentence.)

Several are available on the table at the back of the lecture hall. (Plural pronoun is the subject of the sentence.)

Both archaeologists agree that their earlier finds were misleading. (Pronoun-adjective modifies *archaeologists*.)

Relative Pronouns

Relative pronouns substitute for nouns already mentioned in the sentence and are used to introduce adjective or noun clauses.

To refer to people	
who	whoever
whom	whomever
To refer to things		
that	what	which
To refer to people or things		
that (generally for things)		
whose (generally for people)		

Novelists *who* achieve notoriety quickly often fade from view just as quickly.

Anger *that* is not expressed is often the most damaging.

People *whose* children attend private schools pay for education twice, through taxes and through tuition.

Sometimes the relative pronoun *that* can be left out (understood) in a sentence where the noun-clause relationship is clear without it. As a general rule, use *that* to introduce essential information, but use *which* to introduce information that can be omitted.

An object *that is over one hundred years old* is considered an antique. (The clause is essential to the meaning of the sentence.)

The steamer trunk, *which we found in Aunt Melissa's attic,* belonged to my great grandfather.   (The clause can be omitted without altering the meaning of the sentence.)

Although relative pronouns allow writers to embed information in sentences, too much embedded material can make sentences difficult to read. Use the "search" codes with your word processing program to locate uses of relative pronouns. Decide whether sentences with several pronouns might be more effective if separated.

EXERCISE 6.1 ❯ *Nouns and pronouns*

Underline the nouns and pronouns in each of the following sentences and label each according to type.

1. Acupuncture, a medical treatment, developed centuries ago in China.

2. The acupuncturist uses extremely thin gold needles to pierce the patient's skin.

3. Patients frequently receive sedation before the treatment begins and the needles are implanted.

4. The areas where the needles are inserted do not correspond to the areas of discomfort or pain.

5. Those who have been helped by acupuncture advocate the treatment most strongly.

6. Why should those of us who have not tried acupuncture question their satisfaction?

7. Teams of Western scientists have studied acupuncture and found no physiological explanations for its success.

8. Yet success rates for patients who have faith in the procedure suggest that we can learn more than we already know about the psychological effects of medical treatments.

9. Ironically, while acupuncture has been attracting attention in Europe and America in recent years, its use in China has declined.

10. Some say acupuncture is merely a medical hoax, but others continue to search for scientific explanations for its apparent success.

EXERCISE 6.2 ❯ Nouns and pronouns

Revise the following paragraph, replacing some nouns with pronouns to achieve a smoother style.

Theodore Roosevelt, the twenty-fifth president of the United States, was an individualist. Nonetheless, Roosevelt served the public well. Roosevelt's individualistic tendencies were illustrated first by Roosevelt's attempts at boxing, an uncommon activity for an upper-class gentleman at Harvard. After Roosevelt's graduation, Roosevelt made a trip west, where Roosevelt experimented briefly with ranching and cowboy life. Roosevelt returned to the East to serve in the government, but in 1898 Roosevelt resigned Roosevelt's post as secretary of the navy to organize the Rough Riders, a regiment formed to fight in the Spanish-American War. The Rough Riders found Roosevelt to be an able leader, and though the Rough Riders did not follow Roosevelt up San Juan Hill as legend has it, the Rough Riders did fight with Roosevelt in Cuba. Roosevelt returned to the United States a hero; Roosevelt's notoriety helped Roosevelt to win the mayoral race of New York. Two years later, Roosevelt was elected vice-president in spite of opposition from political bosses and industrial leaders. Political bosses and industrial leaders must have found Roosevelt's freewheeling individualism unsettling and certainly unpredictable. The political bosses and industrial leaders fought Roosevelt in Roosevelt's antitrust actions when Roosevelt became president after McKinley's assassination. Throughout Roosevelt's presidency and the rest of Roosevelt's life, Roosevelt continued to act as an individual but with the public good in mind.

6c	Verbs

A **verb** expresses action (*organize* or *sing*) or state of being (*seem* or *was*). Grammatically complete sentences contain at least one verb, and effectively chosen verbs make writing clear, exact, and interesting.

Types of Verbs

The three types of verbs are **action, linking,** and **auxiliary.**

Action Verbs

Action verbs express both physical and mental activities.

> action verb
> |
> Angela *parked* her car on a designated snow route.

> action verb
> |
> She *thought* the snow would stop.

Action verbs are either intransitive or transitive. **Intransitive verbs** do not need direct objects (a person or thing that receives the action of the verb, like *car* in the first example above) to complete their meaning.

> subj.   intrans. verb
> | |
> The negative ad *campaign backfired.*   (Without a direct object, the sentence is still clear.)

Transitive verbs require direct objects to complete their meaning.

> subj. trans. verb   d.o.
> | | |
> At last, *Bernie earned* her *respect.*   (Without the direct object *respect,* the sentence's meaning would be unclear.)

151

    subj.   *trans. verb*   *d.o.*
Leonardo da Vinci painted very few *works*.   (*Painted* could be either intransitive or transitive, depending on the meaning of the sentence.)

Linking Verbs

Linking verbs express either a state of being or a condition.

Common Linking Verbs			
Forms of to be			
is	be	being	been
am	are	was	were
Other linking verbs			
appear	feel	look	seem	sound
become	grow	make	smell	taste

Forms of *to be* join the subject of a sentence or clause with a complement (either a predicate noun or a predicate adjective), creating a parallel relationship.

With predicate nouns

    linking verb
Rachel *is* the best player on the volleyball team.   (*Rachel* [subject] = *player* [predicate noun]. The predicate noun further identifies Rachel.)

With predicate adjectives

> linking verb
> |

Woodrow Wilson *was* enthusiastic about the League of Nations. (*Woodrow Wilson* [subject] = *enthusiastic* [predicate adjective]. The predicate adjective describes Wilson.)

Auxiliary Verbs

Auxiliary, or **helping, verbs** work with other verbs to create verb tenses or to form questions.

Common Auxiliary Verbs				
***Forms of* to be**				
am	is	were	being	
are	was	been		
Other auxiliary verbs				
will	do	did	may	must
could	should	would	might	

> aux. verb verb
> | |

Ophelia *will enter* from stage right.

> aux. verb verb
> | |

Greenpeace *must oppose* chemical dumping in our waterways.

153

When modifiers are used, they often separate the auxiliary from the main verb. In forming questions, the auxiliary usually precedes the subject. Auxiliary verbs always precede main verbs.

    aux. verb mod.   *verb*
Ophelia *will* probably *enter* from stage right.

aux. verb   *verb*
Must Greenpeace *oppose* chemical dumping in our waterways?

EXERCISE 6.3 ❯ *Verbs*

Underline and label the verbs in the following sentences.

1. Stoics are people who accept their fate without question.

2. They have learned not to concern themselves with what they will be unable to change or to waste time worrying about what is past.

3. Modern stoics have as their model, though they may not know it, a fourth-century Greek philosopher.

4. Zeno and his followers believed that the Fates (goddesses in Greek mythology) determine people's destinies.

5. Modern-day stoics, however, must grapple with Judeo-Christian beliefs that teach us that we have free will.

Forms of Verbs

In English, verbs have three principal parts or forms: the **infinitive,** the **past tense,** and the **past participle.** The infinitive is a verb's primary form (*work, cope*); it is often used with *to.* For regular verbs, the past tense and past participle are formed by adding *-ed* or *-d* to the infinitive (*worked, coped*).

Principal Parts of Regular Verbs		
Infinitive	*Past tense*	*Past participle*
select	selected	selected
inform	informed	informed
cook	cooked	cooked

Many common English verbs are irregular and form the past tense and past participles in a variety of ways. Because there is no predictable pattern for these verbs, it is helpful to become familiar with the principal parts of common irregular verbs.

Principal Parts of Common Irregular Verbs		
Infinitive	*Past tense*	*Past participle*
arise	arose	arisen
awake	awoke, awakened	awakened
be	was/were	been
beat	beat	beaten, beat
begin	began	begun
bend	bent	bent
bite	bit	bitten
blow	blew	blown
break	broke	broken
bring	brought	brought
build	built	built

Infinitive	*Past tense*	*Past participle*
burst	burst	burst
catch	caught	caught
choose	chose	chosen
come	came	come
cost	cost	cost
creep	crept	crept
deal	dealt	dealt
dig	dug	dug
dive	dived, dove	dived
do	did	done
drag	dragged	dragged
draw	drew	drawn
dream	dreamed, dreamt	dreamed, dreamt
drink	drank	drunk
drive	drove	driven
eat	ate	eaten
fall	fell	fallen
fight	fought	fought
find	found	found
fly	flew	flown
forbid	forbade, forbad	forbidden
forget	forgot	forgotten, forgot
freeze	froze	frozen
get	got	got, gotten

Infinitive	Past tense	Past participle
give	gave	given
go	went	gone
grow	grew	grown
hang	hung	hung
hang (to execute)	hanged	hanged
have	had	had
hear	heard	heard
hurt	hurt	hurt
keep	kept	kept
know	knew	known
lay (to put)	laid	laid
lead	led	led
lend	lent	lent
let	let	let
lie (to recline)	lay	lain
lie (to tell an untruth)	lied	lied
lose	lost	lost
make	made	made
read	read	read
ride	rode	ridden
ring	rang	rung
rise	rose	risen
run	ran	run

Infinitive	Past tense	Past participle
say	said	said
see	saw	seen
send	sent	sent
set (to put)	set	set
shake	shook	shaken
shine	shone, shined	shone, shined
shoot	shot	shot
shrink	shrank, shrunk	shrunk, shrunken
sing	sang	sung
sink	sank	sunk
sit (to take a seat)	sat	sat
slay	slew	slain
sleep	slept	slept
speak	spoke	spoken
spin	spun	spun
spring	sprang	sprung
stand	stood	stood
steal	stole	stolen
sting	stung	stung
strike	struck	struck, stricken
strive	strove	striven
swear	swore	sworn
swim	swam	swum
swing	swung	swung

Infinitive	Past tense	Past participle
take	took	taken
teach	taught	taught
tear	tore	torn
throw	threw	thrown
wake (to wake up)	woke, waked	waked, woken
waken (to rouse)	wakened	wakened
wear	wore	worn
wring	wrung	wrung
write	wrote	written

Verb Tenses

English has three simple tenses (**present, past,** and **future**); three perfect tenses (**present perfect, past perfect,** and **future perfect**); and six progressive tenses, one corresponding to each simple and each perfect tense.

Distinguishing among verb tenses will enable you to understand in reading and use in writing the clear, precise time distinctions they express.

Present Tense

The **present tense** indicates an existing condition or state, something occurring at the present time, or a habitual action.

The plums *are* ripe.   (existing condition)

I *hear* a baby crying.   (occurring at the present time)

Marla *plays* the viola.   (habitual action)

Past Tense

The **past tense** indicates that something has already occurred and is in the past.

The architectural plans *arrived* last week.

Future Tense

The **future tense** indicates that something will happen in the future. Form the future tense by adding the auxiliary *will* to the infinitive. (*Shall*, an alternative auxiliary, is rarely used in current American writing.)

Sasha's poem *will appear* in next month's issue of the magazine.

Present Perfect Tense

The **present perfect tense** indicates that something began in the past and continues into the present or that it occurred at an unspecified time in the past. Form the present perfect tense by using the auxiliary *has* or *have* plus the past participle of the verb.

Marcus *has accepted* a football scholarship for next year.   (beginning in the past, continuing to the present)

Inclement weather *has* always *created* problems for farmers.   (unspecified time)

Past Perfect Tense

The **past perfect tense** indicates that an action was completed before some time in the past. Form the past perfect tense by adding the auxiliary *had* to the past participle.

Great cities *had flourished* in the Western Hemisphere long before Spanish explorers reached North and South America.

Future Perfect Tense

The **future perfect tense** indicates that an action will be completed before a certain time in the future. Form the future perfect tense by adding the auxiliaries *will have* (or *shall have*) to the past participle.

By the turn of the century, we *will have depleted* many of the earth's natural resources.

Progressive Tenses

For every basic tense, an equivalent **progressive tense** exists that indicates continuing action. Form the progressive tenses by using a form of the verb *to be* (*is, was, will be, have been, had been,* or *will have been*) and the present participle (*-ing*) form of the verb.

Progressive Tenses	
Present progressive	*is playing*
Past progressive	*was playing*
Future progressive	*will be playing*
Present perfect progressive	*has been playing*
Past perfect progressive	*had been playing*
Future perfect progressive	*will have been playing*

EXERCISE 6.4 ❯ *Verb tenses*

Underline the verbs in the following sentences and label each verb with its tense.

1. In 1947, Kenneth Arnold, a pilot, described saucer-shaped objects that he saw traveling at great speeds.

2. Since then, thousands of people around the world have reported similar incidents of seeing "unidentified flying objects" (UFOs).

3. During the 1950s and 1960s, Project Bluebook, a division of the U.S. Air Force, attempted to explain these sightings and found that most were misinterpreted observations of natural phenomena.

4. By the late 1960s, Project Bluebook had served its purpose — to reassure military and civilian populations that the earth was not being watched or attacked — and was consequently disbanded.

5. Today, some people still claim to see bright, formless objects traveling at great speeds through our skies — and no doubt such claims will continue.

EXERCISE 6.5 ❯ Verbs

The following passage from Benjamin Franklin's letter describing how to reproduce his electrical experiments is written primarily in the present tense. Reconstruct the passage as though Franklin had written a narrative of his procedure. Make appropriate changes in the verbs. (Hint: Many verbs will be in the past tense.)

Make a small cross of two light strips of cedar, the arms so long as to reach to the four corners of a large thin silk handkerchief when extended; tie the corners of the handkerchief to the extremities of the cross, so you have the body of a kite; which being properly accommodated with a tail, loop, and string, will rise into the air, like those made of paper; but this being silk, is fitter to bear the wet and wind of a thunder-gust. To the top of the upright stick of the cross is to be fixed a very sharp-pointed wire, rising a foot or more above the wood. To the end of the twine, next the hand, is to be tied a silk ribbon, and where the silk and the tie join, a key may be fastened. This kite is to be raised when a thunder-gust appears to be coming on, and the person who holds the string must stand within a door or window, or under some cover, so that the silk ribbon may not be wet; and care must be taken that the twine does not touch the frame of the door or window. . . . And when the rain has wet the kite and twine, so that it can conduct the electrical fire freely, you will find it stream out plentifully from the key on the approach of your knuckle. — Benjamin Franklin, "Letter to Peter Collinson"

6d	>	**Adjectives**

An **adjective** modifies or limits a noun or pronoun. Adjectives come in three forms: **positive, comparative,** and **superlative.**

Forms of Adjectives

Positive Adjectives

A **positive adjective** modifies a noun or pronoun without suggesting any comparisons.

These are *clear* instructions.

Comparative Adjectives

A **comparative adjective** compares two people, places, things, ideas, qualities, conditions, or actions.

These are *clearer* instructions than those we had last time.

Superlative Adjectives

A **superlative adjective** compares three or more items.

These are the *clearest* instructions I've ever seen.

Questions Adjectives Answer	
What kind?	*auburn* hair
Which one?	the *fourth* presentation
How many?	*sixteen* guests
Whose?	*Jeffrey's* assessment

Kinds of Adjectives

Regular Adjectives

A **regular adjective** precedes the word it modifies. Several adjectives can modify the same word.

>   adj.   adj.   noun   adj.   adj. noun

There is a *mauve velvet jacket* hanging in *Shirley's hall closet*. (*Mauve* jacket, *velvet* jacket; *Shirley's* closet, *hall* closet.)

》》》 *When adjectives in a series function together as one modifier — when each word alone cannot modify the noun or pronoun — hyphenate the series of words*

In 1982, American car manufacturers reintroduced *two-tone* cars. (not *two* cars or *tone* cars but *two-tone* cars; on the other hand, *American* manufacturers or *car* manufacturers, not *American-car manufacturers*) **《《《**

Predicate Adjectives

A **predicate adjective** follows a linking verb but modifies the subject of the sentence or clause.

>   pred. adj.
> |

The sleeping child was obviously *content*.

⟫ *When adjectives in a series work as a unit but are in the predicate-adjective position, do not hyphenate them.*

Toni's comments were *off the cuff,* but they were sensible. **⟪**

Articles and Demonstrative Adjectives

The **articles** — *a, an,* and *the* — and the **demonstrative adjectives** — *this, that, these,* and *those* — also function as adjectives.

The shortest distance between two points is *a* straight line.

Those forms go in *this* folder.

| 6e | **Adverbs** |

Adverbs modify verbs, adjectives, other adverbs, phrases, clauses, or entire sentences. Adverbs come in three forms: **positive, comparative,** and **superlative.**

Positive Adverbs

A **positive adverb** modifies a verb, an adjective, another adverb, a phrase, a clause, or an entire sentence but does not suggest a comparison.

Erica runs *quickly.*   (modifies the verb *runs*)

Erica runs *very* quickly.   (modifies the adverb *quickly*)

Comparative Adverbs

A **comparative adverb** compares two actions or conditions.

Erica runs *more quickly* than I do.   (modifies *runs,* comparing the two running speeds)

Superlative Adverbs

A **superlative adverb** compares three or more actions or conditions.

> Of all the members of the relay team, Erica runs the *most quickly.* (modifies *runs,* comparing the running speeds of Erica and the group)

Questions Adverbs Answer	
How?	*slowly* approached
When?	laughed *first*
Where?	searched *everywhere*
How often?	praised *repeatedly*
To what extent?	*thoroughly* disliked

⟩⟩⟩ *Although many adverbs end in -ly, many do not, and many words ending in -ly are not adverbs. Use an -ly ending as a guide, but identify adverbs by their function in sentences.*

> The lonely widower was treated well by his neighbors.   *(Lonely* is an adjective; *well* is an adverb.) **⟨⟨⟨**

EXERCISE 6.6 ❯ *Adjectives and adverbs*

Underline the adjectives and adverbs in the following sentences and draw arrows to show the word or group of words that each modifies.

1. American folklore has created a number of important national heroes, among them Abraham Lincoln.

2. Lincoln, the sixteenth president of the United States, was a man destined to become a legend.

3. His solemn, idiosyncratic appearance made him an easily recognizable figure, and his pivotal role during the Civil War clearly made him an important historical character.

4. Yet the reverential anecdotes and the blatant fabrications about him must surely seem questionable.

5. Lincoln's early life, though austere, was not backward, yet the rail-splitting Abe of the rustic log cabin in New Salem far overshadows the sophisticated lawyer that Lincoln clearly was in Springfield.

6. Lincoln belonged to no Christian church, yet he was often depicted in Christ-like terms as an always suffering, always kind, and always patient man.

7. Folklore has undoubtedly skewed the biographical facts of Lincoln's life, but it has created a fascinating — albeit false — vision of a man.

EXERCISE 6.7 ❯ *Adjectives and adverbs*

Underline the adjectives and adverbs in the following paragraph and indicate with an arrow the word or group of words that each modifies.

My favorite spot at Aunt Ruth and Uncle Dan's house is the small, secluded patio just outside their bedroom. Every time I quietly open the sliding doors and step outside, I know I will feel more peaceful. The 8-by-8-foot patio is brick, meticulously set in a herringbone design. A comfortable, well-padded lounge chair provides a place to sit, and a small redwood table is a convenient spot to place my usual drink, a tall glass of Aunt Ruth's lightly spiced tea. Once comfortably seated, I always enjoy the various flowers, my favorite feature. Close to the front edge of the patio are pink, plum, red, and yellow moss roses, gently trailing their waxy green stems onto the dull red bricks. Slightly back, radiating away from the patio, are miniature yellow and orange marigolds, with their dense, round flowers set against dark green, sharp-edged leaves. Close behind those are Aunt Ruth and Uncle Dan's prize roses — white, pink, red, and yellow tea roses that are carefully pruned. The small buds, usually a darker color, contrast noticeably with the large open blossoms that always remind me of fine damask. I always love to escape from the cheerful but noisy family activities to this secluded spot where the flowers are so beautiful. Inevitably, a visit to this floral oasis makes me feel more tranquil than before.

6f > Conjunctions

Conjunctions link words, phrases, or clauses. They show relationships of equivalence, contrast, alternatives, chronology, and cause and effect. Conjunctions may be **coordinating, subordinating,** or **correlative. Conjunctive adverbs,** used only in independent clauses, function similarly to conjunctions.

Coordinating Conjunctions

Coordinating conjunctions link equivalent sentence parts. They are the most commonly used conjunctions.

Coordinating Conjunctions			
and	for	or	yet
but	nor	so	

In a desk drawer in his office, Todd always keeps a needle *and* thread. (joining nouns)

Struggling for modernity *but* ruling in the old style, Peter the Great imposed a tax on beards.   (joining phrases)

Subordinating Conjunctions

Subordinating conjunctions introduce subordinate clauses (those that cannot stand alone as sentences) and link them to independent clauses (those that can stand alone as sentences).

Common Subordinating Conjunctions			
after	because	since	until
although	before	so that	when
as if	even if	that	wherever
as long as	if	unless	while

subordinate clause

While Gilbert was stationed in the Philippines, he returned home once.

subordinate clause

Interest rates will rise *as long as* the national debt grows.

Correlative Conjunctions

Correlative conjunctions always work in pairs and give additional emphasis to parts of sentences. The words, phrases, or clauses joined by these correlative constructions must be in parallel form.

Correlative Conjunctions	
both . . . and	neither . . . nor
either . . . or	not only . . . but also

Both Mobil *and* Atlantic Richfield underwrite programs for the Public Broadcasting Service.

A successful gardener *not only* selects plants carefully *but also* attends to them painstakingly.

Conjunctive Adverbs

Conjunctive adverbs connect ideas in independent clauses or sentences. Like other adverbs, conjunctive adverbs can appear in any position in a sentence. (See sections 22c and 22d for information on punctuating conjunctive adverbs.)

Common Conjunctive Adverbs		
accordingly	however	next
also	incidentally	nonetheless
besides	indeed	otherwise
consequently	instead	similarly
finally	likewise	still
further	meanwhile	then
furthermore	moreover	therefore
hence	nevertheless	thus

Conjunctive adverbs show relationships similar to but with a slight shift in focus or emphasis from those shown by conjunctions. For example, the coordinating conjunctions *but* and *yet* signal a simple contrast between balanced clauses; the subordinating conjunctions *although, even though,* and *though* signal contrast but emphasize one clause over the other; the conjunctive adverb *however* signals contrast but keeps the clauses separate.

Coordinating conjunction

Children learn to use computers with ease, *but* most adults learn with some difficulty.

Subordinating conjunction

Although children learn to use computers with ease, most adults learn with some difficulty.

Conjunctive adverb

Children learn to use computers with ease. Most adults, *however*, learn with some difficulty.

⟩⟩⟩ *Since they are punctuated differently (see section 22c), it is important to distinguish between short conjunctive adverbs and other short conjunctions. A simple method is to count the letters in the word: all conjunctive adverbs contain at least four letters, while coordinating conjunctions contain either two or three letters.* **⟨⟨⟨**

EXERCISE 6.8 **⟩** *Conjunctions*

Use conjunctions to combine the following sets of sentences. Some rewording will be necessary.

1. Geography is the study of land masses. It includes the study of territorial divisions. It includes the study of bodies of water.

2. Geography was once studied as a separate course in public schools. It has now been subsumed by the social studies curriculum in most schools.

3. American students today are not receiving sufficient instruction in geography. They are not making the effort to learn the material.

4. College students in 1950 took a geography test sponsored by the *New York Times.* College students in 1984 took the same test. The comparative scores were startling.

5. Scores in some areas dropped 50 percent. That is not surprising. Seventy-two percent of the 1984 sample group said they had received little instruction in geography.

| 6g | > | **Prepositions** |

Prepositions link words in sentences. **Prepositional phrases** consist of a preposition, a noun or pronoun (the object of the preposition), and, frequently, modifiers.

$$\qquad\qquad\qquad\qquad \overset{\textit{prep.}}{} \overset{\textit{obj.}}{}$$
We seem to be losing the fight *against crime.*

$$\qquad \overset{}{} \overset{\textit{pron.}}{} \qquad \qquad$$
$$\textit{prep.} \quad \textit{adj.} \quad \textit{adj.} \quad \textit{obj.}$$
$$\quad | \qquad | \qquad | \qquad |$$
Because of his heretical views, Galileo was excommunicated.

Common Prepositions		
Single–word prepositions		
about	along	behind
above	among	below
across	around	beneath
after	at	beside
against	before	besides

Common Prepositions		
Single-word prepositions		
between	into	throughout
beyond	like	till
but	near	to
by	of	toward
concerning	off	under
despite	on	underneath
down	onto	until
during	out	up
except	outside	upon
for	over	with
from	past	within
in	since	without
inside	through	
Multiple-word prepositions		
according to	in addition to	in spite of
ahead of	in case of	in side of
as well as	in front of	instead of
because of	in place of	rather than

Prepositional phrases modify specific words or phrases, function-ing sometimes like adverbs (answering questions like *when, where,* or *how often*) and sometimes like adjectives (answering questions like *what kind* or *whose*).

              prep.   *obj.*   *prep.*   *obj.*
Our flight landed *in Montreal ahead of schedule.*   (Adverbial functions: Where did it land? When did it land?)

          prep.   *obj.*   *prep.*   *obj.*
Novels *about families* often describe conflicts *between parents*

obj.
and their children.   (Adjective functions: What kinds of novels? What kinds of conflict?)

EXERCISE 6.9 ❯ *Prepositions*

Underline the prepositional phrases in the following paragraph and label the preposition and object in each phrase.

The dog has got more fun out of Man than Man has got out of the dog, for the clearly demonstrable reason that Man is the more laughable of the two animals. The dog has long been bemused by the singular activities and the curious practices of men, cocking his head inquiringly to one side, intently watching and listening to the strangest goings-on in the world. He has seen men sing together and fight one another in the same evening. He has watched them go to bed when it is time to get up, and get up when it is time to go to bed. He has observed them destroying the soil in vast areas, and nurturing it in small patches. He has stood by while men built strong and solid houses for rest and quiet, and then filled them with lights and bells and machinery. His sensitive nose, which can detect what's cooking in the next township, has caught at one and the same time the bewildering smells of the hospital and the munitions factory. He has seen men raise up great cities to heaven and then blow them to hell. — James Thurber, "A Dog's Eye View of Man"

6h	⟩	**Interjections**

Interjections express surprise or another emotion or provide transitions in sentences.

Okay, I'll try the steamed oysters if you insist.

Oh no! You didn't use aluminum foil in the microwave oven?

Strong interjections may be punctuated like a sentence, with a period or an exclamation point; milder interjections are joined to a sentence with a comma. Because most interjections are conversational and generally do not clarify a sentence's meaning, use them sparingly in formal writing.

EXERCISE 6.10 ❯   *Parts of speech*

Indicate the part of speech of the numbered words and phrases in the following paragraphs. For verbs, name the specific tense.

In the (1) *old* days, when I (2) *was writing* a great deal of (3) *fiction,* there would come, once in a while, moments when I was (4) *stymied.* (5) *Suddenly,* I would find I (6) *had written* (7) *myself* (8) *into* a hole and could see no way out. To take care of that, (9) *I* developed a (10) *technique* which (11) *invariably* worked.

It was simply this — I (12) *went* (13) *to* the movies. Not just any movie. I had to pick a movie which was loaded with action (14) *but* (15) *which* made no demands on the (16) *intellect.* (17) *As* I watched, I did my best to avoid any (18) *conscious* thinking concerning my (19) *problem,* and (20) *when* I came out of the movie I knew exactly what I would have to do to put the story back on track.

It never failed. — Isaac Asimov, "The Eureka Phenomenon"

Revising parts of speech with a word processor

Use your word processor to improve the wording of your sentences. Make a back-up copy of your draft and then experiment with parts of speech.

Substitute pronouns. Examine your draft for sentences where pronouns, rather than nouns, would create coherence and transition and eliminate repetition. Delete selected nouns and replace them with appropriate pronouns.

Change verb tense. To change the method of development of a paper — for example, from explaining a process to narrating an event, or vice versa — use the "delete" feature to change verb tenses to suit your new purpose.

Add clarifying words and phrases. After finishing a draft, make sentences more specific by inserting concrete, vivid adjectives and adverbs; the word-processing program will automatically reformat your sentences to accommodate these changes.

MAKING   C O N N E C T I O N S

If you are like most people, you have given little thought to how you use parts of speech. Their use is so easy and natural in speaking that they can be taken for granted in writing. To improve your writing, look closely at how you use parts of speech. Choose a recent paper and reread it with the following questions in mind.

- Examine your use of nouns and pronouns. Are your nouns as specific as possible? Do you use common nouns when more specific proper nouns are available? Consider replacing some of the general nouns with specific nouns and proper nouns. How and how frequently do you use pronouns? Experiment with ways to balance your use of nouns and pronouns to achieve variety while maintaining clarity.

- Consider your use of verbs. What tenses do you use most and least often? Do you use the full range of available tenses, exploiting the distinctions they make possible? Consider revising verb choices by selecting more precise tenses.

- Think about your use of modifiers. Have you used enough or too many modifiers? Experiment with use of modifiers to achieve clarity. Replace or add modifiers to gain greater clarity and specificity.

- Consider your use of conjunctions. What kinds of conjunctions do you frequently and rarely use? Consider revising several sentences, changing conjunctions and varying sentence patterns. What is the effect on the rhythm and interest of your paper?

7 Understanding Sentences

Sentences contain at least a subject and a verb, and express a complete thought. Although sentences do not depend on groups of words outside themselves to make their meanings clear, they may contain words, phrases, and clauses, in addition to the essential subject and verb, that enhance their internal clarity. This chapter will help you to recognize the parts that make up sentences and to use these parts to form expressive, coherent sentences.

Quick Reference

Learning about parts and kinds of sentences will give you the technical knowledge you need to analyze and revise your writing.

❭ *Sentences must include a subject and a predicate.*

❭ *Phrases cannot stand alone but must be parts of sentences.*

❭ *Subordinate clauses cannot stand alone but must be joined to independent clauses.*

❭ *Use subjects, predicates, phrases, and clauses to create simple, compound, complex, and compound-complex sentences.*

7a ❭ **Distinguish among parts of sentences.**

A **sentence** consists of at least a subject and verb. As the simplest complete expression of meaning, it is therefore the basic unit of written communication. Understanding the parts of sentences will help you to understand how to express your meaning coherently and effectively.

Subjects

The **subject** of a sentence is the person, place, thing, idea, quality, or condition that acts or is acted upon or that is described or identified in the sentence.

> *subj.*
> *Gauguin* fled to the South Pacific in search of unspoiled beauty and primitive innocence.

The subject can consist of one or more nouns or pronouns, together with any related modifiers. The subject generally appears near the beginning of a sentence, but it can appear in other positions as well. **》》》** *Subjects of sentences can never be part of prepositional phrases. The nouns and pronouns in prepositional phrases serve as objects of the preposition and cannot also be subjects.* **《《《**
Subjects can be **simple, compound,** and **complete.**

Simple Subjects

A **simple subject** consists of a single word.

> *simple subj.*
> *Machiavelli* changed the way rulers thought about governing. (*Machiavelli* performed the action, *change.*)

》》》 *Sometimes the subject* you *is unstated but understood in an imperative sentence (a request or command).*

[*You*] Go!

[*You*] Open the door this minute! **《《《**

Compound Subjects

A **compound subject** consists of two or more simple subjects joined by a conjunction.

     compound subject
     ⌐
simple subj.   simple subj.
   Locke and *Descartes* had different views on knowledge.

Complete Subjects

A **complete subject** contains the simple subject plus any words modifying it: adjectives, adverbs modifying adjectives, and prepositional phrases.

            complete subject
  ⌐
    simple subj.
  The *supplies* for a basic design course need not be expensive.

EXERCISE 7.1 ❯ Subjects

Underline the complete subjects in the sentences below. Bracket and label simple subjects; bracket compound subjects and draw an arrow joining the simple subjects within them.

1. The musical, a combination of drama and music, developed as a distinctly American art form.

2. Emerging from vaudeville traditions, productions like George M. Cohan's *Little Johnny Jones* offered engaging tunes like "Yankee Doodle Boy" and "Give My Regards to Broadway" in very predictable plots.

3. However, in 1927, Jerome Kern and Oscar Hammerstein presented *Show Boat,* the first major musical based on a respected novel, and changed musicals forever.

4. *Oklahoma, South Pacific, My Fair Lady,* and *West Side Story* remain the most lasting contributions of the 1940s and 1950s, the golden years of the American musical.

5. In recent decades, British musicals have enjoyed both critical and popular success on Broadway, while American productions have often seemed insipid by comparison.

Predicates

The **predicate** of a sentence expresses the action or state of being of the subject. It states what the subject of the sentence does, what it is, or what has been done to it.

> *predicate*
> As a child prodigy, Mozart *was paraded* through the aristocratic houses of Europe.

A predicate consists of one or more verbs, together with any modifiers or complements. (Complements are discussed on pages 183–84.) Like subjects, predicates can be **simple, compound,** or **complete.** In questions, the parts of the predicate are usually separated by the subject.

Simple Predicates

A **simple predicate** consists of the verb and any auxiliaries.

> *simple pred.*
> Machiavelli *changed* the way rulers thought about governing.

Compound Predicates

A **compound predicate** consists of two or more verbs joined by a conjunction.

compound predicate

simple pred.

Compact discs *have revolutionized* the recording industry and, in all

compound predicate

simple pred.

likelihood, *will replace* albums as the most popular recording form.

Complete Predicates

A **complete predicate** consists of the simple or compound predicate plus all related modifiers — adjectives, adverbs, prepositional phrases, and any complements.

complete predicate

simple pred.

The supplies for a basic design course *need* not *be* very expensive.

EXERCISE 7.2 ❯ Predicates

Underline the complete predicates in the sentences below. Bracket and label simple predicates; bracket compound predicates and draw an arrow joining the simple predicates within them.

1. Professional ice hockey associations were first formed in Canada near the beginning of the twentieth century.

2. The first major league, the National Hockey Association, was founded in 1910 and included teams only from eastern Canada.

3. The following year, the Pacific Coast League organized teams from western Canadian cities, cities from the American northwest, and later other American cities.

4. In 1917, the National Hockey Association was reorganized to form the National Hockey League.

5. Since then, teams from both Canada and the United States have competed throughout the regular season and have vied for the Stanley Cup, the symbol of the League championship.

EXERCISE 7.3 ❯ *Subjects and Predicates*

Underline and label the simple and compound subjects and predi-cates in each of the following sentences.

Most tarantulas live in the tropics, but several species occur in the tem-perate zone and a few are common in the southern U. S. Some varieties are large and have powerful fangs with which they can inflict a deep wound. These formidable looking spiders do not, however, attack man; you can hold one in your hand, if you are gentle, without being bitten. Their bite is dangerous only to insects and small mammals such as mice; for man it is no worse than a hornet's sting.

Tarantulas customarily live in deep cylindrical burrows, from which they emerge at dusk and into which they retire at dawn. Mature males wander about after dark in search of females and occasionally stray into houses. After mating, the male dies in a few weeks, but a female lives much longer and can mate several years in succession. In a Paris museum is a tropical specimen which is said to have been living in captivity for 25 years. — Alexander Petrunkevitch, "The Spider and the Wasp"

Complements

A **complement** completes the meaning of a transitive verb. A **di-rect object** or an **indirect object** completes the action of the verb; a **predicate noun** or a **predicate adjective** follows a link-ing verb and restates the subject or describes its state of being.

Complements follow the verb and are part of the complete predicate. They can be simple or compound.

Direct Objects

Direct objects complete the action of a transitive verb by answer-ing the questions *what* or *whom.*

Senator Packhard supported *the doomed Equal Rights Amendment.*
(*What* did Senator Packhard support?)

Indirect Objects

Indirect objects indicate to whom or for whom the action of the
transitive verb is intended. Indirect objects follow transitive verbs
but always precede direct objects.

The librarian handed *Michael* the bibliography.   (*To whom* did the
librarian hand the bibliography?)

Predicate Nouns

Predicate nouns follow linking verbs and restate or identify the
subject of a sentence.

Agnes De Mille was a skillful and innovative *choreographer.*
(*Choreographer* restates the subject, *De Mille.*)

Predicate Adjectives

Predicate adjectives follow linking verbs and modify the subject
of a sentence.

De Mille's choreography was sometimes *playful,* frequently *surprising,* and often *austere.*   (*Playful, surprising,* and *austere* describe the
subject, *choreography.*)

EXERCISE 7.4 ❯ Complements

*Underline the complements in the sentences below and label them as
direct objects, indirect objects, predicate nouns, or predicate adjectives. Draw an arrow between the parts of compound complements.*

1. The year 1896 was not only a tribute to humanity's best but also a reflection of humanity's worst characteristics.

2. At the Democratic Convention, William Jennings Bryan gave his "Cross of Gold" speech and sparked interest in an uneventful campaign.

3. The British Patent Office granted Guglielmo Marconi a patent for the wireless telegraph.

4. When the United States Supreme Court handed down its *Plessy* v. *Ferguson* decision, it established a "separate but equal" standard that institutionalized racism.

5. Athens, Greece, was the site of the first modern Olympiad.

6. Alfred Nobel was the benefactor of an endowment which began by awarding yearly prizes in peace, science, and literature.

EXERCISE 7.5 ❯ *Complements*

Underline and label the complements in the following paragraph.

Henry Reed was class valedictorian. He was a small, very black boy with hooded eyes, a long, broad nose and an oddly shaped head. I had admired him for years because each term he and I vied for the best grades in our class. Most often he bested me, but instead of being disappointed I was pleased that we shared top places between us. Like many Southern Black children, he lived with his grandmother, who was as strict as Momma and as kind as she knew how to be. He was courteous, respectful and soft-spoken to elders, but on the playground he chose to play the roughest games. I admired him. Anyone, I reckoned, sufficiently afraid or sufficiently dull could be polite. But to be able to operate at a top level with both adults and children was admirable. — Maya Angelou, "Graduation"

Phrases

Phrases are groups of related words that cannot function as independent sentences because they lack subjects or predicates or both; phrases must be part of a sentence. The three most commonly used kinds of phrases are **prepositional phrases, verbal phrases,** and **appositive phrases;** they function as nouns, adjectives, or adverbs. A fourth kind, **absolute phrases,** modifies whole sentences.

Prepositional Phrases

A **prepositional phrase** consists of a preposition, its object or objects (a noun or pronoun), and any modifiers; it functions most often as an adjective or adverb and less often as a noun.

phrase   phrase

prep.   obj. | prep.   obj.

The dog limped *across the yard to the lighted doorway.*   (Both phrases work as adverbs, answering the question "*Where* did the dog limp?")

phrase

prep.   obj.

My anxiety *about the dental work* was intense.   (The phrase works as an adjective, answering the question "*Which* anxiety?")

EXERCISE 7.6 ❯ *Prepositional phrases*

Insert parentheses around the prepositional phrases in the following sentences and then underline the word or words that each phrase modifies.

1. In the last three decades, the once inexact study of weather has become a highly complex science.

2. The National Weather Service currently uses computers to synthesize data it receives from satellites, balloons, ground stations, and airplanes.

3. Once computers at the National Meteorological Center compile this information, it is relayed by a variety of electronic means to regional weather stations where teams evaluate the results.

4. Of particular interest are the findings of the National Severe Storms Forecast Center (NSSFC) in Kansas City, Missouri, for its team channels information about potentially dangerous storms to affected areas.

5. Using data from the NSSFC, local meteorologists issue a wide range of watches and warnings, notably for tornadoes, severe thunderstorms, blizzards, and hurricanes.

6. By providing systematically gathered and carefully organized information, weather forecasters can warn people of danger — saving millions of dollars worth of property and saving thousands of lives.

Verbal Phrases

Verbal phrases combine **verbals** (verb forms used as nouns, adjectives, and adverbs) with complements or modifiers. There are three types of verbals — **gerund phrases, participial phrases,** and **infinitive phrases.** Like verbals, verbal phrases function in sentences as nouns, adjectives, or adverbs.

Verbals. The three types of verbals are **gerunds, participles,** and **infinitives.**

Gerunds are *-ing* forms of verbs that work as nouns.

Reading is my favorite winter sport.

Participles appear in two forms: the present participle (*climbing, going*) and the past participle (*climbed, gone*). See the discussion of participles and the list of irregular verbs on pages 155–59.

Scowling, the tax assessor repeated the question.   (*Scowling* is a present participle modifying *tax assessor.*)

Exhausted, the dancer collapsed into the chair.   (*Exhausted* is a past participle modifying *dancer.*)

Infinitives combine the word *to* with a verb's primary form; they are used as nouns, adjectives, or adverbs.

To win is their only goal.   (*To win* works as a noun — the subject of the sentence.)

The office secretary is an important person *to know*.   (*To know* works as an adjective, modifying *person*.)

Lance was too excited *to sleep*.   (*To sleep* works as an adverb, modifying *excited*.)

Gerund Phrases. **Gerund phrases** combine a gerund and its complements and modifiers; the entire phrase works as a noun.

```
            phrase
    ┌─────────────────────┐
     gerund        obj.
```
Climbing Mount Everest was their lifelong ambition.   (The gerund phrase is the subject of the sentence.)

```
                phrase
        ┌─────────────────────┐
         gerund        obj.
```
I enjoy *playing* chamber music.   (The gerund phrase is the direct object of *enjoy*.)

```
                        phrase
                ┌─────────────────────┐
                 gerund        obj.
```
Harrison reread the instructions for *assembling* the bicycle.   (The gerund phrase is the object of the preposition *for*.)

EXERCISE 7.7   ❯   Gerund phrases

Underline the gerund phrases in the following sentences. Bracket the objects and modifiers.

1. Learning a second language is a complicated task, but it is a rewarding one.

2. The benefits can be as simple as reading a menu in a foreign restaurant, a book in a used-book store, an untranslated quotation in a scholarly work, or a magazine in a library.

3. Working for international corporations is one career option open to people trained in a second language.

4. Traveling outside the United States is especially enjoyable when reading and speaking a country's language is possible.

5. Through studying other languages, people become sensitive to language itself and that sensitivity can increase their effectiveness as thinkers, readers, writers, speakers, and listeners.

Participial Phrases. **Participial phrases** combine a participle and its modifiers; the phrases work as adjectives. Like other adjectives, participial phrases must be placed near the nouns and pronouns they modify.

phrase

part.
Standing on the wooden bridge, Nathan watched small leaves float

phrase

part.
by, *swirling* along in the current.   (The first participial phrase modifies *Nathan;* the second modifies *leaves.*)

phrase

part.
Seated at a table far from the door, Carlos had not noticed his friends' arrival. (The participial phrase modifies *Carlos.*)

EXERCISE 7.8 ❯ *Participial phrases*

Insert parentheses around the participial phrases in the following sentences and label the participles as present or past. Then underline the word that each phrase modifies.

1. Challenged by books like E. D. Hirsch's *Cultural Literacy* and Allan Bloom's *The Closing of the American Mind,* Americans have begun to reassess their educational system.

2. Articles have appeared in the popular media, questioning, on the one hand, the assumptions of these books and, at the same time, criticizing our educational system.

3. Enticed as they are by eye-catching but often misleading headlines and titles, writers have provided misleading clues about the goals of these books.

4. Limited by time and length constraints, television and print journalists have offered elliptical, abbreviated summaries of Hirsch's and Bloom's positions, oversimplifying their statements.

5. Talk-show hosts, by sensationalizing discussions of Hirsch's and Bloom's books, have failed to help viewers address important educational concerns.

6. Such problems in evaluating educational problems, made worse by American tendencies to oversimplify, will persist until Americans consent to read Hirsch's and Bloom's books for themselves.

Infinitive Phrases. Infinitive phrases combine an infinitive and its complements and modifiers; these phrases function as nouns, adjectives, or adverbs. When infinitive phrases are used as adjectives, they should be placed near the nouns they modify. When they work as adverbs, however, they can appear in a variety of positions, as can other adverbs.

phrase

inf.

Rachel must learn *to control* her temper if she wants *to get* along

inf.

phrase

in this office.   (Both infinitive phrases work as nouns. Both are direct objects, describing *what* Rachel must learn and *what* she might want.)

phrase

inf.

To be responsible, we must act without prejudice.   (The infinitive phrase, working as an adjective, modifies *we*.)

phrase

inf.

The experiment was too dangerous *to contemplate* seriously.   (The infinitive phrase, working as an adverb, modifies the predicate adjective *dangerous*.)

EXERCISE 7.9 ❯ *Infinitive phrases*

Underline the complete infinitive phrases in the following sentences and label each phrase as a noun, adjective, or adverb.

1. It is hard to believe how much wood and how many wood products Americans use without being aware of them.

2. To start off our mornings, many of us eat cereals packaged in cardboard boxes while reading newspapers made from wood pulp.

3. To go about our daily routines, we move between rooms built with two-by-fours, walk on hardwood floors, and open wooden doors, often oblivious to the structural uses to which wood is put.

4. We talk on the telephone — to convey messages or simply to converse — without thinking that wood resins are used in the plastic

casing for the phone, let alone that millions of wooden telephone
poles help to make such communication possible.

5. Many of us use pencils to write with, paper to write on, and desks or
   tables to write at — all products of forest-related industries.

6. To conceive of how many trees are necessary to support the activities of even one person is virtually impossible.

Appositives

Appositives explain, describe, define, identify, or restate a noun.
They provide either necessary explanation or nonessential information. In the latter case, the appositive must be separated from
the rest of the sentence with commas.

The painting *American Gothic* has been amusingly used in many advertisements.   (Because *American Gothic,* the appositive, is necessary to the meaning of the sentence, no commas are needed.)

Mitchell, *a hopelessly disorganized person,* was audited by the IRS and
fined one thousand dollars.   (Because the appositive provides nonessential information, it is set off with commas.)

EXERCISE 7.10 ❯ *Appositives*

*Combine the following pairs of sentences to form single sen-
tences containing appositives. Be sure to use commas where
needed.*

Example

The American Kennel Club recognizes over one hundred breeds of
purebred dogs. The American Kennel Club is the primary organization
of dog breeders.

The American Kennel Club, the primary organization of dog breeders,
recognizes over one hundred breeds of purebred dogs.

1. Sporting dogs hunt by smelling the air to locate game. Pointers, setters, retrievers, and spaniels are typical sporting dogs.

2. Working dogs serve or once served as herders, sled dogs, and guards. The group called working dogs comprises twenty-eight separate breeds.

3. Terriers hunt by digging. Their digging is an activity for which their strong front legs seem natural.

4. Nonsporting dogs include nine breeds most usually kept as pets. Many nonsporting dogs are descended from breeds in other classifications.

5. Most toy dogs have been bred down from larger breeds of dogs. Toy dogs are almost always kept only as pets.

Absolute Phrases

Absolute phrases consist of nouns and participles, usually with modifiers, and modify whole sentences rather than individual words. They can be positioned anywhere in a sentence but must be separated from the rest of the sentence by a comma or commas.

Her feet aching from the six-mile hike, Lisa stretched out under the tree to rest.

Lisa stretched out under the tree to rest, *her feet aching from the six-mile hike.*

Lisa, *her feet aching from the six-mile hike,* stretched out under the tree to rest.

EXERCISE 7.11 ❯ *Phrases*

Underline and label the prepositional, gerund, participial, infinitive, appositive, and absolute phrases in the following sentences.

1. Intrigued by the history of Great Britain, many Anglophiles are Americans obsessed by England and English things.

2. To learn about their "adopted" country, Anglophiles often sub-scribe to magazines like *British Heritage*.

3. They read as well materials in books and newspapers that offer in-sight into the English way of life.

4. Many Anglophiles, their daily schedules rearranged, watched the satellite broadcasts of the royal weddings of Charles and Diana and of Andrew and Sarah.

5. Anglophiles, often people who feel displaced in the rush of Ameri-can activities, find pleasure in learning about "that sceptered isle."

6. Visiting England is the lifelong dream of most Anglophiles, but spending time there often spoils illusions that have developed through years of active fantasizing.

EXERCISE 7.12 ❭ Phrases

Place in parentheses and label the prepositional, appositive, and ab-solute phrases in the following paragraph. Then underline the gerund, participial, and infinitive phrases and label each one.

When in the winter of 1845–6, a comet called *Biela* became oddly pear-shaped and then divided into two distinct comets, one of the astronomers who observed them, James Challis of Cambridge, averted his gaze. A week later he took another peep and *Biela* was still flaunt-ing its rude duality. He had never heard of such a thing and for several more days the cautious Challis hesitated before he announced it to his astronomical colleagues. Meanwhile American astronomers in Washington D.C. and New Haven, equally surprised but possibly more confident in their own sobriety, had already staked their claim to the discovery. Challis excused his slowness in reporting the event by say-ing that he was busy looking for the new planet beyond Uranus. When later in the same year he was needlessly beaten to the discovery of that planet (Neptune) by German astronomers, Challis explained that he had been preoccupied with his work on comets. — Nigel Calder, "Heads and Tails"

Clauses

A **clause** contains both a subject and a predicate and can be either **independent** or **subordinate.**

Independent Clauses

An **independent clause** (sometimes called a **main clause**) is grammatically complete and can be used alone as a simple sentence or combined with other clauses to form other sentence types (see pages 198–200).

> *subj.*   *pred.*
> *Eleanor Roosevelt withdrew* her membership from the Daughters of the American Revolution (DAR).

> *subj. pred.*   *subj. pred.*
> The Joad *family lost* their farm, and then *they left* for California. (two independent clauses forming a compound sentence)

Subordinate Clauses

A **subordinate clause** (sometimes called a **dependent clause**) contains a subject and predicate but is grammatically incomplete and must be joined to an independent clause to express a complete idea. Subordinating conjunctions and relative pronouns establish this dependent relationship.

> *conj. subj.   pred.*
> *because* she *objected* to the DAR's discriminatory practices

To make a subordinate clause grammatically complete, join it to an independent clause or revise it into a simple sentence by eliminating the subordinating conjunction or relative pronoun.

> *Eleanor Roosevelt withdrew* her membership from the Daughters of the American Revolution (DAR) *because she objected* to the DAR's discriminatory practices.   (complex sentence)

Or:

> *Eleanor Roosevelt withdrew* her membership from the Daughters of
> the American Revolution (DAR). *She objected* to the DAR's discrimina-
> tory practices. (two simple sentences)

Subordinate clauses function in sentences as nouns, adjectives,
or adverbs, depending on what information they provide.

Noun clause

clause

┌──────────────────────────┐

  subj.   *pred.*

Whoever wrote this paper should pursue graduate study. (used as
the subject of the sentence)

clause

┌────────────────────────────────┐

      subj.   *pred.*

Even the White House knows *that military spending is out of control.*
(used as the direct object of *knows*)

clause

┌──────────────────────────┐

  subj. *pred.*

Sell the land to *whoever agrees not to develop it.*   (used as the object
of the preposition *to*)

Adjective clause

clause

┌──────────────────┐

  subj. *pred.*

The armor *that Mordred wore* was rusty and dented. (modifies *armor*)

Adverb clause

clause

┌──────────────────┐

  subj.   *pred.*

Jessica paints more carefully *than I usually do.* (modifies *carefully*)

EXERCISE 7.13 ❯ Clauses

Underline the subordinate clauses in the following sentences and indicate whether they are used as nouns, adjectives, or adverbs.

1. Wherever I hang my hat is home.

2. Don't count your chickens before they hatch.

3. Absence makes the heart grow fonder.

4. All that glitters is not gold.

5. Fools rush in where angels fear to tread.

EXERCISE 7.14 ❯ Clauses

The following paragraph contains a number of subordinate clauses. Underline them and indicate whether they are used as nouns, adjectives, or adverbs.

When the credits run at the end of a film, audience members who stay to read them discover the names of people whose contributions are sometimes as important to the film as the actors' are. For instance, producers control and organize the entire film production, finding people who will finance the project and finding creative people who will actually make the film. That directors are in charge of the filming is well known, but many people do not realize that directors also choose and coach actors and find locations and select technicians. When the filming is finally completed, editors begin their work. They take thousands of feet of film, select the best shots, and piece together the version of the film that audiences eventually see. Besides the producers, directors, and editors, hundreds of other people are involved in the making of a film. Learning who they are and what they do makes audience members more appreciative of the combined efforts involved in film making.

7b ⟩ **Distinguish among kinds of sentences.**

The four basic sentence types are **simple, compound, complex,** and **compound-complex.** Learning to recognize their different structures and purposes and learning to use them will help you improve the effectiveness of your writing.

Classifying Sentences by Structure

Simple Sentences

A **simple sentence** is an independent clause that contains at least one subject and one predicate. Simple sentences may have compound subjects, compound predicates, and compound complements, however, as well as multiple modifiers and phrases.

>   *subj.*   *pred.*
> Governor O'Brian attended. (simple subject; simple predicate)

>   *subj.*   *pred.*   *d.o.*   *pred.*   *d.o.*
> Governor O'Brian attended the meeting and made the opening speech.
> (compound predicate, each part having its own direct object)

Compound Sentences

Compound sentences contain at least two independent clauses, each with its own subject and predicate. The clauses are usually joined by a comma and a coordinating conjunction, but they can be joined by a semicolon, with no coordinating conjunction.

>   *subj.*   *pred.*   *conj.*   *subj.*   *pred.*
> Bluebirds are getting scarcer, but ornithologists do not know why.

> *subj.*   *pred.*   *subj.*
> Dickens assailed the workhouses in *Oliver Twist;* in *Bleak House* he
>
> *pred.*
> took on the Courts of Chancery.

Complex Sentences

Complex sentences contain one independent clause and one or more subordinate clauses. The clauses are joined by either subordinating conjunctions or relative pronouns.

Subordinate clauses may be positioned at the beginning, middle, or end of the sentence. Each position conveys a different emphasis. Note the placement of commas in the examples.

> *sub. clause*
> *conj.   subj.   pred.*   *subj.*
> Because shortages exist in government-run shops, Soviet citizens

> *ind. clause*
>   *pred.*
> often purchase goods through the black market.

> *ind. clause*
> *subj.   pred.*
> Soviet citizens often purchase goods through the black market

> *sub. clause*
> *conj.   subj.   pred.*
> because shortages exist in government-run shops.

> *sub. clause*
> *conj.   subj.   pred.*
> Soviet citizens, because shortages exist in government-run shops, often purchase goods through the black market. (In this case, the subordinate clause interrupts the independent clause.)

Compound-Complex Sentences

Compound-complex sentences contain at least two independent clauses and one subordinate clause.

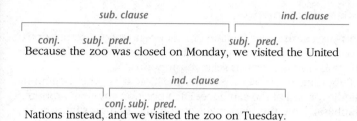

sub. clause | ind. clause

conj.   subj. pred.   subj. pred.
Because the zoo was closed on Monday, we visited the United

ind. clause

conj. subj. pred.
Nations instead, and we visited the zoo on Tuesday.

EXERCISE 7.15 ❯ *Sentences*

*Combine the following groups of simple sentences to form com-
pound, complex, or compound-complex sentences. Create at
least one sentence of each type. Label your revised sentences.*

Example

Hoover Dam supplies water and electricity to Los Angeles and surrounding areas. The dam was originally built to control the flow of the
Colorado River.

Although Hoover Dam currently supplies water and electricity to Los
Angeles and surrounding areas, it was originally built to control the
flow of the Colorado River.   (complex)

1. In the early 1900s, the Palo Verde and Imperial valleys seemed ideal
   for development. At times floods washed away crops. At other
   times crops withered.

2. In 1918, the Bureau of Reclamation submitted a report. The report
   suggested building a dam. The dam would improve water control.

3. Water control was the primary goal for the project. Generating electricity was a secondary goal.

4. The Bureau of Reclamation designed the dam. Six companies
   worked on the project. It was a joint venture that involved an average of 3,500 workers a day.

5. The finished dam is 726 feet high. It is 1,244 feet long. It contains 4,400,000 cubic yards of concrete. That is enough to pave a one-lane road from New York to San Francisco.

Classifying Sentences by Purpose

In addition to classifying sentences by grammatical structure, writers classify sentences by their purpose.

Declarative Sentences

A **declarative sentence** expresses a statement.

"God does not play dice." — Albert Einstein

Exclamatory Sentences

An **exclamatory sentence** expresses an emphatic statement.

"Give me liberty or give me death!" — Patrick Henry

Imperative Sentences

An **imperative sentence** expresses a command.

"Ask not what your country can do for you — ask what you can do for your country." — John F. Kennedy

Interrogative Sentences

An **interrogative sentence** asks a question.

"What *is* the answer? . . . In that case, what is the question?" — Gertrude Stein

EXERCISE 7.16 ❭ *Sentence structures*

Label each sentence in the following paragraph as simple, compound, complex, or compound-complex.

Rodeo, like baseball, is an American sport and has been around almost as long. While Henry Chadwick was writing his first book of rules for the fledgling ball clubs in 1858, ranch hands were paying $25 a dare to a kid who would ride five outlaw horses from the rough string in a makeshift arena of wagons and cars. The first commercial rodeo in Wyoming was held in Lander in 1895, just nineteen years after the National League was formed. Baseball was just as popular as bucking and roping contests in the West, but no one in Cooperstown, New York, was riding broncs. And that's been part of the problem. After 124 years, rodeo is still misunderstood. Unlike baseball, it's a regional sport (although they do have rodeos in New Jersey, Florida, and other eastern states); it's derived from and stands for the western way of life and the western spirit. It doesn't have the universal appeal of a sport contrived solely for the competition and winning; there is no ball bandied about between opposing players. — Gretel Ehrlich, "Rules of the Game: Rodeo"

EXERCISE 7.17 ❭ *Sentence purposes*

Label each of the following sentences as declarative, exclamatory, imperative, or interrogative. Then experiment, rewriting each sentence in each of the three remaining forms.

1. "Tell me what you eat, and I will tell you what you are." — Anthelme Brillat-Savarin.

2. "Education is what survives when what has been learnt has been forgotten." — B. F. Skinner

3. "One only dies once, and it's for such a long time!" — Molière

4. "How can we know the dancer from the dance?" — W. B. Yeats

Revising sentences with a word processor

Writing with a word processor gives you considerable freedom to make sentence-level revisions. Make a back-up copy of your draft, and then experiment with your writing. Consider, for instance, these specific ways that you can use the computer to try different forms and effects:

Combine sentences. Word processors allow you to combine sets of sentences to create varied sentence types without retyping.

De-combine sentences. If, on rereading your draft you decide that some sentences seem too long or complex, use the computer to de-construct them easily into briefer, more readable sentences.

Revise sentence patterns. Using "block" and "move" commands, transform simple sentences into other, more varied sentence types containing appositives, absolute phrases, subordinate clauses, and other patterns. Try recasting some declarative sentences as exclamatory, imperative, or interrogative sentences.

The freedom to rearrange sentences will be a great help to you during revision. You can always return to your original version by using "block" and "move" functions to retrieve sections of your back-up copy.

MAKING   C O N N E C T I O N S

Over the years, you have developed a style even though you may not be aware of it. All writers have a style — determined in part by their subject, thesis, word choice, and sentence structure — and you are no exception.

If you have never analyzed your sentence style before, now is the time to begin. You will discover some interesting facts about the way you write, some that may surprise you. Select a paper that you have written recently, photocopy it, and note in the margins of the copy your responses to the following points:

- Notice sentence patterns. In the margin of the photocopy, note the type of each sentence. Use abbreviations: *s* (simple sentence), *c* (compound sentence), *cx* (complex sentence), and *c-cx* (compound-complex).

- Chart sentence types. Make a chart showing how many of each sentence type you used.

- Analyze sentence patterns. Using the chart and marginal notes, describe what you have discovered about your writing at the sentence level. Consider the pattern and frequency with which you use the sentence types. What are your favorite sentence types? Why do you use them so often? What are your least used patterns? Why do you use them infrequently? Do your sentences form groups of the same type or do they vary?

8   Sentence Variety

Quick Reference

Varied ideas require varied expression. To achieve variety, experiment with alternative methods of constructing sentences.

❭ *Construct paragraphs using a mix of long, short, and medium-length sentences.*

❭ *Use loose, periodic, and balanced sentences to vary rhythm and emphasis.*

❭ *To create interest in your ideas, experiment with new ways to begin sentences.*

❭ *Coordinate and subordinate ideas in sentences to express your exact meaning and emphasis.*

8a   ❭   **Vary sentence length.**

Varying sentence lengths helps writers to achieve effective paragraph rhythm. A paragraph of short sentences can seem undeveloped and choppy; a paragraph of long sentences can seem dense and difficult.

Short Sentences

Although short sentences present one idea clearly, too many of them in succession can make writing seem awkward and simplistic. A few well-placed short sentences, however, can enhance variety and add emphasis.

C • O • N • N • E • C • T • I • O • N • S

Writing is most interesting when it is least predictable. Vivid description, unusual examples, surprising facts, stimulating insights, and original interpretations all contribute to gaining and maintaining reader interest. *What* writers say is further enhanced by *how* they say it. Writing effective as well as substantive sentences greatly improves their effectiveness.

Sentences can be varied by using varied sentence lengths and structures, by coordinating and subordinating some clauses, and by beginning sentences with a variety of words and phrases. By using these techniques, you will write with an unpredictable, appealing rhythm that will intrigue your readers and increase their openness to and appreciation of your ideas.

Our senator maintains two elaborate houses, one in our state and one in Washington. Although I understand the reasons for having two homes, owning two $300,000 residences seems needlessly extravagant. In short, I disapprove.

Medium Sentences

Medium-length sentences allow space to connect ideas and add details, while remaining clear and easy to read. Medium-length sentences are the most versatile and should form the core of your writing.

Although I enjoy televised boxing, I am often dissatisfied with network commentaries. All too often, sportscasters' comments are superficial, pointing out the obvious — like who is winning — rather than helping me to understand the sport.

Long Sentences

Long sentences establish complex interrelationships and include substantial amounts of amplification and clarification. Use long sentences sparingly to emphasize relationships and to incorporate significant details.

> For over a century, the *Statue of Liberty,* in all its majesty, has stood at the entrance to New York Harbor, welcoming immigrants, travelers, and returning Americans and symbolizing the freedoms we value.

EXERCISE 8.1 ❭ *Sentence length*

 Expand, combine, or divide the following sentences to achieve variety and effective expression.

Example

Medieval castles, strongly built of native stone, served as homes for the nobility, but in times of brigandage and war they also served as fortresses and as shelters for the peasants who lived nearby.

Medieval castles served as homes for the nobility. Strongly built of native stone, they also served in times of brigandage and war as fortresses and as shelters for the peasants who lived nearby.

1. Sometimes castles served as prisons, treasure houses, or seats of local governments as well because they were secure and centrally located, although access to castles was sometimes limited because some castles, notably those in central Europe, were built on irregular terrain.

2. Some castles are attractive.

3. Some used drawbridges.

4. Battlements, also called parapets, were the tall, structural walls from which soldiers observed the countryside, and during battles these same soldiers positioned themselves in these lofty places to shoot arrows or hurl rocks at the invaders below.

5. Most people know of castles from films.

| 8b | Vary sentence types. |

Although the four basic sentence structures are **simple, compound, complex,** and **compound-complex,** the effect of these structures varies depending on the types of sentences that writers use: **loose, periodic,** or **balanced.**

Loose Sentences

Loose sentences, the most common type, first present major ideas (the subject and verb) and then provide other information. This pattern is satisfying and easy for readers.

Dr. Zhivago is a typical David Lean film, with panoramic scenes, larger-than-life characters, and universal implications.

Periodic Sentences

Periodic sentences, less common than loose sentences, create suspense and emphasis by placing the main idea or some part of it at the end of the sentence.

After having spent thousands of dollars and hundreds of hours renovating the townhouse, the Petersons sold it.

Balanced Sentences

Balanced sentences use parallel elements — words, phrases, and sometimes whole clauses — to create interest and emphasis.

I practiced; I ran; I lost.

One brother was refined, intelligent, and persuasive, but the other was crude, shrewd, and domineering.

EXERCISE 8.2 ❭   *Types of sentences*

*Label each of the following sentences as loose, periodic, or balanced;
then revise each sentence into one of the other types.*

1. Almanacs, published yearly in book or pamphlet form, include calendars, citations for important dates, information about geography
   and weather, and a myriad of other facts.

2. Almanacs are informative and practical, yet they are also idiosyncratic and entertaining.

3. Though generally associated with colonial American farmers and
   navigators, almanacs have as their precedents the works of an unsuspected group: Persian astrologers.

4. Over the years, sailors have relied on the *Nautical Almanac,* farmers have used the *Old Farmer's Almanac,* and amateur weather
   forecasters have depended on the *Ford Almanac.*

5. With its proverbs, its lists of counties and roads, its advice on planting, its selections of verse, and its astrological information, *Poor
   Richard's Almanac* is probably the best-known early almanac.

6. Contemporary almanacs are best represented by works such as the
   Information Please Almanac, compendiums of widely divergent
   statistics on thousands of topics.

| 8c | ❭ | **Vary sentence beginnings.** |

Although subjects and verbs in subordinate or independent
clauses begin most sentences, writers can create variety by positioning other sentence elements first.

Beginning with Adverbs

Adverbs can appear in many positions in sentences. Using them at
the beginning creates variety.

The ornithologist cautiously approached the eagle's nest.

Cautiously, the ornithologist approached the eagle's nest.

Beginning with Adjectives

When an adjective phrase modifies the subject of the sentence, move it to the beginning of the sentence to create variety.

Jason, exhausted and dirty, collapsed in the armchair.

Exhausted and dirty, Jason collapsed in the armchair.

Beginning with Prepositional Phrases

Move adverbial prepositional phrases to the beginning of the sentence.

The pope did not restrict his travel after the attempt on his life.

After the attempt on his life, the pope did not restrict his travel.

Beginning with Verbal Phrases

Verbal phrases (gerund, participial, and infinitive phrases) make effective beginnings. Make certain, however, that the phrases modify the subject of the first clause; otherwise, you will create a dangling modifier.

The monks, worried that the manuscript might be stolen, placed it in a secret vault.

Worried that the manuscript might be stolen, the monks placed it in a secret vault.

Incorrect

Worried that it might be stolen, the manuscript was placed in a secret vault.   (The beginning phrase cannot modify *manuscript;* therefore, it is a dangling modifier.)

Beginning with Conjunctive Adverbs and Transitional Expressions

Create variety by occasionally placing conjunctive adverbs and transitional expressions at the beginning of sentences.

> The subscription price for *Architectural Record,* for instance, is almost half of the newsstand price.

> For instance, the subscription price for *Architectural Record* is almost half of the newsstand price.

Beginning with Coordinating Conjunctions

Conventionally, coordinating conjunctions join independent clauses in compound sentences, but they can also be used to introduce a sentence closely related to the one preceding it.

> International terrorism has made many world travelers more cautious than they used to be, but some travelers seem naively indifferent to potential threats from terrorists.

> International terrorism has made many world travelers more cautious than they used to be. But some travelers seem naively indifferent to potential threats from terrorists.

》》》 *Some readers object to the use of coordinating conjunctions to begin sentences. If you use this strategy to achieve variety, do so selectively.* **《《《**

EXERCISE 8.3 **》** *Varying sentence structure and beginnings*

Most of the sentences in the following paragraph are loose. To make the writing more varied and interesting, combine some sentences, restructure others into periodic or balanced form, and experiment with different sentence beginnings.

Landscaping serves more than an aesthetic function, even if few people realize it. Small shrubs and bushes protect a building's foundation, sheltering it from summer heat and winter cold. Large shrubs and small trees provide windbreaks for buildings, providing protection, especially in the winter, from strong winds that can affect interior temperatures and subsequently heating costs. Large trees shade a building during the summer, keeping the sun's warming rays off the building's roof and consequently keeping the building cool. Landscaping does improve the looks of a building, often enhancing architectural details and softening harsh lines, but the surprise for many people is that landscaping can pay for itself in energy savings, which means it has practical as well as aesthetic benefits.

| 8d > | **Vary sentence relationships by using coordination and subordination.** |

Coordination joins two or more independent clauses with a comma and one of the coordinating conjunctions: *and, but, for, nor, or, so,* and *yet.* The resulting compound sentences bring balance and emphasis to writing.

Subordination joins at least one independent clause with at least one subordinate clause, forming a complex sentence that indicates the relative importance of ideas. Different subordinating conjunctions (*after, because, when, until,* and so on) create differences in meaning and emphasis.

Coordination

Linking or Contrasting

To avoid a monotonous series of simple sentences while still giving equal stress to the main ideas, join closely related main clauses with a coordinating conjunction. The resulting compound sentence will give your writing an even, balanced rhythm.

Tamiko does not like watching television, *but* she does like shooting video tapes.

Vail had a foot of fresh snow, *but* Katrina postponed her skiing trip.

Varying Conjunctions

Each of the seven coordinating conjunctions links ideas in a slightly different way. For example, although *but* and *yet* both indicate contrast and are roughly interchangeable, they create slightly different impressions for the reader.

Estella was a heartless girl, *but* Pip loved her anyway.

Estella was a heartless girl, *yet* Pip loved her anyway.   (*Yet* expresses contrast more strongly and is more formal than *but*.)

In another example, *for* and *so* indicate a cause-and-effect relationship but require that clauses appear in a different order. Hence, they achieve different effects.

There is no room for delay, *so* there is no room for doubt.   (With *so*, the cause precedes the effect, and the effect is slightly emphasized.)

There is no room for doubt, *for* there is no room for delay.   (With *for*, the effect precedes the cause, and the emphasis shifts slightly to the cause.)

Avoiding Excessive Coordination in a Series of Sentences

The balance of clauses in compound sentences can create a monotonous rhythm if it is overused. Look, for instance, at this series of coordinated sentences:

Several weeks before the last snowfall, the ground thaws, and the wintered-over spinach turns green. Some of the leaves begin to grow, but most remain dormant for a few weeks more. The plants grow rapidly in the middle of March, and by April we are eating fresh spinach salad.

By the third sentence, an annoying and potentially distracting rhythm has developed. Remember not to rely too much on any one sentence pattern.

> Several weeks before the last snowfall, when the ground thaws, the wintered-over spinach turns green. Although some of the leaves begin to grow, most remain dormant for a few weeks more until the middle of March, when the plants grow rapidly. By April we are eating fresh spinach salad.

Avoiding Excessive Coordination Within Sentences

Three or more identically structured clauses in a single sentence can effectively link ideas and create interest and an emphatic rhythm. When clauses are dissimilar in structure or meaning, however, try other methods to join the ideas.

Awkward coordination

> Americans have become concerned about stimulants in foods, and they have started using products without caffeine, and to accommodate them restaurants now regularly serve decaffeinated coffees and teas.   (These clauses lack balance. The first two explain trends among Americans, but the third describes an effect of these trends.)

Effective subordination

> Because Americans have become concerned about stimulants in foods and have started using products without caffeine, restaurants now regularly serve decaffeinated coffees and teas to accommodate them. (The first two clauses are joined and then related to the effect.)

Effective subordination

> Americans, concerned about stimulants in foods, have started using products without caffeine, and to accommodate them restaurants now regularly serve decaffeinated coffees and teas.   (With some necessary rewording, one clause has been reshaped as a verbal phrase.)

Because excessive coordination is distracting and interferes with sentence variety, use your word processor's "search" codes to locate coordinating conjunctions. Determine whether their use is excessive, and experiment with the alternative methods in this chapter for linking ideas and creating variety and emphasis.

EXERCISE 8.4 **›** *Coordination*

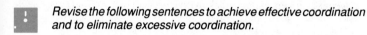

Revise the following sentences to achieve effective coordination and to eliminate excessive coordination.

1. Many American cities are now concerned with maintaining their architectural characters. Building codes control the development of new buildings.

2. Codes often restrict the kinds and sizes of buildings that can be constructed. Architects must design structures that match the scale of existing buildings.

3. Many cities, such as Boston and San Francisco, need the vast commercial space provided by tall office buildings. These skyscrapers often cannot be built in some areas because of protective codes.

4. City dwellers do not want the severe shadows cast by tall buildings. They do not want small, historical, and architecturally interesting buildings dwarfed by monolithic towers.

5. Citizens are now aware that poorly planned cities become unlivable, and, as a result, they have been supportive of new building codes, but city development is now more challenging than it once was, for cities must now grow by controlled, aesthetically consistent patterns.

Subordination

Establishing Levels of Importance

To avoid a monotonous series of simple sentences and to avoid the awkward rhythm of too many compound sentences, join related clauses with a subordinating conjunction. The resulting complex or compound-complex sentence will stress the relative importance of ideas while producing a varied rhythm.

Jessica stripped two coats of shellac and three coats of paint from the table *before* she discovered that the walnut was in excellent condition. (The sentence emphasizes the multiple stages of stripping over the discovery of the wood beneath.)

Because viewers expect quick overviews with many visual aids, television newswriters must plan brief, attention-getting news stories. (The sentence emphasizes the effect on newswriting of viewers' expectations.)

Using Relative Pronouns

Relative pronouns (*that, which, who,* and so on) embed clauses within sentences, adding clarity and producing variety. The information in the embedded relative clause is clearly less important than the information in the independent clause.

One of T. S. Eliot's best poems is "The Love Song of J. Alfred Prufrock," *which* is also one of his earliest.   (The relative clause embeds secondary but useful information.)

Avoiding Excessive Subordination

When too much secondary information is included in a sentence, ideas can become muddled. Consider the following sentence:

Although many films about adolescence concentrate on the awkward and often unsatisfying relationships that exist between teenagers and their parents, most of these films take a satiric approach, presenting parents as fools or tyrants and, as a result, defusing through laughter much of the tension in the real relationships because the depicted relationships are so extreme, so absurd.

Although grammatically correct, this sentence is poorly planned. Revision into three sentences improves its rhythm and clarity.

> Many films about adolescence concentrate on the awkward and often unsatisfying relationships that exist between teenagers and their parents. Most of these films, however, take a satiric approach, presenting parents as fools or tyrants. Because the relationships depicted in these films are so extreme, so absurd, much of the tension of real relationships is defused through laughter.

EXERCISE 8.5 ❯ *Subordination*

> *Use subordinating conjunctions and relative pronouns to combine the following sets of sentences into a coherent paragraph.*

1. Some people never visit art museums or exhibitions. Their only contact with art is through "public art." Public art is sculpture and other works displayed in public places.

2. Monuments are one kind of public sculpture. Statues and placards are the most common kinds of monuments. These monuments commemorate historical events or honor individuals or groups of people, such as veterans.

3. People often walk through plazas and courtyards near government buildings. Sculpture is often displayed in these areas. This sculpture is frequently commissioned by the government.

4. Most people are comfortable with traditional, realistic statuary of people. Many people are less at ease with abstract sculpture.

5. Many people say nonrepresentational sculpture doesn't "look like anything." In time, some grow more accepting. They learn to enjoy modern sculpture's use of form, texture, and material.

6. Sculpture enriches public space. It provides visual and tactile stimulation. It also sometimes provides pleasure. It even supplies topics for conversation.

EXERCISE 8.6 ❯ *Coordination and subordination*

Revise the following paragraph by using coordination and subordination to indicate the relative importance of ideas and to improve the variety of the sentences.

Dermatologists continually warn people about the danger of ultraviolet rays. Many people seem intent on getting dark suntans. During the summer, beaches and pools are crowded with people. These people want to "catch some rays." They smear on creams, lotions, and oils. They can accelerate the sun's natural modification of skin pigments. They want to get deep tans. They lie on towels or stretch out on lounge chairs for hours, oblivious to doctors' stern advice. In most cities, tanning salons are quite popular. "California" tans are not always possible everywhere. For a fee, usually between three and ten dollars, people can lie down and subject themselves to artificial sunlight. This artificial sunlight is produced by ultraviolet bulbs. Many people think a tan looks healthy. Overly dark tans, in fact, cause serious skin damage. This damage can last a lifetime.

Revising for sentence variety with a word processor

Take advantage of the word processor to create needed variety and emphasis in your sentences.

Move sentence elements. Using the "block" and "move" features, shift elements to the beginnings of sentences to create variety. Such moves will require you to change capitalization and punctuation — alterations that are much easier and faster on a word processor than on a typewriter.

Vary sentence structures and lengths. Look for a series of short sentences to combine through coordination or subordination. Look for excessively long sentences to break up. Look for repeated sentence types, and restructure some for greater variety and more effective expression.

MAKING   C O N N E C T I O N S

According to one cliché, "Variety is the spice of life." There's some truth in that tired statement, and it applies to sentences. If you have never considered the variety of your sentences, now is the time to begin.

- Identify the sentence length that you use most often. Why do you write, for example, more medium than short sentences? How did this tendency develop? Through reading? Through instruction?

- Analyze your sentence beginnings. Using a recent paper, note how you began each sentence. What patterns (if any) do you see? Are there ways to vary your sentence beginnings?

- Examine your use of coordination and subordination. What is your typical method for joining clauses? Would alternate ways work equally well? Might other ways work better?

- Plan to vary your sentences. Given your personal writing style, which techniques do you plan to use for achieving sentence variety? Why are those techniques best suited to your writing?

9   Emphasis

Emphasis underscores the significance of main ideas and makes supporting ideas and details clear and vivid. To control emphasis, therefore, is to control meaning. The specific choices that writers make to create emphasis depend on their specific purposes. Among other methods — such as choosing words carefully (see Chapters 13 and 14), constructing cohesive paragraphs (Chapter 4), and using subordination and coordination (Chapter 8) — writers emphasize people and actions by writing active sentences, and they emphasize ideas by writing concisely.

Quick Reference

Emphatic sentences stress the most important ideas, allowing readers to concentrate their attention according to the writer's purpose. Control emphasis in the following ways:

> *Write active sentences to stress the doer of an action.*

> *Write passive sentences to stress the receiver of an action or to stress that the doer of the action is unknown.*

> *Strip sentences of all unnecessary words, phrases, and clauses to highlight words crucial to meaning.*

 Use active and passive sentences to create different kinds and degrees of emphasis.

Active Sentences

Verbs in the active voice create **active sentences:** the subjects of the sentences act.

phrase

subj.   verb   *d.o.*

Lin Su invested two thousand dollars in the commodities market.

Passive Sentences

Verbs in the passive voice create **passive sentences:** the subject of the sentence is acted upon. The subject of a passive sentence would be the complement if the sentence were active. A passive verb requires auxiliaries.

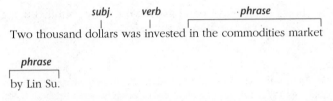

subj.   verb   · phrase

Two thousand dollars was invested in the commodities market

phrase

by Lin Su.

⟩⟩⟩ *A passive sentence does not always specify the person completing the action. When the sentence identifies the person who initiates an action, the person is named in a prepositional phrase beginning with* by. **⟨⟨⟨**

Emphasis

Stressing Who or What Acts

An active sentence emphasizes the doer of an action. It establishes a clear, strong relationship between the subject and verb.

The *restorer damaged* a portion of the fresco when he cleaned it. (The damage is clearly due to the restorer's error.)

When the results of an action are more important than the doer, or when the doer is unknown, passive sentences effectively express the meaning.

Irreparable *damage was done* to the fresco during its restoration.

In most cases, however, clarity, precision, and force make the active voice the better choice. Notice the ambiguity in the following passive sentence:

A portion of the fresco was damaged when the restorer cleaned it.   (It is not clear that the damage was the restorer's fault.)

The choice of an active or a passive verb allows subtle but significant shifts in meaning and emphasis.

Active
The 1980 eruption of Mount St. Helens destroyed over sixty million dollars' worth of property.   (The use of *eruption* with the active verb *destroyed* emphasizes the violence of nature.)

Passive
Over sixty million dollars' worth of property was destroyed by the 1980 eruption of Mount St. Helens.   (This sentence shifts the emphasis to the loss of property.)

Stressing Action

The passive emphasizes action over the doer of the action; thus, it is especially useful for describing universal or widespread conditions or events.

Passive
Open-heart surgery to repair faulty valves is now commonly performed across the United States.   (The surgical procedure is most important here, not the individual doctors who perform it.)

Active

Doctors across the United States now commonly perform open-heart surgery to repair faulty valves.   (This construction emphasizes the doctors who perform the procedures.)

As a general guide to usage, write active sentences when "who is doing what" is most important. When "what is being done" is most important, passive sentences may better serve your purpose.

EXERCISE 9.1 ❯ *Active and passive sentences*

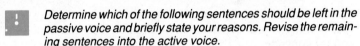 *Determine which of the following sentences should be left in the passive voice and briefly state your reasons. Revise the remaining sentences into the active voice.*

1. Biographies are often written by people who know their subjects well, either from personal contact or through study.

2. The *Life of Samuel Johnson,* a famous early biography, was written by James Boswell, a personal friend of Johnson.

3. In typical fashion, facts, anecdotes, and quotations were recorded in Boswell's diary and then translated into the biography.

4. When people like Benjamin Franklin choose to write their autobiographies, experiences are often presented to create a positive impression.

5. The lives of famous people like Lincoln were once described reverently by biographers.

6. Balanced treatments of positive and negative qualities are frequently presented by contemporary biographers.

7. A multifaceted view of the Roosevelts' relationship is presented in *Eleanor and Franklin,* a biography of the couple by Joseph P. Lash.

8. An essentially negative portrait of Pablo Picasso emerges in the Stassinopoulos-Huffington biography of the twentieth-century artist.

9. Contemporary autobiographies are usually written by well-known people with the help of professional writers.

10. *Iacocca,* a recent autobiography, was written by Lee Iacocca and a co-writer to chronicle Iacocca's rise in the automobile industry.

| 9b | > | **Make your writing as concise as possible.** |

Concise writing expresses meaning in as few words as possible. Such writing is precise, clear, and emphatic. To write concisely, choose concrete, exact words; and avoid needless repetition by eliminating words, phrases, and clauses that do not add meaning. Your sentences need not be short, for some long sentences are concise and some short sentences are not; but, to highlight important ideas, they should contain no extraneous words.

In a first draft, writers may not strive for concision. Rather, they concentrate on developing ideas and connecting them effectively. When revising, however, writers search for the words and expressions that most clearly and concisely express their meaning.

Unnecessary Repetition of Words and Ideas

Deliberate, controlled **repetition,** as in the following example, emphasizes important ideas:

We forget all too soon the things we thought we could never forget. — Joan Didion

But such effects, if overused, can irritate readers and so should be used rarely.

Avoid unintentional, excessive, or monotonous repetition. In revising your writing, delete unnecessary words and rearrange the sentence to read smoothly.

During the 1930s and 1940s, the studio renowned for film musicals was MGM studio.

In the 1930s and 1940s, MGM studio was renowned for film musicals.

Rely on specific word choices to make your ideas clear. Do not elaborate needlessly. **Redundancy,** repeating ideas, adds useless words and irritates readers.

The smile on Karina's face showed that she was pleasantly elated by the reception of her new poem.   (Where else could a smile be but on her face? Could elation be anything but pleasant?)

Karina's smile showed that she was elated by the reception of her new poem.

Eliminating Wordiness

Eliminating Expletive Constructions

Sentences beginning with expletive constructions (*it is, here is, here are, there is,* and *there are*) weaken the impact of ideas by obscuring the subject and verb. Other, stronger words in the sentence can often better express your meaning. Revise your writing to eliminate expletives. Strike them out and use the remaining, substantive words to present the same idea.

There are three kinds of qualifying exams routinely used by the admissions committee.

The admissions committee uses three kinds of qualifying exams.

Eliminating Wordy Expressions

Wordy expressions bog down writing. Phrases like *at this point in time* and *because of the fact that* add unnecessary words without enhancing either sense or sound. Many such expressions can be shortened or have clear, concise substitutes.

Due to the fact that an accident blocked the road, I was late.

Because an accident blocked the road, I was late.

Concise Alternatives to Wordy Expressions	
Wordy	*Concise*
at this point in time	now
by means of	by
in order to	to
in the event that	if
of the opinion that	think
until such time as	until

Eliminating Empty Phrases

Phrases such as *in my opinion, I believe, it seems,* and *I suppose* add little meaning to a sentence but blur its focus and slow its pace. Readers may take these phrases to mean that you are unsure of your ideas or information. Unless your purpose is to compare your opinion with someone else's, such phrases serve no purpose and should be dropped from your writing.

It seems that athletes in triathlons are masochistic.

Athletes in triathlons *seem* masochistic.

Eliminating *to be* Verbs

To be verbs weaken sentences by depriving them of strong verbs and adding words. Many words in English have multiple forms, usually including a verb form that can replace weak *to be* verbs. Examine your sentences containing *to be* verbs for words that might yield verbs.

Research assistants *are responsible for completing* most day-to-day experiments *and recording* the results.

Research assistants *complete* most day-to-day experiments *and record* the results.

Eliminating Nonrestrictive Clauses and Modifying Phrases

Nonrestrictive clauses (clauses not essential to the meaning of the sentence) that contain *to be* verbs can be reduced to appositives (phrases restating a noun or pronoun). Because appositives contain no subject or verb, they are more concise than clauses.

Chemicals found in aerosols have damaged the Earth's ozone layer, *which is our main protection from solar radiation.*

Chemicals found in aerosols have damaged the Earth's ozone layer, *our main protection from solar radiation.*

When it will not affect rhythm or clarity of a sentence, change prepositional and verbal phrases to one-word or multiword modifiers. When multiword modifiers precede a noun, they are often hyphenated.

The colors *of the tapestry* were distorted *by a nearby window made of stained glass.*

A nearby stained-glass window distorted the *tapestry's* colors.

EXERCISE 9.2 ❯ *Concision*

 Through revision, make these wordy sentences concise; note the number of words saved.

1. It is known to scientists who study such matters that an average of four trillion gallons of precipitation falls on the United States each and every day.

2. Falling from the overcast sky, heavy rains and snows fill our lakes, rivers, streams, and waterways, as well as replenish water supplies in our reservoirs.

3. There are some areas of the continental United States that are known to receive annually fewer than five inches of rain each year.

4. Other parts of the United States experience the benefit of more than twenty inches of precipitation or rain in a calendar year.

5. Precipitation — which includes rain, snow, sleet, and drizzle — is crucial to the national well-being of the United States.

6. Most of the people who think about it are aware that water is used to satisfy the needs of people, plant life, and animal life; however, they often fail to consider the fact that water is also in use in important industries.

7. I am of the opinion that water distribution should be under the management of a separate and independent national agency.

8. Until such time as we have a national policy for the management of water supplies, we can expect to have imbalances in the supplies of water in this country.

EXERCISE 9.3 ❯ *Concision*

 Make the following paragraph, bloated with useless words, more concise.

To be capable of understanding the development and use of paper and how that use came about, we must make our way back hundreds of years to China. By most estimates, paper was invented by the Chinese, who created it in 105 B.C. As a matter of fact, it was kept as a secret by the state for hundreds of years. As far as we know, most transcriptions were done on bamboo sheets. The Moors discovered the Chinese invention in A.D. 750. They became aware of it when they were at war with the Chinese. The Moors established and forged the link to Europe. In 1100, there was a paper mill for making paper established in Toledo, Spain. Gradually, the use of paper began to spread across Europe in a slow manner. Paper was able to reach Rome in approximately 1200, and it was a cause for the Catholic Church to feel threatened by the "new" invention. The church opposed the introduction of something that was so unfamiliar. According to the church, documents written on paper were not legally binding due to the fact that the church did not consider paper permanent. Still, paper began to be used by people instead of parchment, which was treated animal skin. People were greatly intrigued and fascinated as well by the new medium, which was cheaper and more convenient than parchment had ever been or could ever be. The use of paper reached English soil by 1400, and then it reached America by 1690. Soon, there was no other universally accepted writing surface that was used everywhere by virtually everyone. At this point in time, we take paper for granted and use it daily. We do not even acknowledge the fact that it was once a revolutionary new invention.

Creating emphasis with a word processor

To create more emphasis in your writing, try these two methods on your word processor.

Find and replace *to be* verbs. Use the "search" commands to check for a variety of *to be* verbs: *am, are, is, was, were,* and others. Not every *to be* verb will need to be replaced, but replacing some with more forceful verbs will make your sentences more emphatic.

Search for and replace expletive constructions. Many word-processing programs allow for multiword searches. If yours does, look for *there is, there are, it is,* and other expletive constructions. Strike them out and revise the sentence by using more forceful subjects and predicates.

MAKING C O N N E C T I O N S

Revising your writing to achieve greater emphasis will be a worthwhile challenge. Using one of your papers, consider these techniques for analyzing and enhancing the emphasis of your writing.

- Identify your weaknesses. Using the divisions of this chapter to guide you, examine your paper and list the ineffective patterns you find.

- Check for active sentences. Examine every sentence in your paper. If you find any in the passive voice, decide whether its use is appropriate. If it is not, revise the sentence.

- Strip your sentences of unnecessary words. Select a single, fairly long paragraph to use for practice. Cut every word that does not add meaning. Try to reduce the paragraph to half of its original length without distorting its meaning.

10 Parallelism

Parallelism brings symmetry to coordinate sentences and sentence elements; symmetry, in turn, enhances clarity. Parallelism requires that ideas of equal importance be expressed in similar ways or that words or phrases used together in similar ways appear in identical grammatical form: nouns with other nouns, verbs with other verbs of the same tense, predicate adjectives with other predicate adjectives, and so on.

Quick Reference

Parallelism creates clarity by stressing the balance between similar words, parts of sentences, or entire sentences.

❯ *Independent clauses joined by coordinating conjunctions must be parallel to be grammatical.*

❯ *Clauses and phrases joined by correlative conjunctions must be parallel to be grammatical.*

❯ *Prepositions, conjunctions, pronouns, and sentence structures arranged in parallel constructions convey meaning clearly and effectively.*

| 10a | **Maintain parallelism in constructions by using coordinating conjunctions: *and, but, for, nor, or, so,* and *yet.*** |

When a coordinating conjunction is used in a sentence, the joined elements should appear in identical grammatical form.

All her employers found Jan to be intelligent, able, and a hard worker. (*Intelligent* and *able* are predicate adjectives; *hard worker,* a predicate noun, is not parallel.)

All her employers found Jan to be *intelligent, able,* and *hard working.*

To have dreams is important, but living them is even more important. (*To have dreams,* an infinitive phrase, and *living them,* a gerund phrase, are not parallel.)

To have dreams is important, but *to live them* is even more important.

>>> *Double-check sentences using coordinating conjunctions to ensure that elements are parallel. If necessary, list elements in the margin of your draft to check their forms against one another.* <<<

| 10b | **Maintain parallelism in sentences by using correlative conjunctions: *both . . . and, either . . . or, neither . . . nor,* and *not only . . . but also.*** |

Correlative constructions present balanced alternatives that require parallel treatment.

Stacy could either go to the library or could develop photographs. (Because *could* appears before *either, could* is not part of the correlative construction. If an auxiliary like *could* does not appear immediately before the first verb, it should not appear before the second verb.)

Stacy could *either go* to the library *or develop* photographs.

The aim of a teacher should be both to inspire and educate.   (In correlative constructions, infinitive forms must be repeated, not mixed with present-tense verbs.)

The aim of a teacher should be both *to inspire* and *to educate.*

>>> *Double-check sentences using correlative conjunctions to ensure that elements are parallel. If necessary, list parallel elements in the margin of your draft to check their forms against one another.* <<<

> 10c

Repeat sentence elements — prepositions, conjunctions, relative pronouns, clauses — for correctness, clarity, emphasis, or effect.

In brief sentences, prepositions and subordinating conjunctions can sometimes be omitted from the second part of a parallel structure. In longer sentences, repeat prepositions and subordinating conjunctions.

Repetition for Correctness and Clarity

Bela Karolyi coached Phoebe Mills, an exceptional performer on the balance beam and who is also an outstanding performer in the floor exercise.   (Use of the coordinating conjunction *and* requires parallel structures in the phrases it links.)

Bela Karolyi coached Phoebe Mills, *an exceptional performer on the balance beam* and *an outstanding performer in the floor exercise.*

Or:

Bela Karolyi coached Phoebe Mills, *who is an exceptional performer on the balance beam* and *who is also an outstanding performer in the floor exercise.*

When the summer days grow increasingly longer and noticeably hotter and work becomes especially frustrating, I head to the cabin at Bishop's Point for a cool and relaxing break.   (The length of the opening subordinate clause makes the parallel construction difficult to follow without repeating the subordinating conjunction, *when.*)

When the summer days grow increasingly longer and noticeably hotter and *when* work becomes especially frustrating, I head to the cabin at Bishop's Point for a cool and relaxing break.

Repetition for Emphasis and Effect

Throughout a paper or paragraph, varied sentence structures help maintain readers' interest. In some cases, however, closely linked ideas expressed in a series of parallel sentences can create clarity and heighten interest.

His voice quavered audibly; his face blushed hotly; his hand trembled violently.

Consider in detail the parallel structures of these elements:

Possessive Pronouns	Subjects	Verbs	Adverbs
His	voice	quavered	audibly;
his	face	blushed	hotly;
his	hand	trembled	violently.

EXERCISE 10.1 ❯ Parallelism

Revise the following sentences to improve parallelism.

1. "As Ye Plant, So Shall Ye Reap" is a moving essay about the plight of migrant workers and which is somewhat controversial.

2. Over the years, César Chávez has used his political power to draw attention to the harsh treatment of these workers, to garner support from politicians, and orchestrate boycotts of selected produce.

3. Not only are migrant workers exploited in the Southwest but also in other parts of the Sunbelt.

4. The work of these laborers, extremely tedious and which needs to be controlled by labor laws, is traditionally undervalued.

5. To supply better wages and providing better working conditions should be our goal.

EXERCISE 10.2 ❯ *Parallelism*

Locate and correct faulty parallelism in the following paragraph.

Americans like to play it safe, so it is not surprising that they want the places where they play to be safe. Not so very long ago, however, amusement parks were poorly supervised, dirty, and they were rather tasteless. On hot summer Saturdays, American families would head to places with names like Chain-of-Rocks Park to have a good time. Once there, they found that the parking facilities were not only randomly planned but also no guards patrolled the area. The parks themselves were poorly maintained, with litter on the sidewalks, with oil running on the sidewalks, and with food having been left to spoil on the tables. The attendants appeared to be people with nothing better to do and who wash or shave only infrequently. They seemed to be alternately indifferent, callous, or they sometimes appeared to be threatening. Probably because of these unappealing qualities and other safety concerns, the amusement parks of an earlier time have been replaced by well-maintained, clean, and attractiveness of today's Six Flags, King's Island, and Disney parks. Yesterday's grimy and chaotic amusement parks have been replaced by today's safe, sanitized theme parks.

Achieving parallelism with a word processor

Use your word processor to identify and revise problems with parallelism.

Locate conjunctions. Because parallelism is most often required in constructions using coordinating and correlative conjunctions, use the "search" code to find them. Search for *and* or *either . . . or,* for instance, and double-check parallelism in sentences containing these words.

Make necessary changes. When you discover elements that are not parallel, use the "delete" code to remove the nonparallel element and then replace it with a parallel one.

MAKING C O N N E C T I O N S

Examine your writing for parallelism. If it lacks parallelism, use your word processor to bring symmetry to your sentences.

- Look for parallel nouns or verbs. Have you used matched subjects or verbs to create symmetry? Have you used parallel forms in successive sentences? Consider where you might have used parallelism but did not.

- Look for parallel modifiers. Have you used parallel adjectives and adverbs? How have they contributed to the meaning and effect of your sentences?

- Look for parallel phrases and clauses. Have you consciously and correctly repeated phrase and clause patterns? Where might you have employed parallelism?

Writers can vary and unify their writing by substituting pronouns for overused nouns. To make their meaning clear, however, writers follow certain patterns of pronoun usage.

Quick Reference

A pronoun must refer clearly to a specific noun, its antecedent; otherwise, the meaning of a sentence can become confused.

❯ *Make sure that a pronoun has one antecedent, not several.*

❯ *Be certain that a pronoun's reference is clear, not vague or general.*

❯ *Make sure that reflexive pronouns have antecedents in the same sentence.*

11a ❯ **Avoid unclear pronoun references.**

Unclear pronoun references result when antecedents are ambiguously placed, broad or vague, or implied rather than stated. Readers associate pronouns with the nearest antecedents. To avoid confusion, be sure that the antecedents of the pronouns you use are specific, clear, and appropriately positioned.

Ambiguous References

Ambiguous references result when more than one noun could be a pronoun's antecedent.

Ambiguous

The scuba instructor gave Patrick a detailed account of the history of the sport. He thought the lecture was a waste of time.   (Did the instructor feel dissatisfied, or did Patrick?)

Clear

Even though he thought the lecture was a waste of time, the scuba instructor gave Patrick a detailed account of the history of the sport. (The rule of nearness suggests that *he* refers to the scuba instructor.)

Vague References

General or broad antecedents result in **vague references** and confused readers.

Vague

The members of Israel's Knesset requested more military aid from the United States. This was approved by Congress.   (Did Congress approve of the request, or did Congress approve the aid?)

Clear

Upon the request of members of Israel's Knesset, Congress approved more military aid.

Implied References

An **implied antecedent** suggests a reference but does so confusingly, leaving to the reader the writer's work of creating clear, precise thought and expression.

Unclear

The Theater-in-the-Round is not very innovative, but they usually do technically polished productions.   (*They* has no direct antecedent.)

Clear

Although the directors at the Theater-in-the-Round are not very innovative, they usually do technically polished productions.

Use reflexive pronouns (those ending in *-self* or *-selves*) to refer only to the subjects of sentences.

Reflexive pronouns serve only as indirect or direct objects.

>   *subj.*   *reflex.*   *indir.*
>   *verb*   *obj.*   *d.o.*
>
> Carlotta Monterey gave herself credit for Eugene O'Neill's stability in his last years.

》》 *Use a personal pronoun in place of a reflexive pronoun if the subject of the sentence is not the antecedent. A reflexive pronoun should never be the subject of a sentence.*

Incorrect
> Wilbur and myself disagreed about the effectiveness of amplified sound on stage.

Correct
> Wilbur and I disagreed about the effectiveness of amplified sound on stage. **《《**

 Use pronouns to refer to antecedents in the same or in the immediately preceding sentence.

When pronouns and antecedents are separated by too many words, references become vague or unclear. Too-frequent use of a pronoun becomes monotonous. Alternate between using a noun and using a pronoun.

> Charlie Chaplin began his work in American films with the
> Keystone Cops. Although ~~Chaplin's~~ ^{his} early roles were limited,
> they gave him a chance to demonstrate his considerable talents.

Chaplin later showcased his talents in a one-reeler titled *The*

Tramp. In that film, ~~Chaplin~~ introduced the character that was
              he

to win him wide acclaim. ~~He~~ later produced, wrote, directed,
                         Chaplin

and starred in such films as *The Kid, City Lights,* and *Modern*

Times.

(Although the entire paragraph is about Chaplin and consequently is
not confusing, it is improved by alternating Chaplin's name with pronouns.)

For clarity, observe the convention of restricting pronoun references to sentences within the same paragraph, even when the reference seems clear.

. . . Chaplin later produced, wrote, and starred in such films as

The Kid, City Lights, and *Modern Times.*
          Chaplin's
~~His~~ importance in Hollywood soon became clear. In fact, he,

Mary Pickford, and Douglas Fairbanks split from their studios to

form the studio United Artists. . . .

EXERCISE 11.1 ❯ *Pronoun reference*

 Clarify the pronoun references in the following sentences.

Example

Although *Macbeth* is based on Scottish history, he modified historical
evidence to create a compelling tragedy.

Although *Macbeth* is based on Scottish history, Shakespeare modified
historical evidence to create a compelling tragedy.

1. In the opening act, the witches tempt Macbeth and Banquo with promises of greatness. They certainly are strange.

2. Teachers have long felt that *Macbeth* is a Shakespearean tragedy that appeals to students. They find *Macbeth* a valuable introduction to Shakespeare's other, more complicated works.

3. Although *Macbeth* has violence at its core, Nedah, Louis, and myself found the Polanski film version bloodier and more perverse than necessary.

4. The elements of Japanese kabuki theater merge well with the symbolic dimensions of *Macbeth*. They make kabuki productions of *Macbeth* very appealing.

5. In the last act of *Macbeth,* it implies that conditions in Scotland will return to normal.

Checking pronoun reference with a word processor

Use "search" codes to locate pronouns; then check for clear antecedents.

Locate personal pronouns. Your subject will determine what pronouns you use most often. Search for these pronouns and examine their use for ambiguous, vague, or implied antecedents.

Locate reflexive pronouns. Search for these pronouns and make certain that their antecedents appear in the same sentences.

MAKING   C O N N E C T I O N S

Pronouns will improve the flow and coherence of your writing, but only if you use them accurately. Examine your writing to see how and how well you use pronouns.

- Mark pronouns and antecedents. Select a recent paper and use a highlighter to mark pronouns and their antecedents. Notice the number of words separating pronouns from antecedents. Do you repeat nouns too frequently? Not frequently enough?

- Check for alternating noun-pronoun patterns. Do you use them to create variety? If you do, what is your pattern for alternating nouns and pronouns? Do you use synonyms for your nouns to create additional variety? How do you keep pronoun references clear?

12   Positioning Modifiers

Modifiers explain, describe, define, or limit a word or group of words. Position modifiers so that the relationship between them and the words they modify is clear.

Quick Reference

Modifiers add vividness and specificity to writing when they are effectively positioned in sentences. Modification is most effective when it adheres to these principles:

❯ *As often as possible, place modifiers near the words they modify.*

❯ *Seldom separate subjects and predicates or predicates and complements with long modifiers.*

❯ *Use modifiers to explain, describe, define, or limit only one word or phrase. If a modifier can conceivably modify several words or phrases, reposition it.*

| 12a | **Place modifiers to create clarity and smoothness in sentences.** |

Modifiers explain, describe, define, or limit a word or group of words. To do so effectively, they must be placed where they create clear meaning.

Positioning Long Modifiers

If a long modifier separates the subject from the verb or the verb from the object, reposition the modifier.

Ineffective

Poe's "The Telltale Heart" is, however disturbing its main premise may be, a spellbinding story.

Effective

However disturbing its main premise may be, Poe's "The Telltale Heart" is a spellbinding story.

Positioning Prepositional Phrases and Subordinate Clauses

Because readers instinctively use nearness as a guide to understanding modification, place prepositional modifiers near the words they modify.

Unclear

Huck and Jim were impressed by the view of the mansion, on the raft. (The mansion was on the raft?)

Clear

On the raft, Huck and Jim were impressed by the view of the mansion.

Unclear

In spite of his successful command of forces in the Pacific, President Truman relieved Douglas MacArthur of his military duties.   (Truman commanded forces in the Pacific?)

Clear

President Truman relieved Douglas MacArthur of his military duties, in spite of his successful command of forces in the Pacific.

Positioning Limiting Modifiers

Limiting modifiers such as *hardly, nearly,* and *only* substantially change the meaning of a sentence. Place them carefully and double-check to see that your intended meaning is clear.

He simply stated the problem.   (Stating the problem is all he did.)

He stated the problem simply.   (He made the problem easy to understand.)

We had time only to meét him.   (We had time for nothing else.)

We had time to meet only him.   (We met no one else.)

Positioning Modifiers near Infinitives

Try not to place a modifier between *to* and an infinitive. Although this usage is common in conversation and is acceptable to some linguists, it is best to avoid split infinitives.

Split infinitive
> After rereading "Ode on a Grecian Urn," Ralph began *to quickly prepare* his report.

Always acceptable
> After rereading "Ode on a Grecian Urn," Ralph quickly began *to prepare* his report.

12b Avoid dangling modifiers.

A phrase that appears at the beginning of a sentence but that does not modify the subject of the sentence is a **dangling modifier.** Sentences with dangling modifiers are unclear and illogical. Eliminate dangling modifiers by repositioning the misplaced phrases.

Dangling
> *Leaping high above the waves,* Michael watched the dolphins. (Michael was not leaping; the dolphins were.)

Clear
> Michael watched the dolphins leaping high above the waves.

Dangling

> *When still in high school,* my father expected me to be home by midnight. (You were not out that late when your father was in high school. You probably were not even born.)

Clear

> When I was still in high school, my father expected me to be home by midnight.

| 12c | **Avoid squinting modifiers.** |

Squinting modifiers are words or phrases that could modify either the words before them or the words after them.

Squinting

> Armand said *before ten o'clock* he would reach the summit. (He spoke before ten o'clock? Or would he arrive before ten?)

Clear

> Armand said he would reach the summit before ten o'clock.

>>> *When a modifier is in an ambiguous position, you may be able to clarify the meaning of the sentence by inserting the relative pronoun* that *in the appropriate position.*

Ambiguous

> Walter said *during the meeting* Monica misrepresented her case. (Did Walter comment during the meeting? Or is that when Monica distorted her case?)

Clear

> Walter said *that* during the meeting Monica misrepresented her case. (Here, *that* clarifies when Monica spoke.)

> Walter said during the meeting *that* Monica misrepresented her case. (Here, *that* clarifies when Walter spoke.) **<<<**

247

EXERCISE 12.1 ❯   *Positioning modifiers*

 The following sentences contain misplaced modifiers. Revise the sentences to make the modification clear and effective.

1. The problems of alcoholism, no matter whether they affect adults, adolescents, or even children, need to be honestly addressed.

2. Drinking is, though acceptable within most groups in American culture, socially, physically, and economically costly.

3. Families and coworkers often fail to honestly assess the drinking habits of alcoholics and, as a result, fail to immediately encourage alcoholics to seek professional help.

4. People who drink often have liver trouble, among other medical and social problems.

5. When inebriated, family members endure the emotional and physical abuse of alcoholics.

6. Alcoholics must admit often that their drinking problems are severe before they can get help.

EXERCISE 12.2 ❯   *Positioning modifiers*

The following paragraph contains a variety of misplaced modifiers. Revise the sentences to make the modification clear and effective.

Helping my uncle with his one-acre garden taught me that victories in the garden are won the hard way. My uncle and I, each morning before it got too hot, would do maintenance work. We would pull small infestations of weeds by hand and then spray, with a postemergent herbicide, larger growths of weeds. Then we would mulch the plants whose foliage did not protect the soil from the sun's drying rays. Using straw and sometimes black plastic sheets, we would, trying not to damage low leaves, encircle the stalks of the plants. Covered with parasitical bugs, we would sometimes have to spray plants with a pyrethrin mixture. Once we got started, we worked often without talking. A few comments seemed to be enough on the growth of the asparagus or the tomatoes. Once, however, Uncle Charles told me during our work sessions I was a conscientious worker when he felt talkative. As the days passed, I began to, because of my own hard work, realize how much effort goes into gardening. I must say that grown with so much care, I now appreciate my fruits and vegetables more than I used to.

Positioning modifiers with a word processor

Use your word processor to improve the effectiveness of modifiers.

Reposition modifiers. When modifiers must be moved, use the "block" and "move" commands to make the changes. You will also need to alter punctuation and mechanics using the "delete" command.

Insert the relative pronoun *that* when *that* is necessary to prevent misreading. Your word-processing program will automatically reformat the sentence.

MAKING   C O N N E C T I O N S

Modifiers help to clarify ideas in writing, but they must be placed carefully to avoid confusion. Identify your patterns for using modifiers and learn to avoid difficulties in modification.

- Notice how often you use modifiers. Using a recent paper, note where and how often you use modifying words, phrases, and clauses.

- Analyze the way you use modifiers. Do you position them correctly? Might any of your modifiers create confusion because of their placement? Do you use some patterns of modification more than you use others?

DICTION

C · O · N · N · E · C · T · I · O · N · S

Diction, the selection and use of words to achieve effective communication, is fundamental to good writing. On one level, word choices clarify ideas and enable writers to express the meaning they want: *enjoying reading* differs from *loving reading; giving a gift* to a politician is quite distinct from *offering a bribe*. On another level, word choices create impressions of the writer: *We shouldn't expect perfection from our children* creates an impression quite different from *Children are not perfect*. The first suggests a writer who has a personal bond with both children (*our* children) and readers (*we*); the second implies a writer who is removed from a personal context. Because of the interplay among diction, meaning, and tone, writers must choose words carefully if they hope to create the impressions they intend in their writing.

The writer's involvement with words is a continuing, intricate interaction of ideas and expression. Formulating a thesis, drafting, revising — each is part of the process of finding the right word and the right combination of words. As you revise your papers, remember that words, alone and in combination, convey both explicit and implicit meanings.

Through **diction,** the choice and use of words for effective communication, writers make their meanings clear to readers. Specific word choices affect the tone of writing, implying writers' perceptions of themselves, their readers, their subjects, and their purposes in writing.

Quick Reference

Selecting appropriate words requires a strong sense of your purpose and your audience.

❯ *Use formal or informal diction, depending on the tone that you want to achieve in your paper.*

❯ *Choose words that your readers will understand.*

❯ *Select words whose denotations suit your meaning and whose connotations suit your purpose.*

❯ *Use specific words that convey your meaning clearly and efficiently.*

❯ *Use idioms correctly; note especially the correct preposition in phrasal idioms.*

| 13a | **Consider your word choices.** |

American English consists of many regional and social dialects that can be broadly classified as standard or nonstandard.

Standard English is just that: standard, established usage for speaking and writing. Writers employ its grammatical principles and accepted word choices for most formal writing, including academic and professional; educated readers expect its use in most of what they read. **Nonstandard English** — often used in conversation, fiction, and informal writing — occasionally uses ungrammatical constructions and colloquial, regional, or personal words and expressions.

In the early stages of writing — in planning, organizing, and writing a rough draft — most writers do not pause to consider their diction, standard or otherwise. However, when writers revise a rough draft, word choices become especially important. Use the following guidelines, the Glossary of Usage starting on page 635, and your dictionary to choose the words that best convey the meaning and tone you want.

Formal Diction

Used in most academic and professional writing, **formal diction** differs somewhat from the word choices of everyday conversation. When addressing certain subjects (death, religion, politics, or culture, for example), writers usually select formal diction.

Formal diction generally excludes slang and contractions and uses the third person (*he, she, it, they*). Writers choose the most exact words to express their meaning and organize words carefully to achieve the desired tone. The following paragraph, informal in the first draft, is revised in the second draft to achieve the formal tone suited to the subject.

Informal diction and tone

The effects of divorce on children change with the kids' ages. Little kids, one to four, often don't get it when their parents yell at each other, but they usually know something's wrong. They tend to get down, stopping eating and talking, or to act up, getting loud and wild. Bigger kids, from four to eight, have a better idea of what's going on. Because they don't know any better, they're always asking embarrassing questions like "Why are you and Mommy yelling at each other?" These kids often get edgy, flunk in school, and carry a heavy load of guilt.

Formal diction and tone

The effects of divorce on children vary with the children's ages. Very young children, from one to four, often do not fully comprehend the problems between their parents, but they usually sense the tension. They may become depressed, not eating or talking, or demand attention through loud misbehavior. Older children, from four to eight, more clearly recognize relationships in turmoil. Lacking social adeptness, they often ask embarrassing and candid questions such as "Why are you and Mommy yelling at each other?" These children may become nervous, do poorly in school, and feel responsible for their parents' problems.

Informal Diction

Informal diction is the language of conversation. Most writers use informal diction naturally, especially for subjects like travel, sports, and popular culture.

Informal diction often includes contractions and uses first-person pronouns (*I, me, my,* and so on) and sometimes includes slang and regionalisms. It can serve your purposes well in a non-academic composition, such as a personal-experience paper. The following paragraph, with its personal point of view, effectively employs informal diction.

When I was about eleven, my parents got a divorce. I wasn't surprised. For months before, I had known something was wrong, although I wasn't sure what. Mom and Dad would alternately argue about trivial matters and then turn silent, not speaking to each other for days. Then one day, Dad just quietly moved out. It was a relief for everyone, and now, ten years later, Mom and Dad are good friends.

Diction and Audience

A good idea supported with pertinent examples and facts may confuse readers if the words you choose do not accurately convey your intended meaning. To assess the appropriateness of your diction for your audience, consider these questions:

How well developed are your readers' vocabularies? If your readers are well educated or well read, their vocabularies are probably extensive, and you have a wide choice of words to use to present ideas. On the other hand, if you suspect that your readers' vocabularies are not well developed, you must adjust your diction to present your ideas clearly yet simply.

Do your readers understand the technical vocabulary of the subject? Readers who are familiar with your subject will understand its technical terminology, and you will be able to use it freely. If readers are not familiar with your subject, however, you cannot assume that they will understand its specialized vocabulary, and you will have to define key words or use everyday equivalents for technical terms.

What level of diction will your readers expect? Most readers expect standard diction in most writing; some prefer formal diction for some topics; others prefer informal diction for all topics. If formal diction suits your purpose, you should comply with readers' expectations by omitting slang, contractions, and regionalisms from your writing. If your purpose justifies informal diction, comply with readers' expectations by choosing words freely. Remember, too, that for some subjects, readers expect a well-chosen blend of formal and informal language, a combination often termed moderate diction. To answer questions about the level of particular words or phrases, refer to the Glossary of Usage starting on page 635, to your dictionary, or to a dictionary of usage.

You cannot completely match your word choices with readers' knowledge, needs, and expectations, but you should make an effort to analyze your audience and write in language that they will understand and appreciate.

EXERCISE 13.1 ❯ *Formal and informal diction*

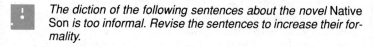

The diction of the following sentences about the novel Native Son *is too informal. Revise the sentences to increase their formality.*

1. Many readers are grossed out when Bigger Thomas bashes the rat in the opening scene of the novel.

2. The Daltons, a filthy rich family, had made a bunch of money by ripping off poor tenants in slum housing.

3. Their daughter Mary and her left-wing friends were into hanging out in restaurants in black neighborhoods.

4. Bigger took off after he accidentally did Mary in.

5. Once the cops nabbed Bigger, he was put on trial and then sent up the river.

13b ❭ **Select words whose denotations and connotations match your meaning.**

Words are defined in two ways, by their denotations and by their connotations.

Denotations

Denotations are dictionary meanings — short, specific definitions. They present the explicit meanings of words and exclude the subtle shades of meaning that words acquire from use in specific contexts.

Connotations

Connotations are the secondary and sometimes emotional meanings of words. They suggest meaning beyond the explicit denotation. Connotations can create difficulties for beginning writers who do not consider the implied meanings of the words they choose. Make sure that the connotations of the words you use match your purpose.

Consider Connotations

Two words often share the same denotation (and hence are synonyms) but have distinct connotations. Connotations can be classified as positive, negative, or neutral.

Positive connotation

The *delegation* of students protested outside the administration building.   (*Delegation* implies an orderly, duly constituted, and representative gathering.)

Negative connotation

The *mob* of students protested outside the administration building. (*Mob* suggests lack of control and implies a threat.)

Neutral connotation

The *group* of students protested outside the administration building. (*Group* simply denotes "a number of people.")

EXERCISE 13.2 ❯ *Connotations*

Revise the following sentences to replace words whose connotations seem inappropriate.

1. Airport security has become restrictive in the last few years, as folks who travel a lot have discovered.

2. At every concourse in major airports, people dawdle in lines, waiting to have their carry-on luggage inspected.

3. At these security checkpoints, people sometimes get peeved about passing their stuff through scanning devices, but every once in a while, someone is flabbergasted when his or her luggage sets off the alarm.

4. The security guards interrogate people whose luggage sets off the alarm to see if they have a reasonable excuse, and then the checking continues.

5. Although these security checks are an annoyance, they help to keep air travel inviolate.

| 13c | **Select abstract or concrete words to suit your meaning.** |

Abstract words name intangibles, such as concepts, qualities, or conditions: *truth, loyalty, laziness, freedom, poverty.* **Concrete words** name tangibles: *fire hydrant, bagel, razor, rabbit, silo.* For some purposes, abstract words effectively present general ideas. The vividness of concrete words, however, adds interest and specificity appropriate to all writing.

Abstract

Poverty demoralizes people.

Concrete

Being unable to pay bills, buy suitable clothing, feed one's children well, and buy some small conveniences demoralizes parents who want comfortable homes for their families.

The diagram following illustrates the continuum of specificity.

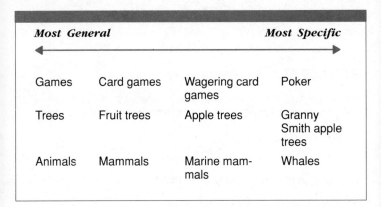

Most General			*Most Specific*
Games	Card games	Wagering card games	Poker
Trees	Fruit trees	Apple trees	Granny Smith apple trees
Animals	Mammals	Marine mammals	Whales

Whales can be made more exact by specifying *blue whales, sperm whales,* and *killer whales.* Although you may not always have this many alternatives, choose the most specific word possible to clarify your meaning.

1. *Women* in *fiction* are sometimes shrewder than *men.*

2. *Heroines* in *novels* are sometimes shrewder than *heroes.*

3. *Romantic heroines* in *nineteenth-century novels* are sometimes shrewder than *their lovers.*

4. *Catherine* in <u>*Wuthering Heights*</u> is shrewder than *Heathcliff.*

Sometimes a generalization best suits your purpose, in which case the third sentence may be the best. However, do not forget the importance of specificity. Readers of the first sentence could easily and justifiably supply their own details, thinking wrongly, for instance, that the writer means that women in contemporary short stories are sometimes shrewder than their fathers. To avoid such misinterpretation, make your meaning clear through using specific diction.

EXERCISE 13.3 ❯ Specific words

> The following sentences present general ideas. Clarify their meanings by replacing general words with specific ones.

1. Politics is expensive.

2. The crowd at the convention was big.

3. Family members of politicians often have personal problems.

4. The candidate won the election.

5. Television influences politics.

| 13d | **Use the established forms of idioms.** |

Idioms, groups of words that together establish an idiosyncratic meaning, are often illogical if examined word for word. For example, *break it up,* commonly understood to mean "stop fighting," does not make sense when examined one word at a time. *Break,* to split into two or more pieces, creates a visual image of fighters separating. *It,* though indefinite, clearly refers to the implied subject, *fight. Up* defies explanation unless it is considered part of the idiom *break up.* Other unanalyzable idioms include *pick up (the house), take a shower, fall in love,* and *catch a cold.* Such idioms have developed along with our language, and although they may not make literal sense, they are understood.

All idioms are not equally acceptable in formal writing. If you use an idiom, use it carefully and use its established form. The correct use of many phrasal idioms, such as those in the following list, depends on using the correct preposition. If you are in doubt about which preposition to use, check the list or your dictionary.

Phrasal Idioms

agree with (someone)

agree to (a proposal)

angry with (*not* angry at)

charge for (a purchase)

charge with (a crime)

die of/die from

differ with (meaning "to disagree")

differ from (meaning "to be unlike")

in search of (*not* in search for)

intend to (*not* intend on)

off (*not* off of)

plan to (*not* plan on)

similar to (*not* similar with)

sure to (*not* sure and)

to search for

try to (*not* try and)

wait for (someone or something)

wait on (meaning "to serve")

Whenever you are confused about the meaning of an idiom, consult a dictionary.

EXERCISE 13.4 ❯ *Idioms*

Select the appropriate idioms for the following sentences.

1. The National Geographic Society (NGS), founded in 1888, is a (type of a/type of) organization with diverse interests and goals.

2. On the one hand, the NGS often goes (in search of/in search for) exotic flora and fauna to describe in articles and broadcasts.

3. On the other hand, NGS also (tries and/tries to) make Americans aware of simple but subtle differences between peoples of different cultures.

4. Although the format for NGS television programs does not (differ with/differ from) that of other nature documentaries, they are nonetheless uniformly more fascinating.

5. With over 10.5 million members, NGS will be (sure to/sure and) flourish into the twenty-first century.

13e > **Use slang and regionalisms selectively.**

Both **slang** and **regionalisms** are exclusive, informal vocabularies, intelligible to a restricted group. In the case of slang, the restriction is generally to a social, professional, or cultural group; in the case of regionalisms, the restriction is to a specific geographic area.

Slang tends to change rapidly and to be in use for only brief periods. In speech, slang can be refreshingly direct and shows that speakers are aware of current language trends. If the use of a slang expression becomes broad enough, the expression may be absorbed into acceptable written English. Until that happens, however, slang has little place in formal writing. Slang is so quickly dated and so informal, and its meaning is so often inexact to those outside the originating group, that it does not communicate very clearly.

That class was *the pits*.   ("A waste," as in peach pits? "A cavity in the ground," as in the La Brea Tar Pits?)

When I saw how far ahead I was, I felt *wicked*.   ("Evil"? Wicked good? Wicked bad?)

Regionalisms are understood within the bounds of a restricted geographic area, but beyond that area their meaning becomes lost. Like slang, regionalisms should be avoided because they can muddle communication.

Early in November, we ordered the *tags* for our car.   (Although *tags* will be clear to readers from some areas of the East, use the more common expression *license plates* to ensure the understanding of readers from other areas.)

EXERCISE 13.5 ❯ *Slang and regionalisms*

Make a list of five slang terms or phrases and five regionalisms in current use. Then write two sentences for each one. In the first sentence, use the slang or regionalism; in the second, translate the slang or regionalism into standard English.

Example:

rip-off (noun)

The insurance plan to supplement Medicare was a *rip-off.*

The insurance plan to supplement Medicare was a *fraud.*

| 13f | **Use euphemisms selectively.** |

Euphemisms are "nice" words substituted for specific words whose connotations are negative, unpleasant, or unappealing. Instead of saying that soldiers were *killed,* a press release might say that they *gave their lives.* Instead of saying that people are being *fired,* a notice might say they are being *let go.* Instead of saying that a customer is *overweight,* a salesclerk might say that she is *full-figured.* Seldom fooled by euphemisms, readers instinctively supply the appropriate translation.

Euphemism	Translation
financial enticements	bribes
the oldest profession	prostitution
corporal punishment	spanking
placed in custody	arrested
hair-color enhancer	dye

Some euphemisms establish a buffer around painful feelings — as when *passed away* replaces *died* — but even this use should be infrequent.

EXERCISE 13.6 ❯ Euphemisms

> Revise the following sentences to eliminate euphemistic words and phrases.

1. Weddings are often not inexpensive displays by people and for people who fail to consider their less-than-genuine behavior.

2. Elaborate and expensive, many weddings must be financed through deferred-payment plans.

3. Even brides who are in the family way often wear traditional white bridal gowns.

4. Many less-than-honest people who do not attend worship services regularly insist on being married in houses of God.

5. Ironically, many of these marriages — begun with such elaborate display — end in marriage dissolutions.

Revising meaning and tone with a word processor

When you are working on a paper, use the word processor's "delete" and "insert" capabilities to adjust the diction.

Make changes as you type the draft. As you reread on the screen, delete words that do not fit naturally in the sentences.

If the right word does not occur to you as you work, use a symbol such as ^ or ~ to mark the place. At a pause in your work, use the "search" function to find the symbols and return to the sentence to consider the appropriate word choice.

Make "hard-copy" changes. Print a copy of the paper, and examine your word choices; then return to your computer to delete ineffective words and substitute better ones.

MAKING C O N N E C T I O N S

Discovering the importance of word choices is a critical step in improving your writing. To further develop your sense of the importance of diction, examine a few of your papers to discover more effective ways to use words.

- Do you typically write formally or informally? Take one paper and briefly list its formal (or informal) language. How was that language suited or ill suited to the topic?

- Can you explain the connotations of the words you use? Select ten important words from your papers. Identify their connotations as positive, negative, or neutral. Choose a few synonyms for each (use a dictionary or thesaurus) and explain how the words you chose vary from their synonyms.

- How specific is your diction? Select ten general words from your papers. For each, construct a continuum like that on page 261, showing at least two additional degrees of specificity. Explain which word best suits the original context of your paper.

- What idiomatic expressions do you use? Select a few idioms from your papers and explain their use as if you were addressing a non-native speaker of English.

14   Choosing Effective Words

Ineffective word choices — such as clichés, pretentious and sexist language, and jargon — weaken writing by distracting or irritating readers and by obscuring ideas. Writers need to be aware of and avoid such problems. This chapter addresses the most common difficulties.

Quick Reference

Avoid hackneyed or imprecise word choices that muddy writing and distract readers from central ideas.

❯ *Eliminate clichés and other trite expressions.*

❯ *Use words to clarify your meaning, not to impress readers; avoid pretentious language and jargon.*

❯ *Use figurative language to enliven and illuminate your writing; avoid overused, illogical, or mixed figures of speech.*

❯ *Avoid sexist language; it is often inaccurate and it may be offensive.*

14a ❯ **Avoid clichés and triteness.**

A **cliché** is an overused expression that has lost its original inventiveness, surprise, and, often, meaning. **Triteness** describes words and phrases that have been overused: they are stale, uninteresting, and frequently vague.

Some writers do make effective use of trite or clichéd language. Consider, for example, the following quotation from Joseph Brodsky's essay "Flight from Byzantium": "Dust! This weird substance, driving into your face! It merits attention; it should not be concealed behind the word *dust.*" *Weird* can seem trite and vague in some contexts, but here it expresses the surprising strangeness Brodsky felt in encountering the common substance dust in a new way and with a new intensity. Readers, however, will be skeptical of clichéd and trite language, and inexperienced writers should avoid using it.

Clichés

Readers finding clichés in your writing will assume that you did not take the time to think through your ideas or consider original ways to express them.

Complete the following phrases.

last but not ———

beat around the ———

fit as a ———

in the final ———

red as a ———

Most people can supply the missing words easily. If you use such phrases in your writing, your readers will find them equally predictable — and boring. Rather than relying on clichés in your own writing, devise phrases that express your meaning exactly, in your own words.

Triteness

Trite words and phrases have been used so often, and so thoughtlessly, that they have lost all appeal and interest. If you discover trite expressions in your writing, strike them out and replace them with less predictable word choices that create interest in and clarify your ideas.

Trite

The report of the Educational Task Force was *very thorough*.   (*Thorough* is so common and used in so many contexts that it hardly clarifies the meaning of the sentence.)

Improved

The report of the Educational Task Force included a general preface, a fifteen-chapter text, and twenty-seven appendixes presenting research data.   (The use of details to explain the features of the report improves the clarity of the sentence.)

Eliminating triteness is especially easy to do on a word processor. Simply delete the trite word or phrase and insert a carefully chosen replacement. If you overuse particular trite expressions, use the "search" function to find and replace them.

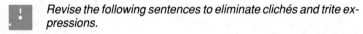

EXERCISE 14.1 **❯** *Clichés and trite expressions*

Revise the following sentences to eliminate clichés and trite expressions.

1. Some monuments have struck a chord with the American people and can remind each and every one of us of the value of public memorials.

2. The *Statue of Liberty* is an awe-inspiring national monument, symbolizing how America opened its arms to European emigrants.

3. The simplicity of the Tomb of the Unknown Soldier and the low-key military display puts a lump in the throats of many visitors.

4. One out-of-the-ordinary monument, St. Louis's Gateway Arch, reaches to the sky in a sweeping curve of shiny stainless steel.

5. With its marble as smooth as glass, the Vietnam Memorial is a plain and simple monument honoring the tens of thousands of soldiers who gave their lives for their country.

14b ▷ **Avoid pretentious language.**

A rich and varied vocabulary is an asset for a writer, but the words used in any given piece of writing must be geared to its specific audience and purpose. Writers who use **pretentious language** use words to impress rather than to communicate with readers. Avoid stilted language, even in formal writing. Not only is pretentious diction dishonest, but it often makes simple ideas difficult to grasp and complicated ideas impossible to understand. If writers do not translate pretentious diction into natural words, readers have to do so.

Pretentious

> *Prior to* the purchase of the *abode,* the Enricos carefully *ruminated* about how *residential payments* would affect their *cash flow.* (The stilted word choices here, some poorly chosen synonyms and some jargon, require a translation.)

Natural

> *Before* the Enricos purchased the *house,* they carefully *thought* about how *mortgage payments* would affect their *finances.* (This sentence uses natural diction and is therefore easily understood on the first reading.)

》》》 *Although a thesaurus, or a book of synonyms, may help you to find alternative ways of stating a point, it should be used carefully. Use only words that are a natural part of your vocabulary, avoid clichés, and never choose words whose connotations you do not understand. Using a thesaurus to find impressive or unusual words results in pretentious writing.* **《《《**

EXERCISE 14.2 **》** *Pretentious language*

> *Revise the following paragraph to eliminate pretentious language and use language that is more natural. (Suggestion: Make this a personal narrative.)*

When one participates in commencement ceremonies, one is often fraught with a mixture of emotions. One senses relief because one's time in high school is terminating. Conversely, one feels uncertain about what lies ahead. Some students will seek employment immediately, other students will approach matrimony, and yet other students will pursue additional academic studies. For this diversity of students, commencement exercises symbolize an uncertain transmutation in their lives.

| 14c | **Avoid jargon.** |

Jargon is the technical vocabulary of a specialized group. Doctors, mechanics, weather forecasters, teachers, carpenters, and publishers all have special words that they use in special contexts. When they write only for their own group, their use of the group's jargon may be acceptable (perhaps even necessary). When writing for a wide audience, however, writers must translate jargon into common terms.

Jargon	*Translation*
urban open space (city planning)	a city park
precipitation (weather forecasting)	rain, snow, sleet
telephone surveillance (law enforcement)	wiretapping
cost-efficient (business)	economical
merchantable dwelling (real estate)	a house that will sell

Jargon

The city council recommends a systematic program of greening for our arterials as a means to revitalize our declining streetscape.

Translation

The city council recommends that we plant trees along our main streets to make them appear less neglected.

EXERCISE 14.3 ❯ *Pretentious diction and jargon*

Translate these pretentious, jargon-laden sentences into natural, clear writing.

1. An excessive proportion of American citizenry improvidently pass their days ignoring quotidian dangers to health.

2. The abundance of vehicular collisions attests to the fact that the people of the United States of America are oblivious to safety-inducing guidelines for automobile management.

3. The numbers of persons who imbibe an excess of distilled spirits is also a depression-inducing statistic.

4. The inhalation of toxic fumes from smoking materials, although prohibited in many business establishments, continues to have a negative impact on the health aspect of the male and female population sectors.

5. The personal and private ownership and use of firearms and related paraphernalia account for the accidental demise of scores of people each twelvemonth.

| 14d | **Use figures of speech cautiously.** |

Figures of speech may be single words, phrases, or longer expressions. They add vitality to writing, most often by making unexpected or suggestive connections between dissimilar things. Metaphors and similes are the most common and useful figures of speech.

Metaphors imply the identity of the things compared.

> Dr. Mantera's criticism of the proposal was all thunder and no lightning.   (The implication is that the criticism was mere noise with no illumination or insight.)

Similes are direct comparisons using the connectives *like, as,* or *as if.*

> Rob accelerated his car, shifting lanes quickly and rounding corners at high speed — as if he were making the final lap at the Indianapolis 500.

Original and apt figures of speech can enliven your writing, but they should be used to illuminate and clarify your ideas, not to decorate them. Be careful to avoid clichés.

Effective metaphor
> Ronald, *a modern Tom Sawyer,* enjoys harmless trickery and mild adventure.

Ineffective metaphor
> After the laughter stopped, Bernice gave Rinaldo an *icy* stare.   (The modifier is a cliché.)

Effective simile
> Cleo is *like a Duracell battery:* she's always starting something, and it lasts longer than we ever expect.

Ineffective simile

Darryl's grades are solid *as a rock*.   ("Solid as a rock" is a cliché.)

Extended or multiple related figures of speech must present a uniform impression, drawing on logically consistent images, locales, experiences, or circumstances. Without this consistency, the image is confused — often laughably so.

Confusingly mixed

Like an agile deer, the politician leaped into the fray.   (Agile deer do leap, but they are shy animals unlikely to seek conflict. Moreover, "leaped into the fray" is a cliché.)

Logically linked

Like an agile deer, the politician leaped over obstacles to the proposal. (The agile deer leaping over obstacles is a logical, consistent image.)

EXERCISE 14.4 ❯ *Figures of speech*

Revise the ineffective figures of speech in the following sentences.

1. Like good soldiers, athletes get down to the work that training sessions require and rise to the occasion.

2. Swimmers fly through lap after lap during practices, building the tireless endurance necessary in races.

3. Like kangaroos, basketball players jump for balls and then fire them down the court, hoping to hone skills to use in games.

4. With catlike speed, sprinters shoot from starting blocks over and over again, trying to perfect an opening move that will put them miles above the rest.

5. Like trains speeding down the tracks, football linesmen practice rushing and tackling, leaving other players in their wake.

| 14e | **Avoid sexist language.** |

Sexist language implies, generally through choices of key nouns and pronouns, that the subject applies only to males or only to females. Because it fails to reflect the diversity of contemporary society, sexist language is narrow-minded and inaccurate.

To avoid sexist language, avoid using sex-specific pronouns when the antecedent is not sex-specific and avoid nouns that arbitrarily or from empty tradition restrict meaning to one sex or the other. When choosing nouns, learn to notice the subtle — and sometimes not so subtle — implications of your choices.

Sexist

A psychiatrist is bound by professional oath to keep his patients' records confidential.   (Many psychiatrists are women, so this statement is not accurate.)

Nonsexist

A psychiatrist is bound by professional oath to keep his or her patients' records confidential.   (The use of *his or her* eliminates the sexist bias in the sentence.)

Nonsexist

Psychiatrists are bound by professional oath to keep their patients' records confidential.   (The use of plural forms avoids sexist language.)

Sexist

According to family records, my forefathers came to the United States from France in 1806.   (Fore*mothers* had to come too, or there would not have been any children.)

Nonsexist

According to family records, my ancestors came to the United States from France in 1806.

EXERCISE 14.5 ❯ *Sexist language*

The following passage was written in 1872, when sensitivity to sexist language was not common. Rewrite the passage to eliminate sexist language — but do not change the meaning of the passage.

The blight which threatens theoretical culture has only begun to frighten modern man, and he is groping uneasily for remedies out of the storehouse of his experience, without having any real conviction that these remedies will avail against disaster. In the meantime, there have arisen certain men of genius who, with admirable circumspection and consequence, have used the arsenal of science to demonstrate the limitations of science and of the cognitive faculty itself. They have authoritatively rejected science's claim to universal validity and to the attainment of universal goals and exploded for the first time the belief that men may plumb the universe by means of the law of causation. — Friedrich Nietzsche, *The Birth of Tragedy*

> 14f > **Avoid neologisms and archaisms.**

Neologisms, recently coined words or word forms, appear in current speech (and in some journalistic and technical writing) and then very often fade away. In formal writing, avoid using new terms unless nothing else expresses your meaning.

Questionable

Personal computers must be *user-friendly.*   (*Computer,* once a neologism, is now standard; *user-friendly* is still jargon, vague to the uninformed, and colloquial.)

Better

Personal computers must be *easy for people to use.*

Archaisms, words once in common use but no longer standard, seem affected and disruptive in contemporary writing.

Words no longer in use — like *yon* ("over there") or *betwixt* ("between"), or words no longer used in a given sense, like *save* in the sense of "except" — make writing artificial and pretentious.

Artificial

> We adults sat and reminisced *whilst* the children played along the shore.   (No one says *whilst* any more, and no one should write it.)

Natural

> We adults sat and reminisced *while* the children played along the shore.

》》》 **Some neologisms are so expressive and apt that they become widely used and universally acceptable.** Stereo, fallout, *and* refrigerator were once newly coined words that have long since become standard. **《《《**

EXERCISE 14.6 **》** *Neologisms and archaic words*

Revise the following sentences to eliminate words or phrases that are either too new or too old to be standard usage.

1. Methinks that romance novels deserve more attention from serious readers than they have often received.

2. Betwixt the covers of romance novels as varied as *Wuthering Heights* and *The Lady and the Highwayman,* readers will find quickly paced stories of intrigue and love.

3. The heroines and heroes of these novels are ofttimes innocent, sincere, and trusting people whose lives are threatened by erstwhile friends who are really enemies.

4. With their inherent reliance on historical context, these infotainment novels provide readers with knowledge of past societies, as well as reading pleasure.

5. Although the reading of romance novels does not require much intellectual input from readers, these books provide innocent pleasure and distraction.

279

Choosing effective words with a word processor

Beyond general uses of word-processing programs to delete and substitute words, consider these specific approaches:

Replace neologisms. As you check a paper by using a spell-checking program, the program will highlight words not found in its dictionary. Neologisms, because they are new and in limited use, will not appear. The spell checker will draw your attention to these words, and you can then decide whether they or standard substitutes best serve your purposes.

Check for sexist use of pronouns. Use the "search" commands to look for masculine pronouns: *he, him, his,* and *himself.* When the antecedent is not exclusively male, change the pronoun to *he or she, him or her,* and so on, or change the antecedent, pronoun, and verb to plural forms.

MAKING   C O N N E C T I O N S

To improve your diction, reevaluate your past writing and develop strategies for making more effective choices in future work.

- Find and eliminate clichés and trite expressions. Examine samples of your writing and make a list of the clichés and trite expressions that you have used in the past. Keep your list and refer to it as you revise later papers.

- Analyze your use of pretentious language. Search through sample papers for pretentious language. Why did you use it? What is its effect? What words or phrases might you replace it with?

- Note your use of jargon. Mark any words that could be considered jargon and decide whether their use was justified. Were they clear to your audience? What other words could you have used?

- Learn to avoid sexist language. Examine several papers for sexist use of restrictive nouns and exclusionary pronouns. Note why such word choices restrict and distort your meaning and replace them with nonsexist choices.

GRAMMAR

Chess, elections, basketball, driving in traffic, and writing have at least one thing in common: all depend on generally accepted rules. People may modify or ignore rules occasionally, but violating underlying assumptions often leads to confusion — or worse.

In writing, grammar provides the rules that govern how words work together to form sentences. But grammar is a way to make your writing understandable and acceptable to readers, not an oppressive set of don'ts. You would not want to play tennis with someone who did not understand or chose to ignore the rule that a ball landing on the line is "fair" or "in play." Rules like this make tennis understandable to everyone who plays, and anyone who has ever played tennis or any other game without using rules knows how chaotic and frustrating that experience can be.

Grammar establishes shared assumptions between writers and readers. Some rules of grammar apply to sentence structure: a complete sentence requires a subject and verb. Some rules apply to word use: *badly* is an adverb, not an adjective. Some grammatical rules are rigidly fixed: do not run two independent clauses together without proper punctuation or connective words. Some are contextual: fragments, though generally unacceptable, can be used selectively to create emphasis. To communicate effectively with readers who know the rules of grammar and expect to see them applied in writing, writers must understand and apply those rules properly.

15 Fragments

Fragments are capitalized and punctuated as if they were sentences, but they are not sentences. They may be phrases lacking subjects or verbs, or they may be subordinate clauses. Four strategies for correcting fragments appear in sections 15a and 15b.

Although fragments are common in speech, notes, rough drafts, and writing that imitates speech, formal writing generally requires complete and grammatical sentences that state ideas fully. The use of fragments for special effect is discussed in section 15c.

Quick Reference

Fragments distract readers and shift their attention away from your ideas to the mechanics of your writing. To avoid this, follow these suggestions:

> ❯ *Make sure that your sentences contain subjects and verbs, the basic sentence elements.*

> ❯ *Be sure to use subordinating conjunctions in complex and compound-complex sentences, not in subordinate-clause fragments.*

> ❯ *Use intentional fragments selectively for special effect, remembering that excessive use distracts and annoys readers.*

15a Revise fragments that are phrases.

Correct fragments that lack subjects or verbs by supplying the missing element or by combining the fragment with a complete sentence.

Fragments Lacking Subjects

Fragments without subjects may be verb phrases (free-standing predicates and complements); they may also be verbal phrases (phrases using gerunds, participles, and infinitives [see Verbs, pages 187–91]). Eliminate these fragments by adding a subject or by joining the fragment to an appropriate sentence.

Fragment

Brian is addicted to reading mystery novels. Reads one a week.

Complete

Brian is addicted to reading mystery novels. *He* reads one a week.   (A subject pronoun has been added.)

Complete

Brian, who is addicted to mystery novels, reads one a week.   (The fragment has been joined to a related sentence.)

Fragment

Jay has one ambition. To travel around the world.

Complete

Jay's one ambition *is* to travel around the world.   (The infinitive phrase is joined to the sentence.)

Fragments Lacking Verbs

Fragments without verbs are usually subjects and related modifiers, appositives, or absolute phrases. Correct these fragments by adding a verb or joining the appositive or absolute phrase to a nearby sentence.

Fragment

Rachel, an avid collector of china figurines. She pays eighty-five dollars for extra insurance coverage.

Complete

Rachel *is* an avid collector of china figurines. She pays eighty-five dollars for extra insurance coverage.   (A verb has been added.)

Complete

Rachel, an avid collector of china figurines, *pays* eighty-five dollars for extra insurance coverage.   (The fragment has been joined to a related sentence.)

 Use your word processor to correct phrasal fragments quickly and easily by inserting subjects or verbs. Be sure to change capitalization and punctuation as required by the new sentence.

15b   **Revise fragments that are subordinate clauses.**

A subordinate clause must be joined to an independent clause to form a grammatical sentence. Correct subordinate-clause fragments by dropping the subordinating conjunction to form a simple sentence or by joining the subordinate clause to one or more independent clauses to form a complex or compound-complex sentence.

Fragment

Some students have to postpone starting college. Because the cost of attending has risen.

Complete

Some students have to postpone starting college. The cost of attending has risen.   (The subordinate conjunction has been dropped.)

Complete

Some students have to postpone starting college because the cost of attending has risen.   (Here the subordinate clause becomes part of a complex sentence.)

Complete

Because the cost of attending college has risen, some students have to postpone starting.

    Your word processor will help you to join phrases and subordinate clauses to related sentences quickly and easily. Use the "block" and "move" features and experiment with ways to reposition these groups of words to form new expressive, grammatical sentences.

| 15c | **Use fragments sparingly for special effect.** |

Fragments can be effective and acceptable, even in final drafts, when they are used to isolate and thus emphasize a key word or phrase. Use this strategy selectively to achieve emphasis or to supply an answer to a question.

G, PG, R, X. These symbols are used to classify films and to restrict the audiences that see them. Although the coding system represents an admirable effort to protect children, does it work? No. Many parents disregard the implied advice of the rating system, and few theater owners adhere to its guidelines when selling tickets.

EXERCISE 15.1 ❭ Fragments

    Eliminate the fragments in the following paragraph by adding subjects or verbs or by combining the fragments with complete sentences.

The National Board of Teaching Standards has been formed recently to address matters of teacher training and certification. Because of inconsistencies that exist among states. Some states require prospective teachers to take a pre-professional skills test. To establish the reading, writing, and mathematical skills of future teachers. But not others. All states require expertise in content areas. Approximates that of traditional majors in each subject area. States require additional work in educational theory and practice. Usually fifteen to twenty semester hours of work. These pedagogical courses, ones emphasizing general principles of teaching and general patterns of learning. No matter how theoretically sound these courses may be, inconsistencies exist. Since states establish their requirements individually. As a result, teachers moving from one state to the other may not be fully prepared to meet requirements. Future teachers need the coordinated efforts of state departments of education. To develop uniform educational programs. Especially with prospects of taking the National Teacher's Exam.

EXERCISE 15.2 ❭ Fragments

 The following paragraph includes a number of fragments. Some are intended for special emphasis, but others are clearly grammatical errors. Correct the ineffective fragments and explain why the others should remain.

New York. St. Louis. Knoxville. New Orleans. Los Angeles. These cities have all hosted those pretentious, glorious, overly expensive, and enjoyable activities known as world's fairs. Filled with exhibits, amusements, and restaurants. World's fairs offer people a chance to learn about the world while enjoying themselves. At these large fairs, nations from around the world build pavilions to showcase their national achievements. Often sending examples of their best technology, art, and historical treasures. Dancers, singers, and musicians. Enjoy seeing native costumes and folk dances that illustrate the diversity of the world's cultures. Sometimes, even specialties of individual fairs have become common later on. St. Louis, the city where the ice-cream cone was invented. It has since become a favorite treat worldwide. World's fairs, originally planned to "bring the world closer together." But do they continue to serve this original purpose? Not really. Because people now travel by airplane and can see the countries of the world. They see much more than can be seen in national exhibits at world's fairs.

MAKING   C O N N E C T I O N S

Fragments affect expression in two ways. First, they can derail meaning when they appear unintentionally, perhaps undermining the reader's confidence in the writer by displaying lack of knowledge of or control over sentence structure. Second, they can enhance meaning when they are used sparingly to emphasize material and surprise readers.

- Find and correct unintentional fragments in your written work. Return to a few graded papers on which fragments were marked. Note the kinds of fragments that you write and then correct them.

- Consider using fragments for emphasis. Examine your papers to see whether selected use of fragments to isolate information or to respond to questions that you have posed might create needed emphasis. Remember to use this pattern selectively.

16

Comma Splices and Fused Sentences

Comma splices and fused sentences contain two or more independent clauses that are not properly punctuated. In a **comma splice** (also called a **comma fault**), the independent clauses are incorrectly joined with only a comma. In a **fused sentence** (also called a **run-on sentence**), independent clauses are placed one after the other, with no punctuation.

Correct comma splices and fused sentences by changing the punctuation or structure of the sentence.

Quick Reference

Comma splices and fused sentences are never acceptable in writing because they incorrectly merge ideas.

> *Use a period to separate the independent clauses in comma splices or fused sentences.*

> *Use a semicolon, a comma and a coordinating conjunction, or a subordinating conjunction (and a comma if necessary) to join independent clauses.*

> *Remember that conjunctive adverbs may be used only within independent clauses or sentences, not to join them as coordinating or subordinating conjunctions do.*

| 16a | **Separate the independent clauses in a comma splice or a fused sentence by using a period to form two sentences.** |

Comma splice

Many artists and musicians are extremely fashion conscious, they view their clothes as a form of self-expression.

Separate sentences

Many artists and musicians are extremely fashion conscious. They view their clothes as a form of self-expression.

| 16b | **Join the independent clauses in a comma splice or a fused sentence by using a semicolon to form a compound sentence.** |

Fused sentence

In the 1950s, members of English departments felt their programs were too diverse they split into departments of literature, composition, linguistics, and speech communication.

Compound sentence

In the 1950s, members of English departments felt their programs were too diverse; they split into departments of literature, composition, linguistics, and speech communication.

| 16c | **Correct a comma splice or a fused sentence by using a comma and a coordinating conjunction to form a compound sentence or by using a subordinating conjunction to form a complex sentence.** |

Use the coordinating conjunctions (*and, but, for, nor, or, so,* and *yet*) with a comma to link independent clauses grammatically to form a compound sentence. Use subordinating conjunctions (*although, because, since, while,* and others) to join independent clauses to form complex or compound-complex sentences.

Comma splice

The sky diver hurtled toward the ground, she felt no fear.

Compound sentence

The sky diver hurtled toward the ground, but she felt no fear.

Fused sentence

NASA delayed the shuttle launch the ground crew wanted to check the on-board computers again.

Complex sentence

NASA delayed the shuttle launch because the ground crew wanted to check the on-board computers again.   (When the subordinate clause ends the sentence, a comma is unnecessary if the meaning is clear.)

Fused sentence

Many cabinet members work for only four to eight years with the president they continue to work in Washington as consultants to major firms.

Complex sentence

Although many cabinet members work for only four to eight years with the president, they continue to work in Washington as consultants to major firms.   (When the subordinate clause begins the sentence, a comma is required.)

16d	**Do not mistake conjunctive adverbs for coordinating or subordinating conjunctions.**

Conjunctive adverbs (*besides, furthermore, however, nevertheless, still, then, therefore,* and others) logically connect ideas, but they do not link independent clauses grammatically as coordinating conjunctions do. When a conjunctive adverb appears in a comma splice or fused sentence, correct the sentence by using a period or semicolon to separate the independent clauses.

Comma splice

Corporate mergers are often like marriages, however, some unfriendly ones are like abductions.

Correct

   Corporate mergers are often like marriages. However, some
   unfriendly ones are like abductions.

Correct

   Corporate mergers are often like marriages; however, some unfriendly
   ones are like abductions.   (The use of the semicolon establishes a
   closer link between the ideas.)

EXERCISE 16.1 ❯ *Comma splices and fused sentences*

*Correct these faulty sentences by changing their punctuation or
structure.*

1. *Rock 'n' roll* is a generic term used to describe a wide variety of musical styles, nonetheless, each musical style remains distinct.

2. The term *pop music* was coined in the 1950s, it describes music that
   cuts across socio-ethnic lines and appeals to a wide audience.

3. *Acid rock* describes the amplified, electronic music of mid-1960s
   artists in this subgenre of rock music were often part of the counterculture of drugs.

4. *Disco*'s emphasis on highly synthesized electronic music with an
   insistent rhythm made it popular dance music, nevertheless, its
   popularity faded in only a few years.

5. Black American music, sometimes called *soul music* and sometimes
   rhythm and blues, developed from gospel music its acceptance in
   conservative white culture attests to the power of music to break
   down barriers.

6. With its emphasis on shock value, *punk rock* created a brief sensation in the world of music people soon grew tired of being shocked
   by performers who often lacked musical skill.

EXERCISE 16.2 ❯ *Comma splices and fused sentences*

  Correct the comma splices and fused sentences in the following paragraph by adding periods, commas and coordinating conjunctions, semicolons, or subordinating conjunctions.

Book censorship in American high schools has become a standard practice these days, individuals and groups have applied pressure to school boards everywhere. The books that have been censored range widely in subject they range widely in literary quality as well. No book seems to be beyond the reach of book censors. Books treating sexual situations, like *A Farewell to Arms,* have been banned, books that contain questionable language, like *The Catcher in the Rye,* have been banned, too. *The Grapes of Wrath* has been censored in some communities because of its presentation of socialist ideology, *Lord of the Flies* has been removed from libraries because of its violence. Even a book like *Huckleberry Finn* is now being brought into question it has racially demeaning dialect. The American Library Association has come to the defense of these books, however that has not kept them on bookshelves and reading lists in many American high schools.

Revising comma splices and fused sentences with a word processor

Use a word processor to revise comma splices and fused sentences, taking advantage of its ability to make small changes that do not require the retyping of whole sentences.

Separate faulty sentences. Divide comma splices and fused sentences into separate simple sentences. Be sure to change capitalization and punctuation.

Insert coordinating conjunctions to join independent clauses correctly.

Join clauses with subordinating conjunctions. Use the "block" and "move" functions to experiment and find the best placement for clauses and coordinating conjunctions. You may also need to add commas.

MAKING   C O N N E C T I O N S

Comma splices and fused sentences have no place in your writing. They are grammatically incorrect and never used to achieve emphasis.

- Locate comma splices and fused sentences in your papers. Examine your graded papers to find examples of these sentence errors.

- Evaluate the mistakes that led to each error. Is there a pattern that you can avoid? For example, are your comma splices and fused sentences the result of misused conjunctive adverbs?

- Revise your comma splices and fused sentences. Experiment with alternative methods for correcting these sentence errors. Try simple sentences. Try compound sentences. Try complex or compound-complex sentences. Remember, the best solution for each error will take account of the context, the structure, and the tone of the entire paragraph.

17　Agreement

Subjects and verbs agree in number; pronouns and antecedents
agree in number and gender.

> ## Quick Reference
>
> *Errors in subject-verb or pronoun-antecedent agreement
> are easy to correct if you remember these basic
> principles.*
>
> ❯ *Verbs must agree in number with the subject of the
> clause or sentence. Do not be misled by intervening
> words.*
>
> ❯ *Let the meaning of the subject (singular or plural)
> guide your choice of verbs; watch especially
> compound subjects with* and *or* or, *indefinite pronouns,
> collective nouns, and plural words with a singular
> meaning.*
>
> ❯ *Make sure that pronouns have clear antecedents with
> which they consistently agree in both number and
> gender.*
>
> ❯ *Let the intended number of the antecedent guide your
> choice of pronouns; watch especially compound
> subjects with* and *or* or, *indefinite pronouns, collective
> nouns, and plural words with a singular meaning.*

| 17a | **Subjects and verbs must agree in number.** |

Verbs agree with the subject of the sentence, not with intervening
words. Words that separate subjects and verbs, especially nouns

that serve as objects of prepositions, should not influence your choice of verbs.

The *swallows* of Capistrano *are* becoming noticeably less predictable. (*Capistrano,* a singular noun in a prepositional phrase, does not affect verb choice.)

Compound Subjects Joined by *And*

Compound subjects joined by *and* require plural verbs.

      compound subj.   plural verb

The *defendant* and her *counsel were* both angered by the verdict.

》》》 *Compound subjects that are seen as one unit are singular and require a singular verb.*

"*Tragedy and triumph*" *describes* Britain's lonely resistance to Hitler during the grim days of 1940. **《《《**

Subjects Joined by *Or, Nor, Either . . . Or,* or *Neither . . . Nor*

Or, nor, and so on do not indicate multiple subjects; they indicate alternative subjects. The verb, therefore, should agree with the number of the subjects considered individually.

Singular subjects

    Either walking or running strengthens the heart.   (Walking *strengthens;* running *strengthens.*)

Plural subjects

    Recordings or books as gifts *please* most people.   (Recordings *please;* books *please.*)

When a compound subject contains both plural and singular elements, the verb agrees with the nearer element.

Singular and plural elements
   Neither the designer nor the *engineers accept* the prototype.

Plural and singular elements
   Neither the engineers nor the *designer accepts* the prototype.

》》》 *When a singular noun follows a plural noun in a compound subject, the required singular verb, though grammatically correct, may seem awkward. If a sentence seems awkward, revise it.*

The prototype satisfies neither the engineers nor the designer. **《《《**

Indefinite Pronouns

Indefinite pronouns (*anyone, each, either, everybody, none, someone,* and others) have no specific antecedents. Some, such as *both* and *all,* are plural and require plural verbs, but most are singular and require singular verbs. Be especially careful using pronouns like *everyone* or *everybody,* which require singular verbs even though *every-* sounds plural; *-one* or *-body* should guide you.

Somebody attends to the correspondence while she is gone.

Both assign papers during the first week of class.

Everyone brings her or his book to class on Friday.

》》》 Every *and* each *used as adjectives require singular verbs, even when the subject is compound.*

Every man, woman, and child *was* evacuated before nightfall.   (*Every* emphasizes the people individually, so a singular verb is appropriate.)

Each actor and musician *was* asked to stand to be acknowledged. (*Each* emphasizes individuals and requires a singular verb.) **《《《**

Collective Nouns

Collective nouns stressing group unity require singular verbs; collective nouns stressing the individuality of group members require plural verbs.

Group unity

The *committee votes* by a show of hands.   (The committee as a whole follows this procedure.)

Individuality of group members

The Supreme Court act according to their individual consciences. (Each member acts separately, so the plural form is correct.)

》》》 *If collective nouns stressing individuality sound awkward with plural verbs, revise the sentence by including "members of" or a similar phrase that clearly requires a plural verb.*

The Supreme Court justices act according to their individual consciences. **《《《**

Expletive Constructions

Expletive constructions (*here is, here are, there is,* and *there are*) depend for meaning on the noun complement (the noun that follows the construction); the verb in the expletive phrase must agree in number with the noun. A singular noun requires *is;* a plural noun requires *are.*

Here *is* the first *chapter* of my forthcoming novel.

There *are* many unimaginative *programs* on television.

Your word processor will help you locate and check your
uses of expletive constructions. Use the "search" codes to
find *here is, here are, there is,* and *there are.* Make sure that
the verb in each expletive agrees with its noun complement.

Relative Clauses

The relative pronouns (*who, which,* and *that*), when used as the
subject of a clause, agree in number with their antecedents.

> Flooding in the spring is a *threat* that *requires* our attention.   (*That*
> refers to *threat,* a singular predicate noun. Consequently, the relative
> clause requires a singular verb.)

> People once believed in the *pseudo-sciences* of physiognomy and
> astrology, which *have* now lost their credibility.   (*Which* refers to
> *pseudo-sciences,* a plural object of a preposition. The verb in the rela-
> tive clause must, therefore, be plural.)

Linking Verbs

Linking verbs agree with the number of the subject, not the number of the predicate noun.

> A major *expense* of operating a school *is* salaries for administrators,
> teachers, and custodians.   (Although *salaries* is plural, the subject of
> the sentence is *expense,* a singular noun. Therefore, the verb must also
> be singular.)

Plural Nouns with Singular Meanings

Plural nouns such as *news, politics, electronics,* and *mumps* often
have singular meanings. When used in a singular sense, they require singular verbs.

Fractions, measurements, money, time, weight, and volume
considered as single units also require singular verbs.

301

Plural noun

   Geriatrics successfully *discredits* the prejudice that senility is inevitable in the elderly.   (*Geriatrics* is a single discipline and requires a singular verb.)

Plural unit

   Six hundred dollars seems a reasonable price.   (The dollar amount, considered *one* price, requires a singular verb.)

>>> *Common exceptions to this principle are* scissors *and* trousers. *Though units, they are considered plural. When used with the phrase a* pair of, *however,* pair *dominates and requires a singular verb.*

   The *scissors need* sharpening.   (The logic is that scissors have two functional parts, making the plural verb appropriate.)

   This *pair* of scissors *needs* sharpening.   (The word *pair* emphasizes that the parts act as a single unit, making the singular verb necessary.) **<<<**

Titles

Even when the words in a title are plural, the title of a single work requires a singular verb.

   Leaves of Grass illustrates the best and worst characteristics of nineteenth-century American verse.   (*Leaves of Grass* is the title of one long poem, so a singular verb is required.)

Words Used as Words

Words used as words require singular verbs. This rule applies even when the word discussed is plural.

Media often inaccurately *substitutes* for *medium*.   (*Media,* a plural noun, requires a singular verb when discussed as a word.)

In news broadcasts, *persons has become* a standard but annoying substitute for the word *people*.   (*Persons,* a plural noun, when discussed as a word requires a singular verb.)

EXERCISE 17.1 ❯ *Subject-verb agreement*

Select the verb that maintains subject-verb agreement.

1. Archaeologists (studies/study) the buildings, tools, and other artifacts of ancient cultures.

2. Every archaeologist, especially field researchers, (know/knows) of a historic site ruthlessly desecrated by treasure-seekers.

3. Despite international agreements, unscrupulous museums or a wealthy private collector (compete/competes) for every major artistic discovery, stolen or not.

4. But laws and international policing (reduce/reduces) yearly the number of destroyed sites and stolen artifacts.

5. Excavations — better controlled than ever by teams of university archaeologists, students, local workers, and national representatives — (proceed/proceeds) slowly these days, avoiding the damage inflicted by yesterday's "grave robbers."

6. *Digs* (is/are) the current jargon used to describe an excavation site.

7. Recent decades (has seen/have seen) few finds of the historical significance of the discovery of Tutankhamen's tomb in 1922, but research in various locales (continue/continues).

8. For archaeologists, five or ten years (seem/seems) a reasonable time to work at a single site, so new finds will be made — but made more slowly than in the past.

EXERCISE 17.2 ❯ *Subject-verb agreement*

 The following paragraph contains many errors in subject-verb agreement. Correct the misused verbs and then draw arrows to the subjects with which each verb agrees.

There is more and more adults attending college at a later age. Their motives, either to change careers or to get the education they missed, varies. Anyone walking on a college campus see students in their thirties, forties, fifties, and even sixties carrying books and talking with friends. Almost every class and laboratory now include at least one of these "non-traditional" students. Because their home and job situations and their preparedness differs from those of eighteen- and twenty-one-year-olds, these students face problems that surprises a younger student. Some of these adults organizes their schooling around full-time jobs. Others care for families, as well as attends class. Nobody going to college and getting a degree find it easy, but an adult student with adult responsibilities have extra problems to cope with. As this situation becomes more common, everyone adjust, however, a process that already have begun. Even the media recognize this trend in American education. With humor and sympathy, *Kate and Allie* provide insights into the problems adults face when attending college. Who knows? Given a chance today, maybe even Lucy Ricardo or John Walton might enroll in a class or two.

| 17b | **Pronouns and their antecedents must agree in number and gender.** |

Singular antecedents (the words to which pronouns refer) require singular pronouns; plural antecedents require plural pronouns.

*sing.
antecedent* *sing.
pronoun*

Genghis Khan ruled *his* vast empire with great cruelty.

*plural
antecedent* *plural
pronoun*

Children need encouragement and guidance from *their* parents.

Pronouns must also agree with the gender of their antecedents.

   fem. antecedent   *fem. pronoun*
      | |

Queen Elizabeth II rules *her* empire as a constitutional monarch.

Plural pronouns do not specify gender, but singular pronouns specify masculine, feminine, or neuter gender.

Pronoun Forms			
	Subjective	*Objective*	*Possessive*	*Reflexive*
Masculine	he	him	his	himself
Feminine	she	her	hers	herself
Neuter	it	it	its	itself

Pronoun-Antecedent Agreement and Sexist Language

The masculine pronouns (*he* and its variations) were once acceptable substitutes for antecedents whose gender was undetermined and thus might be either male or female. This usage is unacceptable today, even in formal writing, because it excludes women without justification and consequently reinforces stereotypes.

To avoid this problem, use plural antecedents and pronouns when possible or rephrase the sentence. Do not use a plural pronoun like *their* with a singular antecedent; this creates a problem in pronoun-antecedent agreement. Another possible solution, using pronouns in pairs (*he or she, his or hers, he/she,* and so on) should be used sparingly, since it can lead to distracting repetition and awkward rhythm in sentences.

Sexist

   A good *surgeon* carefully explains procedures to *his* patients.

Nonsexist but incorrect

   A good *surgeon* carefully explains procedures to *their* patients.   (The plural *their* does not agree with the singular *surgeon*.)

Nonsexist and correct

   Good *surgeons* carefully explain procedures to *their* patients.   (Here a plural noun is used with a plural pronoun.)

Nonsexist and correct

   Good *surgeons* carefully explain procedures to patients.   (Here the possessive pronoun is omitted without substantial loss of meaning.)

Nonsexist and correct

   A good *surgeon* carefully explains procedures to *his or her* patients.

To express generalizations based on individual experiences, use a specific antecedent instead of a general noun. That, in turn, will dictate a specific pronoun choice and help you to avoid sexist language.

   Dr. Knepper, like all good surgeons, carefully explains procedures to *his* patients.

Compound Antecedents Joined by *And*

Compound antecedents joined by *and* require plural pronouns.

compound antecedent   *plural pronoun*

Female *whales and dolphins* fiercely protect *their* young.

Antecedents Joined by *Or, Nor, Either . . . Or,* or *Neither . . . Nor*

Compound subjects joined by these words present alternative, not multiple, subjects, so pronouns refer to each subject individually.

Singular antecedents
   Neither Gladstone nor Disraeli graciously accepted criticism of *his* plans for the British government.   (Gladstone/*his*; Disraeli/*his*)

Plural antecedents
   Did *the Greeks or the Romans* consider Zeus *their* principal god? (Greeks/*their*; Romans/*their*)

When part of a compound antecedent is singular and part is plural, the pronoun agrees with the nearer antecedent.

Singular and plural antecedents
   The dean or the *students* must modify *their* terms.   (students/*their*)

If the construction sounds awkward, place the singular noun first or consider rewriting the sentence.

Correct but awkward
   The students or the *dean* must modify *her* terms.   (dean/*her*)

Better

If the *dean* will not change *her* terms, the *students* will have to change *theirs.*   (dean/*her*; students/*theirs*)

Indefinite Pronouns as Antecedents

Indefinite pronouns (*anyone, each, either, everybody, none,* and others) are usually singular in meaning and take singular pronouns. However, some indefinite pronouns (*all, most, some,* and others) are plural in meaning and take plural pronouns. Let the number of the indefinite pronoun guide you.

Anyone who works as a war correspondent risks *his or her* life frequently.   (*Anyone* refers to people one at a time, as does the pronoun cluster *his or her.*)

All signed the petition, and then *their* regional representative sent it to national headquarters.   (*All* refers to the signers in the aggregate, so the plural *their* is correct.)

Collective Nouns

When collective nouns stress group unity, they take singular pronouns; when collective nouns stress the group as a collection of individuals, they take plural pronouns.

Group unity

The *audience* showed *its* approval by applauding loudly.   (The audience is perceived as a single unit, creating a unified response.)

Individuality within the group

The *audience* raised *their* voices in song.   (This sentence stresses the many voices of the audience members.)

EXERCISE 17.3   ❯   *Pronoun-antecedent agreement*

Insert appropriate pronouns in the following sentences.

1. Greeks, Romans, Egyptians, Indians, and virtually every other civilized group had one or more methods of keeping ————— dwellings cool in summer months.

2. For example, all of these peoples hung water-soaked mats in ————— doorways to develop cooling moisture.

3. Leonardo da Vinci, with ————— usual inventiveness, created the first mechanical fan in about 1500, ————— power provided by running water.

4. The 1838 British House of Commons was the first to enjoy systematic control of ventilation and humidity during ————— sessions.

5. Neither Alfred Wolff (in 1902) nor Willis Carrier (in 1911) realized the impact ————— work would have on later generations.

6. After 1931, a passenger riding on the Baltimore & Ohio railroad could travel to ————— destination in air-conditioned comfort.

7. When Stuart Cramer first used the phrase *air conditioning* in 1906, ————— almost certainly didn't know that ————— newly coined term would be in universal use today.

8. Few people who live in temperate climates or who work in high-rise buildings would want to give up ————— air conditioning in the summer.

EXERCISE 17.4   ❯   *Pronoun-antecedent agreement*

Most pronouns in the following paragraph have been omitted. Insert appropriate pronouns, maintaining correct pronoun-antecedent agreement.

   Everyone who works in the United States must pay _____ income
taxes on or before April 15. An employee of a traditional business has
_____ taxes withdrawn in each pay period and at the end of the year
receives _____ yearly statement, the W2 form. Neither employees nor
the employer can decide how _____ tax accounts will be handled, but
employees determine what percentage of taxes will be taken from
_____ wages. For a self-employed taxpayer, the procedure for determining _____ taxes is not so clear. Artists, writers, free-lance contractors, and other people whose incomes fluctuate must estimate _____
incomes for the year and pay _____ taxes in installments. Anyone
who has ever tried to estimate how productive _____ will be in the
next year can appreciate the difficulty a self-employed person has in estimating how much _____ will owe at the end of the year. In the past,
the self-employed were granted some leniency in paying _____ taxes.
However, in 1987, in spite of objections from some of _____ constituents, Congress voted to penalize people whose estimated tax payments
were less than 90 percent of _____ taxes due.

Maintaining agreement with a word processor

Use the computer's capabilities to discover and correct errors in subject-verb and pronoun-antecedent agreement.

Use the "search" function to locate *and* and *or* and related conjunctions. Check for agreement problems.

Check pronouns and antecedents. Use the "search" codes to locate specific pronouns. Once you have located them, check the sentence to make sure that the antecedent and pronoun are correctly matched in number and gender. If they are not, change either the pronoun or the antecedent. Check masculine pronouns carefully to avoid sexist use.

Revise agreement errors. Use the "delete" and "insert" capabilities to change verbs and pronouns that do not agree with their subjects or antecedents.

Experiment with solutions to agreement errors. Convert all nouns to plurals, for example, to avoid problems with sexist use of pronouns.

MAKING   C O N N E C T I O N S

Agreement errors interfere with communication, but they can
be easily avoided once you discover your chronic patterns of
agreement problems.

- Note the kinds of agreement errors that you make.
  Review your graded papers and catalog the agreement
  errors that you discover. Are your agreement errors
  related to subjects and verbs or to pronouns and
  antecedents? Does a pattern emerge? Do you use *he* in a
  sexist way? Do you have special trouble with collective
  nouns?

- Revise sentences that contain agreement errors. Review
  the rules governing agreement and then experiment with
  solutions to your agreement problems.

18 Pronoun Case

The case of a pronoun indicates the pronoun's grammatical relationship to the other words in the sentence. Pronoun case is indicated by changes in form (*I, me, or mine,* for example) or by changes in position in the sentence, as in the following example.

```
subj.     obj.  poss.
case      case  case
  |         |     |
I gave them his address.
```

Nouns and pronouns used as subjects or predicate nouns are in the **subjective case.** Nouns or pronouns used as direct objects, indirect objects, or objects of prepositions are in the **objective case.** Nouns or pronouns used to show ownership are in the possessive case.

Case Forms of Personal Pronouns			
	Subjective	*Objective*	*Possessive*
Singular			
1st person	I	me	my, mine
2nd person	you	you	your, yours
3rd person	he, she, it	him, her, it	his, hers, its
Plural			
1st person	we	us	our, ours
2nd person	you	you	your, yours
3rd person	they	them	their, theirs

Case Forms of *Who* and Related Pronouns		
Subjective	*Objective*	*Possessive*
who	whom	whose
whoever	whomever	

Most pronouns and all nouns in the subjective case (*someone, Alicia*) form the possessive case by adding *'s* (*someone's, Alicia's*). The objective case is most frequently indicated by change of position.

Personal pronouns and relative pronouns produced with variations of *who* change forms in all three cases.

》》》 *Do not confuse possessive-case pronouns that do not use an apostrophe (*his, her, its, ours, your, yours, their, theirs, *and* whose*) with contractions that sound the same:* it's *("it is"),* there's *("there is"), and* who's *("who is").* **《《《**

| 18a | **Pronouns used as subjects or as predicate nouns require the subjective-case form.** |

Subjective case
Although *he* got a *D* in freshman composition, Faulkner went on to become one of America's most honored writers.

When a sentence has a compound subject, isolate the parts of the subject to help you choose the appropriate pronoun.

Compound subject
Just after sunrise, Kendal and *she* waded into the stream to fish. (Kendal waded; *she* waded; consequently, *Kendal and she* waded.)

A predicate noun restates the subject and so requires the subjective case. Sometimes, however, this construction sounds excessively formal. Observe this pronoun-case rule in formal writing, but consider revising your sentence for less formal writing contexts. For example, invert the subject and predicate noun.

We discovered that "the mad scribbler" was *he*.   (The predicate noun, signaled by the linking verb *was,* must be in the subjective case.)

We discovered that *he* was "the mad scribbler."   (This sentence sounds less formal but is still correct.)

18b	**Pronouns used as direct objects, indirect objects, or objects of prepositions require the objective-case form.**

A direct object answers the question *whom* or *what.* An indirect object answers the question *to whom* or *for whom.* Pronouns that answer these questions should be in the objective case.

Direct object

Susan B. Anthony challenged sexist and racist assumptions; we should respect *her* for that.

Indirect object

Although Rasputin was feared by the Russian nobility, Czar Nicholas and Czarina Alexandra gave *him* their absolute trust.

Object of preposition

The Medici family supported the arts in Renaissance Florence; many of the greatest works of Michelangelo, Leonardo, and Botticelli were created for *them.*

》》》 *When a preposition has a compound object, isolate the parts of the object to help you choose the appropriate pronoun.*

The contract had to be signed by both *him* and Eileen.   (by *him;* by Eileen) **《《《**

18c > **Pronouns showing ownership or modifying a gerund require the possessive-case form.**

Possessive Pronouns Used with Nouns

The possessive pronouns *my, your, his, her, its, our, your,* and *their* modify nouns. They act as adjectives in sentences and are sometimes called pronoun-adjectives.

> Although *my* exam scores and Wilma's were better than *Sasha's* scores, *her* speeches were clearly the best.   (The pronouns in the possessive case serve as pronoun-adjectives.)

Possessive Pronouns Used Alone

The possessive pronouns *mine, yours, his, hers, its, ours, yours,* and *theirs* are sometimes used alone as subjects, predicate nouns, direct objects, indirect objects, or objects of prepositions.

> The blue car outside is *mine; his* is the red one.   (Both pronouns are in the possessive case, but *mine* works as a predicate noun and *his* as a subject.)

Possessive Pronouns Modifying a Gerund

When modifying a gerund (an *-ing* verb that functions as a noun), pronouns must be in the possessive case, serving as pronoun-adjectives.

> I was annoyed by *his* interrupting the speaker.   (The annoyance resulted from the person's *interrupting,* not from the person himself.)

> The director commented that *their* dancing was the best part of the musical number.   (The best part was their *dancing,* not them.)

18d	**Sentence structure determines the case of pronouns in appositives, with nouns, and in elliptical constructions.**

Pronouns in Appositives

When a pronoun in an appositive restates the subject of a clause, use the subjective case. When a pronoun in an appositive restates an object, use the objective case.

> The two assistant managers, Gerald and *he,* were responsible for preparing the quarterly reports.   (Because *Gerald and he* restates the subject of the sentence, the pronoun must be in the subjective case.)

> Certificates of merit were given to the runners-up, Abigail and *her.* (*Abigail and her* restates *runners-up,* the object of the preposition, so the pronoun must be in the objective case.)

We or *Us* with Nouns

When using *we* or *us* with a noun, choose the case that would be correct if the noun were omitted.

> I think that *we* bicyclists should demand special cycling lanes on campus.   (Without *bicyclists,* the clause reads *we should,* a correct use of the subjective case.)

> Organizational policy prohibits *us* committee members from meeting informally.   (*Members* is a direct object, so the adjoining pronoun must be in the objective case.)

Pronouns in Elliptical Constructions

In **elliptical constructions** (constructions in which words are omitted or understood), use the case that would be appropriate if all the words were included. If the pronoun used alone sounds too formal, add the omitted words.

The Piersons arrived twenty minutes later than *we.*   (The complete thought is that they arrived twenty minutes later than *we arrived.*)

EXERCISE 18.1 ❯ *Pronoun case*

Supply the correct pronouns in the following sentences.

1. Hans Christian Andersen, the son of a shoemaker, began _____ adult life as an actor.

2. _____ failed on the stage, but because the king granted _____ a scholarship, Andersen was able to begin _____ writing career.

3. _____ writing of novels, plays, and long poems is almost completely forgotten, but almost everyone knows a few of _____ best fairy tales.

4. Ironically, Andersen did not set out to write fairy tales, but _____ wrote _____ first four to make money quickly.

5. Those stories succeeded beyond _____ expectations, and subsequently European nobility and royalty honored _____ for _____ work.

6. Although Andersen's tales may not be as well known as those of the brothers Grimm, _____ use of irony and humor, rather than violence, makes _____ work very appealing.

7. "The Emperor's New Clothes," one of _____ most ironic tales, alienated _____ from some of _____ noble patrons.

8. Today's readers, however, can enjoy the irony without insult and take delight in what was, for _____, a troublesome piece.

9. The best children's writers — and _____ is among them — delight us as children and intrigue us as adults, providing in simple tales some lessons on life.

10. If you think about Andersen as a failed actor who became a world-famous writer of fairy tales, you'll discover why "The Ugly Duckling" was one of _____ favorites; in a professional sense, at least, it was _____ story.

18e ⟩ **Distinguish between the subjective-case forms** *who* **and** *whoever* **and the objective-case forms** *whom* **and** *whomever.*

Use the subjective-case forms *who* and *whoever* as subjects of sentences, clauses, and questions. Use the objective-case forms *whom* and *whomever* as direct objects, indirect objects, and objects of prepositions.

Who and *Whoever*

Who among us has not heard of the lost city of Atlantis?   (*Who* is the subject of the question.)

Salvador Dali was an artist *who* took delight in shocking his contemporaries.   (*Who* is the subject of the clause.)

The foundation will offer a scholarship to *whoever* writes the most creative essay.   (*Whoever* is the subject of the clause; although the preposition *to* might suggest that the objective case is required, the whole clause, not the word *whoever,* is the object of the preposition.)

Whom and *Whomever*

Whom should we invite to speak to the alumni?   (*Whom* is the direct object of *invite.*)

The board will approve the appointment of *whomever* we select. (*Whomever* is the direct object of the last clause.)

Use the "search" feature to locate *who, whoever, whom,* and
whomever. Then double-check the sentence to be sure that
you have used them correctly. If you have not, use the
"delete" and "add" functions of your word processor to make
necessary changes.

EXERCISE 18.2 ❭ *Pronoun case*

Use who, whom, whoever, *and* whomever *correctly in the following
sentences.*

1. The Better Business Bureau, a nonprofit organization, was founded
   to help people _____ are victims of questionable business methods and deceptive advertising.

2. Consumers should first address complaints to _____ has acted in
   an unbusinesslike manner.

3. The Better Business Bureau is a group to _____ consumers can
   turn if they still are not satisfied.

4. The Better Business Bureau will answer questions and suggest
   strategies to _____ calls, but it will not take legal action against
   suspected businesses.

5. Since the Better Business Bureau refers cases to government agencies, however, it helps ensure that businesspeople _____ are unethical do not continue to exploit consumers.

EXERCISE 18.3 ❭ *Pronoun case*

*Indicate whether the italicized pronouns in the following paragraph
are in the subjective, objective, or possessive case. Be ready to explain your decisions.*

When *I* came out of prison, — for some one interfered, and paid that
tax, — *I* did not perceive that great changes had taken place on the

common, such as *he* observed *who* went in a youth and emerged a tottering and grey-headed man; and yet a change had to *my* eyes come over the scene, — the town, and State, and country, — greater than any that mere time could effect. *I* saw yet more distinctly the State in which *I* lived. *I* saw to what extent the people among *whom I* lived could be trusted as good neighbors and friends; that *their* friendship was for summer weather only; that *they* did not greatly propose to do right; that *they* were a distinct race from *me* by *their* prejudices and superstitions, as the Chinamen and Malays are; that in *their* sacrifices to humanity *they* ran no risks, not even to *their* property; that after all *they* were not so noble but *they* treated the thief as *he* had treated *them,* and hoped, by a certain outward observance and a few prayers, and by walking in a particular straight though useless path from time to time, to save *their* souls. This may be to judge *my* neighbors harshly; for *I* believe that many of *them* are not aware that *they* have such an institution as the jail in *their* village. — Henry David Thoreau, "Civil Disobedience"

MAKING   C O N N E C T I O N S

Clear writing uses pronoun case accurately.

- Accurate use of pronoun case depends on an understanding of subjects and complements in clauses and sentences. Review this material in section 7a.

- Review your own writing. Examine some recent papers for problems with pronoun case. When you discover errors in case, consider their cause and revise your sentences.

- Make a list of case rules that you apply accurately; make a list of those that cause you problems. Use this list as a guide when revising future papers.

19   Verb Tenses

Tenses are the forms of verbs that indicate when things happened or existed in relation to when they are described. Tenses also indicate whether an action or state of being continued over time or whether it has been completed. Tenses are formed through the use of auxiliary verbs and changes in verb endings.

Quick Reference

Verbs, along with subjects, form the core of sentences. The use of effective verbs will strengthen your writing.

❯ *Use the correct verb tense and form to express your meaning accurately.*

❯ *Use present tense to describe beliefs, scientific principles, works of art, and repeated or habitual actions.*

❯ *Use sequences of tenses correctly to clarify the time relations in your writing.*

❯ *Use verb mood correctly to indicate your opinion on the factuality or probability of your sentence.*

Regular Verbs

Regular verbs form tenses according to consistent patterns. (For an example of a full conjugation of the verb *to learn*, see page 324.)

To Learn	
Present tense	learn(s)
Past tense	learn*ed*
Future tense	*will* (or *shall*) learn
Present perfect tense	*have* (or *has*) learn*ed*
Past perfect tense	*had* learn*ed*
Future perfect tense	*will* (or *shall*) *have* learn*ed*
Progressive tenses	
Present progressive	am (are) learning
Past progressive	was (were) learning
Future progressive	will be learning
Present perfect progressive	has (have) been learning
Past perfect progressive	had been learning
Future perfect progressive	will have been learning

Irregular Verbs

Irregular verbs form tenses through changes in word form.

To Go	
Present tense	go(es)
Past tense	went
Future tense	will (or shall) go
Present perfect tense	have (or has) gone
Past perfect tense	had gone
Future perfect tense	will (or shall) have gone

C • O • N • N • E • C • T • I • O • N • S

The correct grammatical use of verbs assures precision in expressing occurrence and continuance of actions or states of being. Beyond that grammatical role, however, verbs help to create expressive, forceful sentences, making your writing clear, vivid, and interesting.

When you write, and especially when you revise, select strong, specific verbs that exactly express your meaning. The statement *Tornadoes damaged the town,* for example, suggests minor loss of property and minimal effect; but if the losses were extensive and the effect catastrophic, using a stronger verb will better express the meaning: *Tornadoes devastated the town.* Overuse of common, general verbs, such as *to be* and *to go,* can flatten prose: *Rachel went to class.* More specific verbs — such as *hurried, ran, strolled, sauntered, ambled* — allow writers to create clear and exact meanings not conveyed by *went.*

During revision, then, examine your verb choices: use strong, specific verbs that clearly and effectively express your ideas.

》》》 *The progressive tenses of irregular verbs (* I am going, I was going, *and so on) are formed regularly.* **《《《**

| 19a | **Use the simple tenses to describe actions or conditions occurring or completed within the time specified.** |

The simple tenses are the **present, past,** and **future.**

Present Tense

Use the present tense to describe events occurring or conditions existing in the present.

He *concedes* your point.

In addition, there are some special uses of the present tense.

Repeated or Habitual Actions

Use the present tense to describe a habitual or frequently repeated action or series of actions or to explain standard procedures.

Air traffic controllers *work* long, tension-filled shifts.

Deposit a coin into the slot; *wait* for the tone; then *dial* the number.

General Beliefs and Scientific Principles

Use the present tense to assert accepted beliefs.

Every child *deserves* adequate nutrition, clothing, housing, and a good education.

Express scientific and other principles in the present tense.

The force of gravity *determines* the flow of water in rivers and streams.

Do unto others as you would have them *do* unto you.

Descriptions of Works of Art

Use the present tense to describe and discuss works of art — literature, music, dance, painting — prehistoric through contemporary.

In Coleridge's *Rime of the Ancient Mariner,* the narrator *learns* and compulsively *repeats* to others the lesson of the sacredness of all life.

Picasso's *Guernica contains* images of chaos and terror.

Past Tense

Use the past tense to describe actions completed or conditions that existed in the past. In writing, you use the past tense more

often than any other tense because much of what you write about
has already occurred.

Henry Ford *created* the Model T but, more importantly, *perfected* the
industrial assembly line.

Future Tense

Use the future tense to describe actions or conditions that will or
are expected to occur or exist in the future.

The committee *will hold* its next meeting in Geneva, Switzerland.

| 19b | **Use the perfect tenses to describe actions or conditions in relation to other actions or conditions.** |

The perfect tenses are the **present perfect, past perfect,** and **future perfect.**

Present Perfect Tense

Use the present perfect tense to describe actions that occurred or
conditions that existed at an unspecified time in the past or that
began in the past and continue to the present.

Since I *took* a music appreciation class, Beethoven's piano concertos
have been favorites of mine.   (*Took* is in the past tense because the
class is over; *have been* is in the present perfect tense because the pref-
erence began in the past and continues to the present.)

Past Perfect Tense

Use the past perfect tense to describe past actions or conditions
that were completed before some other past action or condition.

Until Lincoln *was elected* in 1860, the Republican party *had achieved*
very little since its founding in 1854.   (*Had achieved* establishes the
limited success of Republicans before the other past event, Lincoln's
election.)

Future Perfect Tense

Use the future perfect tense to describe actions that will be completed or conditions that will exist in the future but before a specific time.

Almost all businesses *will have converted* to computerized bookkeep-
ing by the turn of the century.   (The "turn of the century" is in the
future. Converting to computerized booking will also be in the future,
but before A.D. 2000.)

| 19c | Use the progressive tenses to describe actions or conditions beginning, continuing, or ending within the present, past, or future. |

Progressive tenses stress the continuing nature of actions or
conditions.

The Japanese *are sharing* a large part of the costs for operating the
United Nations.   (The present progressive tense shows a continuous
action.)

The American government *has been supporting* the United Nations
since its founding.   (The present perfect progressive tense describes
a continuing process that began in the past.)

》》》》 *To avoid unnecessary wordiness, use the progressive tenses only
when necessary to express continuing actions or states.*

The president was trying to avert an increase in the minimum wage.

The president tried to avert an increase in the minimum wage. **《《《**

19d ▷ **Use tenses in logical sequences to show precisely and accurately the relationships among actions and conditions.**

Verb tense signals chronology, indicating when actions occurred or conditions existed in relation to when they are described. Logical sequences of tenses clarify the relationship among actions and conditions.

Sequences of present and past tenses cause few problems for writers, but more complicated verb-tense sequences may. Use the following rules for guidance.

Infinitives

Infinitives (*to swim, to subscribe, to record*) assume the tense indicated by the main verb.

> Brainwashing *attempts to convince* people *to give up* their beliefs. (The infinitives coordinate with the present-tense verb.)

> Fidel Castro *led* the revolution *to overthrow* Cuba's dictator and subsequently *guided* the country's efforts *to institute* Communist reforms. (The infinitives automatically coordinate with the past-tense verbs.)

Present Participles

The present participle, like the infinitive, assumes the tense of the main verb.

> *Having* a fixed rate of interest, bonds *appeal* to wary investors more than stocks do.

> *Speaking* to the American people in his first inaugural address, Franklin Roosevelt *reassured* them that "the only thing we have to fear is fear itself."

Past Participles and Perfect Participles

Past participles (*hurried, welcomed, driven*) and perfect participles (*having hurried, having welcomed, having driven*) indicate that the action or condition they describe occurred before that of the main verb.

> *Dressed* as a man, Aurore Dupin (who used the pen name George Sand) *attended* the theater when women were not allowed to go.

> *Having won* a record nine gold medals in Olympic swimming, Mark Spitz retired from competition.

Use of Tenses in a Subordinate Clause

Past Tense or Past Perfect Tense in a Subordinate Clause

When the verb in an independent clause is in the past or the past perfect tense, the verb in the subordinate clause must also be in the past or the past perfect tense.

> Once scientists *discovered* that fluorocarbons damage the ozone layer that protects the Earth from ultraviolet radiation, environmentalists *protested* against their use in commercial products.   (The use of the past tense *protested* in the independent clause establishes that this series of actions took place in the past.)

> Before bacteria and viruses *were* discovered, diseases *had been explained* in superstitious ways.   (The use of the past perfect *had been explained* establishes that nonscientific explanations existed before the scientific ones.)

Present, Future, Present Perfect, or Future Perfect Tense in a Subordinate Clause

When the verb in the independent clause is in the present, future, present perfect, or future perfect tense, any tense can be used in the subordinate clause. These tenses and combinations of tenses create numerous possibilities for expressing chronological relationships precisely and accurately. Be sure to arrange the tenses logically so that your meaning is clear.

Some scientists currently *think* that exercise *will prolong* life.

Although Molière's *Tartuffe was written* in 1665, its comments on religious hypocrisy and exploitation still *have* meaning today.   (Literature of the past still speaks to contemporary audiences.)

| 19e | Use the mood of a verb to indicate your opinion on the probability or factuality of your sentence. |

Verbs in English may have one of three moods: indicative, imperative, or subjunctive. Grammatical mood does not refer to or equal psychological mood; the word *mood* in the grammatical sense derives from "mode," meaning "manner," the way in which something appears, is done, or happens.

Definition and Use of Moods

Using the **indicative mood,** writers make statements or ask questions about conditions or actions that they consider facts.

Air travel is one of the safest modes of transportation.

Using the **imperative mood,** writers make statements (commands) about actions or conditions that they consider should or must become facts.

Buckle your seat belt and observe the no-smoking sign.   (The subject, *you,* is omitted or understood, as is generally the case in the imperative.)

Using the **subjunctive mood,** writers make statements or ask questions about actions or conditions that they doubt, wish for, or consider hypothetical or contrary to fact.

If the terminal were redesigned, airport security would be easy to maintain. (Note that *both* clauses express conditional, nonfactual states: The terminal has not been redesigned, and security is not easy to maintain.)

》》》 *Clauses beginning with* if *use the indicative when they describe factual conditions, as in the following example:*

If the terminal was redesigned, it was difficult to see any improvement. (Both clauses are in the indicative past tense because they describe actual events and perceptions.) **《《《**

The subjunctive, which can sound extremely formal and even stilted, is now rarely used in English, except for conditional expressions, such as the example above, and other idiomatic expressions, such as the following:

Let it *be*.

God *save* the Queen!

I move that the committee secretary *forward* the report to the mayor.

He asks that his privacy *be* respected.

Forming the Moods

Most expressions in English are in the indicative mood, which is formed using any and all of the verb tenses covered in 19a through 19c above. The imperative mood is formed using the present tense, as in the example above.

Only the subjunctive has distinct forms. The verb *to be* in the subjunctive differs from its indicative forms in both the present and the past tense; the forms, identical in the singular and plural, are, respectively, *be* and *were*.

If the report *be* true, let us act quickly.   (present tense)

If she *were* in charge, she would have acted.   (past tense)

Subjunctive forms for verbs other than *to be* differ from the indicative only in the third person singular of the present tense, in which the *-s* ending is dropped.

May the weather *continue* clear.

This last example illlustrates the sometimes excessively formal tone of statements in the subjunctive. Often, a correct version in the indicative can be substituted.

If the report is true, we should act quickly.

I hope that the clear weather continues.

》》》 *If you choose to use the subjunctive, remember to use the correct forms and to use them consistently in related clauses or sentences.* **《《《**

EXERCISE 19.1 **》** *Tenses*

Revise the following sentences, written primarily in the present tense, by changing them into the past tense.

1. The design team for the theater production meet to review the script for the play.

2. They talk about specific concerns and mention any special needs they should consider.

3. The discussion turns to potential problems in lighting the production, as it always does, because the theater — a renovated movie house — is modified less than is needed.

4. The lighting designer says, once again, that the theater will need major electrical work before a computerized lighting system can be installed.

5. Completing the discussion of lighting, the team turns its attention to the set for the play.

6. The play chosen — *Who's Afraid of Virginia Woolf?* — requires a single set, one room in a history professor's house.

7. The designers describe productions they have seen.

8. The costumer describes a production that was done in Baltimore.

9. The lighting designer remembers a collegiate production she saw in Iowa.

10. The director says he wants this set to be more realistic in its details than others he has seen.

11. As is usually the case, the team leaves after the first meeting, having made only a few key decisions.

EXERCISE 19.2 ❯ Tenses

Identify the tenses of the numbered verbs in the following paragraphs. Be prepared to explain why each tense is used.

Are owls truly wise? The Greeks (1) *thought* so, identifying them with Athena, goddess of wisdom. In medieval illustrations, owls (2) *accompany* Merlin and share in his sorcery. In fairytales they rival the fox for cunning. Children's picture books (3) *show* them wearing spectacles, mortarboard, and scholar's gown. Soups and other confections made from owls (4) *have been credited* with curing whooping cough, drunkenness, epilepsy, famine, and insomnia. The Cherokee Indians used to bathe their children's eyes with a broth of owl feathers to keep the kids awake at night. Recipes using owl eggs (5) *are reputed* to bestow keen eyesight and wisdom. Yet these birds are no smarter, ornithologists (6) *assure* us, than most others. A museum guide in Boston once (7) *displayed* a drowsy-looking barn owl on his gloved wrist, (8) *explaining* to those of us assembled there how small the bird's brain actually was. "You (9) [*will*] *notice* the head of this live specimen appears to be about the size of a grapefruit," he said, "but it's mostly feathers." Lifting his other hand, he (10) *added,* "The skull, you (11) *see,* is the size of a lemon. There's only room enough inside for a bird-brain, not enough for Einstein!" We all laughed politely. But I was not convinced. Sure, the skull (12) *was* small. The lower half was devoted to jaw and most of the upper half to beak and eye-holes. Yet enough neurons could be fitted into the remaining space to enable the barn owl to catch mice in total darkness. They can even snatch bats on the wing, these princes of nighttime stealth. We have to invent sonar for locating submarines, radar for locating airplanes; neither (13) *is* much use with mice or bats. Barn owls can also see dead — and therefore silent — prey in light one-hundredth as bright as we would need. Like the ability to saw a board square or judge the consistency of bread dough, that might not amount to scholarship, but it (14) *is* certainly a wisdom of the body. It (15) *has worked* for some sixty million years. — Scott Sanders, "Listening to Owls"

EXERCISE 19.3 ❯ *Mood*

Where appropriate, revise the verbs in the following sentences to correct their use of mood.

1. Increasingly, working parents in the United States are asking that every employer acknowledges the childcare problem.

2. A single parent especially often wishes a company-operated childcare facility was available at or near his or her place of work.

3. Lateness would probably decline if a parent was able to make one trip to a single location, instead of a trip to a childcare facility and then a separate trip to work.

4. If Congress was to partially subsidize childcare facilities, many companies might help their employees by providing on-site childcare.

5. But even if a company was to provide on-site childcare, problems in assuring sufficient daycare facilities would still exist.

MAKING C O N N E C T I O N S

Verbs supply most of the force in your writing, emphasizing actions and thought processes. Consider how effectively you have used verbs to create meaning.

- Examine the tenses of your verbs. Highlight and label the verbs in one of your papers. How do the tenses help to establish your meaning?

- Revise previous verb-tense errors. Using a recent paper, review your use of verbs, correcting any errors and concentrating on the use of tense sequences to convey your exact meaning.

- Practice using various tenses. Select five of the verbs that you have used in a paper and conjugate them in the three simple and three perfect tenses. Then, using one of the verbs that you conjugated, write a sentence using each of the verb forms — a total of six sentences. Notice how the different tenses create different meanings.

- Consider your use of mood in your writing. Do you use the imperative mood for instructions, commands, or forceful encouragement? Do you use the subjunctive mood correctly to signal speculations or conditional statements? Use mood to create or emphasize these special effects in your writing.

20   Adjectives and Adverbs

Most writers naturally use adjectives and adverbs correctly. Occasionally, however, they misuse adjectives and adverbs because they do not think carefully about which word they are modifying. The following guidelines should help to solve most problems in adjective and adverb usage.

> ### Quick Reference
>
> *Adjectives and adverbs refine the meaning of a sentence, but to do so effectively they must be used correctly.*
>
> ❯ *Use adjectives to modify nouns and pronouns.*
>
> ❯ *Use adverbs to modify verbs, adjectives, and other adverbs.*
>
> ❯ *Use positive adjective and adverb forms when no comparison is made; use comparative forms to compare two items; use superlative forms to compare three or more items.*
>
> ❯ *Distinguish between troublesome adjective and adverb pairs.*

20a   Adjectives modify nouns and pronouns.

Make sure that the word modifying a noun or pronoun is an adjective. Isolate the word and its modifier, placing the modifier first, to see if the pair sounds correct. When you are uncertain, consult a dictionary to find the correct adjective form.

Treasure Island, an *adventure* novel by Robert Louis Stevenson, is a classic of *adolescent* fiction.   (*Adventure* modifies *novel; adolescent* modifies *fiction.*)

Jim Hawkins, the *young* hero, is *resourceful* and *brave.*   (*Young* modifies *hero; resourceful* and *brave* modify *Jim Hawkins.*)

20b ▷ **Adverbs modify verbs, adjectives, and other adverbs.**

Make sure that the word modifying a verb is an adverb. Isolate the pair of words to see if the pair sounds correct. The adverb should make sense before or after the verb. When you are uncertain of a word's adverb form, consult a dictionary.

H. G. Wells, a political and social reformer in Victorian England, is *best* known *today* for two brief works: *The War of the Worlds* and *The Time Machine.*   (*Best* and *today* both modify *is known.*)

Adverbs that modify adjectives and other adverbs are intensifiers, stressing the specific modifications of the primary modifier. Because some intensifiers — *very, especially, really,* and *truly* — are used so frequently, they may have the paradoxical effect of weakening the impact of your statement. Use them only when they are necessary to your meaning.

Unfortunately, Wells' ingenious science fiction has spawned some *very* bad science fiction films.   (*Very* intensifies the adjective *bad.*)

⟫⟫⟫ *This sentence would be improved if the writer substituted a single, stronger adjective (for example,* appalling *or* dreadful*) or a more specific, descriptive adjective (for example,* boring, unbelievable, *or* exploitative*) for* very bad. ⟪⟪⟪

Use positive, comparative, and superlative adjectives and adverbs correctly.

Positive Adjectives and Adverbs

Positive adjectives and adverbs imply no comparisons: *recent, soon, clearly, fortunate*.

$$\text{adj.} \qquad \text{adj.}$$
The set for *The Passion of Dracula* was *ornate* and *eerie*.

$$\text{adv.}$$
The scene changes were made *quickly*.

Comparative Adjectives and Adverbs

Comparative adjectives and adverbs establish differences between two similar people, places, things, ideas, qualities, conditions, or actions. Adjectives and adverbs form comparatives in two ways. One-syllable modifiers add the suffix *-er: sooner, paler*. (See also the table of irregular adjectives and adverbs on page 341.) Multisyllable modifiers use *more* or *less* to form the comparative: *less easily, more recent.*   **》》》** *A number of two- and three-syllable adjectives use the -er form (and -est for the superlative). Use the -er and -est forms with multisyllable words that have the following characteristics:*

"Voiced" last syllables: *pretty, narrow*

L sound in the last syllable: *simple*

Accent on the last syllable: *severe*

Consult a dictionary if you are unsure of how to form a specific comparative or superlative. **《《《**

comp. adj.   comp. adj.
| |

The set for *The Passion of Dracula* was *more ornate* and *eerier* than anyone expected.

comp. adv.
|

The scene changes for this production were made *more quickly* than they were for *Hedda Gabler*.

Superlative Adjectives and Adverbs

Superlative adjectives and adverbs compare a person, place, thing, idea, quality, condition, or action with three or more similar items. Superlatives are the most emphatic adjective and adverb forms. One-syllable words form the superlative by adding the suffix *-est : soonest, palest.* Multisyllable adjectives and adverbs generally form the superlative by using *most* or *least: least easily, most recent.* (But see also the note on exceptions under the discussion of comparative forms on page 339.)

super. adj.   super. adj.
| |

The set for *The Passion of Dracula* was the *most dramatic* and *eeriest* one I have seen.

During this production season, the scene changes in *Dracula* were
super. adv.
|
made *most quickly*.

Several adjectives form the comparative and superlative irregularly, using neither suffixes nor helping words, but changing their spellings completely.

Positive	*Comparative*	*Superlative*
bad	worse	worst
good	better	best
little	less littler	least littlest
many much some	more	most
well	better	best
badly	worse	worst

Double Comparatives and Superlatives

Only one change is needed to form the comparative or superlative of an adjective or adverb. To use both a suffix and a helping word is unnecessary and incorrect.

Incorrect

Madonna rose to superstardom *more faster* than even she expected.

Correct

Madonna rose to superstardom *faster* than even she expected.

Incorrect

Kliban's cartoons of cats are the *most funniest* ones I have seen.

Correct

Kliban's cartoons of cats are the *funniest* ones I have seen.

Incomparable Adjectives

Because of their meanings, some adjectives cannot suggest comparisons of any kind. Examples of such words are *central, dead, empty, impossible, infinite, perfect, straight,* and *unique.* Use only the positive form of such modifiers.

Incorrect

James Joyce's *Ulysses* was the *most unique* novel I have read. (*Unique* means "one of a kind.")

Correct

James Joyce's *Ulysses* is a *unique* novel. (This sentence uses *unique* in its proper, positive form.)

Correct

James Joyce's *Ulysses* was the *most unusual* novel I have read. (*Unusual* is a quality that can be compared.)

| 20d | Distinguish carefully between troublesome adjective and adverb pairs. |

Use *bad,* the adjective form, to modify nouns and pronouns, even with sensory or linking verbs (*appear, feel, look, smell, taste, sound,* and forms of *to be*). Use *badly* only to modify a verb.

That was a *bad* rendition of *Rhapsody in Blue.*

After sitting in the sun for two hours, Monica felt *bad.*

After dozens of art classes, Anita still painted *badly.*

Use *good,* the adjective form, only to modify a noun or pronoun. Use *well* as an adverb to mean *satisfactory;* use *well* as an adjective to mean *healthy.*

Marco was a very *good* pianist.

The rehearsal went *well* last night.

Although Anton had a slight fever, he said he felt *well* enough to play in Saturday's game.

Other troublesome adjective and adverb pairs appear in the Glossary of Terms.

EXERCISE 20.1 ❯ *Adjective and adverb forms*

Select the appropriate adjective or adverb forms in the following sentences.

1. Current methods of building construction will make homes (affordable/more affordable/most affordable) than they were in the past, without sacrificing quality.

2. Although prefabricated homes have always been (easily/more easily/most easily) constructed than conventionally built homes, they were not always built (good/well).

3. Now, however, factory construction of major structural elements is (increasing/increasingly) impressive.

4. Many home units — like kitchens and bathrooms — are being constructed with their plumbing and wiring embedded in wall units; then these "core construction blocks" are fitted together (quick/quickly/more quickly) in various ways.

5. Because installing plumbing and wiring is (costly/more costly/most costly) than other phases of construction, these "core blocks" keep on-site construction costs (low/lower/lowest).

6. With the money saved from structural costs, a homeowner can concentrate on architectural trim and interior design work that can make his or her home (unique/more unique/most unique).

EXERCISE 20.2 ❯ Adjectives and adverbs

Correct the errors in adjective and adverb use in the following paragraph.

Tapestries, fabrics with pictures woven into them, were used in medieval churches and palaces more often as decorations but sometimes as insulation in the chilly buildings. The most unique tapestries were produced in Arras, France, where the art of weaving pictures reached its perfectest form in the 1400s. The tapestry makers of Arras worked so good that the word *arras* was soon used as a synonym for *tapestry.* The tapestries that have survived from the 1400s and 1500s are in various states of repair. Some, like the set of tapestries called *The Hunt of the Unicorn,* are in real sound condition. Their colors are still vibrant. The more famous panel of the set shows a unicorn sitting within a circular fence, surrounded by flowers and foliage of the brightest colors. Unfortunately, other tapestries have been treated bad over the centuries, and their colors are faded or their yarns damaged. Weaving tapestries is a most complex craft that has been sporadically and more simplistically revived in the last hundred years, but we will probably never approximate the more intricate and reverential nature of tapestries done in the late Middle Ages.

Using the word processor to evaluate adjective and adverb use

Beyond basic strategies for revision, a word processor can help you to solve special problems with adjectives and adverbs.

Search for intensifiers. Use the "search" codes to find words like *very, really,* and *especially.* Eliminate all of the intensifiers that do not convey crucial meaning.

Search for comparatives and superlatives. Use the "search" codes to find *more, most, less,* and *least.* Then make sure that the comparative or superlative form is aptly chosen. With some word-processing programs, you can search for specific sets of letters, not just separate words. If your program has that capability and if you have special problems with comparatives and superlatives, consider searching for *-er* and *-est* combinations.

MAKING   C O N N E C T I O N S

Adjectives and adverbs can add liveliness and meaning to writing, but only if they are used selectively and accurately. Examine your patterns of adjective and adverb use.

- Tabulate your use of adjectives and adverbs. Choose a recent paper and highlight the adjectives and adverbs, list them, or count the number of each that you used. These strategies will show you where and how often you use adjectives and adverbs.

- Evaluate your use of adjectives and adverbs. What patterns do you discover? Do you overuse intensifiers? Do you miss opportunities to use adjectives and adverbs to add specificity and clarity to your writing? Do you use positive, comparative, and superlative forms correctly?

PUNCTUATION

Punctuation refers to the use of small marks that have an enormous impact on writing. We are so accustomed to seeing punctuation marks that we may fail to realize how vital a role they play in written communication.

In Nicholas Udall's play *Ralph Roister Doister* (ca. 1550), Ralph hires a letter writer to write to his beloved; the letter reads in part:

Do and say what you will; you shall never please me
But when you are merry; I will be all sad
When you are sorry; I will be very glad
When you seek your heart's ease; I will be unkind
At no time; in me shall you much gentleness find. (3.5.69 – 73)

But when Ralph copies the letter in his own handwriting, he alters the punctuation, with disastrous results:

Do and say what you will, you shall never please me;
But when you are merry, I will be all sad;
When you are sorry, I will be very glad.
When you seek your heart's ease, I will be unkind;
At no time in me shall you much gentleness find. (3.4.56 – 60)

Mistakes in punctuation do not always produce such a total subversion of meaning, with its potentially tragic or, in this case, comic results. But every writer depends on the long and short pauses, the bracketing and organization of information achieved through punctuation, in order to control and communicate emphasis and meaning.

21 End Punctuation

Three marks of punctuation end sentences: the period (.), the question mark (?), and the exclamation point (!). These forms of punctuation usually end sentences that have expressed complete thoughts; they also serve a few other purposes.

> ### Quick Reference
>
> *End punctuation clearly and simply indicates the end of a sentence and its intended effect.*
>
> ❯ *Use periods to end sentences that make statements, issue commands, or ask indirect questions.*
>
> ❯ *Use question marks to end sentences that ask direct questions.*
>
> ❯ *Use exclamation points to end sentences that express strong feeling.*

21a ❯ **Use periods after sentences making statements, issuing commands, or asking indirect questions.**

Statement

Cigarette smoking is hazardous to your health.

Command

Stop smoking today.

Indirect question

The Surgeon General asked whether the students understood the risks of smoking.   (The sentence implies that the Surgeon General asked a question; but the sentence itself is not a question. The word order of the main subject and verb indicates that the sentence is a statement.)

| 21b | **Use question marks after direct questions.** |

A question mark is one of two indicators of direct questions; the other is inverted word order of the subject and any part of the verb. (Indirect questions end with periods and use normal word order; see section 21a.) The verb in a question may include a helping verb not necessarily present in a statement.

Question

Did the president know of the illegal actions of his advisers?

Statement

The president knew of the illegal actions of his advisers.

》》》 *Some writers use question marks in parentheses to indicate uncertainty. This usage should be avoided in formal writing.*

The Chinese invented paper in A.D. 105(?) but kept it a state secret for hundreds of years.

Better

The Chinese invented paper around A.D. 105 but kept it a state secret for hundreds of years. **《《《**

21c ⟩ **Use exclamation points after sentences and strong interjections to express strong feeling or indicate special emphasis.**

An exclamation point may follow a sentence or an interjection.

Sentence

"I know not what course others may take; but as for me, give me liberty or give me death!" — Patrick Henry

Interjection

"Well! Some people talk of morality, and some of religion, but give me a little snug property." — Maria Edgeworth

Exclamation points should be used sparingly, especially in formal writing. Not many sentences or interjections require the emphasis that exclamation points provide.

EXERCISE 21.1 ⟩ *End punctuation*

 Add the end punctuation required in the following paragraph, capitalizing where necessary to indicate new sentences.

Harry Truman, the thirty-third president, was a spirited leader with a penchant for candor he assumed the presidency in 1945, after Franklin Roosevelt's death, and until he left office in 1953 repeatedly challenged assumptions about how presidents ought to behave his presidency was marked by controversy Truman made the decision to drop nuclear bombs on Hiroshima and Nagasaki; he supported the Marshall Plan to help Europe recover from the devastation of World War II; he sent American troops to Korea a sign of his unquestioning acceptance of responsibility for key decisions one of Truman's favorite slogans became nationally known: "the buck stops here" another of his favorites was "if you can't stand the heat, get out of the kitchen" supporters, using

Truman's own flavorful language often shouted this refrain: "give 'em hell, Harry" Truman made many difficult decisions and never attempted to avoid the controversy that resulted or to blame others for his decisions was he a great president that is a judgment best left to history, but he certainly was an honest and an interesting one

Word processing and end punctuation

A word processor will help you to avoid problems with overuse or incorrect use of question marks and exclamation points.

Find and check your use of question marks. Use "search" commands to locate question marks. Check the sentence to make sure that the subject and verb are inverted. If you discover a question mark following an indirect question, revise the sentence or the punctuation.

Find and replace most exclamation points. Use the "search" commands to locate all exclamation points in your papers. For all but the most necessary and emphatic uses, delete the exclamation points and replace them with periods.

MADING   C O N N E C T I O N S

Examine patterns in your use of end punctuation.

- Consider your use of question marks. Questions can
  effectively vary the rhythm and emphasis of your writing. Do
  you ask and then answer questions? Do you challenge your
  readers to answer questions? Do you ask unanswerable
  questions? How does your use of questions affect the
  interest, tone, and clarity of your writing?

- Consider your use of exclamation points. Exclamation
  points can be used effectively to add emphasis, drama,
  irony, and other special effects to your writing, but they are
  most effective if used sparingly. Find any exclamation points
  in your recent writing. Does the context honestly require the
  use of an exclamation point? Could emphasis have been
  achieved by using more forceful diction or varied sentence
  structure or rhythm? How would your meaning be affected if
  the exclamation point were changed to a period?

22 Commas

Commas separate and clarify the relations among single words, phrases, and clauses. If commas do not appear where they are needed, thoughts can merge or overlap confusingly.

Confusing

As the speaker finished his audience stood to cheer.   (Without a comma after *finished,* the sentence momentarily suggests that the speaker finished the audience.)

Clear

As the speaker finished, his audience stood to cheer.

Quick Reference

Use commas to clarify and separate sentence elements.

❯ *Use commas to separate items in a series.*

❯ *Use commas to separate clauses in compound sentences.*

❯ *Use commas to set off introductory subordinate clauses in complex and compound-complex sentences.*

❯ *Use commas to set off introductory words and phrases that serve as adverbs.*

❯ *Use commas to set off nonrestrictive information.*

❯ *Use commas to set off statements that signal direct quotations.*

C•O•N•N•E•C•T•I•O•N•S

Correct comma use provides readers with the signals they need to understand your writing. The word *comma* comes from a Greek word meaning "to cut," and correctly placed commas divide without severing the coherent parts that contribute to the meaningful whole of the sentence.

In addition to correct comma use, writers strive for effective comma use. Commas are the most frequently used form of internal sentence punctuation because of their great flexibility in revealing meaning and enhancing expression. Commas both separate and relate parts of sentences, indicating clearly the writer's intended effect of subordination, parallelism, or balance. And they create both stress and pause, encouraging the reader to follow the pattern and rhythm of the writer's thoughts and expression.

Learning correct and effective comma use will enable you to improve your communication of your ideas to readers.

| 22a | **Use commas to separate three or more items in a series.** |

Separate a series of three or more parallel words, phrases, or clauses with commas. Although some writers omit the comma immediately preceding the conjunction, a comma there is always correct and may prevent confusion.

Nouns or Verbs in a Series

The faces of George Washington, Thomas Jefferson, Abraham Lincoln, and Theodore Roosevelt are carved into Mount Rushmore.   (Commas separate each noun in the series.)

A good reporter asks questions directly, listens attentively, and takes notes accurately and quickly.   (Commas separate all verbs in the series.)

Adjectives and Adverbs in a Series

When several adjectives independently modify a single noun, use commas to separate each one. Similarly, when adverbs separately and equally modify a verb or an adjective, separate them with commas. No comma separates the last modifier in the series from the word modified.

The ancient, dilapidated depot is slated for demolition.   (*Ancient* depot; *dilapidated* depot; each adjective functions independently.)

The ornithologist slowly, calmly, and carefully approached the injured goose. (*Slowly* approached; *calmly* approached; *carefully* approached; each adverb functions independently.)

》》》 *To test the independence of modifiers, reverse the order of the modifiers or substitute* and *for each comma. If the sentence still makes sense, the adjectives or adverbs are* coordinate *and should be separated by commas. If the sentence does not make sense, the modifiers are* cumulative *and do not require commas (see section 23d).*

The dilapidated and ancient depot is slated for demolition.   (The modification is clear, and the sentence makes sense.) **《《《**

Phrases and Clauses in a Series

Phrases

Letters by Churchill, to Churchill, and about Churchill have become important and valued historical documents.

Clauses

At the turn of the century, the need for social reforms erupted into pitched battles as muckrakers exposed business corruption, industrial leaders challenged their accusations, and politicians sided with the powerful industrialists.

EXERCISE 22.1 ❯ *Commas*

Insert commas where needed in the following sentences.

1. Computers are now commonplace equipment in homes schools and businesses.

2. It is amazing how quickly completely and smoothly most people have become acclimated to the new technology.

3. Computerized cash registers are now common in grocery stores at movie houses in discount stores and even at gas stations.

4. Computers in public and private libraries have made it possible for people to search for books print lists of available materials and complete research quickly.

5. Today our mail comes with computer labels our bank statements arrive with spread-sheet accounts of transactions and even our grocery store receipts have computer lists of products we've bought.

22b ❯ **Use commas to separate clauses in compound and compound-complex sentences.**

Compound Sentences

Most independent clauses joined by a coordinating conjunction must be separated by a comma. When the clauses are brief and when no confusion is likely, the comma may be omitted. Using a comma, however, is always correct.

> Price supports for dairy products greatly help farmers, and consumers benefit as well.   (Without a comma after *farmers,* the initial reading might inappropriately link *farmers* and *consumers* as direct objects.)

Making mistakes is common but admitting them is not.   (Because these clauses are brief and because confusion is unlikely, the comma may be omitted.)

⟩⟩⟩ *Do not mistakenly place a comma before every coordinating conjunction. Place a comma only before coordinating conjunctions that link independent clauses. Conjunctions that connect only two words, two phrases, or two dependent clauses usually do not require commas.* **⟨⟨⟨**

Compound-Complex Sentences

One comma separates the independent clauses in a compound-complex sentence. When a compound-complex sentence begins with a subordinate clause, however, a comma must also be used to show where the subordinate clause ends and the independent clause begins.

> Once people learn to use computers and laser printers, personal publishing becomes possible, and many small organizations print their own materials.

EXERCISE 22.2 **⟩** *Commas*

Combine these simple sentences to form compound, complex, or compound-complex sentences. Insert any necessary commas.

1. *Buffalo* is the name usually used to refer to American bison. It is a common name used to describe several hundred kinds of large wild oxen worldwide.

2. Water buffalo in India have been domesticated for centuries. South African buffalo have resisted domestication and run wild. Small buffalo on Pacific islands remain wild as well.

3. In North America, especially on the Great Plains, huge herds of buffalo once roamed. By 1900, the bison population of approximately 20 million was reduced to fewer than six hundred.

4. William Hornaday, an American zoologist, worked to protect the remaining bison. He felt their extinction would be shameful. He encouraged the National Forest Service to build fenced areas for small herds.

5. Today, bison are kept in captivity. They cannot be trained or domesticated. They are of zoological rather than practical interest.

| 22c | **Use commas after most introductory words, phrases, and subordinate clauses.** |

Introductory Words

Because conjunctive adverbs (*however, subsequently,* and others) and some adverbs are nonrestrictive sentence elements, they must be set off by commas. (See Nonrestrictive Words, pages 362–63.)

Conjunctive adverb

> *Subsequently,* testimony proved that President Nixon was deeply involved in illegal activities.

 A conjunctive adverb used to link compound sentences joined by a semicolon should be followed by a comma.

> Impeachment proceedings seemed imminent; therefore, Nixon resigned from office. ◀◀◀

Adverb

> First, children require good nutrition to grow and learn properly. (The comma prevents confusion; without it, readers might think that *first* is an adjective modifying *children.*)

Introductory Phrases

When a transitional expression (*for example, in other words, in fact,* and others) or an opening prepositional or verbal phrase is used as an adjective or adverb, separate the phrase from the rest of the sentence with a comma.

Transitional expression
> *For example,* most organization newsletters are now generated by laser printers to achieve the look of typeset copy without the cost.

Prepositional phrase
> After twenty years of promoting feminist causes, the National Organization for Women has achieved some of its goals but continues to address new ones.   (The comma signals the end of the introductory phrase and the beginning of the main idea of the sentence.)

>>> *If an introductory prepositional phrase is brief and if the meaning is clear without a comma, the comma may be omitted.*

> In April Americans pay income taxes. <<<

Verbal phrase
> Crouching in a makeshift hut of sticks and grasses, Jane Goodall observed the chimpanzees at play.   (The introductory participial phrase is adjectival, modifying *Goodall.*)

Introductory Subordinate Clauses

When a subordinate clause begins a sentence, use a comma to separate it from the independent clause that follows.

> Because mosquitoes are such a problem in southern coastal cities like New Orleans, city workers spray with insecticides each evening. (The comma marks the end of the subordinate clause.)

EXERCISE 22.3 ❯ *Commas*

Insert commas where needed in the following sentences.

1. Built during the third and fourth centuries the catacombs of Rome are the most famous in the world.

2. Intended for use as burial sites the passages and rooms were used for other purposes too.

3. According to legend early Christians kept the bodies of Saint Peter and Saint Paul hidden for a time in the catacombs.

4. In addition Christians often took refuge in the catacombs because the catacombs were protected by Roman law.

5. Curiously use of the Roman catacombs ceased in A.D. 400.

22d	**Use commas to separate nonrestrictive information from the rest of a sentence.**

Restrictive information, essential to the meaning of a sentence, supplies the distinctions that give ideas the specificity intended by the writer. Such information is not set off by commas. Nonrestrictive information does not supply distinctions central to the meaning of a sentence. Because nonrestrictive information can be omitted, it is set off by commas from the rest of the sentence. Nonrestrictive elements may be single words, phrases, or clauses.

Nonrestrictive Words

Conjunctive Adverbs

Use commas to set off conjunctive adverbs. When they appear at the beginning or end of a sentence, use one comma to set them off. When they appear in the middle of a sentence, use two commas.

At end of sentence

Many people admired Nixon's command of international policy. They remained suspicious of his politics, however.

In midsentence

Newspaper reports suggested Nixon's involvement in Watergate. The president, however, claimed he had committed no crimes.

The words *yes* and *no,* mild interjections, and names in direct address

Use commas to separate the words *yes* and *no,* interjections, and names in direct address from the rest of a sentence.

Yes and direct address

"Yes, Virginia, there is a Santa Claus." — Francis Church   (The comma after *yes* separates it from the rest of the sentence; the comma after *Virginia* separates this name used in direct address.)

Interjection

Okay, so it was Franklin who said, "In this world nothing is certain but death and taxes."

Nonrestrictive Phrases

Transitional Expressions

Transitional expressions (*for example, as a result,* and so on) are nonrestrictive and should therefore be separated from the rest of the sentence. Use a single comma if the expression appears at the beginning or end of a sentence; use two commas if it appears in the middle of a sentence.

Nixon has, in fact, remained an astute commentator on foreign affairs.

363

Absolute Phrases

Absolute phrases modify entire sentences. Because these phrases are nonrestrictive, they must be set off by commas. Use a single comma if the phrase appears at the beginning or end of a sentence; use two commas if it appears in the middle of a sentence.

At end of sentence

   Franklin Roosevelt was the first president to fly in a commercial airplane, a fact unknown to most people.

In midsentence

   Gandhi, the goal of Indian independence achieved, retired from public life.

Prepositional and Verbal Phrases

When prepositional and verbal phrases supply information that is not essential to the meaning of a sentence, use commas to set them off from the rest of the sentence.

Prepositional phrase

   J. D. Salinger, above all else, values his privacy.   (The prepositional phrase *above all else* requires commas because it can be omitted without substantially altering the sentence's meaning.)

Verbal phrase

   M*A*S*H*, challenging idealized assumptions about war, achieved surprising success.

Appositives

Appositives restate proper nouns. Nonrestrictive appositives add clarifying but not essential information and are set off by commas.

Frank Lloyd Wright, an architect in the early twentieth century, felt that the design of a building should be suited to its surrounding.

Nonrestrictive Clauses

Nonrestrictive clauses that begin with a relative pronoun *(which, who, whose, whom, whoever,* and *whomever)* can be omitted without substantially changing the meaning of a sentence. Because they are not essential, nonrestrictive clauses must be set off by commas.

The Starry Night, which is prominently displayed in the Museum of Modern Art in New York, exemplifies Van Gogh's use of rich colors applied in bold strokes.   (The information in the relative clause is set off by commas because it does not add to the essential meaning of the sentence.)

Picasso, who became one of the most successful and wealthiest artists in the world, started out ignored and impoverished during his early days in Paris.

 Use commas to set off sentence elements that express contrast.

Because words and phrases that provide contrasting details do not function grammatically as parts of a sentence, they should be separated from the rest of a sentence by commas.

Shaw's first love was music, not theater.

The BBC, unlike American public television networks, is completely financed by the government.

EXERCISE 22.4 ❯ *Commas*

Insert commas where needed in the following sentences.

1. *Beowulf* which is one of the earliest examples of Anglo-Saxon literature still appeals to those who like adventure stories not only to scholars.

2. The character Beowulf with a combination of heroic and religious qualities goes to the aid of Hrothgar the leader of a noble tribe.

3. The most famous episode of *Beowulf* the battle between Beowulf and the monster Grendel is a marvelous mix of supernatural and traditional Christian elements.

4. *Beowulf* is a historical-literary milestone; it is however a popular classic as well.

5. The plot elements of *Beowulf* — fights with supernatural beasts and tests of moral strength for example — remain standard elements in today's science fiction films perhaps explaining why *Beowulf* remains so popular.

| 22f | **Use commas to set off expressions that signal direct quotations.** |

Commas separate expressions such as *he said* and *she commented* from the quotations they identify. These expressions can be used at the beginning, in the middle, or at the end of a quotation. Note that the comma precedes the opening quotation mark.

In an ongoing battle of wits, Lady Astor once said to Winston Churchill, "Winston, if you were my husband, I should flavor your coffee with poison."

"Madam," Churchill replied, "if I were your husband, I should drink it."

Or:

"Madam, if I were your husband, I should drink it," Churchill replied.

 Use commas according to convention in numbers, dates, addresses, place names, and titles.

For easy reading and comprehension, most numbers of one thousand or more are divided by placing a comma between groups of three digits, moving from the right.

1,271   1,300,000

Dates written in month-day-year order require a comma between the day and the year, and in sentences a comma must also follow the year.

December 7, 1941, marked the beginning of America's involvement in World War II.

If dates are written in day-month-year order, or if only the month and year are given, no comma is needed.

Martin Luther King, Jr., was born on 15 January 1929; his birthday has been designated a national holiday.

The stock market crash of late October 1929 precipitated the Great Depression.

Addresses written on one line or within a sentence require commas after the street name and between the city and state. Zip codes follow, with two spaces before and no comma after when written on a single line. When written within a sentence, zip codes appear without extra space before and with a comma after. (See Business Writing, Appendix D.)

709 Sherwood Terrace, Champaign, Illinois 61820

Information on the water rights issue is available by writing the newspaper directly at *Courier-Journal,* 822 Courier Road, Wendel, Vermont 05753, to the attention of the editor.

Parts of place names are separated by commas even when they include only city and state or city and country. Within a sentence, a comma also follows the last item in the place name — essentially making the last item an appositive.

Marietta, Georgia   Ontario, Canada

Nestled in the bluffs along the Mississippi River, Elsa, Illinois, is always 10 to 15 degrees cooler than nearby towns and cities.

Titles and academic and professional degrees that follow an individual's name should be set off with commas.

Adele Zimmerman, professor emerita, spoke at the alumni luncheon on Saturday.

Fernando Rivera, M.D., and Sean Mullican, Ph.D., coordinated the county's alcohol-abuse program.

》》》 *When roman numerals follow the name of a private individual, monarch, ship, and so on, no commas are required.*

Louis XIV of France was known as the "Sun King" because of the splendor of his court.

Commas are required with the abbreviations Sr. *and* Jr., *however.*

Louis Gosset, Jr., won critical acclaim for his sensitive portrayal of an extraterrestrial being. **《《《**

EXERCISE 22.5 ❯ Commas

Insert commas where needed in the following paragraphs.

A. Although zoos provide opportunities to see many exotic animals up close the facilities for the animals do not always allow them to pursue or visitors to observe natural habits. Rhesus monkeys very small primates do not seem cramped in small places; they do not appear to suffer or experience any ill effects from their confinement. Chimpanzees however seem noticeably depressed in areas that do not allow them to move about freely. Orangutans highly intelligent primates also seem despondent. However the jungle cats tigers and leopards seem to suffer most. They pace in their cages or lie inactive and inattentive. These large primates and big cats which are usually among a zoo's main attractions require more space and some distance from the crowds of eager spectators. In recent years zoo keepers who have the animals' best interests in mind have begun building habitats for these larger animals. Most zoos have paid for these building projects which can be quite elaborate from general funds. Other zoos have launched major advertising campaigns hoping for individual donations. Still others stressing commitment to the community have appealed to major corporations. These large building projects should continue for they provide improved living conditions for large wild animals. As we maintain zoos that entertain and educate people we must also remember that the animals that live there should not suffer for our benefit.

B. Alaska the forty-ninth state joined the Union on January 3 1959. The largest state geographically covering 586412 square miles Alaska is also the least populated with only 479000 people. In fact the entire state has fewer people than many American cities of moderate size let alone Chicago Los Angeles or New York. Yes the contrast in physical size and population presents an anomaly but Alaska's history is full of such anomalies. Juneau its capital city has approximately twenty thousand people making it roughly the same size as Texarkana Arkansas; Augusta Maine; and Winchester Nevada. Alaska has fewer schools than many other states but has the highest teachers' salaries in the nation. Contradictions such as these have always been present. In 1867 when William H. Seward secretary of state arranged the purchase of Alaska for $7200000 most people thought the purchase was foolish. But "Seward's Folly" as the acquisition was called turned out to be not at all foolish. Rich deposits of minerals oil and natural gas have made Alaska one of America's greatest assets. (For more information on Alaska write to the Alaskan Chamber of Commerce 310 Second Street Juneau Alaska 99801.)

Word processing and commas

If you have problems with comma use, a word processor will provide a convenient means for eliminating them.

Check your comma use. Use "search" commands to locate the commas in your writing. Be sure that a comma rule justifies each use; check the position of the comma in relation to the items it separates or sets off from other sentence elements.

Add commas when necessary. Reread your final draft carefully, checking for places where needed commas are missing. Use the computer's ability to insert commas and automatically reformat the altered sentence. Check spacing and capitalization.

MAKING   C O N N E C T I O N S

Analyzing and improving your use of commas will enable you to control the meaning of your sentences.

- Examine your comma use. Look at your papers, noting particularly commas that have been added by peer editors or teachers.

- Discover patterns of omission. What kinds of patterns emerge when you analyze your omissions of needed commas? Do you sometimes forget to separate items in a series? Do you frequently omit commas needed in complex sentences?

- Concentrate on particular comma rules. Identify the comma rules that give you the most trouble. Review carefully the explanations and examples of those rules, perhaps preparing a reference card for use when you proofread.

---

23   Unnecessary Commas

Commas help to establish meaning by separating elements in sentences. Thus, the use of commas where they are not needed confuses, distracts, and annoys readers and interferes with the communication of ideas.

Quick Reference

Too many unnecessary commas can be as confusing as too few necessary commas.

❯ *Do not place commas between subjects and verbs or between verbs and complements.*

❯ *Do not use a comma before a coordinating conjunction joining only two words, phrases, or clauses.*

❯ *Do not use commas to set off restrictive sentence elements.*

❯ *Do not use commas before quotations introduced by* that *or* if.

23a	**Do not use a comma between a subject and its verb or between a verb and its complement.**

In general, no punctuation should break the subject-verb or verb-complement pattern in a sentence. Insert commas only when they are necessary because of intervening elements, such as non-restrictive phrases or clauses, appositives, coordinate modifiers, and transitional words.

Subject and verb

Governments in many countries, control the prices of consumer goods.   (The comma interrupts the subject-verb pattern.)

Governments in many countries control the prices of consumer goods.

Governments in many countries, especially those in the Communist bloc, control the prices of consumer goods.   (The pair of commas is required because a nonrestrictive phrase has been added.)

Verb and complement

Black markets generally develop, in countries where consumer goods are scarce.   (The comma interrupts the verb-complement pattern.)

Black markets generally develop in countries where consumer goods are scarce.

 Do not use a comma before a coordinating conjunction that joins only two words, phrases, or dependent clauses.

Words

The Federal Reserve controls the twelve Federal Reserve banks, and regulates the prime interest rate.   (The comma incorrectly separates the elements of a compound verb: controls *and* regulates.)

The Federal Reserve controls the twelve Federal Reserve banks and regulates the prime interest rate.

Phrases

The Federal Reserve's goals are to stabilize the national economy, and to help establish international monetary policies.   (The comma incorrectly separates two infinitive phrases joined by *and*.)

The Federal Reserve's goals are to stabilize the national economy and to help establish international monetary policies.

Clauses

Economists note that low interest rates encourage spending, but that they can also fuel inflation.   (The comma incorrectly separates two clauses, each beginning with *that*.)

Economists note that low interest rates encourage spending but that they also fuel inflation.

》》》 *Remember that a comma is required between the independent clauses of a compound sentence.*

Low interest rates encourage spending, but they also fuel inflation.

See Chapter 16 for more information and examples. **《《《**

23c	Do not use a comma before the first or after the last item in a series.

Commas separate items in a series, but unless the series is part of a nonrestrictive phrase, no commas should separate the series as a unit from the rest of the sentence.

To earn extra money, to gain experience, and to make important contacts, are reasons recent graduates in education often work as substitute teachers.   (The infinitive phrases form a series that is the subject of the sentence. The commas after *money* and *experience* are appropriate, but the comma after *contacts* separates the compound subject from the verb.)

To earn extra money, to get more experience, and to make important contacts are reasons that recent graduates in education often work as substitute teachers

---

23d — Do not use commas with cumulative modifiers.

Cumulative modifiers — adjectives and adverbs that build upon each other to create meaning — should not be separated by commas. They differ from coordinate modifiers, which modify words separately and require separation with commas.

> A pulsar is a rotating, neutron star.   (The comma separates cumulative adjectives: *neutron* modifies *star;* but *rotating* modifies the phrase *neutron star.*)

> A pulsar is a rotating neutron star.

To test whether modifiers are cumulative, change their order. If the new order makes no sense, the modifiers are cumulative and no commas should be used. The example above would not make sense if it were written "A pulsar is a neutron rotating star."

23e — Do not use commas to set off restrictive elements in sentences.

Because restrictive elements — whether they are single words, phrases, or clauses — are essential to the meaning of a sentence, they should not be set off by commas.

Words

> The musical play, *West Side Story,* is based on Shakespeare's *Romeo and Juliet.*   (The commas are incorrect because *West Side Story* is necessary to the meaning of the sentence.)

> The musical play *West Side Story* is based on Shakespeare's *Romeo and Juliet.*

Phrases

Audience members continued to arrive, until well into the first
act.   (Because the phrase is essential to the meaning of the sentence,
no comma should be used.)

Audience members continued to arrive until well into the first act.

Clauses

Composers and lyricists, who adapt well-known plays, usually strive
to maintain the spirit of the original works.   (The commas are not
needed because the relative clause is essential; it identifies a particular
group of composers and lyricists.)

Composers and lyricists who adapt well-known plays usually strive to
maintain the spirit of the original works.

| 23f | **Do not use a comma before an indirect or a direct quotation introduced by *that* or *if*.** |

Because a quotation preceded by the word *that* or *if* functions as
a complement, a comma would improperly separate verb and
complement.

Mark Twain commented, that Wagner's music is more respected than it
should be.   (The subordinate clause following *said* is the direct object of *said*.)

Mark Twain commented that Wagner's music is more respected than it
should be.

But:

Mark Twain commented, "Wagner's music is better than it sounds."

23g	**Do not use a comma after *such as* or *like* or before *than*.**

Such as and *like* are prepositions that introduce examples in prepositional phrases; because these examples serve as objects, no comma is needed. *Than* signals a comparative construction, and it is illogical to separate with a comma the two items compared.

Some humanistic studies such as, philosophy, art history, and dramatic arts require a more scientific approach, than most people think.   (The comma after *such as* inappropriately separates the preposition from its objects; the comma preceding *than* interrupts a comparative construction. The commas after *philosophy* and *art history* correctly separate items in a series.)

Some humanistic studies such as philosophy, art history, and dramatic arts require a more scientific approach than most people think.

EXERCISE 23.1 ❯ *Unnecessary commas*

The following sentences contain far too many commas. Eliminate those that break the flow of the sentences or that obscure the logical connections between ideas.

1. Primary colors like, red, blue, and yellow are the most often used colors in national flags.

2. Interestingly enough, Libya's bright, green, flag is the only solid colored flag, in current use.

3. The small, Arab republic, Qatar, has a simple, black, and white flag.

4. Many countries — such as, Bahrain, Canada, Denmark, Indonesia, Japan, Monaco, Singapore, and Tunisia — use only red, and white, in their flags.

5. Most national flags use three, or four, bold colors, and use simple geometric shapes in their designs.

6. However, the ornate flag, of Sri Lanka, uses four colors, and black, and an elaborate design.

7. Only a few national flags, vary from the traditional, rectangular shape, including those of, Nepal and Switzerland.

8. The most frequently used colors, for flags, are red, white, and blue.

9. The U.S. flag, contains fifty, small, white stars on a blue field, and thirteen, alternating stripes of red and white.

10. As symbols of nations, flags serve, ideological, and political purposes — uniting citizens in times of peace, as well as in times of war.

EXERCISE 23.2 ❯ Unnecessary commas

!   Delete the unnecessary commas from the following paragraph.

We went fishing, the first morning. I felt the same, damp, moss covering the worms, in the bait can, and saw the dragonfly alight on the tip of my rod, as it hovered a few inches from the surface of the water. It was the arrival of this fly, that convinced me, beyond any doubt, that everything was as it always had been, that the years were a mirage, and there had been no years. The small, waves were the same, chucking the rowboat under the chin as we fished at anchor, and the boat was the same boat, the same color green, and the ribs broken in the same places, and under the floor-boards the same fresh-water leavings and débris — the dead helgrammite, the wisps of moss, the rusty discarded fishhook, the dried blood from yesterday's catch. We stared, silently at the tips of our rods, at the dragonflies that came and went. I lowered the tip of mine into the water, tentatively, pensively dislodging the fly, which darted two feet away, poised, darted two, feet back, and came to rest again a little farther

up the rod. There had been no years, between the ducking of this dragonfly and the other one — the one that was part of my memory. I looked
at the boy, who was silently watching the fly, and it was my hands that
held his rod, my eyes watching. I felt dizzy, and didn't know which rod, I
was at the end of. — E. B. White, "Once More to the Lake"

 Word processing and unnecessary commas

If you use unnecessary commas, use the word processor to
help you avoid this problem.

Check your comma use. Use "search" commands to
locate the commas in your writing. Check each use,
making sure that a comma rule justifies it.

Delete unnecessary commas. The word-processing
program will automatically reformat sentences for you.

MAKING   C O N N E C T I O N S

Examine your papers to discover patterns for your comma usage.

- Note any corrections in comma use. Review your graded papers, looking for notes or markings that indicate the use of unnecessary commas.

- Try to discover patterns. If unnecessary commas clutter your papers, where do they most often appear? Once you discover your patterns of comma misuse, you can work to avoid these problems in later papers.

- Revise at least one of the paragraphs you analyzed above, preferably one containing a large number of your most typical comma error. Eliminate the unnecessary commas and punctuate the paragraph correctly, making the punctuation serve your tone, sentence structure, and meaning.

24 Semicolons and Colons

Semicolons perform various functions, sometimes acting as commas (separating items in a series) but more often acting as periods (separating closely related independent clauses).

A colon in effect says, "Notice what follows." Colons formally introduce lists, clarifications, and quotations.

> ### Quick Reference
>
> *Use semicolons and colons selectively according to convention.*
>
> ❭ *Use semicolons to join closely related independent clauses.*
>
> ❭ *Use colons to introduce lists, clarifications, and quotations*
>
> ❭ *Do not allow colons to separate verbs from complements or prepositions from objects.*

24a ❭ **Use a semicolon between closely related independent clauses not joined by a coordinating conjunction and before a conjunctive adverb that connects independent clauses.**

The use of a semicolon to link closely related independent clauses emphasizes the close relationship between the clauses.

Only a few hundred people in the United States know how to work with neon tubing; most of them are fifty years old or older.

»» *Remember that the clauses linked by a semicolon must be independent; otherwise, you will create a sentence fragment.* **«««**

The use of a conjunctive adverb in addition to a semicolon further stresses the interrelationship of the independent clauses.

Neon signs were once common at stores, restaurants, and gas stations across the country; however, in the sixties and seventies these sometimes garish advertisements fell into disfavor.   (The conjunctive adverb emphasizes the contrast.)

»» *Remember to include a comma after the conjunctive adverb.* **«««**

| 24b | **Use semicolons to separate equivalent sentence elements that contain commas.** |

Items in a Series

When items in a series contain commas, use semicolons to separate them.

Sculptors creating works for outdoor display generally use native stone like sandstone, granite, or limestone; metals or alloys like bronze, cast iron, or steel; or imported stone like marble.   (This use of semicolons helps readers identify the elements of the series.)

»» *Heavily punctuated series can become awkward to read. If your sentence contains too many pauses, break it into briefer, smoother sentences.*

Sculptors creating works for outdoor display generally use native stone like sandstone, granite, or limestone. Other frequently used materials include metals or alloys like bronze, cast iron, or steel or imported marble. **«««**

Independent Clauses

A semicolon effectively marks the break between independent clauses containing commas.

> Much of the sculpture commissioned for public plazas is artistically innovative, visually exciting, and technically impressive; but often it does not appeal to the general public because they have grown accustomed to traditional, realistic statuary.   (The semicolon clarifies the balance of the two-part sentence.)

》》》 *Separate clauses into independent sentences if doing so would make reading them easier. Some rewording may be necessary.*

> Much of the sculpture commissioned for public plazas is artistically innovative, visually exciting, and technically impressive. Nevertheless, it often does not appeal to the general public because they have grown accustomed to traditional, realistic statuary. **《《《**

24c **Do not use semicolons when other punctuation is required.**

With a Subordinate Clause

Use a comma, not a semicolon, after a subordinate clause at the beginning of a complex or compound-complex sentence.

Incorrect
> Because it had a strong, centralized government; the Roman Empire was able to maintain relative stability, peace, and prosperity for nearly four centuries.   (The semicolon obscures the relationship between the clauses.)

Correct
> Because it had a strong, centralized government, the Roman Empire was able to maintain relative stability, peace, and prosperity for nearly four centuries.

To Introduce a List

Use a colon or a dash, not a semicolon or a comma, to introduce a list.

Incorrect

Historians cite several reasons for the decline of Rome; expanded citizenship, the deterioration of the army, barbarian invasions, economic decentralization, and inefficient agriculture.

Correct

Historians cite several reasons for the decline of Rome: expanded citizenship, the deterioration of the army, barbarian invasions, economic decentralization, and inefficient agriculture.

24d	**Use colons to introduce elements formally or emphatically.**

Selective use of colons adds clarity and emphasis to writing. Excessive use may be distracting.

To Introduce a Series

The part of the sentence that precedes a colon must be an independent clause, and the items in the series should never be direct objects, predicate nouns or adjectives, or objects of prepositions.

The names of six of the Seven Dwarfs reflect their personalities and habits: Bashful, Dopey, Grumpy, Happy, Sleepy, and Sneezy.   (The colon emphasizes the list; the words that precede the colon form a complete sentence.)

To Introduce an Independent Clause That Explains the Preceding Clause

When a complete sentence is needed to explain the meaning of the preceding sentence, use a colon to clarify the relationship. The first word following the colon usually begins with a lower-case letter, which identifies the clause as a clarification. However, the first word following the colon may begin with a capital letter.

> Good song lyrics are like good poetry: both express ideas in rhythmic, elliptical form.   (Without the second sentence, the meaning of the first would not be completely clear; the colon points to the explanatory relationship.)

To Introduce an Appositive at the End of a Sentence

Appositives (restatements of nouns or pronouns) are given special emphasis when they are introduced with colons. This use of the colon stresses the appositive as a necessary explanation of a key word in the main sentence.

> Early astronomers and astrologers assigning names to planets drew primarily on one source: mythology.

To Introduce a Direct Quotation

Direct quotations are formally introduced by colons. Both the introduction and the quotation must be independent clauses. The first word of the quotation is capitalized. (See Quotation Marks, pages 430–31).

> The educational sentiment that Mark Twain articulated would shock many humorless educators: "It doesn't matter what you teach a boy, so long as he doesn't like it."   (The colon, preceded by a complete sentence, emphasizes Twain's comment.)

24e > **Use colons to separate numerals in time references and Bible citations and to separate titles from subtitles.**

Hours and minutes given in numerals are separated by a colon. When the reference is to hours only, spell out the number.

The next flight to Tel Aviv leaves at 2:15 A.M.

We expect to be home by nine o'clock.

Chapter and verse in citations of books of the Bible are separated by a colon.

Genesis 3:23   Luke 12:27

Titles and subtitles are separated by a colon.

Nancy McPhee's *Book of Insults Ancient and Modern: An Amiable History of Insult, Invective, Imprecation, and Incivility (Literary, Political, and Historical) Hurled Through the Ages and Compiled as a Public Service* is a collection of amusing comments, criticisms, and rejoinders.

24f > **Do not use a colon between a verb and its complement or between a preposition and its object.**

Colons should not separate basic sentence elements. To test the accuracy of colon placement, change the colon to a period and drop the words that follow. If the remaining sentence is complete, the colon is correctly placed. If the remaining sentence is incomplete, delete or move the colon or rephrase the sentence.

Incorrect

The names of Enrico's cats are: Winston Churchill, T. S. Eliot, Eudora Welty, and Eleanor Roosevelt.   (*The names of Enrico's cats are* is a fragment; the colon separates the verb from its complement.)

Correct

The names of Enrico's cats are Winston Churchill, T. S. Eliot, Eudora Welty, and Eleanor Roosevelt.

Incorrect

Enrico named his cats after: Winston Churchill, T. S. Eliot, Eudora Welty, and Eleanor Roosevelt.   (*Enrico named his cats after* is a fragment; the colon separates the preposition *after* from its objects.)

Correct

Enrico named his cats after Winston Churchill, T. S. Eliot, Eudora Welty, and Eleanor Roosevelt.

Correct

Enrico named his cats after historical figures and writers: Winston Churchill, T. S. Eliot, Eudora Welty, and Eleanor Roosevelt.   (The prepositional phrase is complete, and the list of names adds clarification.)

EXERCISE 24.1 ❭ *Semicolons and colons*

Correct the errors in semicolon and colon usage in the following sentences.

1. The Mediterranean Sea is bordered to the south by: Egypt, Libya, Tunisia, Algeria, and Morocco.

2. The major ports on the Mediterranean Sea are: Barcelona; Spain, Marseille; France, Naples; Italy, Beirut; Lebanon, Alexandria; Egypt, and Tripoli; Libya.

3. Because the Bering Sea borders both the Soviet Union and the United States; it is often patrolled by military ships from each country.

4. In the Western Hemisphere, gulfs are more common than seas: however, several seas are located off the northernmost coasts of North America.

5. Four seas are named for colors; the Yellow Sea, the Red Sea, the White Sea, and the Black Sea.

EXERCISE 24.2 ❯ *Semicolons and colons*

The following paragraph uses the semicolon as its only form of internal punctuation. Revise the punctuation, reserving the semicolon for places where it works better than any other mark of punctuation.

Ninety-six percent of Americans have eaten at one of the McDonald's restaurants in the last year; slightly more than half of the U.S. population lives within three minutes of a McDonald's; McDonald's has served more than 55 billion hamburgers; McDonald's commands 17% of all restaurant visits in the U.S. and gets 7.3% of all dollars Americans spent eating out; McDonald's sells 32% of all hamburgers and 26% of french fries; McDonald's is the country's largest beef buyer; it purchases 7.5% of the U.S. potato crop; McDonald's has employed about 8 million workers — which amounts to approximately 7% of the entire U.S. work force; and McDonald's has replaced the U.S. Army as America's largest job training organization. — John Love, *McDonald's: Behind the Arches*

Word processing and semicolons and colons

Because semicolons and colons must be used so infrequently and so carefully, you probably will want to check each use. A word processor will help you do that easily.

Locate semicolons. Use "search" commands to locate places where you have used semicolons. Make sure that they separate independent clauses or items in a series that contain commas.

Locate colons. Use "search" commands to locate colons. Double-check their use, especially making sure that they do not separate verbs from their complements or prepositions from their objects.

MAKING   C O N N E C T I O N S

Semicolons and colons create emphasis. Turn to your own writing to see if you have used semicolons and colons to full advantage.

- Consider your use of semicolons and colons. Look at several of your papers to see whether you have used semicolons and colons clearly and effectively. Note especially places where a semicolon would have expressed a relationship between two independent clauses more clearly than a period. Revise some of your sentences, using semicolons and colons.

- Experiment with semicolons and colons. Using samples of your previous writing or a current assignment, revise a few paragraphs, trying various patterns of semicolon and colon use. Can closely connected sentences be joined effectively with a semicolon? Can clarifications be emphasized by introducing them with a colon? Experimenting with new patterns of punctuation may help you to create variety in your writing and to communicate more fluently.

25   Apostrophes

Apostrophes show possession (usually with an added *s*) and indicate the omission of letters or numbers from words or dates. Errors in the use of apostrophes are easily corrected.

Quick Reference

Apostrophes have two uses: to show possession and to indicate omission.

❯ *Use an apostrophe and an* s *to form the possessive case of words not ending with* s.

❯ *Use only an apostrophe to form the possessive of words ending with* s.

❯ *Use an apostrophe to indicate the omission of letters in contractions and numbers in dates.*

❯ *Do not use apostrophes with possessive pronouns (*yours, theirs*); do not confuse the possessive pronoun* its *with the contraction* it's *("it is").*

25a   **Use apostrophes to form the possessive case.**

Words Not Ending with *S*

Form the possessive of words not ending with *s* by adding an apostrophe and an *s*.

Wyoming*'s* state capitol   Pasteur*'s* discovery

Rockefeller*'s* legacy   a week*'s* wages

everybody's last choice   the atom's nucleus

Saturday's game   *A Room of One's Own*

Words Ending with *S*

Many singular nouns end with an *s*: *virus, Chris, albatross*. Most plural nouns also end in *s*: *clocks, scientists, cats*. Both singular and plural nouns ending in *s* form the possessive by adding an apostrophe only; an additional *s* is unnecessary.

Dickens' *Bleak House*   a United Nations' task force

Paris' night life   Brahms' *Requiem*

⟫⟫⟫ *To check whether the possessive form you have used is correct, mentally eliminate the apostrophe and s or the apostrophe. The word remaining should be the correct one for your meaning. For example, the phrase* earthquake's destruction *without the apostrophe and s refers to only one earthquake; the phrase* earthquakes' destruction *without the apostrophe refers to multiple earthquakes.* **⟪⟪⟪**

Compound Words and Joint Possession

Show possession in compound words or joint possession in a series by adding an apostrophe and *s* to the last noun only.

brother-in-law's objection

General Motors, Ford, and Chrysler's combined profits

the United States and Canada's trade agreement

⟫⟫⟫ *If possession in a series is not joint but individual, each noun in the series must be possessive.*

Angela's, Bert's, and Lionel's fingerprints   (Each person has a separate set of fingerprints.)   **⟪⟪⟪**

Use apostrophes to indicate the omission of letters from contractions and of numbers from dates.

With apostrophe	*Complete form*
shouldn't	should not
I'll	I will *or* I shall
it's	it is
the '89 champions	the 1989 champions

》》 *Use contractions and dates with numbers omitted in informal writing only. In formal writing, present words and dates fully.* **《《**

25c > **Do not use apostrophes with possessive pronouns.**

Possessive pronouns do not require the addition of an apostrophe. Do not be confused by those *(yours, ours, his,* and others) that end in *s.*

Incorrect
    a belief of her's

Correct
    a belief of hers

EXERCISE 25.1 》 *Apostrophes*

 Correct the use of apostrophes in the following sentences. Add needed apostrophes and delete unnecessary ones.

1. Even before people kept record's or conceived of science as a field of study, chemistry exerted its influence on their lives.

2. Early civilizations understanding of elements was primitive — the Greeks' and Romans' four elements were air, earth, fire, and water — but their applications of chemical principles were sophisticated.

3. Today, perhaps, its difficult to understand how much the development of the alloy bronze revolutionized human's lives.

4. During the Middle Ages, alchemists discovered how many chemical compounds work, even though trying to turn metals to gold was a chief preoccupation of their's.

5. By the seventeenth century, scientists studies were more methodical and practical, as was illustrated by Robert Boyles studies' of gases, for example.

6. Even before the development of sophisticated microscopes, John Daltons' theories of atomic elements explained chemical's reactions.

7. Dmitri Mendeleev, Russias foremost early chemist, explained the relationships among elements and devised the periodic tables that still appear on student's tests in classes' in introductory chemistry.

8. Marie Curie's and Pierre Curie's discovery of radium in 1898 further expanded scientist's understanding of chemistry.

9. Alfred B. Nobels' bequest of $9 million made possible awards in science and literature; one of the first five prizes in 1901 was an award for achievement in chemistry.

10. Chemist's work today is aided by sophisticated technology, but their search for knowledge has been shared by scientists' of generation's past.

MAKING C O N N E C T I O N S

- Consider your uses of apostrophes. Locate and analyze your use of apostrophes in one of your papers. Do you use possessive forms accurately? Do you use contractions frequently? Is their use appropriate to your purpose and the required tone of your writing? Do you use apostrophes in contractions correctly?

- Experiment with possessive forms. Possessives are formed with apostrophes, as in *Mary Cassatt's pastel drawings*; but possession can also be expressed in prepositional phrases, as in *the pastel drawings of Mary Cassatt*. Experiment with these alternate methods. Note how the different forms affect the rhythm, concision, and emphasis of the phrase. Be sure to use apostrophes correctly when forming possessives.

Dashes, hyphens, parentheses, brackets, and ellipsis points serve specialized though important purposes in writing. Used effectively, they help to create emphasis and establish meaning.

> ### Quick Reference
>
> *Use specialized marks of punctuation carefully to emphasize elements of your sentences and to clarify your meaning.*
>
> ❯ *Use dashes to introduce parenthetical information, to set off material that contains commas, and to mark interruptions in thought, speech, or action.*
>
> ❯ *Use hyphens to divide words, to form some compound words, and to join some prefixes and suffixes to root words.*
>
> ❯ *Use parentheses in pairs to introduce parenthetical information and numbered or lettered sequences.*
>
> ❯ *Use brackets to indicate alterations to direct quotations.*
>
> ❯ *Use ellipsis points to indicate omissions in direct quotations and to indicate hesitation or suspended statements.*

26a ❯ **Use the dash selectively to introduce parenthetical comments, to set off series, and to indicate breaks or shifts in thought, speech, or action.**

A dash, made by typing two hyphens with no space before or after, introduces parenthetical information emphatically and

C • O • N • N • E • C • T • I • O • N • S

Writers use the specialized forms of punctuation with their purposes and readers in mind. Though sometimes the necessary or even the only possible form with which to punctuate a given sentence construction, these marks are most often used in place of other, more common punctuation for particular effects. The special forms of punctuation achieve their effects largely because they are used infrequently. Larger and more pronounced than most punctuation marks, they draw attention to themselves; they disrupt the flow and rhythm of sentences, creating their own accelerated, retarded, or syncopated rhythms. These changes of rhythm help writers to create and control emphasis and to focus readers' attention.

Because their expressiveness is disruptive and potentially distracting, use special forms of punctuation selectively to avoid diminishing their effectiveness.

clearly, sets off a series at the beginning or end of a sentence, and marks interruptions in thought, speech, or action.

Parenthetical Comments

Parenthetical comments may be single words, phrases, or clauses inserted into a sentence to explain, amplify, or qualify the main idea. Parenthetical comments are grammatically independent of the rest of the sentence. They are frequently marked by parentheses, but those requiring special emphasis are set off with dashes.

American military advisers did not acknowledge the strength and tenacity of the Viet Cong — a costly error.

The reports of atrocities — in particular the My Lai Massacre — changed American attitudes about the war.

397

Appositives (phrases renaming nouns or pronouns) that contain commas may be set off by dashes (in place of commas) for greater clarity.

> Several presidents — Eisenhower, Kennedy, Johnson, and Nixon — were embroiled in political debates about the necessity of American involvement in Vietnam.   (Because the appositive contains three commas, dashes mark the appositive more clearly than commas would mark it.)

A Series

A list of items placed at the beginning of a sentence for special emphasis is followed by a dash.

> The Tiger, the Mako, the Great White — these "man-eating" sharks deserve our respect more than our fear.

A dash may be used to introduce a list informally.

> *Jaws* portrayed most people's reactions to sharks — ignorance, fear, and irrationality.   (In formal writing, use a colon to introduce a list.)

Shifts or Breaks in Thought, Speech, or Action

> Andrew Wyeth's monochromatic paintings — why does he avoid color? — are popular with the American public.   (The dashes mark a shift in thought.)

> Because of cover stories and related articles in scholarly and popular magazines, interest in Wyeth's "Helga" paintings and drawings was intense for several months — and then suddenly subsided.   (The dash marks a break in action.)

Selective Use

The use of dashes to show emphasis and discontinuity disrupts the rhythm of writing. Often, other punctuation serves as well.

Too many dashes

The thunderstorm — coming from the southwest — looked threatening — with black and blue clouds and flashes of lightning. Within a matter of minutes — five to be exact — it was upon us. Around our house, the trees — delicate dogwoods, tall maples, and stout pines — bent in the heavy winds — their branches swaying violently. The black sky, the growing roar, the shaking house — all signaled the approach of a tornado — we headed for the basement.   (Only two uses of the dash are required in this paragraph, with the appositive in the third sentence and with the introductory list in the last. The other uses are technically correct, but the use of fewer dashes would call less attention to the mechanics of the paragraph and allow readers to focus on the events described.)

Better

The thunderstorm coming from the southwest looked threatening, with black and blue clouds and flashes of lightning. Within five minutes, it was upon us. Around our house, the trees — delicate dogwoods, tall maples, and stout pines — bent in the heavy winds, their branches swaying violently. The black sky, the growing roar, the shaking house — all signaled the approach of a tornado. We headed for the basement.

EXERCISE 26.1 ❯ *Dashes*

Use dashes to combine each set of sentences into a single sentence.

1. The Distinguished Service Cross, the Navy Cross, the Silver Star, the Distinguished Flying Cross, the Bronze Star, and the Air Medal are awards given to members of the armed forces. These awards all recognize heroism.

2. Soldiers may be recognized for heroic behavior several times. They do not receive additional medals. Instead, they receive small emblems to pin on the first medal's ribbon.

3. Since 1932, the Purple Heart has been awarded to members of the armed forces who were wounded in combat. The medal is gold and purple, heart-shaped, and embossed with George Washington's image.

4. General George Washington established this military decoration in 1782. It was called the Badge of Military Merit. It wasn't given between 1800 and 1932.

5. The Congressional Medal of Honor is our nation's highest military award. The award was authorized in 1861 for the navy and in 1862 for the army.

 Use hyphens to divide words at the ends of lines, to form some compound nouns and adjectives, and to link some prefixes and suffixes to root words.

Word Division

Hyphens are used to divide words that do not fit in their entirety at the ends of typed or printed lines. Because hyphens must be placed between syllables, one-syllable words cannot be broken. Check your dictionary when you do not know where to divide a word. Other conventions of hyphenation dictate that one or two letters not be isolated on a line and that proper nouns not be divided. When it is not possible or acceptable to hyphenate a word, move the whole word to the next line.

Incorrect

Because of excavation difficulties, the archaeologist thought he'd quit the project.

Correct

Because of excavation difficulties, the archaeologist thought he'd quit the project.

Incorrect

Every year some natural disaster seems to strike Bolivia.   (Proper names should not be divided; two
letters should not be isolated on a single line.)

Correct

Every year some natural disaster seems to strike
Bolivia.

Many word processors can hyphenate words, providing an
alternative to the sometimes awkward spacing that appears
with justified right margins or the ragged edge that appears
with unjustified margins. However, consider the workability
of the word processor's hyphenation before using it. ■
Check the hyphenation pattern. Does the program introduce
hyphens only between syllables? If it does not, do not use
the "hyphenation" feature. ■ Check proper names. A
word-processing program will not distinguish proper names
from other words and will inappropriately hyphenate them.
Check for hyphenated proper names and move any you find
to the next line.

Compound Forms

A compound noun is a pair or group of words that together function as a single noun. Noun compounds may be open (*beer mug*),
closed (*headache*), or hyphenated (*hurly-burly*). If you are unsure about how to present a compound noun, consult a dictionary. If the compound does not appear, it should be spelled open.

father figure	grandfather	mother-in-law
raw silk	snowmobile	go-between
medical examiner	notebook	razzle-dazzle

When modifiers preceding a noun work together to create a single meaning, hyphens emphasize their unity. When the same modifiers follow the noun, hyphens usually are not needed.

Hyphens necessary	*Hyphens unnecessary*
out-of-the-way resort	a resort that is out of the way
long-term investment	an investment for the long term

》》 *When an adverb ending in -ly is the first word of a compound, omit the hyphen.*

Margaret Atwood is a highly inventive writer. **《《**

When spelled out, fractions and cardinal and ordinal numbers from twenty-one through ninety-nine require hyphens. This rule applies whether the numbers are used as nouns, modifiers, or complements.

eighty-two recipes

forty-first president

three-fourths of the taxpayers

one hundred thirty-three bandages

Prefixes and Suffixes

Use hyphens to form words with the prefixes *all-*, *ex-*, and *self-* and with the suffix *-elect*. Other prefixes (*anti-*, *extra-*, *inter-*, *mid-*, *non-*, *over-*, *post-*, *pre-*, and *un-*) and suffixes (*-fold*, *-like*, and *-wide*) are generally spelled closed.

Hyphenate	*Spell closed*
all-consuming ambition	*anti* body
ex-department chairperson	*extra* sensory
self-restraint	*mid* point
president-elect	state *wide*

When prefixes are joined to proper nouns or to compounds consisting of more than one word, hyphens are required. The proper nouns are capitalized.

un-American

post-World War II

non-native speakers

pre-Columbian

When a prefix has the same last letter as the first letter of the root word (or when a suffix has the same first letter as the last letter of the root word), hyphens are sometimes used for clarity.

anti-intellectual

bell-like

When the omission of a hyphen would result in ambiguity, a hyphen should be used.

release ("let go")	re-lease ("to lease again")
reform ("to improve")	re-form ("to form again")
unionized ("formed into a union")	un-ionized ("not ionized")

EXERCISE 26.2 ❯ *Hyphens*

> **!** Add or delete hyphens to correct the use of hyphens in the following sentences. (Some of the hyphens are used correctly.)

1. In the United States, senators are elected to six year terms, presidents (and their vice presidents) to four year terms, and members of Congress to two year terms.

2. Although these electoral guidelines are un-changed, little else about modern day elections has remained the way our national founders conceived them.

3. In pre-computer elections, hand-tabulated ballots were the norm, and results often were not certain for days.

4. Today, with computer-aided counting, officials post fully three fourths of election returns by mid-night of election day.

5. Television-networks quickly project the results of today's elections, usually on the basis of less than one fiftieth of the ballots cast.

6. Consequently, presidents elect now make victory speeches before mid-night on election day, rather than at mid-morning on the following day. Times have clearly changed.

26c ❯	**Use parentheses selectively, always in pairs, to introduce parenthetical comments and numbered or lettered sequences.**

Parenthetical Comments

Use parentheses to set off information that is only casually related to the flow of ideas in the rest of the sentence; essential information deserves direct presentation. Do not include long explanations parenthetically.

Joan of Arc (only seventeen at the time) led military troops to help return the rightful king of France to the throne.   (The information about Joan of Arc's age supplements the main idea; it is appropriately set off by parentheses.)

Parentheses are less emphatic and more disruptive than dashes, which are used for a similar purpose. The overuse of parentheses makes writing seem uneven, incoherent, or immature. To avoid such problems, use parentheses only when no other strategy or punctuation will serve your purpose.

Choppy

The compass (scratched and cracked) should have been replaced (years ago), but Joaquín (reluctant to spend the money) preferred to keep it as it was.   (The rhythm of the sentence is broken by the disruptive use of parenthetical details, some of which should be incorporated in the main sentence.)

Better

The scratched and cracked compass should have been replaced years ago, but Joaquín, reluctant to spend the money, preferred to keep it as it was.

⟩⟩⟩ *Although you should use such complex patterns of punctuation sparingly, add clarifications of elements in parentheses using brackets, as in the following example:*

HMS ("Her [or His] Majesty's Ship") *Reliant* **⟨⟨⟨**

Numbered or Lettered Sequences

The numbering or lettering of steps can help clarify the steps of a complicated sequence of events or a process. Such lists, however, may be more distracting than helpful. Use them with care.

Freezing green beans involves six steps: (1) snap the ends off the beans; (2) wash the beans thoroughly in water; (3) blanch the beans for two to three minutes in boiling water; (4) cool them in ice water; (5)

drain them for several minutes and then pack them into freezer containers; (6) seal the containers, label them, and put them in the freezer.

| 26d | **Use brackets selectively, always in pairs, to indicate alterations in a direct quotation.** |

Brackets indicate alterations in quoted material. If your typewriter does not have brackets, leave spaces when you type and insert brackets by hand.

Clarification

When quotations out of context are not clear, use brackets to add clarifying information. Add only information that makes the original meaning clear; never add contradictory information or negative comments.

> Davies commented, "The army nurses' judgment in triage [where the medical staff decides which patients to treat first] is paramount, for they must determine a soldier's medical stability in a matter of seconds."   (The bracketed material explains a key term, and the brackets indicate that the writer, not Davies, defined *triage*.)

> "If architectural preservationists are unsuccessful in their efforts, most [theaters built in the early 1900s] will probably be demolished by the end of the century," Walter Aspen noted.   (In place of the bracketed material, the original read "of these fascinating buildings," an unclear reference outside of the original context.)

Alteration of Syntax

Use brackets to indicate changes in the syntax of a quoted passage. Make only minor changes — changes in verb tense, for instance — that allow you to insert a passage smoothly into the context of your writing. Do not alter the meaning of the original.

Immigrants were sometimes confused or ambivalent about a new life in the United States. As a journalist noted in 1903, "Each day, thousands of immigrants [moved] through the turnstiles at Ellis Island, uncertain but hopeful."   (The brackets show a change from the present tense *move,* which was appropriate in 1903, to the past tense *moved,* which is appropriate in current contexts.)

Notation of Error

When a direct quotation contains an error in grammar or fact, you must still transcribe the wording of the original exactly. However, to indicate for readers that you recognize the error and have not introduced it yourself, insert the word *sic* (Latin for "thus") in brackets following the faulty element.

Adderson noted in her preface, "The taxpayers who [sic] the legislation will protect are the elderly, the handicapped, and those in low-income families."   (*Sic* notes that the writer recognized Adderson's misuse of *who* for *whom.*)

》》》 *To avoid seeming overly critical or pedantic, use* sic *only when necessary for clarity. The writer of the sentence above, for example, could have avoided using* [sic] *by rephrasing the sentence.*

Adderson noted in her preface that those protected by the legislation are "the elderly, the handicapped, and those in low-income families." **《《《**

26e | **Use ellipsis points to indicate omissions from quoted material and to indicate hesitating, trailing, or incomplete statements.**

Ellipsis points are three *spaced* periods. Other marks of punctuation (periods, question marks, exclamation points, commas, and so on) are separated from ellipsis points by one space. Place ellip-

sis points either before or after the original punctuation, depending on the original sentence.

Omissions from Quoted Material

Use ellipsis points in quoted material to indicate where you have
omitted extraneous information, parenthetical details, or unnecessary clarifications. Never omit words to change the original
meaning of a source.

Original version

"The Ninth Street Station is a superb example of ornate woodworking
and stonework. Typical of Steamboat-Gothic architecture, it was designed in 1867 by Fielding Smith. It is a landmark we should endeavor
to preserve."

Acceptable cut version

"The Ninth Street Station is a superb example of ornate woodworking
and stonework. . . . It is a landmark we should endeavor to preserve."
(Note the retention of the period at the end of the first sentence.)

Original version

"Theaters, such as the magnificent edifices built by the Lowe and Fox
families, aging public buildings, and deteriorating commercial buildings in prime business locations are often demolished to provide space
for new office buildings with little architectural interest."

Acceptable cut version

"Theaters . . . , aging public buildings, and deteriorating commercial
buildings in prime business locations are often demolished to provide
space for new office buildings with little architectural interest."   (The
ellipsis points mark the omission of secondary material; the comma
before *aging* is retained to separate the items in the series.)

Original version
  "This is a great movie if you enjoy meaningless violence, gratuitous sex, inane dialogue, and poor acting. It is offensive by any standards."

Dishonest cut version
  "This is a great movie . . . by any standards."   (This is a misquotation.)

Hesitating, Trailing, or Incomplete Statements

More common in dialogue, especially in fiction, than in expository writing, the use of ellipsis points to indicate hesitating, trailing, or incomplete thoughts and statements can be effective if it is used sparingly.

Woody Allen's *Stardust Memories* was . . . boring.

From the back of the crowded elevator Chie shouted, "I have important news about. . . ." But the doors closed before she could finish.

EXERCISE 26.3 ❯   *Parentheses, brackets, and ellipsis points*

> *Correct the faulty use of parentheses, brackets, and ellipsis points in the following sentences.*

1. To install a cable converter, simply follow these directions: 1) remove the converter from the box; 2) attach the blue adapter wires to your television set; 3) plug the converter into an electrical outlet; 4) select a channel and test the equipment by turning it on.

2. "The benefits (to those who subscribe to cable services) are amazingly varied, from more programs to better programs," explained Ms. Abigail Fitzgerald, a cable network spokesperson.

3. Most cable subscribers would agree that they are offered more...
   but is it better?

4. Professor Martínez, media specialist at ASU, commented: "Much of
   what's offered is junk . . . When *Mr. Ed, Car 54,* and *The Munsters*
   make it to national rebroadcast, we have to question the uses to
   which cable is put. Of course, that's the long-standing issue (in television broadcasting)."

5. Then again, people (the American people in particular) have always enjoyed (really enjoyed) some mindless entertainment (*unchallenging* is, perhaps, a better word) to relieve the tension (and
   frustration) of the day.

EXERCISE 26.4 ❯ *Punctuation review*

Punctuate the following paragraph.

The Postal Reorganization Act signed into law by President Nixon on
August 12 1970 created a government-owned postal service operated under the executive branch of the government the new US Postal Service is
run by an eleven-member board with members appointed by the president of the Senate for nine-year terms the Postmaster General who is no
longer part of the president's cabinet is selected by the members of the
board since 1971 when the system began operating four men have
served as Postmaster General Winton M Blount E T Klassen Benjamin F
Bailar and William F Bolger but has the postal system changed substantially since the PRA went into effect on July 1 1971 no not to any great
extent first class second class third class and fourth class these still represent the most commonly used mailing rates however some services have
been added for instance Express Mail which tries to rival Federal Express
Purolator and other one-day delivery services guarantees that packages
will arrive at their destinations by 300 the day after mailing the prices are
steep as one might expect in addition the Postal Service has instituted
nine-digit zip codes in some areas for all practical purposes however the
business at 29990 post offices throughout the US continues in much the
same way it did before the PRA

Word processing and specialized punctuation

Use a word processor to experiment with varied punctuation and to help you locate and check the correct use of specialized marks of punctuation.

Locate dashes, hyphens, parentheses, brackets, and ellipsis points in your writing. Use "search" codes to find each form of punctuation. Check sentences carefully to make sure that you have used these special punctuation marks correctly.

Experiment with varied punctuation. Because word-processing programs allow you to modify your work without completely retyping, experiment with alternative forms of punctuation to create various kinds of emphasis.

MAKING C O N N E C T I O N S

Explore the possibilities of using specialized marks of punctuation. Practice using each kind. Although you will not want to overuse these specialized forms in papers that you plan to submit, practice using them by overusing them. Return to a paper completed earlier and use dashes in every position possible, for instance. By experimenting with overuse, you will discover uses that do, in fact, improve your sentences.

MECHANICS

C · O · N · N · E · C · T · I · O · N · S

Mechanics describes a set of principles and content-determined patterns that helps writers to convey ideas. It constitutes an important code shared by writers and readers. Consider, for example, how italics, quotation marks, and changes in capitalization affect the meaning of the phrase *the sound of music* in these sentences.

We could hear the sound of music as we entered the lobby. (This phrase conveys only the denotation of the combined words.)

Rodgers and Hammerstein's *The Sound of Music* is a perennial favorite in regional musical theaters. (Capitals and italics indicate that the subject of this sentence is a play.)

"The Sound of Music" as sung by Julie Andrews is perhaps the best-known song from the film version of the musical play. (Capitals and quotation marks indicate that the subject of this sentence is a song.)

The use of mechanics, then, is not merely mechanical. Rather, correct choices in mechanics, determined by sentence content, help readers to understand a writer's meaning.

27 Capitals

Capitals indicate the beginnings of sentences, signal proper nouns and proper adjectives, and identify important words in titles. Appropriate capitalization contributes to the clarity and correctness of your writing. Since unnecessary capitalization is confusing and annoying to readers, make sure when capitalizing a word that an upper-case letter is required.

> **Quick Reference**
>
> *Capitals are used to create special emphasis.*
>
> ❯ *Capitalize the first word in every sentence.*
>
> ❯ *Capitalize proper nouns and proper adjectives.*
>
> ❯ *Capitalize first, last, and important words in titles.*

27a ❯ Capitalize the first word in every sentence.

Subtitles in foreign films can be as distracting as they are helpful.

⟫⟫ *When a complete sentence follows a colon, capitalizing the first word is optional.*

The Declaration of Independence presents an idea we should remember: *All* people are created equal.   ⟪⟪

Apply this rule when quoting a complete sentence.

The senator remarked, *"Initiating* dialogue among national leaders is an important step in solving problems in the Middle East."

»»» *In long, interrupted quotations, only words that begin sentences are capitalized.*

> *"Prospects* for peace in the Middle East exist," the senator reiterated, "only if leaders negotiate in good faith." **«««**

| 27b | > | **Capitalize proper nouns and proper adjectives.** |

Proper nouns and proper adjectives refer to specific people, places, and things and are therefore capitalized.

> In August, the Benton Teachers' Association voted to strike.   (specific name, capitals required)

But:

> In August, the teachers' union voted to strike.   (general noun, no capitals required)

Treat the pronoun *I* as a proper noun.

> I want to sail to the Bahamas, but I've got to earn some money first.

Names of specific individuals, races, ethnic groups, nationalities, languages, and places

Proper Nouns	Proper Adjectives
Samuel Johnson	Shakespearean sonnet
Caucasian	Egyptian border
Chicano	Hispanic traditions
New Yorker	of German descent
Portuguese	Portuguese trade

Kenya	Belgian lace
Southern Alps	Alpine village
African-Americans	African-American organization

》》》 *Registered trade names and trademarks, even those for common objects, must be capitalized.*

Coke   Scotch tape   Kleenex   Xerox **《《**

Names of historical periods, events, and documents

the Age of Reason

the Battle of Bull Run

the Declaration of Independence

Names of days, months, and holidays

Monday   August   Valentine's Day

Do not capitalize the names of seasons (*winter, spring, summer,* and *autumn*).

Names of organizations and government branches and departments

Phi Beta Kappa

Greenpeace

the House of Representatives

the Department of Transportation

Names of educational institutions, departments, specific courses, and degrees

Brown University	Belleville High School
Department of Education	School of Nursing

1. art 426 (or english 426) is an interdisciplinary course that offers a survey of important artists and writers.

2. the course is team-taught by dr. nicholas bradford of the english department and ms. marlene jacobs of the art department.

3. during the fall of last year, i took the course to fulfill a humanities requirement.

4. we read a portion of dante's *divine comedy* — but not in italian — and saw slides of michelangelo's frescoes on the ceiling of the sistine chapel, both presenting perspectives on italian religious views.

5. we saw numerous paintings depicting the nativity, the crucifixion, and the ascension and read several religious poems.

6. turning our attention from europe, we saw *habuko landscape* by sesshu, a sixteenth-century japanese painter, and read samples of haiku poetry to learn of the spare but elegant images both create.

7. italian and flemish artists dominated the months of october and november.

8. we learned, however, that by the 1800s, neo-classicism had emerged and artistic dominance had shifted to france, where it remained for over a century; we read corneille's *phaedre* and saw representative paintings by david and ingres.

9. Over thanksgiving break, i took an optional field trip with ms. jacobs and several other students; we went to the art institute of chicago, her alma mater, to view their collection.

10. by the time we studied abstract art, national and artistic boundaries had been broken and painters like picasso and poets like t. s. eliot could be said to draw upon the same aesthetic traditions.

11. when ms. jacobs first said, "the fine arts are symbiotic, each reciprocally influencing the other," i wasn't sure i understood what she meant. now i think i know.

MAKING   C O N N E C T I O N S

Capitals, used properly, add clarity to sentences, but if overused create confusion.

- Consider your use of capitals. Review your written work, looking particularly for instances where necessary capitals were omitted. Are sentences confusing? What is the effect of any unnecessary capitals you may have used?

- Classify your incorrect uses of capitals. List the capitalization errors you find in your sentences so that you can refer to the list as you write and revise.

28 Italics

Italics distinguish titles of complete published works (except articles, essays, and short stories and poems, which require quotation marks): books; journals, magazines, and newspapers; works of art, the specific names of ships, trains, aircraft, and spacecraft; foreign words used in English sentences; and words or phrases requiring special emphasis.

In a printed text, italics are indicated with slanted type (*like this*), but in a typed or handwritten text, italics are indicated with underlining (like this). The meaning is the same.

Quick Reference

Use italics to create your intended meaning.

❯ *Use italics to distinguish some titles, generally those of complete works.*

❯ *Italicize the specific names of ships, trains, aircraft, and spacecraft.*

❯ *Italicize unfamiliar foreign words and phrases.*

❯ *Italicize words used as words, letters as letters, and numbers as numbers.*

❯ *Italicize words to create special emphasis.*

28a ❯ **Italicize the titles of most complete published works.**

The titles of books, journals, magazines, newspapers, pamphlets, plays, and long poems are italicized. Parts of long works, such as chapter titles, and titles of articles, essays, and short stories and poems are presented in quotation marks. Titles of long musical compositions, albums, films, radio and television programs, paintings, statues, and other artworks are also italicized.

Books

Joseph Heller's *Catch-22*

Zora Neale Hurston's *Their Eyes Were Watching God*

》》》 The Bible, books of the Bible (Song of Solomon, Genesis), and legal documents (the Constitution) are not italicized, although they are capitalized. **《《《**

Magazines and journals

Business Week

American Scholar

Charles Simic's essay "Reading Philosophy at Night" from *Antaeus*

Newspapers

the *Kansas City Star*

the *New York Times*

Long poems

John Milton's *Paradise Lost*

Walt Whitman's *Leaves of Grass*

But: Elizabeth Bishop's brief poem "In the Waiting Room"

Long musical compositions

Igor Stravinski's *Firebird Suite*

Giacomo Puccini's opera *Madame Butterfly*

Albums

Kathleen Battle and Christopher Parkening's *Pleasures of Their Company*

the Beatles' *Abbey Road*

Tracy Chapman's "Fast Car" from her album *Tracy Chapman*

Plays

Neil Simon's *Brighton Beach Memoirs*

Edward Albee's *Zoo Story*

Films

Rainman

The Wizard of Oz

Radio and television programs

All Things Considered

Cheers

》》》 Although italic type is required for the name of a television series, the titles of episodes (daily, weekly, or monthly segments) are enclosed in quotation marks.

"Antarctica: Earth's Last Frontier" airs Tuesday at nine on *NOVA*. **《《《**

Paintings

Pablo Picasso's *Three Musicians*

Georgia O'Keeffe's *Black Iris III*

Statues

Rodin's *The Thinker*

Michelangelo's *David*

Pamphlets

NCTE's *How to Help Your Child Become a Better Writer*

Roberta Greene's *'Til Divorce Do You Part*

28b ▷ **Italicize the specific names of ships, trains, aircraft, and spacecraft.**

Only specific names are italicized and capitalized. The names of vehicle types and models are capitalized but not italicized. Abbreviations such as *SS* ("Steamship") and *HMS* ("Her [or His] Majesty's Ship") are not italicized.

Ships

Queen Elizabeth II

HMS *Wellington*

Andrea Doria

But: Starcraft Marlin, cruiser series XL

Trains

Orient Express

Stourbridge Lion

Aircraft

The Spirit of St. Louis

The Spruce Goose

But: Boeing 707

Spacecraft

Apollo I

Sputnik II

<table>
<tr><td>28c</td><td>Italicize unfamiliar foreign words and phrases in English sentences.</td></tr>
</table>

If a foreign word or phrase is likely to be unfamiliar to your readers, italicize it.

> Andrea Palladio made frequent use of *trompe l'oeil* effects and murals in his villa designs.

The English language has borrowed extensively from the vocabularies of other languages. Some terms — such as *coffee, coupon, kasha, cliché,* and *kindergarten* — are fully assimilated into standard American usage and do not require italics. A standard college dictionary will help you to distinguish among unfamiliar, familiar, and assimilated foreign words. If a foreign word or phrase is not found in the dictionary (*cinéma vérité, perestroika*), it is likely to be recently imported or unfamiliar to your readers and should be italicized. If a foreign word or phrase is labeled in the dictionary as foreign (*adiós, coup de théâtre*), it may be unfamiliar to your readers; italics are optional. A word that is not labeled need not be italicized, even though the etymology indicates that it has been borrowed (*coup d'état, kibbutz*). **▶▶▶** *When using any but the most common foreign terms, observe all conventions of spelling, including accents and other marks, found in the original language.* **◀◀◀**

<table>
<tr><td>28d</td><td>Italicize words used as words, letters used as letters, and numbers used as numbers.</td></tr>
</table>

> "The *s* was put in *island,* for instance, in sheer pedantic ignorance." — Bergen Evans

> According to numerology, the numbers *5, 7, 12,* and *13* have occult significance.

28e > **Use italics selectively for emphasis.**

Italics may be used to call attention to words requiring emphasis, to signal a contrast, and to ensure close and careful examination of words by the reader.

> "It makes a world of difference to a condemned man whether his reprieve is *upheld* or *held up*." — Bergen Evans

Use italics very selectively to create emphasis. Emphasis should be created by effective diction and sentence structure. Overuse of italics dilutes emphasis and may distort the tone of your writing. By mimicking heavily stressed speech, overuse of italics may create an impression of irony or even cynicism that you do not intend. (See also section 29d.)

EXERCISE 28.1 > *Italics*

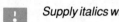

Supply italics where they are needed in the following sentences.

1. E. D. Hirsch's Cultural Literacy: What Every American Needs to Know — especially its appended list — has created a fascinating controversy since its publication.

2. For instance, Herman Melville's name is on the list, but his famous novel Moby Dick is not.

3. The statues David and the Pietà in St. Peter's Church in Vatican City are listed, but their creator Michelangelo does not appear.

4. Many of the foreign phrases — including ancien régime, bête noire, coup d'état, déjà vu, faux pas, fin de siècle, and tête-à-tête — are French, although a large number are Latin.

5. The Niña, Pinta, and Santa Maria do not appear, but the unfortunate Lusitania and Titanic do.

6. The maudlin poem *Hiawatha* and its author Henry Wadsworth Longfellow both appear, but *Paradise Lost*, the brilliant epic poem, appears without its author John Milton.

7. *Birth of a Nation* is the only film on the list not produced first as a book or play with the same name.

8. The absence of *I Love Lucy*, *The Dick Van Dyke Show*, *The Mary Tyler Moore Show*, *All in the Family*, and *M*A*S*H* makes it clear that popular television culture does not concern Hirsch.

9. Oddly enough, the ampersand (&) appears on the list.

10. Including the novel *Tobacco Road* on the list but not the play *Who's Afraid of Virginia Woolf?* seems arguable, but the enjoyment in lists is in disagreeing with them.

Word processing and italics

Word processors allow you to use italics easily, without extra typing.

Choose between slanted italic print and underlining. With some word processors and some printers, italic automatically prints as underlining. Some, however, give you the choice of using slanted italic. Before you choose slanted italic, look at a sample print-out. If the slanted type is difficult to read, choose underlining instead; the meaning will be the same.

Insert codes for slanted italic or underlining carefully. Once you enter a code, be sure to toggle out of the code; otherwise, your printer will continue the italics. If your word processor uses control marks in the text, rather than more visible contrasting bars, give this special attention.

Do not use codes for boldface in place of codes for italics. Many people enjoy experimenting with the typefaces made available by word processors and compatible printers, but boldface print is not an acceptable substitute for italics.

Accents and other diacritical marks are available on most word processors and printers. Learn how they work on yours and practice using them.

MAKING   C O N N E C T I O N S

Adding italics helps to create meaning by distinguishing specific words and phrases. Learn to use italics correctly and effectively to enhance the clarity of your writing.

- Consider the uses of italics most common to your writing. Do you write frequently about films, books, paintings, or television series? Are you interested in music and inclined to write about albums?

- Take advantage of the ways italics clarify meaning by distinguishing one kind of work from another. For instance, *Tommy,* the rock musical by The Who, is distinguished from "Tommy," one of the songs in the musical, and from Tommy, the title character. Consider similar distinctions that you might want to make in your own writing.

Quotation marks set off direct quotations and identify the titles of unpublished and short works and chapters and other sections of long works.

Quick Reference

Use quotation marks in one of three ways:

❯ *Use quotation marks to set off direct quotations.*

❯ *Use quotation marks with the titles of brief works, parts of longer works, and unpublished works.*

❯ *Use quotation marks to indicate ironic or special use of a word.*

29a ❯ **Use quotation marks with direct quotations and with dialogue.**

Direct Quotations

Direct quotations represent spoken or written words exactly; quotation marks indicate where the quoted material begins and ends. In contrast, indirect quotations—often introduced by *that* for statements or *if* for questions—report what people say or ask without using their exact words. Quotation marks are not needed with indirect quotations.

> John Kenneth Galbraith commented, "In the affluent society no useful distinction can be made between luxuries and necessities."   (The exact words are enclosed in quotation marks.)

But:

> Galbraith argues that, in an affluent society, the necessary and the desirable become inextricably mixed. (The paraphrase of Galbraith's comment needs no quotation marks, though it does require attribution and documentation.)

Dialogue

In dialogue, a record of a conversation between two or more people, quotation marks indicate the exact words used by each speaker in turn. By convention, each change of speaker begins a new paragraph.

> . . . I felt that I was getting a better sense of the language from novels than from grammars. I read hard, discarding a writer as soon as I felt I had grasped his point of view. At night the printed page stood before my eyes in sleep.
>
> Mrs. Moss, my landlady, asked me one Sunday morning:
>
> "Son, what is this you keep on reading?"
>
> "Oh, nothing. Just novels."
>
> "What you get out of 'em?"
>
> "I'm just killing time," I said.
>
> "I hope you know your own mind," she said in a tone that implied that she doubted if I had a mind.—Richard Wright, "The Library Card"

 29b ⟩ **Place punctuation marks with quotation marks according to convention.**

Periods and Commas

Periods and commas appear before closing quotation marks.

> One of Flannery O'Connor's most haunting stories is "The River."

> "The Circus Animals' Desertion," a late poem by William Butler Yeats, describes his growing frustration with poetry.

Semicolons and Colons

Semicolons and colons always follow closing quotation marks.

> As a young poet, T. S. Eliot showed his brilliance in "The Love Song of J. Alfred Prufrock"; readers and critics responded to it enthusiastically.

> One word describes Lewis Carroll's "Jabberwocky": nonsense.

Question Marks and Exclamation Points

Question marks and exclamation points must be placed to maintain the meaning of the sentence. If the material in quotation marks (whether a direct quotation or a title) ends with a question mark, then the closing quotation mark appears last. If your sentence is a question that contains material in quotation marks, then the question mark appears last. The same principles apply to the use of exclamation points with quotation marks.

> Was it Archibald MacLeish who wrote "A world ends when its metaphor has died"?   (The quotation is contained within the question.)

> Have you read Ralph Ellison's "Did You Ever Dream Lucky?"   (The question mark inside the quotation marks serves both the question in the title and the question posed by the sentence.)

⟫⟫⟫ *If a quotation ends with a question mark or exclamation point, any other punctuation normally required by the sentence structure may be omitted.*

> I just read Ralph Ellison's "Did You Ever Dream Lucky?"

> "Which is the right road?" he asked, but he received no reply.   (A comma is unnecessary following the question mark.)   **⟪⟪⟪**

Use quotation marks with the titles of brief works, parts of long works, and unpublished works.

Articles, short stories, short poems, essays, and songs are brief works whose titles should appear in quotation marks. Chapter or unit titles and episodes of television series require quotation marks because they are parts of long works. Titles of unpublished papers or dissertations of any length are placed in quotation marks.

Articles

"Good News Is No News" in *Esquire*

"The New World Through New Eyes" in *Smithsonian*

Short stories

Charles Baxter's "A Fire Story"

Isaac Bashevis Singer's "Gimpel the Fool"

Poems

Emily Dickinson's "Because I Could Not Stop for Death"

Theodore Roethke's "My Papa's Waltz"

Essays

Joan Didion's "Why I Write"

James Thurber's "University Days"

Songs

Sarah Vaughn's "How Long Has This Been Going On?"

George and Ira Gershwin's "Summertime"

Chapter or unit titles

"Theatre of the Orient" in O. G. Brockett's *History of the Theatre*

"Nightmare" in *The Autobiography of Malcolm X*

Episodes of television programs

"The Death of Chuckles the Clown" from *The Mary Tyler Moore Show*

"Captain Tuttle" from *M*A*S*H*

Unpublished papers and dissertations

"Prohibition in the New England States"

"The Poetic Heritage of John Donne"

| 29d | **Use quotation marks sparingly to indicate an ironic or other special use of a word.** |

Words should be used according to their accepted meanings. The use of quotation marks to indicate irony may confuse and annoy readers. The use of quotation marks with nonstandard words— slang, regionalisms, or jargon—shows that you understand the words' potential inappropriateness in a sentence but does not justify their use. Either use the word with assurance or choose another word. (See also section 28e.)

Ironic use

Who needs enemies with "friends" like these?   (Clearly *friends* is being used ironically. The phrase *so-called friends* would convey the same meaning more clearly.)

Disavowal

The negotiator asked for our "input."   (Placing *input* in quotation marks suggests that the writer knows it is unacceptable jargon, but the disavowal does not make the word acceptable. Unless you are quoting directly, use a better word, such as *reactions, responses,* or *thoughts.*)

EXERCISE 29.1 ❯ *Quotation marks*

Place the needed quotation marks in the following sentences. Pay attention to their positioning with other punctuation.

1. Running on Empty? an article in *National Wildlife,* stresses that water management should be a universal concern.

2. The opening chapter of *The Grapes of Wrath* contains this central image: The rain-heads [thunderclouds] dropped a little spattering and hurried on to some other country. Behind them the sky was pale again and the sun flared. In the dust there were drop craters where the rain had fallen, and there were clean splashes on the corn, and that was all.

3. Dry as Dust, a local documentary on the plight of the Depression farmers, had special meaning in 1988, when water shortages occurred throughout the midwestern states.

4. The very real fear of drought was softened during the Depression by ironic songs like What We Gonna Do When the Well Runs Dry?

5. Nadene Benchley's dissertation, Deluge or Drought: The Crisis in Water Management, ought to be published, for it contains information many people need to know.

MAKING C O N N E C T I O N S

Quotation marks are a relatively specialized form of punctuation. Nonetheless, consider how you use them or how you can use them to improve the clarity, variety, and effectiveness of your writing.

- Consider your present uses of quotation marks. How and how often do you use them? Do you use them correctly? Do you use them effectively?

- Consider special uses for quotation marks. Do you use dialogue in your writing to recreate conversations and to create variety? What effect might such dialogues create? Try incorporating brief dialogues in your journal, in notes, or in papers (especially narrative, descriptive, persuasive, or research papers using interviews). What is their effect?

30 Numbers and Abbreviations

Quick Reference

Use numbers and abbreviations according to convention.

❯ *In most instances, write out numbers expressible in one or two words.*

❯ *Use figures for exact numbers starting with 101.*

❯ *Use figures for measurements, technical numbers, and fractions.*

❯ *Use abbreviations sparingly in formal writing; if you use them, use standard abbreviations and forms.*

| 30a | **In most writing contexts, use the written forms of numbers expressible in one or two words.** |

Numbers Expressible in Words

Unless you are writing scientific or technical material, cardinal and ordinal numbers expressible in one or two words should be written out. This rule applies to numbers *one* through *one hundred* (*first* through *one hundredth*) and to large round numbers like *four thousand* (*four thousandth*) and *nine million* (*nine millionth*).

The Soviet Union has four cities — Moscow, Leningrad, Tashkent, and Kiev — with populations of more than two million.

❯❯❯ *Numbers from twenty-one through ninety-nine must be hyphenated.* ❮❮❮

Numbers at the beginning of a sentence must be spelled out — no matter how many words are needed. If the number is long and awkward, revise the sentence.

Incorrect

115 seniors attended graduation.

Correct

One hundred fifteen seniors attended graduation.

Better

We counted 115 seniors at graduation.

Numbers Expressible in Figures

Exact cardinal and ordinal numbers starting with 101 should be expressed in figures.

The Rogun Dam, the tallest in the world, stands 1,066 feet high.

| 30b | **Use abbreviations sparingly in formal writing and only in contexts in which their meaning is clear.** |

With few exceptions, abbreviations should not be used in formal writing. Commonly used personal titles such as *Ms., Mr.,* and *Dr.* are acceptable; also acceptable are some commonly used and easily recognizable abbreviations such as *JFK* and *NAACP.* If you are unsure whether your readers will recognize an abbreviation, spell out the words.

If you choose to use a common abbreviation for a person or organization in formal writing, the first mention should include the full name, followed by the abbreviation in parentheses.

Other Numbers Expressible in Figures	
Addresses	316 Ridge Place; 1111 West 16th Street
Dates	24 December 1948 (*or* December 24, 1948); 150 B.C.; A.D. 1066
Divisions of books and plays	chapter 3; volume 9; act 2; scene 4
Exact dollar amounts	$3.12; $546 million; $7,279,000
Measurements	8 by 10
Identification numbers	332-44-7709; UTC 88 22495
Percentages	82 percent; 100 percent
Fractions	3/4
Scores	101 to 94
Times	3:15 A.M.; 7:45 P.M. (*but* four-thirty in the morning; nine o'clock)

The Potato Chip/Snack Food Association (PC/SFA) is an international trade association. Like other trade associations, the PC/SFA monitors government actions that affect the business of its members.

》》》 *Many common abbreviations may be written without periods. Check your dictionary for acceptable forms.* **《《《**

Certain specialized writing situations — technical directions, recipes, entries for works cited pages, résumés — use abbreviations to save space; but formal, academic writing should not. Instead, write the words out completely.

Acceptable Abbreviations

Well-known personal names	LBJ (Lyndon Baines Johnson); FDR (Franklin Delano Roosevelt)
Personal titles	John Walton, Jr.; Rebecca Santos, Ph.D.; Ms. Ella Beirbaum; Harold Blankenbaker, M.D.; Dr. Asha Mustapha; Rev. Joshua Felten; Gov. Michael S. Dukakis (*but* Governor Dukakis)
Names of countries	USA, US (*or* U.S.A., U.S.); UK (*or* U.K.); USSR (*or* U.S.S.R.)
Names of organizations and corporations	UNESCO; GE; FAA; AT&T
Words with figures	no. 133 (*or* No.)
Time of day	1:05 P.M. (*or* p.m.)
Dates	1200 B.C.; A.D. 476

Use the spell checker of your word-processing program to help you discover irregular abbreviations. ■ Run the spelling program. Because spelling programs include only a sampling of abbreviations, only the most common, most generally accepted ones are part of the dictionary. Reconsider your use of any abbreviations that the speller brings to your attention. ■ Check a dictionary in special instances. If you want to use the abbreviation anyway, check a dictionary to make sure that it is correct.

Unacceptable Abbreviations		
	Not	*But*
Business designations	Co. Inc.	Company Incorporated
Units of measurement	lb. cm	pound centimeter
Names of days and months	Fri. Oct.	Friday October
Academic subjects	psych. Eng.	psychology English
Divisions of books and plays	p. chap. sc. vol.	page chapter scene volume
Names of places	L.A. VT	Los Angeles Vermont
Personal names	Wm. Robt.	William Robert
Latin phrases	cf. (*confer*) e.g. (*exempli gratia*) et al. (*et alii*) etc. (*et cetera*) i.e. (*id est*)	compare for example and others and so on, and others that is

Numbers and Abbreviations n/ab 30b

EXERCISE 30.1 ❱ *Numbers and abbreviations*

Correct the misuse of number forms and abbreviations in the following sentences.

1. Doctor Ruth Waller, an econ. prof. at UCLA, has written 26 articles and 2 books about Asian-American trade relations.

2. 1 of her books and 14 of her articles are on reserve at the ISU library — to be read by students in Econ. two-hundred and thirty-six.

3. Statistics in one article show that Japan's labor force is well diversified, with eleven percent in agriculture, thirty-four percent in manufacturing, and forty-eight percent in services.

4. Statistics also show that the Am. labor force is not as well diversified: we have seventy percent in services, with close to one-third of those in info. management.

5. By Fri., Dec. twelfth, each of us in the class must prepare a report on a US co. that is affected by Asian-American trade.

EXERCISE 30.2 ❱ *Numbers and abbreviations*

Correct the misuse of number forms and abbreviations in the following paragraph.

Walter E. Disney, better known as Walt, was born Dec. fifth, 1901, in Chicago. After early work at the Chicago Academy of fine arts and at a Commercial Art firm in MO, he moved to Hollywood in nineteen-twenty-three. It was there that he revolutionized US entertainment. 1928 was the year he produced "Steamboat Willie," a short cartoon that introduced Mickey Mouse, as well as the use of soundtracks with cartoons. 10 years later, his studio produced the 1st feature-length animated cartoon, *Snow White and the 7 Dwarfs,* and 2 years later, *Pinocchio.* The success of Disney's films stemmed from their innovations, i.e. their use of animated forms, color, music, voices, and story. After more than 12 successful films, Disney began work in television in 1950. In 55, Disneyland opened outside L.A., and Disney's theme parks created a new standard for amusement parks. Few would have suspected, in nineteen-twenty-six, that the man whose first cartoon creation was Oswald the Rabbit would change entertainment in the US of A.

MAKING   C O N N E C T I O N S

Inconsistencies and errors in the use of numbers or abbreviations can be avoided or revised easily if you learn the rules that apply to the type of writing you do.

- Review your written work. What samples of number and abbreviation use do you find? Do you discover any inappropriate, incorrect, or inconsistent uses?

- Make a list of your regular uses of numbers and abbreviations. Taking this list as a pattern, make a brief personal guide, perhaps on an index card, to refer to as you write and revise.

---

31 Spelling

Many writers have spelling problems. Although these can sometimes be solved by reliance on familiar spelling rules (for example, *i* before *e*, except after *c*), spelling rules in English have many exceptions because English words derive from so many language groups. When you are uncertain of the spelling of a word, immediately consult a dictionary. Also develop practical strategies for overcoming spelling problems.

> ## Quick Reference
>
> *Problems in spelling can be solved in a number of ways.*
>
> ❱ *Learn to use general spelling rules.*
>
> ❱ *Use dictionaries to determine meaning and spelling.*
>
> ❱ *Use correct pronunciation to guide spelling.*
>
> ❱ *Check the spelling of technical terms carefully.*

31a ❭ **Learn to use the general rules that guide spelling.**

Although rules for spelling in English have many exceptions because English incorporates words from many languages, a few basic rules are helpful.

Forming Plurals

The letters that end a singular word dictate how its plural is formed.

Ending letters	Plural ending	Samples	
Consonant plus o	Add *-es*	potato	potatoes
		fresco	frescoes
Vowel plus o	Add *-s*	radio	radios
		stereo	stereos
Consonant plus y	Change *y* to *i* and add *-es*	victory	victories
		melody	melodies
Vowel plus y	Add *-s*	monkey	monkeys
		survey	surveys
s, ss, sh, ch, x, *or* z	Add *-es*	bonus	bonuses
		by-pass	by-passes
		dish	dishes
		catch	catches
		tax	taxes
		buzz	buzzes
Proper name with y	Add *-s*	Gary	Garys
		Germany	Germanys

Adding Prefixes

Some prefixes (*dis-, mis-, non-, pre-, re-, un-,* and others) do not change the spelling of the root word.

  similar   dissimilar   restrictive   nonrestrictive

See pages 402–403 for exceptions to this rule.

Adding Suffixes

The pattern for adding suffixes depends on the letters that end the root word and those that begin the suffix.

Last letter of root word	First letter of suffix	Pattern	Examples
Silent **e**	Consonant	Retain the *e*	achieve*e*ment resolute*e*ly
Silent **e**	Vowel	Drop the *e*	griev*i*ng siz*a*ble
Silent **e** *preceded by a "soft"* **c** *or* **g**	Vowel	Retain the *e*	noti*ce*able chang*e*able
Single consonant in one-syllable word with one vowel	Vowel	Double the consonant	si*tt*ing cli*pp*ing

Distinguishing Between *ie* and *ei*

This familiar, useful poem explains the order of *i* and *e*.

> Write *i* before *e*
> Except after *c*
> Or when sounded like *ay*
> As in *neighbor* and *weigh*

 Use dictionaries to determine meanings and spellings.

Spelling Dictionaries

Spelling dictionaries provide the correct spellings of thousands of words. These specialized dictionaries dispense with pronunciation guides, notes on word origins, definitions, and synonyms.

They generally indicate syllable breaks, however, which are helpful for hyphenating words at the ends of lines. People who have good vocabularies but spell poorly benefit from spelling dictionaries because they offer a quick way to confirm, for example, that *separate* is spelled with two *a*'s and two *e*'s and *develop* does not end with an *e*.

Standard Dictionaries

Words that sound alike, such as *mail* and *male*, may have very different meanings and spellings. Knowing which word has your intended meaning will lead you to the correct spelling. To determine that a word has your intended meaning and that you have spelled it correctly, use a standard dictionary.   **》》》** *When reading a dictionary definition to select the proper word and spelling, be sure to read all the definitions to find the one you need.* **《《《**

The sample from *The American Heritage Dictionary, Second College Edition* (Boston: Houghton, 1985) shown in Figure 1 illustrates common features of a dictionary entry.

31c ⟩	**Use correct pronunciation as a guide to correct spelling.**

The omission of letters in casual speech generally does not interfere with comprehension. Habitual mispronunciation, however, may lead to incorrect spelling. To ensure correct spelling when you write, sound out problem words, stressing all the letters but especially those omitted in speech. For instance, people often pronounce *accidentally* as if it were spelled "accident*ly*." Slowing down to sound out all the letters — *ac·ci·den·tal·ly* — will prevent this spelling problem.

Figure 1   A sample dictionary entry.

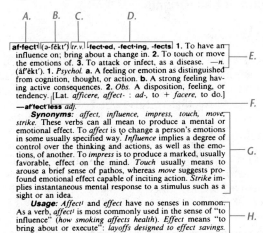

A.   B.   C.   D.

af·fect¹ (ə-fĕkt′) *tr.v.* **·fect·ed, -fect·ing, -fects** **1.** To have an
influence on; bring about a change in. **2.** To touch or move
the emotions of. **3.** To attack or infect, as a disease. —*n.*
(ăf′ĕkt′). **1.** *Psychol.* **a.** A feeling or emotion as distinguished
from cognition, thought, or action. **b.** A strong feeling having active consequences. **2.** *Obs.* A disposition, feeling, or
tendency. [Lat. *afficere, affect-* : *ad-*, to + *facere*, to do.]
—**af·fect′less** *adj.*

> **Synonyms:** *affect, influence, impress, touch, move,*
> *strike.* These verbs can all mean to produce a mental or
> emotional effect. To *affect* is to change a person's emotions
> in some usually specified way. *Influence* implies a degree of
> control over the thinking and actions, as well as the emo-
> tions, of another. To *impress* is to produce a marked, usually
> favorable, effect on the mind. *Touch* usually means to
> arouse a brief sense of pathos, whereas *move* suggests pro-
> found emotional effect capable of inciting action. *Strike* im-
> plies instantaneous mental response to a stimulus such as a
> sight or an idea.

> **Usage:** *Affect*¹ and *effect* have no senses in common.
> As a verb, *affect*¹ is most commonly used in the sense of "to
> influence" (*how smoking affects health*). *Effect* means "to
> bring about or execute": *layoffs designed to effect savings.*

A. Spelling and syllabification
B. Pronunciation (guide at bottom of dictionary page)
C. Part of speech
D. Spelling variations (past tense, present participle, plural)
E. Numbered definitions
F. Word origins
G. Synonyms and antonyms
H. Usage note

31d ▷ **Carefully check the spelling of technical words and British variants.**

Technical Words

If you use specialized words, check them individually. Their spellings are sometimes difficult because we use such words infrequently. Keep a note card handy with a list of the correct spelling of any technical words that you use often.

British Variants

Dictionaries list alternative spellings for some common words, and many times any choice is acceptable if applied consistently. When alternatives are identified as *American* (*Am.*) and *British* (*Brit.*), however, use the American spelling.

American Words with British Variants	
American	*British*
center	centre
color	colour
encyclopedia	encyclopaedia
judgment	judgement

⟩⟩⟩ *When using a proper name, maintain the original spelling even if it is British.*

Great Britain's *Labour Party* favors the nationalization of many industries.   (Although the American spelling is *labor,* the proper name of the political party uses the British spelling.) ⟨⟨⟨

448

Word processing and spelling

If you use a word processor for writing, take advantage of its spelling program. A spelling program searches a manuscript for words not appearing in its dictionary and highlights them for your attention. Be aware, though, of several minor limitations of some spelling programs.

A spelling program cannot distinguish an error in the choice of homonyms (words that have the same sound but different meaning). As long as a word appears in the program's dictionary, the program will not highlight the word. For instance, the use of *pail* for *pale* and *blew* for *blue* would go unnoticed.

A spelling program cannot identify typing errors if they produce words that are in the dictionary of the program. For instance, the use of *quite* instead of *quiet* would go unnoticed because *quite* is a recognizable English word.

The dictionaries for spelling programs are necessarily general so that many people can use them for many types of writing. Highly specialized words — proper names and technical terms, for instance — may not be included. In such cases, add these specialized words to the word list of the dictionary or check them individually.

Always proofread your writing carefully for spelling errors that are not identifiable by the spelling program.

The following list contains words that many people misspell. Use this list as a brief spelling dictionary as you write.

Commonly Misspelled Words

abbreviate	a lot	arranging
absence	although	article
absolutely	altogether	assassin
absurd	always	assassination
accelerate	amateur	assess
accidentally	ambiguous	association
accommodate	among	athlete
accomplish	amount	athletics
according	analysis	attempt
accumulate	analyze	attractive
accustom	annual	audible
achievement	Antarctic	audience
acknowledgment	anxiety	authorities
acquaintance	apartment	automobile
acquire	apparatus	auxiliary
across	apparent	awkward
address	appearance	bachelor
adoption	appropriate	balance
aggravate	archaic	balloon
aggression	arctic	barring
alleviate	argument	bearing
alley	arising	because
allotted	arithmetic	becoming
allowed	arouse	before

Commonly Misspelled Words

beggar	cemetery	completely
beginning	certain	compulsory
believe	changeable	concede
beneficial	changing	conceivable
benefited	characteristic	conceive
biscuit	chief	condemn
boundaries	choose	condescend
breathe	choosing	condition
brilliant	chose	conjunction
bulletin	chosen	conquer
buoyant	climbed	conscience
bureau	column	conscientious
buried	coming	conscious
burying	commission	considered
business	commitment	consistent
busy	committed	contemptible
cafeteria	committee	continuous
calendar	companies	control
candidate	comparatively	controlled
carrying	compel	convenient
casualties	compelled	cooperate
category	competent	copies
ceiling	competition	corner
celebrity	complaint	corpse

Commonly Misspelled Words

costume	definition	dissatisfy
countries	democracy	dissipate
courteous	dependent	distribute
courtesy	descendant	doctor
cozy	describe	dominant
cries	description	dormitory
criticism	desirable	dropped
criticize	despair	drunkenness
cruelty	desperate	echoes
cruise	destruction	ecstacy
curiosity	develop	efficient
curriculum	developed	eighth
custom	development	eligible
cylinder	diary	eliminate
dealt	dictionary	embarrass
debater	diet	eminent
deceitful	difference	emphasize
deceive	digging	employee
decide	disappearance	encouraging
decision	disappoint	encyclopedia
defendant	disastrous	enthusiastic
deferred	discipline	entrepreneur
deficient	discussion	environment
definite	disease	equipment

Commonly Misspelled Words		
equipped	fiery	guarantee
equivalent	finally	guard
especially	financial	guardian
eventually	financier	guest
exaggerate	forehead	guidance
exceed	foreign	handicapped
excel	foremost	handkerchief
excellent	forfeit	harass
exceptional	forty	hearse
excitement	frantically	height
exercise	fraternity	heroes
exhaust	freshman	hesitancy
exhilaration	friend	hindrance
existence	fulfill	hoarse
experience	furniture	hoping
explanation	gaiety	human
extensive	generally	humane
extracurricular	genius	humorous
extremely	genuine	hundredths
exuberance	glorious	hurries
fallacy	government	hygiene
familiar	grammar	hypocrisy
fascinate	grandeur	hysterical
February	grieve	illiterate

Commonly Misspelled Words

illogical	interpret	loneliness
imaginary	interrupt	losing
imagination	irrelevant	magazine
imitative	irresistible	magnificent
immediately	irreverent	maintain
implement	itself	maintenance
impromptu	judgment	maneuver
inadequate	judicial	manual
incidentally	khaki	manufacture
incredible	kindergarten	mathematics
indefinitely	knowledge	mattress
independent	knowledgeable	meant
indicted	laboratory	medicine
indispensable	laid	messenger
inevitable	later	millennium
influential	latter	millionaire
initiate	legitimate	miniature
innocent	leisure	minute
inoculate	library	mischievous
intellectual	license	misspelled
intelligence	lightning	modifies
intentionally	likable	modifying
intercede	likely	momentous
interest	literature	mortgage

Commonly Misspelled Words

mosquitoes	occurred	peaceable
mottoes	occurrence	perceive
mountainous	o'clock	perceptive
murmur	official	perform
muscle	officious	perhaps
mysterious	omission	permissible
naive	omit	perseverance
naturally	omitted	persuade
necessary	opinion	phrase
necessity	opportunity	physical
neither	optimistic	physician
nervous	organization	pierce
nevertheless	original	planed
nickel	orthodox	planned
niece	ought	playwright
ninety	outrageous	pleasant
ninth	overrun	politics
noticeable	paid	possesses
notorious	pamphlet	possessive
obedience	parallel	possible
obliged	parliament	potatoes
obstacle	particularly	practice
occasionally	partner	prairie
occur	pastime	precede

Commonly Misspelled Words

predominant	quarter	repetition
prefer	questionnaire	replies
preference	quiet	representative
preferred	quizzes	reservoir
prejudice	realize	resistance
preparation	really	restaurant
prevalent	recede	reverent
primitive	receipt	rhetoric
privilege	receive	rheumatism
probably	receiving	rhythm
proceed	recognize	ridiculous
professor	recommend	sacrifice
prominent	refer	sacrilegious
pronounce	reference	safety
pronunciation	referred	salary
propaganda	referring	sanctuary
propeller	regard	sandwich
protein	regional	scarcely
psychology	relevant	scene
pursue	religion	scenic
pursuing	religious	schedule
putting	remembrance	scrape
quantity	reminiscence	secretarial
quarantine	rendezvous	secretary

Commonly Misspelled Words

seize	statute	tangible
sense	stomach	tasting
sensible	stopped	technical
sentence	strength	technique
separate	strenuous	temperament
severely	stretch	tenant
shining	struggle	tendency
shriek	studying	than
siege	subordinate	therefore
sieve	subtle	thorough
similar	succeed	though
sincerely	success	thought
sincerity	successful	till
skeptical	suffrage	tired
slight	superintendent	together
sophomore	supersede	tournament
source	suppress	toward
specifically	surely	traffic
specimen	surprise	tragedy
sponsor	suspense	transferred
spontaneous	swimming	tremendous
statement	symmetry	tries
statue	synonymous	truly
stature	taboo	twelfth

Commonly Misspelled Words

typical	vengeance	which
tyranny	victorious	whole
unanimous	view	wholly
undoubtedly	vigilant	whom
unnecessary	vigorous	wiry
until	village	woman
usage	villain	women
useful	volume	won't
using	warrant	worried
usually	warring	worrying
vacancy	weird	writing
vacuum	welfare	written
valuable	where	yacht

MAKING C O N N E C T I O N S

Among writers' obligations to readers is correct spelling: misspellings distract and annoy readers and interfere with the effectiveness of writing.

- Scan the list of commonly misspelled words (pages 450–58) and underline the words that cause you trouble. Write the words on a four-by-six-inch index card for handy reference when you proofread your papers.

- Review your graded papers and make a list of the words you have misspelled. Add these, along with any specialized terms you commonly use, to your personal spelling list.

- Note the words frequently highlighted as misspelled by your word-processing program. Add them to your personal spelling list.

- Prepare a four-by-six-inch card for each of your courses, listing important names and terms, especially those that give you spelling problems.

RESEARCH

C·O·N·N·E·C·T·I·O·N·S

People do research almost every day, gathering facts, ideas, and information on subjects beyond their personal experience and outside the range of common knowledge. They search directories to find telephone numbers; they check listings to find out when a television program will be broadcast; they consult brochures to determine the best stereo equipment to buy. In academic contexts, research is a more formal and extended inquiry.

In some ways, college research papers resemble other papers. They must be logically organized, clearly developed, grammatically correct, and ultimately interesting and convincing. In some ways, however, research papers are distinct. Research papers explore topics, making use of facts, ideas, examples, explanations, and observations gathered from sources outside the writer's or most readers' previous or usual experience, and therefore research papers require clear and accurate documentation. Documentation — notes acknowledging the sources of the words and ideas supporting the statements in a research paper — systematically distinguishes the researcher's ideas from those of others.

Writing a research paper requires more than compiling facts and mastering the rules of documentation. Learning to research and write about a topic means learning to collect, analyze, and selectively use information to make or clarify a point — or to make a discovery.

A central method of enlarging knowledge, research is a means of entering others' minds and of entering more deeply into your own. Both the responsibility and the pleasure of research come from its nature: research is the open-minded search for and evaluation of information that will contribute to your understanding of some aspect of society, culture, or the world.

32 Choosing and Researching a Topic and Taking Notes

To begin work on a research paper, you need to select a topic to research and write about. The possibilities are many, but some kinds of topics will have more value for you than others because of your interests and experiences. Explore alternative topics, keeping an open mind, and base your selection on a reasoned judgment. Consider topics related to your fields of study; consider topics related to your personal interests; consider topics that raise questions you would like to explore. Whatever your final choice, make sure you are committed to it because you will spend hours reading and thinking and writing about it.

Quick Reference

❯ *Choose a general subject that is interesting, specific, and challenging.*

❯ *Narrow the subject to a specific topic by restricting its time period, its locale, or its special circumstances.*

❯ *Write a working thesis statement to guide your research.*

❯ *Compile a preliminary list of sources and evaluate their potential usefulness.*

❯ *Take clear, consistent, and complete notes.*

❯ *Avoid plagiarism by accurately identifying material quoted or paraphrased from any source.*

Research papers can take two forms: factual, objective surveys of all the literature available on a topic, or interpretive analyses of selected evidence arrayed to support the writer's viewpoint and ideas. An interpretive paper, though primarily concerned with the writer's own ideas and interpretations, cannot ignore contrary evidence. Writers of such papers must be thorough and fair even though they must take a position on their material. Part of the challenge — and pleasure — of research is the constant need to reexamine your evidence in the light of new evidence and your ideas in the light of new ideas. In psychology, sociology, economics, and some other courses, you may be required to write the first type of paper. Ask your instructor for guidelines and, if possible, for an example of a good paper of this type. Since most college research papers, particularly those for composition courses, are of the second type, this text focuses on interpretive research papers.

As you gather and read materials related to your topic, you will be taking notes to record information and ideas to use when you write the final paper. You will find the process of reading source materials and taking notes rewarding and enlightening if the topic intrigues and has value for you.

 Choose a subject and narrow it to a specific topic.

Choosing a General Subject

Unless your instructor has assigned a general subject for your research paper, you must begin your work by selecting one. Your major or minor field of study or an academic subject that you enjoy or know well is a good broad subject to begin with. Any subject that you know well or have an interest in can lead you to a good topic. A student who works for Exxon, for example, might write about company policies on or responses to ecologically damaging oil spills.

Guidelines for Assessing General Subjects

The subject should be interesting enough that you are willing to spend hours thinking, reading, and writing about it.

The subject should be of a scope broad or narrow enough to be treated adequately in the space recommended or required.

Enough material should be available to research the subject completely within the time available. Very recent events do not make good subjects because adequate materials are not generally available.

The subject should be challenging but should not require special knowledge that you do not have and do not have time to acquire.

The subject should not be overused; overused subjects are likely to be uninteresting to readers and difficult to research because of the high demand for the source materials.

When you have selected a general subject that meets the above requirements, you should consult with your instructor to be sure that it meets the requirements of the assignment.

Michele, who intends to major in psychology and minor in English, considered these general subjects:

Counseling juvenile delinquents

Using psychological concepts to teach literature

The uses of IQ tests

She eliminated the first because it seemed to require knowledge and experience that she did not have. The first of the remaining subjects seemed too broad. IQ testing was also broad, but it could be narrowed easily, and with a nationally recognized psychology program at her school, Michele knew she could find a wide range of materials.

EXERCISE 32.1 ❯ *General subjects*

List five possible subjects for a research paper. Test them against the guidelines given on page 464. (If you have difficulty with this assignment, skim the index of a textbook in your major or minor field for interesting subjects.)

Example

1. Stained-glass windows

2. Housing and architecture

3. Public sculpture

4. Impressionist art

5. Art in contemporary society

Narrowing a General Subject to a Specific Topic

With a general subject in mind, begin to narrow its focus. A focused topic will help you to determine your thesis. It will also help you to avoid wasting valuable research time reviewing and reading materials that will not fit into the final paper. An hour or two spent skimming reference books to narrow a subject often saves many hours later.

Begin by reading general sources in the library's reference room — various encyclopedias, specialized dictionaries, and fact books — to discover the scope and basic themes and details of your general subject. (See the selected list of general reference works on pages 470–73.) Use this information and the following strategies to narrow your subject to a specific topic:

Limit the scope of your paper to a specific, manageable time span. For example, restrict the topic *assembly-line automobile production* to the *1920s* or *1970s*.

Limit the scope of your topic to a single, specific location. For example, focus the topic *revitalization of cities* on *midwestern cities* or *St. Louis.*

Limit your topic to a specific set of circumstances. For example, the topic *the U.S. presidency* might focus on *the U.S. presidency in wartime.*

These strategies can be combined to achieve even greater focus. For example, a student might research *assembly-line automobile production in Korea in the 1970s* or *the U.S. presidency during the conflict in Vietnam.*

To obtain a general knowledge of IQ testing and to find some themes or details to help her to narrow the general subject, Michele skimmed some of the relevant reference books in the college library. She found that her general subject could be effectively narrowed by examining the uses of IQ tests in particular periods, such as the 1920s or 1950s, or by discussing the uses of IQ tests in the United States or in a specific area of the United States. Michele also found many special circumstances that applied to her subject; for example, she noted evidence of cultural bias in the compilation, administration, and interpretation of the tests. Narrowing the subject by combining the problem of bias with a specific location gave Michele many additional topics. One of them was the effect of cultural bias in the use of IQ tests in the multi-ethnic communities of southern California.

Michele was most interested, however, in what she read about the evolving concept of intelligence and its effect on the form and use of the tests and in efforts to change limited and stigmatizing ways of assessing intelligence. She was unsure whether a historical or a contemporary perspective would be more effective, but she decided to begin with this topic and to let a structure emerge as she gathered information.

EXERCISE 32.2 ❯ *Specific topics*

Select three subjects from your responses to Exercise 32.1 and write three focused topics by identifying a particular time, place, or special circumstance.

Example

1. Stained-glass revivals in the nineteenth and twentieth centuries

2. The universal appeal of the Impressionists

3. Blockbuster exhibitions and the role of art in contemporary American society

---

| 32b | ❯ | **Write a working thesis statement.** |

In the same way a working thesis statement guides your planning and drafting for other papers, it guides your planning and drafting for your research paper. For a research paper, which involves intensive reading and thinking, the working thesis statement also helps you to select and evaluate materials.

Your focused topic, stated as a complete statement or question and anchored with details derived from your preliminary research (see pages 481–83 and section 32e), should yield an effective working thesis statement. A student working with the focused topic *the U.S. presidency during the conflict in Vietnam* might develop the following thesis:

> During the conflict in Vietnam, the presidency was forced to a new level of accountability by the peace movement and the media.

After writing your working thesis statement, evaluate its effectiveness. (For more information on thesis statements, see section 1e.) An effective thesis statement has three essential characteristics and may have three optional characteristics:

Essential Characteristics

Identify a specific, narrow topic.

Present a clear opinion on, not merely facts about, the topic.

Establish a tone appropriate to the topic, purpose, and audience.

Optional Characteristics

Qualify the topic as necessary, pointing out significant opposing opinions.

Clarify important points, indicating the organizational pattern.

Take account of readers' probable knowledge of the topic.

》》》 *A thesis statement can make research seem a deductive process, one beginning with a general conclusion to support. But research should also be inductive, shaped by and building to a conclusion based on information discovered. Therefore, a question may sometimes be more effective than a statement as a guide to research. When researching, allow new ideas and unexpected information to lead you in promising new directions. Keep an open mind by using your working thesis not as something to be proved but as a controlling idea to be confirmed, refuted, or modified on the basis of your reading in the weeks or months ahead.* **《《《**

From her general reading and discussions with her psychology professor, Michele decided to research the misuse of IQ tests over the years in light of the current emphasis on responsible use. Before beginning her focused search for specific, relevant materials, she reviewed her preliminary research notes and formulated her working thesis statement:

IQ tests, their use, and the concept of intelligence itself have been constantly challenged, refined, and redefined by scientists and edu-

cators seeking to use the tests wisely, not to label people but to help them overcome weaknesses and build on strengths.

Michele planned to use this thesis statement to guide her research; it would help her to eliminate sources that treated unrelated aspects of intelligence testing and direct her toward relevant sources. She kept in mind, however, that her thesis statement would likely change as she learned more about her topic.

> A word processor allows you to revise your working thesis statement easily as you complete your research. ■ Draft alternative working thesis statements. Work freely and quickly, typing as many variations of your thesis statement as possible. In trying to express the thesis statement in alternative ways, you may discover different approaches to your work. ■ Revise your working thesis statement as you learn more. Because the computer allows you to add and delete freely, without retyping, review and revise your thesis statement frequently as you continue your research, acknowledging changes in your interpretation of the topic.

EXERCISE 32.3 ❯ *Working thesis statements*

Type three working thesis statements with which you might begin your research. Discuss them with other students or with your instructor to determine which promises to lead to the most productive research and the best paper.

Example

1. The revivals of use of stained glass in the nineteenth and twentieth centuries owe something to a romantic view of the unromantic Middle Ages, when stained glass first came into widespread use.

2. The art of the Impressionists, based on idealized images of leisure and pleasure, has natural appeal and wins easy acceptance in a century desperately dedicated to increasing and pursuing both.

3. Entertainment or aesthetic experience? Opinion is divided over the usefulness of blockbuster exhibitions and their ultimate effect on museums and the public. Visitors arrive in record numbers to see Van Gogh, Renoir, Gauguin, but what are they seeing and why?

32c ▷ Begin your research in the library.

If you have not done so already, take a tour of your college library with a staff member. On your own, after a tour or using a map or guide to the library, locate and explore the card catalog area (which includes both traditional and computerized catalogs), the reference room, the periodical and newspaper sections, the stacks and reserve area (where books are shelved), and the circulation desk (where books are checked out). Locate and learn to use microfilm, microfiche, or other viewing devices. Talk to library staff members about other services offered by the library, such as interlibrary loans and computerized databases.

General Reference Works

The reference room in your library contains a number of useful general reference works: major encyclopedias, almanacs, atlases, dictionaries, and compendia of biography, etymology, and quotations. The following lists indicate the variety of material available.

General References

Contemporary Authors. 123 vols. 1967 to date.

Current Biography. 1940 to date.

Facts on File Yearbook. 1940 to date.

National Geographic Atlas of the World. 5th ed. 1981.

New York Times Atlas of the World. 2nd rev. ed. 1983.

Who's Who. 1849 to date.

The World Almanac and Book of Facts. 1868 to date.

Encyclopedias

Collier's Encyclopedia. 24 vols. 1981.

Encyclopedia Americana. 30 vols. 1985.

Encyclopedia International. 20 vols. 1982.

New Encyclopaedia Britannica. 30 vols. 1986.

Art and Music

Apel, Willi. *The Harvard Dictionary of Music.* 2nd rev. ed. 1969.

Encyclopedia of World Art. 15 vols. 1959-68.

Sadie, Stanley, ed. *The New Grove Dictionary of Music and Musicians.* 20 vols. 1980.

Thompson, Oscar. *International Cyclopedia of Music and Musicians.* 11th ed. 1985.

Trachtenberg, Marvin, and Isabelle Hyman. *Architecture: From Prehistory to Post-Modernism.* 1986.

Economics and Business

Greenwald, Douglas. *The McGraw-Hill Dictionary of Modern Economics.* 3rd ed. 1984.

Munn, Glenn G. *Encyclopedia of Banking and Finance.* 8th ed. Ed. Ferdinand L. Garcia. 1983.

Sloan, Harold S., and Arnold Zurcher. *A Dictionary of Economics.* 5th ed. 1970.

History

American History Association. *Guide to Historical Literature.*
1961.

Cambridge Ancient History. 12 vols. 1923–39.

Cambridge Mediaeval History. 9 vols. 1911–36.

Freidal, Frank, and Richard K. Showman, eds. *Harvard Guide to
American History.* Rev. ed. 2 vols. 1974.

Langer, William Leonard. *An Encyclopedia of World History:
Ancient, Medieval, and Modern.* 5th ed. 1972.

New Cambridge Modern History. 14 vols. 1957–80.

Language and Literature

Baugh, Albert C., ed. *A Literary History of England.* 2nd ed.
1967.

Drabble, Margaret, ed. *The Oxford Companion to English Literature.* 5th ed. 1985.

Encyclopedia of World Literature in the Twentieth Century. Ed.
Leonard S. Klein. Rev. ed. 4 vols. 1984.

Hart, James D., ed. *The Oxford Companion to American Literature.* 5th ed. 1983.

*Modern Language Association International Bibliography of
Books and Articles on the Modern Languages and Literatures.* 1922 to date.

The Oxford English Dictionary. Ed. J. A. Simpson and E. S. C.
Weiner. 2nd ed. 20 vols. 1989.

Spiller, Robert E. *Literary History of the United States: Bibliography.* 1974.

Philosophy and Religion

Edwards, Paul, ed. *Encyclopedia of Philosophy.* 4 vols. 1973.

Ferm, Vergilius, ed. *An Encyclopedia of Religion.* 1976.

Science and Math

Belzer, Jack, et al., eds. *Encyclopedia of Computer Science and Technology.* 14 vols. 1975–80.

Considine, Douglas, ed. *The Encyclopedia of Chemistry.* 4th ed. 1984.

Gellert, W., et al., eds. *VNR Concise Encyclopedia of Mathematics.* 1977.

Gray, Peter. *The Encyclopedia of Biological Sciences.* 2nd ed. 1981.

The McGraw-Hill Encyclopedia of Science and Technology. 5th ed. 15 vols. 1982.

Thewlis, J., ed. *Encyclopedic Dictionary of Physics.* 9 vols. 1961–75.

Social Sciences

Brock, Clifton. *The Literature of Political Science.* 1969.

Eysenck, Hans Jurgen, ed. *Encyclopedia of Psychology.* 2nd ed. 3 vols. 1979.

Mitzel, Harold, ed. *Encyclopedia of Educational Research.* 5th ed. 4 vols. 1982.

Sills, David L., ed. *International Encyclopedia of the Social Sciences.* 17 vols. 1977.

Winick, Charles. *Dictionary of Anthropology.* 1977.

Card and Computerized Catalogs

Card Catalogs

Card catalog entries list books in each of three formats — author, title, and subject. In a **divided catalog,** cards are filed separately by type. A divided catalog may interfile author and title cards and place only subject cards in a separate catalog. In a **dictionary catalog,** author, title, and subject cards are filed together. Each book in the library's collection is cataloged in at least three ways, making your search for materials easier. For instance, if you need a book by Carl Sagan but cannot remember the title, look under *S* in a dictionary catalog or an author catalog for cards listing the library's holdings of Sagan's books. Similarly, if you want a book titled *The Unheavenly City* but cannot remember the author's name, look under *U* in a dictionary catalog or title catalog to locate the book. (Titles beginning with *a, an,* and *the* are filed under the first letter of the following word.) To locate books on a subject like "solar energy," look under *S* in a dictionary catalog or subject catalog.

Individual catalog cards provide basic information about a book: author, title, publisher, publication date, and call number (the number indicating the book's exact location in the library). They also indicate whether a book contains any special features such as maps, illustrations, or bibliographies. (See Figure 1.) **》》》**
Note accurately the call number of any book you are interested in seeing. Books are shelved by call number, so this information is essential to locate books in the stacks. **《《《**

Figure 1 Author, title, and subject cards

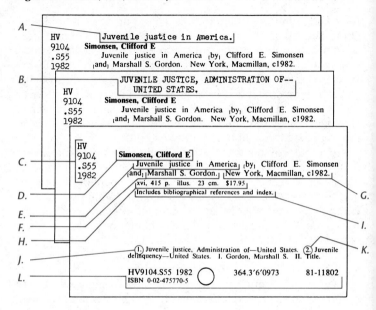

A. *Title card heading*

B. *Subject card heading*

C. *Library of Congress number*

D. *Author card heading*

E. *Title of book*

F. *Name of second author*

G. *Publication information: city, company, date*

H. *Technical information: number of pages in preface, number of textual pages, illustrations, book size, price*

I. *Additional information: textual apparatus*

J. *First subject classification*

K. *Second subject classification*

L. *Library of Congress number, ISBN number, Dewey Decimal number, On-line Computer Library Center number*

Computerized Catalogs

Increasing numbers of libraries list all or part of their holdings in computerized catalogs. In some libraries, books acquired after a certain date appear *only* in the computerized catalog; in other cases, older holdings may not yet have been entered in the computerized catalog. Be sure to check with a librarian to find out how to use the computerized catalog in your library, what it covers, and what will be found only in the card catalog. Computerized catalogs provide the same basic information as card catalogs: author, title, subject, call number, and so on.

A computer system can display simultaneously the information that would occupy several catalog cards. For instance, to research insomnia, you would type the necessary operating commands and then type the subject name, *insomnia.* Within seconds, the computer screen will display the names of the library's books on insomnia. When the list is too long to fit on one screen, you must type a command to see the rest of the list.

Computerized catalogs also make it possible to print out shelf-position lists — print-outs that include a fixed number of sources with call numbers preceding or following a selected call number. Such a printed list is a handy reference when you are beginning research.

Computer searching saves a great deal of time and energy. Take advantage of the new technology if it is available to you.

Periodical Indexes and Bibliographies

Periodicals — magazines, journals, and newspapers — are published at regular intervals, are often intended for expert or informed audiences, and offer up-to-date, specialized discussions of topics. These sources add depth, timeliness, and focus to your research.

Magazines, such as *The New Yorker, U.S. News & World Report,* and *Scientific American,* provide commentary and current information for general audiences. Journals, such as *Critical Inquiry, American Psychologist,* and *October,* are professional or scholarly publications written by and for experts in a given field; they contain specialized, technical information. Magazines usually appear monthly or weekly while journals may appear monthly or quarterly.

A Guide to Magazine Articles

The *Readers' Guide to Periodical Literature* lists articles appearing in hundreds of magazines. Usually located in the reference or the periodicals section, the *Readers' Guide* is printed regularly, is bound yearly, and covers most general-interest magazines. Your library may also have the *Readers' Guide* available on a computerized system.

The *Readers' Guide* alphabetically lists entries by author, title, and subject. Its condensed format uses many abbreviations, which are listed and explained at the front of each volume. Figure 2 (page 478) shows an excerpt from the *Readers' Guide.*

Guides to Journal Articles

To find articles in journals, use the various specialized indexes and bibliographies. Normally located in the reference room, these indexes and bibliographies list entries alphabetically by author, subject, and sometimes title. Indexes and bibliographies differ somewhat in format, but the excerpt from the *Education Index* shown in Figure 3 (page 479) is a fairly representative sample.

Indexes and bibliographies are shelved in the reference room by the call numbers of their subjects. Available guides include the following:

Agricultural Index, 1919–64

The American Humanities Index, 1975 to date

American Indian Index, 1953–68

Figure 2   Sample entries from the *Readers' Guide to Periodical Literature*

A. —— **POLITICAL FORECASTING**
        See also
        Public opinion polls ———————————————— B.
C. ——— Beyond the cold war. C. Krauthammer. *The New Republic*
        199:14-15+ D 19 '88
        Election prediction: Michael Dukakis will win. M. S.
        Forbes, Jr. il *Forbes* 142:33 N 14 '88
        The next four years [special section] bibl f il *Foreign*
        Affairs 67:1-134 Wint '88/'89 ———————————— D.
        Precipitation and presidents [cover story] R. Marshall.
F. ——— il *Weatherwise* 41:263-5 O '88 ————————————— E.
        Vultures [Democrats after losing race by M. Dukakis]
        M. Kondracke. *The New Republic* 199:10+ N 7 '88
        When optimists attract [H. Zullow's political forecasting
        method based on candidates' optimism measurement]
        D. Gelman. il *Newsweek* 112:80 O 17 '88
        POLITICAL INTEREST GROUPS *See* Special interest
        groups

A. *Subject heading*
B. *Cross reference*
C. *Article title*
D. *Special information: bibliography, footnotes, illustrations*
E. *Author*
F. *Publication information: magazine title, volume number, page numbers, month, year*

Applied Science and Technology Index, 1958 to date

The Art Index, 1929 to date

Bibliography and Index of Geology, 1961 to date

Biography Index, 1949 to date

Biological and Agricultural Index, 1964 to date

Book Review Index, 1965 to date

Business Periodicals Index, 1958 to date

Figure 3   Sample entries from *The Education Index*

A. ——— Intelligence, Artificial
                 See also
B. ———   Expert systems (Computers)
                 Hypertext
C. ——— Artificial intelligence: a promise of productivity gain
             at the keyboard? G. C. Whyte. *Bus Educ Forum*
             43:11-12 D '88
         Figuring out the rules for how the brain works. J. A.
             Turner. por | *Chron Higher Educ* 35:A3 O 26 '88
D. ——— Investigating AI with BASIC and LOGO. A. Mandell
             and R. Lucking. See issues of The Journal of Computers
             in Mathematics and Science Teaching
         Intelligence, Social *See* Maturity, Social
         Intelligence, Superior *See* Mentally superior
         Intelligence quotient
             Cognitive development and reading achievement in
             pervasive-ADD, situational-ADD and control children.
             M. Boudreault and others. | bibl | *J Child Psychol*   ——— F.
E. ———   *Psychiatry Allied Discip* 29:611-19 S '88
             Effect of intrauterine growth retardation (IUGR) on the
             psychological performance of preterm children at
             preschool age. R. Matilainen and others. bibl *J Child
             Psychol Psychiatry Allied Discip* 29:601-9 S '88

A. *Subject heading*
B. *Cross references*
C. *Article title*
D. *Special information: portraits*
E. *Author*
F. *Publication information: journal title, volume number, page numbers,
   month, year*

Catholic Periodical Index, 1930–33, 1939 to date

Cumulated Drama Index, 1909–49

Dramatic Index, 1909–49

Education Index, 1958 to date

Engineering Index, 1884 to date

Film Literature Index, 1974 to date

General Science Index, 1978 to date

Humanities Index, 1974 to date

Index to Legal Periodicals, 1908 to date

Index to U.S. Government Periodicals, 1974 to date

Industrial Arts Index, 1913–57

MLA International Bibliography of Books and Articles on Modern Languages and Literatures, 1922 to date

Music Index, 1949 to date

Social Sciences Index, 1974 to date

United Nations Documents Index, 1950 to date

Guides to Newspaper Articles

In the reference or the periodicals area, you will find the *New York Times Index, Wall Street Journal Index, London Times Index, Washington Post Index,* and other indexes listing articles published in the newspaper named in the index title. These guides are compiled yearly and arranged alphabetically by subject. If you find a relevant reference in one index, check other newspaper indexes for articles on the subject printed on the same day or a few days before or after. The section from the *New York Times Index* shown in Figure 4 is typical of newspaper indexes.

Figure 4   Sample entries from the *New York Times Index*

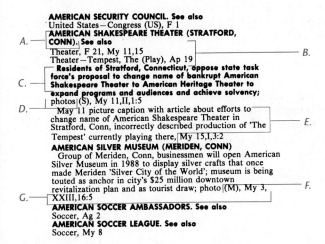

A.   *Subject heading*

B.   *Cross references*

C.   *Entry of unusual interest* (boldface type)

D.   *Photograph information*

E.   *Abstract of an important news story*

F.   *Note on length of the article:* (L) *means over three columns;* (M) *means one to two columns;* (S) *means less than one column*

G.   *Publication information: month, day, newspaper section number, page number, column number*

32d ▷ **Compile and evaluate a preliminary list of sources.**

Compiling a Preliminary List of Sources

A preliminary list of sources generally includes books and a variety of journal, magazine, and newspaper articles. Begin to note possible nonprint sources as well — for example, class notes, interviews, and television documentaries.

On separate 3-by-5-inch note cards, jot down information about each potential source. Note its location. For books, note call number, author, and title. For articles, write down the complete index or bibliography entry. For interviews, documentaries, class notes, and so on, indicate date, title, speaker or producer, and any other relevant identifying information. In addition to the information that is essential for locating or identifying a source, note any special features, such as maps or bibliographies, that might make the source especially useful.

Evaluating a Preliminary List of Sources

Review your preliminary list of sources, using the following guidelines to evaluate their potential usefulness:

Does the author have special credentials? An *M.D., M.A., Ph.D.,* or notice of an affiliation with a university or other organization following the author's name may indicate authority and expertise in the subject at hand.

Does the title of the work suggest a focus appropriate to your topic? The phrasing of a title or subtitle can indicate the author's subject and his or her attitude toward it. A title like *Latin American Civilization: Colonial Period* does not reveal its author's thesis or attitude, whereas *The Colonial Heritage of Latin America: Essays on Economic Dependence in Perspective* does reveal to an extent the book's approach to its subject.

Is the publishing company a reputable one? Most of the books you use have been published by university, academic, or trade presses. You will soon recognize the important publishers in your field.

Are the periodicals well respected by authorities in the field? You may not be able to evaluate a periodical thoroughly, but, depending on your subject and purpose, you will be able to determine the most reliable sources. For example, on issues of national and international importance, the *New York Times* or *Washington Post* are often more authoritative than local newspapers. You will learn which periodicals in your field are most respected by noting which are most frequently cited in the notes and bibliographies of the other works you consult. For academic research papers, the use of popular periodicals, such as *U.S.A. Today* and *Time,* should be kept to a minimum.

Is the publication date recent? For some topics, the currentness of a source is unimportant, but for most topics, sources older than ten or fifteen years are of little value.

Using these guidelines, Michele evaluated Walter Fenno Dearborn's *Intelligence Tests: Their Significance for School and Society* (Boston: Houghton, 1928). Her first instinct was to reject the book because of its publication date; she thought that its information would be outdated. However, Dearborn's credentials as a medical doctor with a Ph.D. and as director of the Psycho-Educational Clinic at Harvard University convinced her that the book deserved a closer look.

EXERCISE 32.4   ❯   *Preliminary list of sources*

Prepare a preliminary list of sources for your paper. Using the card catalog, find at least four books on your topic, including one published within the last two years and one providing an overview of the topic. Using the Readers' Guide, *the appropriate subject index, and one or more newspaper indexes, find at least six articles on your topic. Using the nonprint resources of your library and other local resources — such as businesses, government agencies, and civic and cultural organizations — find two nonprint sources, including one potential interview.*

| 32e | **Evaluate your sources.** |

Before you begin to read your sources carefully, leaf through them quickly, noting their organization, content, and any tables, maps, photographs, or other illustrations. Do not read each source thoroughly or take notes at this stage; follow the guidelines given below for making a preliminary, general assessment of the usefulness of the materials you have gathered. Once you have a general sense of your sources, you can then read them carefully and take complete and consistent notes, following the guidelines given in section 32f.

Evaluating Books

Books will probably provide the most thorough treatment of your subject, but you should evaluate each one quickly to see if it meets the needs of your research before taking the time to read it closely. After considering the title and subtitle carefully and any information provided about the author's credentials and other writings, review the table of contents. Consider how material is divided and arranged and how much space is allotted to topics that relate to your paper.

Skim the preface, introduction, or the first chapter to get a sense of the author's general approach and the context. Frequently, authors explain their reasons for writing, their strategies for presenting information, or their general interpretations of material in the preface, introduction, or first chapter. These explanations can help you to assess the source's potential value for your paper.

Examine any special sections or appended materials: in-text illustrations, tables, charts, graphs, or diagrams; bibliographies; sections containing special supporting material, such as case studies or lists of additional readings. Reviewing these sections gives you a sense of the book's content and approach. Nontextual materials can be quite useful in providing details, illustrations, and leads to other sources.

Skim a portion of the text that specifically relates to your topic. Do not read it carefully yet, but instead note how the author has developed the content. For example, does the author use examples and facts or narration and description based on personal experience? Does the author explain and support assertions, document facts, and present balanced discussions? Also note the author's style. Is it varied, lively, and interesting? What technical and other vocabulary and tone does it employ? A quick analysis of content and style can reveal whether a source treats the topic seriously and in depth or superficially. (For more information about evaluating sources and forms of argument, see Chapter 5, "Critical Thinking and Writing.")

Evaluating Articles in Periodicals

Articles in magazines, journals, and newspapers can provide you with a great deal of information. To save time, you need to evaluate the potential usefulness of each article you might wish to use before you read it carefully and take notes.

First, read the title and subtitle carefully, assessing what they reveal about the author's content, approach, and tone. Check any note on the author (this may appear at the bottom of the first page or at the end of the article or in a separate section of the journal or magazine). These notes usually state the author's credentials and other publications, which may give you insight into the author's interests and attitudes.

Read any headings that are used to separate sections of the article. Note whether any of the headings indicates content specifically related to your topic.

Skim the article to assess its content and form of presentation. Without pausing over details, skim the article to see if it is specific, current, and complete, and if its style indicates an approach to the topic that will be useful to you.

Check for related materials in the same periodical. Sometimes lists of suggested readings or of people or organizations to contact appear with an article. Issues of periodicals are sometimes organized in whole or in part around a theme, so that a number of articles in the periodical may relate to your topic.

EXERCISE 32.5 ❯ *Evaluating a source*

Look briefly at four sources — two books and two articles from periodicals — and write a brief paragraph describing each. Note especially each source's potential usefulness for your paper.

| 32f | **Take complete, consistent notes.** |

Establish a uniform system for taking notes. Many researchers use 4-by-6-inch index cards because they are large enough to hold complete notes and easy to distinguish from 3-by-5-inch works cited cards. (For more on works cited cards, see section 33b.) Some writers prefer the generous space of legal pads or loose-leaf paper even though in later stages of planning and writing notes on paper are often more difficult to handle than those on cards.

Use new cards for new ideas; during planning, this will make it easier for you to organize — and reorganize — your notes. At the top of each card, record the following information to help you to identify your sources easily and avoid plagiarism: the author of the source, title (if you are using more than one source by any given author); and the page number of the material you are noting. Make notes on one side of the card only, so that later you do not overlook any information. Fit material on one card, if possible; but if additional cards are necessary, note the author's name, the number of each card, and the total number of cards at the top (for example, "Johnson, Card 2 of 3").

Keep your working thesis in mind as you take notes. Some researchers like to keep a rough outline handy, so that they can take notes with the overall structure of their argument in view and can mark cards with key words to indicate where information fits. **⟫⟫⟫** *Be alert as you take notes to unexpected information and ideas that alter or expand your working thesis in new and interesting ways.* **⟪⟪⟪** You will want to make note of relevant information (facts, examples, and details) and of ideas (the thoughts and conclusions offered by your sources to interpret or organize their information). You can take notes on both types of material in any of three ways: summaries, quotations, and paraphrases. The sample note cards in figures 5, 6, 7, and 8 present information from this passage from Stephen Jay Gould's *The Mismeasure of Man* (New York: Norton, 1981):

[Terman] reified average test scores as a "thing" called general intelligence by advocating the first of two possible positions (1906, p. 9): "Is intellectual ability a bank account, on which we can draw for any desired purpose, or is it rather a bundle of separate drafts, each drawn for a specific purpose and inconvertible?" And, while admitting that he could provide no real support for it, he defended the innatist view (1906, p. 68): "While offering little positive data on the subject, the study has strengthened my impression of the relatively greater importance of endowment over training as a determinant of an individual's intellectual rank among his fellows."

Goddard introduced Binet's scale to America, but Terman was the primary architect of its popularity. Binet's last version of 1911 included fifty-four tasks, graded from prenursery to mid-teen-age years. Terman's first revision of 1916 extended the scale to "superior adults" and increased the number of tasks to ninety. Terman, by then a professor at Stanford University, gave his revision a name that has become a part of our century's vocabulary — the Stanford-Binet, the standard for virtually all "IQ" tests that followed (175).

Summaries

Summaries present the substance of a passage in condensed form. They are useful means of recording facts, best noted in list or other abbreviated form, as in Figure 5; examples, perhaps noted as a sketch of the original, as in Figure 6; or long arguments, perhaps noted in outline form. Summaries should be entirely in your own words. When taking notes, read the passage carefully, determine what information and ideas you want to record, and express them in lists of words, brief phrases, or short sentences. Do not use any of the original passage without enclosing it in quotation marks. Use quotation marks carefully at the note-taking stage to avoid inadvertently using others' words in your paper without giving proper credit.

Quotations

Quotations reproduce another's work word for word, with the original's exact spelling and punctuation. Quotations should not be overused in your writing and should be sparingly used in your notes. Assess the value of a quotation before you copy it. Ask yourself the following questions:

Is the author's style so distinctive that I could not say the same thing as well or as clearly in my own words?

Is the vocabulary technical and therefore difficult to translate into my own words?

Is the author so well known or so important that the quotation will lend authority to my argument?

Does the author's material raise doubts or questions or make points with which I disagree?

If you answer "yes" to any of these questions, then make note of the quotation. If the material does not fulfill any of these criteria but is significant nonetheless, paraphrase it instead.

Figure 5

Gould *Tests & Tasks*

Mismeasure, p. 175
—Binet's 1911 test, 54 tasks, toddlers to teenagers
—Terman's 1916 revision, upward to "superior adults," 90 tasks
—Terman, professor at Stanford U.

Figure 6

Gould *Stanford-Binet Test*

Mismeasure, p. 175
Terman made the Binet test more comprehensive, renamed it the Stanford-Binet, and helped to popularize it in the United States.

Always enclose quotations within quotation marks and double-check your note against the original. The copy must be *exact*. Figure 7 shows a sample quotation card.

 Because you can introduce errors each time you write or type a quotation, use a word-processing program to avoid extra recopying or retyping. ■ Prepare a separate file for quotations. Type each quotation into the file and double-check its accuracy against the original. Be sure to label each quotation completely with author, title, and page number. ■ Copy quotations into the draft as needed, leaving a copy in the quotation file in case you change your mind about where or how much of the quotation to use. The use of control codes to copy quotations avoids retyping, which saves time and prevents the introduction of errors.

Figure 7

Gould   *Preconceptions*

<u>*Mismeasure*</u>*, p. 175*

Terman said in 1906:
"While offering little positive data on the subject, the study has strengthened my impression of the relatively greater importance of endowment over training as a determinant of an individual's intellectual rank among his fellows."

⟫⟫⟫   *When a quotation continues from one page to the next in a source, indicate where the break occurs when you copy the quotation onto your note card (a double slash [//] is a useful indicator for this). This notation is important because when you use the quotation in your paper, you may use only part of it, and you must be able to cite the page reference accurately.* ⟪⟪⟪

Paraphrases

Paraphrases restate a passage in another form and other words; but, unlike summaries, they contain approximately the same amount of detail and the same number of words as the original. If a passage contains an important idea but does not meet the requirements for quotation, restate the idea in your own words, sentence structure, and sequence. When you finish the paraphrase, check it against the original passage to be sure the idea has been completely restated. If you use any phrases or sentences from the original, place them in quotation marks. Intentional or not, unacknowledged borrowing from a source is plagiarism, and most schools impose severe penalties on students who plagiarize.

Figure 8, on page 492, shows a sample paraphrase card.

EXERCISE 32.6 ❭   *Taking notes*

Using the books and articles that your evaluation of your preliminary list of sources determined would be useful, begin taking notes. Summarize, paraphrase, and directly quote from your sources, and make sure that each note card accurately reflects the source and provides full identifying information.

Figure 8

Gould   *Stanford-Binet, 1916*

<u>*Mismeasure*</u>*, p. 175*

*Terman was the person responsible for the concept of
"general intelligence" and the widespread use of Binet's IQ
tests. When Terman worked at Stanford, he revised Binet's
test (1911), nearly doubling the number of questions, and
named it the Stanford-Binet (first revision, 1916). It became
the model for later IQ tests.*
—the name "became part of our century's vocabulary"

32g ⟩ **Do not plagiarize.**

Plagiarism is the use of someone else's words, ideas, or line of
thought without acknowledgment. Even when, as is frequently
the case, plagiarism is inadvertent — the result of careless note
taking, punctuating, or documenting — the writer is still at fault
for dishonest work, and the paper will be unacceptable. You will
remember the seriousness of the offense of plagiarism, and work
to avoid committing it, when you remember that the word *plagiarism* comes from the Latin for "kidnaping." To avoid plagiarizing,
learn to recognize distinctive content and expression in source
materials and learn to take accurate, carefully punctuated and
documented notes.

Common Knowledge

Some kinds of information — facts and interpretations — are known by many people and are consequently described as **common knowledge.** That U.S. presidents are elected for four-year terms is commonly known, as is the more interpretative information that the U.S. government is a democracy with a system of checks and balances among the executive, legislative, and judicial branches of government. But common knowledge extends beyond these very general types of information to more specific information within a field of study. In English studies, for example, it is a commonly known fact that George Eliot is the pseudonym of Mary Ann Evans and a commonly acknowledged interpretation that drama evolved from a Greek religious festival honoring the god Dionysus. Documenting these facts in a paper would be unnecessary because they are commonly known in English studies, even though you might have discovered them for the first time.

When you are researching an unfamiliar subject, distinguishing common knowledge that does not require documentation from special knowledge that does require documentation is sometimes difficult. The following guidelines may help.

What Constitutes Common Knowledge

Historical facts (names, dates, and general interpretations) that appear in many general reference books. For example, George Washington was the first president of the United States, and the Constitution was adopted in 1787.

Literature that cannot be attributed to a specific author. Two examples are *Beowulf* and the Bible; the use of specific editions or translations still may require acknowledgment.

General observations and opinions that are shared by many people. For example, it is a general observation that children learn by actively doing, not passively listening, and a commonly held opinion that reading, writing, and arithmetic are the basic skills to be learned by an elementary school child.

Unacknowledged information that appears in multiple sources. For example, it is common knowledge that the earth is approximately 93 million miles from the sun and that the *gross national product* is the market value of all goods and services produced by a nation in a given year.

If a piece of information does not meet these guidelines or if you are uncertain about whether it is common knowledge, always document the material.

EXERCISE 32.7 ❯ *Common knowledge about your topic*

Make a list of twenty facts, ideas, or interpretations that are commonly known or held about your topic. Beside each item, note into which category of common knowledge it falls.

Special Qualities of Source Materials

A more difficult problem than identifying common knowledge involves using an author's words and ideas improperly. Improper use is often the result of careless summarizing and paraphrasing. To use source materials without plagiarizing, learn to recognize their distinctive qualities:

Special Qualities of Sources

Distinctive prose style: the author's choices of words, phrases, and sentence patterns

Original facts: the result of the author's personal research

Personal interpretations of information, the author's individual evaluation of his or her information

Original ideas: those ideas that are unique to that author

As you work with sources, be aware of these distinguishing qualities and make certain that you do not appropriate the prose (word choices and sentence structures), original research, interpretations, or ideas of others without giving proper credit.

Look, for instance, at this paragraph from Stephen Jay Gould's book:

> If Binet's principles had been followed, and his tests consistently used as he intended, we would have been spared a major misuse of science in our century. Ironically, many American school boards have come full cycle, and now use IQ tests only as Binet originally recommended: as instruments for assessing children with specific learning problems. Speaking personally, I feel that tests of the IQ type were helpful in the proper diagnosis of my own learning-disabled son. His average score, the IQ itself, meant nothing, for it was only an amalgam of some very high and very low scores; but the pattern of low values indicated his areas of deficit.
>
> The misuse of mental tests is not inherent in the idea of testing itself. It arises primarily from two fallacies, eagerly (so it seems) embraced by those who wish to use tests for the maintenance of social ranks and distinctions: reification and hereditarianism (155).

Now look at the following examples of plagiarism and acceptable summaries and paraphrases.

Summaries

Plagiarized

— *tests are often misused.*

— *that's not <u>inherent in the idea of testing</u>.*

— *people use IQ tests for <u>the maintenance of social ranks and distinc-tions</u>.*

(The underlined phrases are clearly Gould's. To avoid plagiarism, either place key phrases in quotation marks or rewrite them entirely in your own words and form of expression.)

Acceptable

— *tests are not the problem; the problem is the way people use them.*

— *the problems develop from unscientific methodology, which is "embraced by those who wish to use tests for the maintenance of social ranks and distinctions."*

(Here, the words and phrases are the writer's, not Gould's. Quotation marks enclose Gould's phrase.)

Paraphrases

Plagiarized
Had Binet's ideas about testing been used, and his IQ tests given as he intended, we would not have seen one of this century's misuses of science. Oddly enough, some school boards in the United States have gone back to Binet's original use of the tests: they are being used to assess children with special needs.

(Changing a few words while retaining the basic phrasing and sentence structure of the original is not acceptable paraphrasing. Gould's thought pattern and prose style still mark the passage.)

Acceptable
We have seen IQ tests misused because scientists have not followed Binet's guidelines for using his tests. Today, some learning disabled students are being assessed effectively, however, because schools are using IQ tests as Binet intended.
— *"American school boards have come full cycle."*

(Here, the paraphrase presents Gould's idea but does not mimic his sentence structure; the quoted material records a specific phrase for possible use later. Remember that summaries and paraphrases, as well as quotations, require full citations.)

Avoiding plagiarism takes conscious effort, and that effort takes time. Be aware of the special qualities in your source materials, and take notes carefully. By preparing notes properly and then documenting completely, you will avoid plagiarism, which can invalidate your paper and perhaps have other serious consequences, as well.

EXERCISE 32.8 ❯ *Practice in note taking*

Take notes on the following sets of paragraphs as you would if you were researching their subjects. Include a summary, a quotation, and a paraphrase from each set. Do not plagiarize.

McLoughlin, Merrill, et al. "Men vs. Women." *U.S. News & World Report.* 8 Aug. 1988: 50–56. [The following paragraphs appear on page 52.]

If God created man first, He or She apparently took advantage of hindsight when it came to women. Except for the moment of conception (when 13 to 15 males are conceived for every 10 females), the distaff side simply has a better chance at survival. Spontaneous abortions of boys outnumber those of girls. More males than females die during infancy, youth and adulthood. In every country in the world where childbirth itself no longer poses mortal danger to women, the life expectancy of females exceeds that of males. And in the United States, the gap is growing. A baby girl born today can look forward to nearly 79 years — seven more than a baby boy.

Why? Some of the answers seem to lie deep in the genes. Others doubtless float in the hormones that carry messages from organ to organ, even, some researchers believe, "imprinting" each human brain with patterns that can affect the ways it responds to injury and disease. The research suggests that females start out with some distinct biological advantages.

Fleming, Stuart. "Limning: A Noble Approach to Painting." *Archaeology* May/June 1987: 60, 61, 73. [The following paragraphs appear on page 60.]

During the early years of the seventeenth century, the English philosopher Francis Bacon faced a dilemma. He had gained some public popularity for his outspoken views on social morality, yet thoroughly distrusted the notion that any good could come from having the common people better educated. At the same time, men of science and fellow counselors at court, whom he identified as having the intellectual potential of advanced scholarship, seemed to be entrapped by false traditions of logic and rhetoric. He decried the fact that the dynamic mood of the European industry was being totally ignored by academia. For Bacon, the study of trades and practical experiment held the key to establishment of a universal truth, and he condemned the contrary attitude of his colleagues as one of "vain and supercilious arrogancy."

These seeds of a philosophy that would inevitably elevate the status of craftsmen did not fall on barren ground among the English artistic community. This group well remembered how the Italian Renaissance had enabled painters to shed the social stigma attached to artisans and gain artistic status of a kind previously reserved for poets.

Sagan, Carl. *The Dragons of Eden: Speculations on the Evolution of Human Intelligence*. New York: Random, 1977. [The following paragraphs appear on pages 189 and 191; a double slash (//) indicates the page break.]

In general, human societies are not innovative. They are hierarchical and ritualistic. Suggestions for change are greeted with suspicion: they imply an unpleasant future variation in ritual and hierarchy: an exchange of one set of rituals for another, or perhaps for a less structured society with fewer rituals. And yet there are times when societies must change. "The dogmas of the quiet past are inadequate for the stormy present" was Abraham Lincoln's description of this truth. Much of the difficulty in attempting to restructure American and other societies arises from the resistance by groups with vested interests in the status quo. Significant change might require those who are now high in the hierarchy to move downward many steps. This seems to them undesirable and is resisted.

But some change, in fact some significant change, is apparent in Western society — certainly not enough, but more than in almost any other society. Older and more static cultures are // much more resistant to change. In Colin Turnbull's book *The Forest People,* there is a poignant description of a crippled Pygmy girl who was provided by visiting anthropologists with a stunning technological innovation, the crutch. Despite the fact that it greatly eased the suffering of the little girl, the adults, including her parents, showed no particular interest in this invention. There are many other cases of intolerance to novelty in traditional societies; and diverse pertinent examples could be drawn from the lives of such men as Leonardo, Galileo, Desiderius Erasmus, Charles Darwin, or Sigmund Freud.

MAKING C O N N E C T I O N S

Choosing and researching a topic and taking notes are complex, demanding processes that require careful thought. It may help you to plan your research if you consider how research activities relate to other writing that you have done.

- Consider your process for selecting a topic. Compare and contrast your method of choosing a research topic with your method of choosing a topic for a personal experience or expository paper. Speculate on the reasons for these similarities and differences.

- Consider how your research differed from other research that you have done — for example, in high school or to find a job. Make two lists. In one, list important aspects of your previous research experience; in the second, note the similarities and differences you experienced in your college research work.

- Consider how what you have learned about evaluating sources applies to nonresearch materials. Using the guidelines that you have used to test the quality of research sources, evaluate a textbook for another course or a general-interest book or article. Which of the principles of evaluation apply? What other criteria are more useful?

- Consider how the notes you take in class resemble those you take during formal research. Review a few weeks of notes from another class; distinguish notes that are in the form of summaries, paraphrases, and quotations. What have you learned from taking notes for a research paper that might help you to take better class notes? What have you learned in taking class notes that might improve your research notes?

33 Preparing Works Cited Entries

The research process is painstaking, especially when it comes to recording complete and accurate information about sources for use in documenting the final paper. Careful documentation and a complete works cited list provide readers with full information on sources cited in the paper. (See section 34d for information on in-text citations.)

To be useful to readers, citations must be clear and consistent. Therefore, very specific rules of documentation have been devised and must be applied.

Quick Reference

Begin preparing your works cited entries, using the formats shown below, as soon as you begin taking notes. Use 3-by-5-inch cards, a new one for each entry, and keep them current and in a safe place or create a works cited file on your word processor.

❯ *A book by one author*

> *Author's last name, first name. <u>Book title</u>. Additional information. City of publication: Publishing company, publication date.*

❯ *An article by one author*

> *Author's last name, first name. "Article title." <u>Periodical title</u> Date: inclusive pages.*

Guidelines for preparing entries for other types of sources appear on the pages that follow.

| 33a | **Follow the standard citation format required by your subject.** |

Most writing in English and other humanities courses uses the documentation format described in Joseph Gibaldi and Walter S. Achtert's *MLA Handbook for Writers of Research Papers,* third edition (New York: MLA, 1988). This documentation format, known as MLA style, is simple, clear, and widely accepted. Some subjects, however, require other styles of documentation, so always ask instructors, especially in nonhumanities courses, whether MLA style is acceptable. In addition to the *MLA Handbook,* frequently used style guides include the following:

Frequently Used Style Guides

CBE Style Manual. 5th ed. Bethesda: Council of Biology Editors, 1983.

The Chicago Manual of Style. 13th ed. Chicago: U of Chicago P, 1982.

Handbook for Authors. Washington, DC: American Chemical Soc., 1978.

Publication Manual of the American Psychology Association. 3rd ed. Washington, DC: American Psychological Assn., 1983.

Style Manual for Guidance in the Preparation of Papers. 3rd ed. New York: American Inst. of Physics, 1978.

Turabian, Kate. *A Manual for Writers of Term Papers, Theses, and Dissertations.* 5th ed. Chicago: U of Chicago P, 1987.

The most widely used of these alternate styles is that of the American Psychological Association (APA), often the preferred style for writing in the social sciences. Guidelines for using APA style appear in Appendix B.

33b	**Prepare accurate and complete works cited entries.**

Because works cited entries direct readers to sources used in researched writing, these entries must be as complete as possible and presented in a consistent and recognizable format. If the following guidelines do not cover a source you want to use, consult the *MLA Handbook* (see section 33a).

Place works cited entries on 3-by-5-inch note cards, one entry to a card. Carefully copy all information directly from the source, and enter it in the exact format that will eventually be required for your works cited page. Keep cards up-to-date and in a safe place.

Information for Citations

Citations vary in the information they include, but all must follow a consistent arrangement. When you must combine forms (to list a translation of a second edition, for example), use these guidelines to determine the format of the combined entry.

1. *Author (s)*. For books, use the name or names with the spelling and in the order shown on the title page. For periodicals, take the author's name from the article itself (it may be at the beginning or the end of the article), not from the contents page. If no author, individual or corporate, is listed, make a note of that fact; the work will be listed by title on the works cited page.

2. *Title*. List titles from part to whole. If you are citing part of a book (for example, a single essay in a collection), list the title of the part before the book title; list the title of an article before the periodical title. Take the title of a book from the title page and the title of a part or an article from the first page of the part or article. Use complete titles, including subtitles.

3. *Additional information*. Include any of the following information (in the order presented here) if it is listed on the

title page of a book or the first page of an article: editor, translator, compiler, edition number, volume number, name of series.

4. *Facts of publication.* For books, take the publisher's name and the place of publication from the title page and the date of publication from the copyright page (immediately following the title page); use the publisher's name in abbreviated form (see examples in section 33c), the first city listed if more than one is given, and the most recent date shown. For periodicals, take the volume number, issue number, and date from the masthead, found at the top of the first page of newspapers or within the first few pages in journals and magazines, often in combination with the table of contents.

5. *Page numbers.* When citing a part of a book or an article, provide inclusive page numbers. Look these up for yourself; do not rely on the table of contents.

Format for Citations

Whether handwritten or typed, works cited entries must consistently follow this format:

1. Begin the first line of the entry at the left margin, and indent all subsequent lines five spaces.

2. Invert the first author's name so that it appears last name first (to make it easy to alphabetize and locate on the works cited list). List additional authors in first-last name order.

3. When no author is named, list the source by title.

4. Cite the complete title; use a colon followed by a single space to separate the title from any subtitle.

5. Separate major sections of entries (author, title, and publication information) with periods. A title ending with a question mark or an exclamation point does not require a period. (See example on page 513.)

6. Double-space entries.

Book by one author

```
Sagan, Carl.  The Dragons of Eden: Speculations on the

    Evolution of Human Intelligence.  New York:

    Random, 1977.
```

Magazine article by one author

```
Diamond, Jared.  "The Price of Human Folly."  Discover

    Apr. 1989: 73-77.
```

Using a word processor to prepare citations is especially helpful because entries can easily be added, changed, or deleted as your research continues, and programs have features that simplify typing. ■ To block-indent second and subsequent lines of each entry, use the program's "block-indent" feature (also called a *hanging paragraph*), instead of using a five-space tab to indent each second and subsequent line individually. ■ Revise entries to adjust the spacing, punctuation, and position of information. Word processors allow you to insert, delete, and rearrange information without retyping. ■ Prepare entries in a separate file. Place works cited entries in a separate file so that you will have easy access to them. Add items to the file in alphabetical order. You can later use "block" and "move" codes to correct alphabetization and then to append the complete file to your research paper.

33c ⟩ **Follow the appropriate citation forms for books.**

A Book by One Author

```
Bloom, Allan.  The Closing of the American Mind.  New
     York: Simon, 1987.
```

A Book by More Than One Author

```
Vidich, Arthur J., and Joseph Bensman.  Small Town in
     Mass Society: Class, Power and Religion in a Rural
     Community.  Princeton: Princeton UP, 1968.
```

(A comma follows the first author's first name. The names of other listed authors are not inverted. The letters *UP*, without periods, abbreviate *University Press*.)

```
Winks, Robin W., et al.  A History of Civilization:
     Prehistory to the Present.  7th ed.  Englewood
     Cliffs: Prentice, 1988.
```

(Using *et al.* (meaning "and others") saves space when a work has four or more authors (the Winks book has four). Do not underline *et al.*

A Book with No Author or Editor Named

```
The Chicago Manual of Style.  13th ed.  Chicago: U of
     Chicago P, 1982.
```

(When no author or editor is named, list the work by title. Alphabetize under *c*, disregarding the article *the*.)

A Book by a Corporate Author

American Psychological Association. <u>Thesaurus of</u>

<u>Psychological Index Terms</u>. 5th ed. Washington,

DC: APA, 1988.

(The American Psychological Association, or APA, is both author and publisher of this work.)

An Edition Other Than the First

Corbett, Edward. <u>Classical Rhetoric for the Modern</u>

<u>Student</u>. 3rd ed. New York: Oxford UP, 1988.

A Work in Several Volumes

Doyle, Arthur Conan. <u>The Complete Sherlock Holmes</u>. 2

vols. New York: Doubleday, 1930.

(The entry cites the entire series; *volumes* is abbreviated.)

Churchill, Winston S. <u>The Birth of Britain</u>. New York:

Dodd, 1966. Vol. 1 of <u>A History of the</u>

<u>English-Speaking Peoples</u>. 4 vols.

(This entry cites a single, separately titled volume in a series.)

Granville-Barker, Harley. <u>Prefaces to Shakespeare</u>.

Vol. 2. Princeton: Princeton UP, 1975. 2 vols.

(This entry cites a single volume of a series without separate volume titles. The number of the cited volume follows the title; the total number of volumes ends the entry.)

A Work in a Collection by the Same Author

Cohen, Arthur A. "The Monumental Sculptor." <u>Artists</u>

   <u>and Enemies: Three Novellas</u>. Boston: Godine,

   1987. 41–124.

(Note that the page numbers, *41–124,* stand alone without the word or abbreviation for *pages.*)

A Work in a Collection by Different Authors

Tizard, Barbara. "The Impact of the Nuclear Threat on

   Children's Development." <u>Children of Social</u>

   <u>Worlds: Development in a Social Context</u>. Ed.

   Martin Richards and Paul Light. Cambridge:

   Harvard UP, 1986. 236–56.

Chaucer, Geoffrey. <u>The Canterbury Tales</u>. <u>The</u>

   <u>Riverside Chaucer</u>. Ed. Larry D. Benson. 3rd ed.

   Boston: Houghton, 1987. 23–328.

(Editors' names must be included in entries when they are listed on the title page.)

Articles In Encyclopedias and Other Reference Works

Williams, Edgar Trevor. "Victoria and the Victorian Age."

   <u>Encyclopaedia Britannica: Macropaedia</u>. 1986 ed.

(List articles from reference works by author's name if it is provided and by title if it is not. If the author's initials appear with the article, check the list of contributors for the full name. Reproduce the spelling of titles of reference works exactly, including, as above, any British spellings. Page numbers are not needed when the reference work is arranged alphabetically.)

"Spock, Benjamin." Who's Who. 1989.

(This unsigned article is listed by title, reproduced exactly as given in the heading of the reference.)

Moray, Neville. "Attention." The Oxford Companion to

the Mind. Ed. Richard L. Gregory. New York:

Oxford UP, 1987.

(Well-known reference works, such as standard dictionaries and encyclopedias, require no information other than the title, edition number [if any], and date. Less well known or recently published reference works, such as this one, should have full publication information.)

A Work in a Series

O'Connor, Flannery. Wise Blood. Collected Works. Ed.

Sally Fitzgerald. The Library of America Ser.

New York: Literary Classics of the United States,

1988. 3–131.

Strachey, Lytton. Landmarks in French Literature.

Oxford Paperback's University Ser. 42. New York:

Oxford UP, 1969.

(If a work is part of a series, the series title and any number are indicated on the title or copyright page. Abbreviate *series*.)

A Reprint

Palmer, John. The Comedy of Manners. 1913. New York:

Russell and Russell, 1962.

(Reprints are identified as such on the copyright page. List the original publication date after the title, and list the date of the reprinted edition after the publisher's name.)

A Translation

Emphasis on the Work

Mann, Thomas. Death in Venice. Trans. Kenneth Burke.

New York: Modern Library, 1970.

(Abbreviate *Translated by* as *Trans.*)

Aristotle. Rhetoric. Trans. W. Rhys Roberts.

Aristotle: Rhetoric and Poetics. New York: Modern

Library, 1954.

(Placing the translator's name after the title of part of a longer work indicates that the translator translated only that part.)

Emphasis on the Translation

Shepley, John, trans. Interview with History. By

Oriana Fallaci. Boston: Houghton, 1976.

(Use this form only when you are discussing the techniques of translation. Abbreviate *translator* as *trans.*)

A Government Document

United States. Cong. Joint Economic Committee. New

Dimensions in Rural Policy: Building upon Our

Heritage. 99th Cong., 2nd sess. Washington: GPO,

1986.

(Information about sessions and specific committees appears on the title page, which is often the cover of government documents.)

A Preface, Introduction, Foreword, or Afterword

Schorer, Mark. Introduction. Pride and Prejudice. By

Jane Austen. Ed. Schorer. Boston: Houghton,

1956.

(Use this form to cite the introduction specifically.)

A Pamphlet

How to Feed Your Baby: The First Year. Evansville:

Mead Johnson, 1980.

(Editorial standards for pamphlets are less consistent than those for books, and some information may be missing. Use *n.p.* for "no place of publication" or "no publisher" and *n.d.* for "no date." The abbreviations are not underlined in the entry.)

A Published Dissertation

Rollins, Jeremy. The Philanthropic Legacies of the

Robber Barons: Carnegie, Rockefeller, and

Vanderbilt. Diss. Syracuse U, 1986. Ann Arbor:

UMI, 1980. 9413756.

(The title page indicates whether a dissertation has been published. If it has been, italicize the title. If University Microfilms International [UMI] is the publisher, include the order number, found on the title or copyright page.)

An Unpublished Dissertation

```
Shapiro, Barbara.  "Structure and Form: The

     Architectural Development of Frank Lloyd Wright."

     Diss.  U of Illinois, 1988.
```

(The title page provides all necessary information. Enclose the title in quotation marks because the material is unpublished.)

| 33d | **Follow the appropriate citation forms for periodicals.** |

An Article in a Monthly Magazine

```
Schell, Jonathan.  "Speak Loudly, Carry a Small Stick:

     Foreign Policy in an Age of Ambivalence."

     Harper's Mar. 1989: 39-49.
```

An Article in a Journal with Continuous Paging Through a Single Year

```
Pinsker, Sanford.  "Comedy and Cultural Timing: The

     Lessons of Robert Benchley and Woody Allen."  The

     Georgia Review 42 (1988): 822-37.
```

(The title of the periodical is followed, without intervening punctuation or the abbreviation *vol.*, by the volume number and then by the year in parentheses. Page numbers, without an abbreviation for *pages*, follow a colon.)

An Article in a Journal with Separate Paging in Each Issue

Thym, Jurgen. "The Composer as Evangelist." American
    Choral Review 30.2 (1988): 7-29.

(When issues are paged separately, a period separates the volume number and issue number; both are necessary.)

An Article in a Weekly Magazine or Newspaper

A Weekly Magazine

Lewis, Geoff. "Is the Computer Business Maturing?"
    Business Week 6 Mar. 1989: 68-78.

(Abbreviate the month and use the date format as shown above to eliminate a comma. Only May, June, and July are not abbreviated.)

A Weekly Newspaper

Barrett, Wayne, and Lynnell Hancock. "Ten Ways to Save
    the Schools: The Decentralization Debate Begins."
    The Village Voice 28 Mar. 1989: 21-28.

An Article in a Daily Newspaper

Frankel, Glenn. "Camp David Accord's Unfulfilled
    Promise." The Washington Post 25 Mar. 1989: A9.

(Editions, such as *morning* or *evening,* when specified in the masthead, must be cited after the date, as in the next entry. Section and page numbers are separated with a colon — *1:9.* If sections are identified by letter, as above, no colon is used.)

An Editorial

```
"U.S. Judges, Held Hostage."  Editorial.  The New York
     Times 24 Mar. 1989, national ed.: sec. 1:20.
```

A Letter to the Editor

```
Weber, Catherine S.  Letter.  Newsweek 13 Mar. 1989:
     11-12.
```

(Do not use titles that publishers may include to get readers' attention. If the letter appears in a journal or newspaper, follow the appropriate format for those types of periodicals after the designation "Letter.")

A Review

```
Davis, Nancy.  Rev. of The American Perception of
     Class, by Reeve Vanneman and Lynn Weber Cannon.
     Contemporary Sociology 18.1 (1989): 26-28.
```

| 33e | **Follow the appropriate citation forms for nonprint sources.** |

Finding the documentation information for nonprint sources is usually easy, but sometimes it requires ingenuity. Album jackets provide the manufacturers' catalog number and copyright date. Printed programs for speeches or syllabuses for course lectures provide names, titles, locations, and dates. Information about films or television programs can be obtained from opening or closing credits or from reference books such as *Facts on File* or *American Film Record.* If you have difficulty documenting nonprint sources, ask your instructor or a librarian for help.

A Lecture or Speech

```
Gould, Stephen Jay.  "Pattern and Pathway of Life's

     History."  University Speaker Series Lecture.

     Indiana State University.  Terre Haute, 14 Mar.

     1989.


Bush, George.  Inaugural Address.  Washington, 20 Jan.

     1989.


Mitten, David M.  Class lecture.  "Greek Art and

     Architecture in the West: Southern Italy, Sicily,

     and Campania."  Harvard University.  Cambridge, 15

     May 1989.
```

(Use a descriptive word, such as *lecture* or *address*, without underlining, if a lecture or speech has no title.)

A Work of Art

```
Gauguin, Paul.  The Brooding Woman.  Worcester Art

     Museum, Worcester, MA.
```

(The title was provided by the artist.)

```
Achilles Painter.  Muses on Mount Helicon.  Private

     collection, Lugano, Switz.
```

(This entry provides the artist and subject designations that art historians have given this anonymous, untitled vase painting.)

Graphic Work (Maps, Charts, Tables)

Periodic Table of Elements.   Table.   McGraw-Hill

Encyclopedia of Science and Technology.   6th ed.

1987.

A Film

Casablanca.   Dir. Michael Curtiz.   With Humphrey Bogart

and Ingrid Bergman.   Warner, 1943.

(List films by title, with the director's name immediately following.)

Schulberg, Budd, screenwriter.   On the Waterfront.

Dir. Elia Kazan.   With Marlon Brando and Eva Marie

Saint.   Horizon-American, 1954.

(If your paper emphasizes the work of a particular contributor, list the film under his or her name.)

A Television Broadcast

Special Programs

The Great American Fourth of July and Other Disasters.

Writ. Jean Sheperd.   American Playhouse.   PBS.

WGBH, Boston.   16 Mar. 1982.

(List special programs by title, followed by the name of the writer, director, or producer — whichever contributor suits your purpose. Capitalize but do not underline the series title.   Include the name of the network and the date on which the program was broadcast.)

Regular Programs

"Politics, Privacy, and the Press." <u>Ethics in America</u>.

PBS. WNET, New York. 4 Apr. 1989.

(Episodes of regular programs are listed by title, placed in quotation marks. After the appropriate contributor's name [if any], include the title of the series, underlined.)

A Radio Broadcast

<u>All Things Considered</u>. Natl. Public Radio. WBUR,

Boston. 30 Mar. 1989.

A Recording

The Beatles. <u>Sgt. Pepper's Lonely Hearts Club Band</u>.

Capitol, SMAS 2653, 1967.

(Alphabetize this entry by *Beatles*, not *The*. Use *n.d.* if no date is shown on the recording's label or packaging.)

Parker, Charlie. "Don't Blame Me." <u>The Very Best of</u>

<u>Bird</u>. Audiotape. Warner, J5A 3198, 1977.

(Song titles are enclosed in quotation marks. Media other than long-playing records are noted after the title of the complete recording.)

Mozart, Wolfgang Amadeus. Serenade in B Flat, K. 361,

"Gran Partita." Compact disk. Netherlands Wind

Ensemble. Philips, 420 711-4, 1986.

(Designations of musical works by type, key, or number are neither underlined nor quoted.)

```
Netherlands Wind Ensemble.  Serenade in B Flat, K. 361,

    "Gran Partita."  By Wolfgang Amadeus Mozart.

    Compact disk.  Philips, 420 711-4, 1986.
```

(This entry emphasizes the performers rather than the composer.)

A Performance

```
The New Moon.  By Sigmund Romberg.  With Richard White,

    James Billings, and Leigh Munro.  Cond. Jim

    Coleman.  New York City Opera.  Wolf Trap, VA.

    23 June 1989.
```

(In addition to title, author, location, and date, provide whatever other information suits the purpose of your paper.)

An Interview

```
Haroldson, Thomas B.  Telephone interview.  14 Dec.

    1988.
```

(List entries for interviews by the last name of the person interviewed; include the type — *personal* or *telephone,* for example — and the date of the interview.)


```
Doctorow, E. L.  Interview.  Fresh Air.  Natl. Public

    Radio.  WBUR, Boston.  14 Mar. 1989.
```

(For a broadcast interview, indicate the program, network, local station, and date on which you heard the interview.)

Computer Searches

```
"Salk, Jonas."  American Men and Women of Science.

     15th ed.  Bowker, 1983.  Dialog file 314, item

     0112528.
```

(Information about the original source, presented according to convention, is followed by the access numbers that are used to retrieve information stored by computer services.)

EXERCISE 33.1 ❯ *Compiling a works cited page*

From these ten sets of scrambled information, produce ten sample works cited cards. Keep them to use in a later exercise.

1. pages 47–48; Margaret Mead; *Redbook;* "Double Talk About Divorce"; May 1968.

2. 2nd edition; edited by J. Gipson Wells; "Some Thoughts on Divorce Reform"; Paul Bohannan; in *Current Issues in Marriage and the Family;* 1979; New York; Macmillan Publishing Company; pp. 249–63.

3. *Marriage in the United States;* originally published in 1867; Auguste Calier; Arno Press; New York; 1972; 3rd edition.

4. KNOW, Inc.; Pittsburgh; *'Til Divorce Do You Part;* 1972; pamphlet; Roberta Greene.

5. Page 3; "Data Shows Marriages Up, Divorces Down"; section A; March 16, 1983; *Washington Post.*

6. 1984 edition; "Divorce and Separation"; *Facts on File.*

7. Radnor, Pennsylvania; *Inside Divorce: Is It What You Really Want?;* Chilton Book Company; 1975; Edmond Addeo and Robert Burger.

8. Columbia Pictures; starring Dustin Hoffman and Meryl Streep; 1979; *Kramer vs. Kramer;* directed by Robert Benton.

9. Personal interview with Rebecca Stahl; February 19, 1988.

10. Number 1; pages 1–10; "Divorce Is a Family Affair"; March 1971; volume 5; Jack C. Westman and David W. Cline; *Family Law Quarterly.*

MAKING   C O N N E C T I O N S

No doubt, citations have long been a part of your reading and, in all likelihood, your writing as well. The third edition of the *MLA Handbook,* published in 1988, uses streamlined forms, making citations easy to read and interpret; knowing how the new forms differ from forms used in the past will help you to understand sources and use the correct form in your own research.

• Examine the citation pages of research papers that you wrote before 1988. Note particularly the changes. The old format used single-, not double-spacing and the heading "Bibliography," rather than "Works Cited." The new format simplifies forms, omitting unnecessary details, and simplifies and sometimes even eliminates abbreviations.

• Make a list of key changes that you note. Use an index card to record changes in citation forms that you use frequently.

• Examine citation pages in source materials that are five or more years old. To appreciate the clarity and simplicity of MLA forms in the third edition, look at these older materials and compare them to the examples given on pages 506–19.

After weeks of gathering information, organizing and writing the research paper may seem an enormous undertaking. It is. It is also an exciting stage in your work because you now are ready to bring your information and your ideas together in a clear and convincing paper.

Quick Reference

❯ Reread your notes and organize them into groups that correspond to logical divisions of your topic.

❯ Write a rough draft based on this organization, working with one group of notes at a time.

❯ Integrate source material smoothly with your ideas.

❯ Use parenthetical notes to provide readers with information about your sources.

❯ Revise the rough draft to clarify organization and content, to improve style, and to correct technical errors. (See Chapter 3, "Revising," for revision checklists.)

❯ Prepare and submit the final copy according to your instructor's or other standard guidelines.

34a Organize your notes.

The basic patterns of organizing a research paper resemble patterns used for other papers. (See Chapter 4, "Paragraphs," to review patterns of organization.) Your note taking has given you a

C • O • N • N • E • C • T • I • O • N • S

Researched writing requires extensive and detailed inquiry into a topic, and careful documentation of this inquiry requires use of the perhaps unfamiliar elements of parenthetical notes and the works cited list. Aside from the research process itself and these special elements, however, writing the research paper should seem reassuringly familiar. Writers of research papers organize their planning materials, mostly notes on sources, the same way they would any other type of paper: by reviewing and grouping materials into coherent and meaningful subtopics and by composing informal and formal outlines to rough out and refine this organization. Writers of research papers draft their work as they would any paper: although they must incorporate parenthetical notes, their primary concern is to explore and express their thoughts on their topics, while responding to and integrating the thoughts and information derived from their research. When revising, writers of research papers have the same goals and take the same steps as they would for any paper: they revise content, striving for a clear, unified, coherent, and complete statement of their ideas; they revise style, striving for balanced, clear, and appropriately emphatic expression of their ideas; and they revise punctuation, mechanics, and documentation, striving for a presentation that does not distract or detract from the communication of their ideas.

Remember as you organize, write, and document your research paper that all you have learned about writing will be useful — even as you learn new ways to think and write — for any type of writing you do in the future.

wealth of material; now you need to arrange that material in the way that will best present your thesis to your readers.

Reread Your Notes

To begin, review your notes. Though time consuming, rereading all notes will help you to see the scope of your materials and the connections among ideas distilled from your sources. A complete grasp of your materials is crucial as you revise your thesis statement, prepare an outline, and sort your materials.

Revise Your Thesis Statement

Examine your working thesis statement. Based on the information gathered during research, test the validity of your thesis statement:

Does it identify your topic clearly?

Does it present a valid judgment?

Does it incorporate necessary qualifications and limitations?

Does it state or imply that you have acknowledged opposing views?

Is it worded effectively?

If you cannot respond "yes" to these questions, revise the thesis statement.

Use the Revised Thesis to Develop a Rough Outline

Once your thesis statement is clearly and effectively worded, type a clean copy and use it to help you construct a rough outline for your paper. What major categories does the thesis statement imply? Use them as the basis of a rough outline with which to sort your note cards into meaningful groups dictated by your thesis and ideas. Michele's thesis statement, in revised form, looked like this:

In a process that began with the first intelligence test and continues today, the tests, their use, and the concept of intelligence itself have been constantly challenged, refined, and redefined by scientists and educators seeking to use the tests wisely, not to label people but to help them overcome weaknesses and build on strengths.

This thesis statement clearly implies at least three major areas of emphasis: the history of intelligence tests, uses of the tests, and new directions in their use. Allowing for an introduction and conclusion and placing in rough order the most important of her discoveries about her topic, Michele created this rough outline:

Introductory paragraphs/thesis statement

History of tests

   — *Binet and Simon*

   — *Terman*

   — *Otis*

   — *Wechsler*

Uses of tests

   — *Learning context*

   — *Social misuses*

   — *Judicial misuses*

New directions

   — *Current trends/new directions*

Concluding paragraphs/where should we be heading?

》》》 *Remember that you can revise your outline if you discover a better way to arrange materials as you write the rough draft.* **《《《**

Although you are only sketching your research paper when you are composing a rough outline, preparing it on a word processor has advantages. ■ Type your rough outline on your word processor and then take a break. Return to the outline and print it out, examining it, and then make any necessary changes. Revise it and print a new copy. It will be much easier to evaluate your outline if it is typed rather than handwritten. ■ Write alternative versions. Prepare different versions of the rough outline, experimenting with the arrangement of information and ideas. Print two versions side by side and compare their clarity, balance, and emphasis. ■ Save the rough outline. The structure of the rough outline — and even some of its phrasing — can be used later in devising your formal outline.

Sort Your Notes

Using the major headings of your rough outline, sort your notes. First, find a roomy place — a large table in the library, the floor in your family room, the bed in your room. Make label cards using the major topics from your rough outline. Spread them out and then sort your note cards into the appropriate major topic groups.

If a note fits in more than one group, place the card in the most appropriate group and place a cross-reference card (for example, "See Parker quotation, p. 219 — in *childhood*") in each of the other appropriate groups. Expect to have a stack of notes that do not logically fit into any group. Label them *miscellaneous* and set them aside. You may see where they fit as you continue working. Use paper clips, binders' clips, rubber bands, or envelopes to keep groups of notes together.

Allow a few days to organize and perhaps reorganize your notes. Sorting cards involves analyzing, reconsidering, and re-arranging. Expect temporary chaos.

Prepare a Formal Outline

After sorting cards into major topics, use the topics to decide on
the arrangement of information within sections of your paper.
Take each group of cards and organize them into a clear, logical
sequence. Creating a formal outline is generally the most useful
way to accomplish this. (To review outlining, see section 2b.)

Through a formal, detailed outline derived from her notes,
Michele evolved the structure of her paper, including chronological organization of material on test history and topical organization of material on test uses. Her formal outline appears on pages
549–55.

Using the word processor, expand your rough outline to
produce the formal outline of your paper. ▪ Introduce the
elements of a formal outline: roman numerals, upper-case
letters, arabic numerals, and lower-case letters to indicate
levels of detail. ▪ Add clarifying information. Insert
details that will guide you in writing the rough draft.
▪ Insert your revised thesis statement. Using the "block"
and "move" codes, copy your thesis statement into the file
that contains your formal outline and place it at the top,
below the title. ▪ Use the "outline" feature of your word
processor to arrange material easily into the correct format.

34b ⟩ **Write the rough draft.**

With notes, revised thesis, and formal outline in hand, you are
ready to begin writing the rough draft. The rough draft of a research paper, like the rough draft of any paper, will be messy and
inconsistent, sketchy in some places and repetitive in others. That
is to be expected. In fact, writing the draft of a research paper may
present even more problems than writing other papers because of
its greater length and complexity. To help with the process of
drafting the research paper, remember the drafting strategies that

you developed in writing other kinds of papers. (For a complete discussion, see section 2c.)

General Drafting Strategies

Gather all your materials together.

Work from your outline.

Remember the purpose of your paper.

Use only ideas and details that support your thesis statement.

Remember your readers' needs.

Do not worry about technical matters.

Rethink and modify troublesome sections.

Reread sections as you write.

Write alternative versions of troublesome sections.

Periodically give yourself a break from writing.

Beyond these general principles, which apply to all writing, there are specific principles that apply to writing a research paper and take into account its special requirements and demands:

Drafting Strategies for Research Papers

Allow ample time to write. Begin writing as soon as you can and write something every day.

Work one section at a time. Work steadily, section by section. When you come to a section that is difficult to write or for which you need more information, leave it for later and move on to the next section. Remember to look for necessary new material as soon as possible.

Give special attention to introductory and concluding paragraphs. Ideas for introductory and concluding paragraphs may occur at any time during the writing process. Consider several strategies and select the one most clearly matched to the tone and purpose of your paper.

Give special attention to technical language. Define carefully any technical language required in your paper. Thoughtful definition and use of important technical terms will help you to clarify your ideas as you draft your paper.

Think of your paper by section, not by paragraph. Because of the complexity of material in a research paper, discussions of most topics will require more than one paragraph. Keep that in mind and use new paragraphs to present subtopics.

Use transitions to signal major shifts within your work. The multiparagraph explanations required for key points can make it difficult for readers to know when you have moved from one key point to another. Consequently, emphasize transitions in your draft; you can refine them during revision if they are too obvious.

Incorporate your research notes smoothly so that they are an integral part of your paper. Material from sources should support, not dominate, your ideas. Incorporate source material as needed to support your thesis; do not simply string notes together with sentences. (For a complete discussion of incorporating research notes, see section 34c.)

As you write, remember that a research paper should present your views on a subject, based on outside reading and interpretation; it should not just show that you can collect and compile what others have said about the subject. Develop your own ideas fully. Be a part of the paper: add comments on sources and disagree with them when necessary. Do not be a stenographer. Be a thinker and a writer.

If possible, compose at the computer. "Add," "delete," "move," and "reformat" features will give you flexibility as you prepare your rough draft. You will also be able to print "clean" pages to review and revise later. ■ Drafting a research paper is a complex process, but a few suggestions may simplify your work. ■ Create a file for your draft and copy your thesis statement into it. ■ Copy quotations from your quotation file into the paper as you need them. By copying quotations into the file, rather than retyping them, you will save time and avoid introducing new errors.

■ Keep in mind the kinds of changes that you can easily make during revision. You will be able to move or change words, phrases, sentences, paragraphs, or whole sections; check spelling; change format and spacing; use "search and replace" procedures; and add full documentation.

  Incorporate notes smoothly into the research paper.

The information from your note taking — summaries, quotations, and paraphrases — must be incorporated smoothly into your research paper, providing clarifications, explanations, and illustrations of important ideas. Use your notes selectively to substantiate your points, not simply to show that you have gathered materials, and provide your own commentary on the central ideas. Your readers should know why you have included the source material you did.

Summaries

Summaries are probably the easiest kind of researched material to incorporate in your paper because such information fits into your own sentences. Remember that sentences containing summarized facts and ideas require parenthetical notes (see section 34d) that identify the sources of the information. Information that is common knowledge, however, does not require an identifying note (see section 32g for a discussion of common knowledge).

Quotations

Use quotations selectively to add clarity and emphasis to a research paper, not to pad its length. Overquoting reduces the effectiveness of a paper because it suggests that the writer has depended too heavily on other people's ideas.

Never "float" a quotation and expect readers to know why it was worth quoting. Instead, frame the quotation with your own ideas and provide a brief evaluative comment. The examples given below demonstrate an effective pattern for introducing quotations: identify the author and source (book, article, interview, and so on) and explain the quotation's relevance to the discussion. Numerous verbs may be used to introduce quotations.

Verbs Used to Introduce Quotations

add	explain	reply
answer	mention	respond
claim	note	restate
comment	observe	say
declare	reiterate	stress
emphasize	remark	summarize

Quotations of prose and poetry can be either brief and included within the text of a paragraph or long and set off from the paragraph text.

Brief Prose or Verse Quotations

Include prose quotations of four or fewer typed lines (approximately forty-five words) within the paragraph text. Enclose them in quotation marks. For example:

Binet's IQ test has been under attack for decades.   Yet
many of the most vocal critics have not objectively
considered Binet's intended use for the test.   According to Stephen Jay Gould, in The Mismeasure of Man,
Binet designed his test "as a practical guide for
identifying children whose poor performance indicated a
need for special education" (152).

To vary the pattern, references can be placed at the end of
the quoted material or, if not disruptive, in the middle of it. For
example:

Binet's IQ test has been under attack for decades.   Yet
many of the most vocal critics have not objectively
considered Binet's intended use for the test.   "He
devised his scale," Stephen Jay Gould states in The
Mismeasure of Man, "as a practical guide for identifying children whose poor performance indicated a need
for special education" (152).

To use very brief segments of a quotation, a phrase or a part of a
sentence, incorporate the material into your own sentence structure. Although derived from the same passage as the quotation
used above, this example demonstrates use of only part of the
original:

Binet's IQ test has been under attack for decades.   Yet
many of the most vocal critics have not objectively
considered Binet's original use for the test.   Stephen
Jay Gould, in his book The Mismeasure of Man, stresses

```
that Binet's primary purpose was to separate "children

whose poor performance indicated a need for special

education" (152).
```

Punctuate such quotations according to the requirements of the entire sentence. Do not set such quotations apart with commas unless your sentence structure requires commas.

Incorporate verse quotations of three or fewer lines in the same way. Use quotation marks and indicate the poem's line divisions with a slash (/) preceded and followed by one space. Retain the poem's pattern of capitalization.

```
Tennyson stresses Ulysses' longing to pursue unreach-

able goals, even in the face of old age and death: "And

this gray spirit yearning in desire / To follow knowl-

edge like a sinking star, / Beyond the utmost bound of

human thought" ("Ulysses" 30-32).
```

Long Prose or Verse Quotations

To incorporate prose quotations of five or more typed lines, or approximately forty-five words, set the quotation off from the body of the paragraph. Indent the quotation ten spaces from the left margin and double-space it; do not enclose it within quotation marks. If a clause introduces the quotation, follow it with a colon, as in this example:

```
Binet's IQ test has been under attack for decades. Yet

many of the most vocal critics have not objectively

considered Binet's intended use for the test. Stephen

Jay Gould offers this clarification in The Mismeasure

of Man:
```

```
          Not only did Binet decline to label IQ as

          inborn intelligence; he also refused to

          regard it as a general device for ranking all

          pupils according to mental worth. He devised

          his scale only for the limited purpose of his

          commission by the ministry of education: as a

          practical guide for identifying children

          whose poor performance indicated a need for

          special education. (152)
```

To quote four or more lines of poetry, follow the pattern for long prose quotations: indent ten spaces, double-space the lines, and omit quotation marks. Follow the poet's line spacing as closely as possible, as in this example:

```
Dante Gabriel Rossetti presents a lush, sensuous view

of the afterlife in his poem "The Blessed Damozel":

          The blessed damozel leaned out

               From the gold bar of heaven;

          Her eyes were deeper than the depth

               Of waters stilled at even;

          She had three lilies in her hand,

               And the stars in her hair were seven.

               (1-6)

Such images of heaven must have shocked tradition-bound

Victorians.
```

Punctuation with Quotations

Single Quotation Marks. Quotations within brief quotations are to be enclosed within single quotation marks. Place the material you are quoting in double quotation marks (" ") and change the source's punctuation to single quotation marks (' '), as in this example:

```
Gould explains Binet's IQ scoring this way: "The age

associated with the last tasks he could perform became

his 'mental age,' and his general intellectual level

was calculated by subtracting this mental age from his

true chronological age" (149-50).
```

》》》 *In long quotations that are indented ten spaces and not enclosed within quotation marks, any quotation marks within the source material remain double.* **《《《**

Brackets. Use brackets to clarify words or phrases in a quotation. For example, the bracketed phrase in the passage below substitutes for the word *he,* which was used in the original but has no antecedent in the quotation or its introduction.

```
Gould explains Binet's IQ scoring this way: "The age

associated with the last tasks [a school boy] could

perform became his 'mental age,' and his general intel-

lectual level was calculated by subtracting this mental

age from his true chronological age" (149-150).
```

Bracketed information can substitute for the original word or words or appear in addition to the original material: "the tasks he [a school boy] could perform." If your typewriter does not have brackets, leave space for them and add them neatly by hand.

》》》 *If a quotation requires extensive use of brackets, use another or express the information in your own words.* **《《《**

Ellipses. Use ellipsis points (three spaced periods) to show where words are omitted from a quotation. Omissions from the middle of a sentence do not require any punctuation other than ellipses. Omissions from the end of a sentence, however, require a fourth period (the sentence's end punctuation). The first period immediately follows the last letter of the last word.

```
Gould notes: "[Binet] devised his scale . . . as a

practical guide for identifying children whose poor

performances indicated a need for special education"

(152).
```

》》》 *It is not necessary to use ellipses at the beginning or end of a quote because readers know that quotations come from more complete sources. However, readers cannot be expected to know when something has been omitted from the middle of a passage.*

Unnecessary ellipses

> Gould notes that Binet developed ". . . a practical guide for identifying children whose poor performances indicated a need for special education" (152). **《《《**

Paraphrases

Notes that paraphrase a source's ideas in your own words can simply be incorporated into your paper where they fit. A one-sentence paraphrase should be followed immediately by a parenthetical note. Longer paraphrases, especially background information taken from a single source, should be placed in a separate paragraph with parenthetical documentation at the end. So that readers do not assume that the documentation applies only to the ideas expressed in the last sentence, identify the author and source at the beginning of the paragraph. For example:

```
Stephen Jay Gould, in The Mismeasure of Man,

provides a useful summary of Binet's position on IQ

testing.  According to Gould, Binet opposed theories

that heredity set limits on a student's achievement.

For him, a student's score on the test did not estab-

lish his or her worth as a student or as a person.

Rather, Binet wanted to use IQ tests to pick out slow

learners and help them through better planned and

better focused education (152).
```

34d > Use parenthetical notes to document your research.

A research paper must include internal documentation to identify clearly which materials come from which sources and where facts, quotations, or ideas appeared in original sources. In the past, note numbers (one half-space above the line) at the end of sentences indicated when information, ideas, and quotations came from source materials. Those note numbers corresponded to full citations placed either at the bottom of the page (footnotes) or gathered at the end of the paper (endnotes). Numbered notes are still seen in older books and articles. Simplified, less repetitive methods of citation are more commonly used today.

Acknowledging the repetitive nature of full note citations, the Modern Language Association (MLA), following the lead of the American Psychological Association, now briefly identifies sources in the paper in parentheses. See section 33a for a discussion of MLA and other style guides.

Consistency of References

Parenthetical references must correspond to an entry in the list of works cited. If a works cited entry is listed under the author's name, the text reference must cite the author, not the title, editor, translator, director, or any other agent. Readers can thus match information in parenthetical references with the information in works cited entries.

Basic Forms of Parenthetical Notes

To avoid disrupting the text, parenthetical notes use the briefest possible form to identify the relevant source: the name of the author or the title under which the source appears in the list of works cited and, for print sources, a page number. In the interests of clarity and economy, writers may incorporate some of the necessary information into their sentences. For example:

```
Between 1851 and 1861, more than 150,000 white settlers

moved westward into land previously claimed by the

Santee Sioux (Brown 38).
```

Or:

```
Brown notes that between 1851 and 1861, more than

150,000 white settlers moved westward into land previ-

ously claimed by the Santee Sioux (38).
```

In-text references can also be used to identify specific authors, when citing more than one author with the same last name ("Dee Brown notes"), or to identify specific works, when citing more than one source by the same author ("In *Bury My Heart at Wounded Knee,* Brown notes"). In these cases, the parenthetical note contains only the page number, as in the second example given above.

Print Sources

For any print materials listed by author's name (books, articles, pamphlets, and so on), generally use the author's last name and the page number.

```
Coexisting with illiteracy we often find innumeracy,

"an inability to deal comfortably with the fundamental

notions of number and chance" (Paulos 3).
```

Or:

```
John Allen Paulos states that coexisting with illitera-

cy we will find innumeracy, "an inability to deal

comfortably with the fundamental notions of number and

chance" (3).
```

In some special circumstances, the rule of including the author's last name and the page reference is superseded:

Special circumstance	*Rule and sample*
Two authors with the same last name	Include first and last name: (John Paulos 3), distinct from (Miguel Paulos 217)
Two works by the same author	Include a shortened version of the title: (Paulos, *Innumeracy* 3), distinct from (Paulos, *Mathematics* 76)
Two authors	Include both last names: (Vidich and Bensman 321)
Three authors	Include all last names, separated by commas: (Adams, Atwan, and Ford 17)
Four or more authors	Include the last name of the first author and *et al.,* without underlining: (Lewis et al. 27)
Corporate author	Include the organization as "author": (APA 256)
Multivolume works	Include the volume number after the author's name: (Churchill 1: 8)
Reference books	Include the author's name or a shortened form of the title, depending on how the work appears in the works cited list; no page numbers are required: (Williams) or ("Primates")
Poetry or drama in verse	Include the author's name, a short title (if necessary), and line (not page) numbers: (Arnold, "Stanzas" 67–72)

⟩⟩⟩ *Remember that any information given in the text should be omitted from the parenthetical reference.* ⟨⟨⟨

Nonprint Sources

Cite nonprint sources, for which no page numbers can be given, by title or "author" (lecturer, director, writer, producer, performer, or interview respondent), as they appear in the list of works cited. Such citations, however, are often clearer if worked into the text of your paper.

```
A depressing and patronizing view of homemakers has

even permeated musical theater, where this image

emerges:

            Here's to the girls who play wife

            Aren't they too much!

            Keeping house but clutching

            A copy of "Life"

            Just to keep in touch.   (Sondheim, "Ladies")
```

Or:

```
A depressing and patronizing view of homemakers has

even permeated musical theater, where this image

emerges in Stephen Sondheim's "The Ladies Who Lunch":

            Here's to the girls who play wife

            Aren't they too much!

            Keeping house but clutching

            A copy of "Life"

            Just to keep in touch.
```

>>>   *Because nonprint sources require such limited information in parenthetical notes, it is often possible to incorporate all needed information in the written text.*   <<<

Punctuating Parenthetical Notes

Without disrupting the text, place parenthetical notes as close as possible to the material they explain — usually at the end of the sentence but before the end punctuation. Allow one space before the opening parenthesis.

Paraphrases and Summaries

```
Jefferson and Latrobe modified the original design of

the White House by adding terraces in 1807 (Pearce 17).
```

Brief Quotations

For brief quotations, place the note *outside* the quotation marks but *before* the end punctuation, a change from the usual pattern of placing end punctuation before the closing quotation marks.

```
Individual occupants, from Jefferson to Roosevelt, have

modified the building to suit their tastes.  Thus,

present features of the White House "form a living link

with the building's past" (Pearce 17).
```

Long Quotations

For long, set-off quotations (indented ten spaces and not enclosed in quotation marks), place a period at the end of the quotation, followed by two spaces and then the parenthetical note not followed by additional punctuation.

The limited press coverage of the Kitty Hawk flight was
probably the result of earlier notable failures:

> Just nine days before Kitty Hawk, the
> secretary of the Smithsonian Institution,
> Samuel Langley, had tried to launch a winged
> contraption from the roof of a houseboat on
> the Potomac River in Washington, D.C. . . .
> But while boatloads of reporters and
> government officials watched expectantly,
> the craft had left its catapult and plunged
> nose first into the Potomac. (<u>Century</u> 88)

34e ⟩	**Revise the rough draft into a final draft.**

After writing the draft of the paper, set it aside for at least two or
three days and longer if possible. Then reread it carefully. Consider the paper's organization, content, and style. Your ideas should
be clearly expressed, logically organized, and effectively supported with appropriate and illuminating facts, quotations, and
paraphrases smoothly and accurately incorporated. Leave time in
your schedule to rework your paper, strengthening undeveloped
sections by expanding them, clarifying confusing sections by rewriting them, and focusing overly long sections by cutting unnecessary material. For more information on this stage of the writing
process, see Chapter 3, "Revising."

Evaluate the Rough Draft

Using the guidelines given below, assess your rough draft or consider having a peer editing session with someone in your class. Make revisions according to your assessment of the paper's strengths and weaknesses.

Introduction

Is the title interesting, accurate, and appropriate?

Is the introductory strategy interesting and appropriate to the tone and subject of the paper?

Is the thesis statement clear?

Is the length of the introduction proportionate to its importance and to the length of the entire paper?

Organization

Is the organizational pattern appropriate to the subject?

Are topics and subtopics clearly related to the thesis?

Is background information complete and well integrated?

Are interpretations of and conclusions from research clearly stated?

Content

Is the thesis statement clearly developed throughout?

Are topics adequately supported by facts, ideas, and research?

Are quotations and paraphrases well chosen to support the thesis?

Is material from sources smoothly and accurately incorporated?

Style

   Is the tone of the paper consistently serious and appropriate for a college paper?

   Are sentences clear and logical?

   Are sentences in the active voice when possible?

   Are sentences varied in length and type?

   Is the diction appropriate and consistent?

   Are any unfamiliar terms clearly explained?

Mechanics

   Is correct grammar used throughout?

   Is spelling correct throughout?

   Are capitals, italics, and punctuation used correctly throughout?

   Are parenthetical notes correctly placed and punctuated?

Conclusion

   Does the conclusion restate the main ideas of the paper or offer a final interpretation or illustration of them, without repetition?

   Does the concluding strategy leave the reader with the impression of a thorough, thoughtful paper on a meaningful subject?

Prepare the List of Works Cited

Separate the source cards containing the works cited entries for *sources used in the paper* and alphabetize them. Double-check the form of the entries (see section 33b), and then type the list of works cited, starting on a new page. (See page 589 for an illustration of the correct format.)

If you have more than one source by the same author, do not repeat the name for each source. Arrange the sources in alphabetical order by title and type the full name in the first entry and three hyphens followed by a period in place of the name in subsequent entries:

```
Gould, Stephen Jay.  Ever Since Darwin: Reflections in

     Natural History.  New York: Norton, 1977.

---.  The Mismeasure of Man.  New York: Norton, 1981.

---.  The Panda's Thumb: More Reflections in Natural

     History.  New York: Norton, 1980.
```

> If you have prepared your citations on the computer, your job will be simple: all you will need to do is add the heading "Works Cited," alphabetize the entries, and double-check the form of each entry. (See the example on pages 589–91.)

| 34f | **Prepare and submit the final manuscript.** |

The manuscript format for the research paper varies only slightly from that for other papers. (See Appendix A, Manuscript Form.) The margins, the heading, and the paging are the same, and double-spacing is still required throughout. Because the research paper has additional parts and because parenthetical notes complicate typing, however, allow extra time to prepare the final copy. Do not assume that typing and proofreading a research paper is a one-night process.

Type carefully. Type at an unhurried pace, proofreading and correcting pages before you remove them from the typewriter. Keep the finished pages nearby to double-check when necessary. Type the list of works cited, if you have not already done so, using the guidelines given on pages 544–45. When the final copy is complete, proofread it carefully for typing errors and make any small corrections neatly in black ink.

> If you have prepared your paper using a word processor, you will be able to make final changes quickly and easily. ■ Insert paging codes. If you have not already done so, create a "header" that includes your last name and a page code. ■ Print a draft copy. Examine this copy to check the general presentation and format. If you need to alter anything — move a list so that it all appears on the same page, for example — do so now. ■ Print a high-quality copy to submit. Use a letter-quality printer, if possible, to produce the final manuscript.

After preparing the final manuscript of your paper, make a high-quality photocopy as insurance against damage or loss. **》》》** *If you have worked on the computer, you can print yourself an extra copy; you should make a disk copy, and perhaps a back-up disk copy as well, as insurance against loss.* **《《《**

If your instructor suggests a specific way to present the manuscript, follow those guidelines carefully and completely. If your instructor does not suggest a specific procedure, secure the pages with a paper clip in the upper left corner (outline first, then text, and then works cited pages) and place them in a 9-by-12-inch manila envelope with the identifying information from the first page of the paper typed on the outside. It is important to protect the manuscript in this way against damage or loss of pages.

34g A sample research paper.

The following paper, written by a freshman in a composition class, demonstrates many important aspects of writing and documenting a research paper.

An Optional Outline

Not all instructors will expect an outline with the final copy of the research paper, but some will. On those occasions when you must submit an outline, place it at the beginning of the paper.

Examine Michele Newton's outline for her paper on intelligence testing, considering especially these important features:

1. On each page, the student's last name and the page number are given in the upper right corner.

2. A standard heading is provided, with the student's name, course number, instructor's name, and the date.

3. The complete title of the paper is given.

4. The introduction (and conclusion), separated from the outline, appear without roman numerals.

5. The full thesis statement is presented.

6. A traditional outline format is used. Roman numerals indicate major divisions; upper-case letters, arabic numerals, and lower-case letters indicate subdivisions.

1.

2. Michele Newton

   English 105

   Dr. Robert Perrin

   6 April 1990

3.   Intelligence Testing:

                    Avoiding the Sargasso Sea

4. INTRODUCTION

5. <u>Thesis statement</u>: In a process that began with the
   first intelligence test and continues today, the
   tests, their use, and the concept of intelligence
   itself have been constantly challenged, refined, and
   redefined by scientists and educators seeking to use
   the tests wisely, not to label people but to help
   them overcome weaknesses and build on strengths.

6. I. Alfred Binet and Theodore Simon produced the
       first well-known intelligence test (1905).

       A. Test design

           1. Individually administered

           2. Thirty subtests

       B. Innovations

           1. Subtests to produce average score

           2. Concept of intelligence quotient

               a. Mental age

               b. Chronological age

7. Roman numeral divisions are complete sentences; subdivisions are in topic-outline form.

An outline of a research paper serves as a "table of contents" and clearly and completely describes the information presented in the paper.

7. II. Lewis M. Terman revised the Binet-Simon test to create the Stanford-Binet (1916).

    A. Test emphasis

        1. Arithmetical skills

        2. Verbal skills

        3. Social variables

    B. Uses of the test

        1. Identify the retarded

        2. Label the feeble-minded

        3. Characterize criminals and delinquents

        4. Acknowledge superior children

        5. Determine vocational fitness

  III. David Wechsler developed the Wechsler-Bellevue Intelligence Scale (1939) and the Wechsler Intelligence Scale for Children (1949).

    A. Test design

        1. Academic tests

            a. Verbal

            b. Arithmetical

        2. Performance tests

    B. Innovations

        1. Composite scores

        2. Increased reliability

IV. Historically, intelligence tests have been given and interpreted outside a learning context.

    A. Anthony--Mexican American five-year-old

        1. Average score (national group)

        2. Exceptional score (Spanish-speaking group)

    B. Cultural and social biases

        1. Deprives children

        2. Limits possibilities

        3. Deprives society

V. The social consequences of misused IQ scores should not be ignored.

    A. Undue emphasis on scores

        1. Low scorers--not challenged

        2. High scorers--often pressured

    B. Uncertain predictors

VI. The judicial system has misused the results of IQ tests.

    A. Carrie Buck (1927)

        1. Scored in feeble-minded range (standards then)

        2. Sterilized by court order

    B. Supreme Court ruling until 1972

VII. Current trends in intelligence testing suggest flexibility in test design and caution in the use of tests.

    A. Alternative methods

        1. Sensory tests

        2. Observations

        3. Ongoing assessment of patterns

    B. Attempts to redefine general intelligence

        1. Academic

           a. Verbal

           b. Arithmetical

        2. Spatial

        3. Physical

        4. Musical

        5. Social

        6. Interpersonal

    C. Applied intelligence

        1. Contextual

        2. Adaptable

        3. Insightful

CONCLUSION

1. Begin page numbering on the first page. In the upper right corner, one-half inch from the top of the paper, type your last name, followed by a space, and then the page number. Position the page number flush against the one-inch margin on the right.

2. Use the same heading for the research paper that you use for other papers: the writer's name, course number, instructor's name, and date. Double-space the heading and place it within the normal one-inch margins in the upper left corner.

3. Two line spaces down from the heading, center the title. If the title runs to a second line, center both lines. Allow two line spaces between the title and the first paragraph of the paper.

4. Michele introduces her paper with a long quotation. It is indented ten spaces from the left. The ellipsis points indicate the omission of the phrase "for example." The parenthetical note follows the closing period.

5. Michele provides a transition from the introductory quotation and establishes a historical context for her discussion.

1. Michele Newton

2. English 105

   Dr. Robert Perrin

   6 April 1990

3.   Intelligence Testing:

        Avoiding the Sargasso Sea

4.   If . . . the impression takes root that

   these tests really measure intelligence,

   that they constitute a sort of last judg-

   ment on the child's capacity, that they

   reveal "scientifically" his predestined

   ability, then it would be a thousand times

   better if all the intelligence testers and

   all their questionnaires were sunk without

   warning in the Sargasso Sea. (Eysenck and

   Kamin, Controversy 90)

       Walter Lippmann, a prominent columnist and

   social philosopher of the first half of the twentieth

5. century, wrote this provocative statement in 1922.

   But during their eighty years of use, intelligence

   tests have always generated controversy. Today,

   psychologists and educators continue to debate what

   the tests can measure, how they should be designed,

6. Michele merges a brief quotation with her sentence. The parenthetical note includes only the author's name because the material appeared in an encyclopedia, for which page references are not required. The full quotation reads, "Binet conceived intelligence as the sum of all thought processes involved in mental adaptation."

7. After describing historical definitions of intelligence, Michele provides a current definition, establishing a transition to her thesis statement.

8. Michele's thesis statement comes at the end of her introductory paragraphs. It is presented in one sentence but establishes the qualified opinion that will focus her paper.

9. Michele begins the body of her paper by describing the early work of Alfred Binet and Theodore Simon, the first people to devise intelligence tests. This opening establishes the chronological-historical context for her later discussions.

and how their results should be used--and not
misused.

 At the turn of the century, when the first
intelligence tests were administered in large num-
6. bers, intelligence was thought to be the "sum of all
thought processes involved in mental adaptation"
7. (Durost). Today, although there are many definitions
of intelligence, most theorists agree that intelligence is expressed through the potential of the
person being tested, rather than through the sum of
8. fully developed skills. In a process that began with
the first intelligence test and continues today, the
tests, their use, and the concept of intelligence
itself have been constantly challenged, refined, and
redefined by scientists and educators seeking to use
the tests wisely, not to label people but to help
them overcome weaknesses and build on strengths.

9. Alfred Binet, director of the psychology laboratory at the Sorbonne, and Theodore Simon, a noted
French physiologist, were looking in new directions
when they designed and administered the first
well-known intelligence tests to French school children in 1905 (Guilford 4). The thirty subtests of

10. Michele summarizes the general skills tested by the 1905 Binet-Simon scale; this general information is considered common knowledge.

11. Rather than quoting long sections of Guilford's book, Michele composed a brief list of representative subtests. Because her list was not a quotation, she did not indent it ten spaces but aligned it with the left margin as is done with tables and charts. Michele identifies the source of the paraphrased information in her list with a parenthetical note. Notice that no punctuation separates the author's name from the page number.

12. Dearborn's interpretation of the innovations in the Binet-Simon test covers three pages in the original source. Michele chose to summarize it briefly and give Dearborn credit for the interpretation.

the 1905 Binet-Simon Intelligence Scale were designed
10. and individually administered to measure memory,
reasoning, numerical facility, comprehension, time
orientation, and the ability to combine ideas into
meaningful patterns of thought. The following subtests, abstracted from the complete Binet and Simon
test, indicate the skills expected of the average
five-year-old:

11. Recognize food (choice between wood and chocolate)

Seek food (in response to chocolate wrapped in paper)

Follow simple orders to repeat gestures

Point to objects (head, nose, etc.)

Recognize objects in pictures

Name objects in pictures

Repeat three digits

Resist suggestions

Define simple words   (Guilford 4-5)

Binet and Simon improved on earlier tests in two
ways: (1) the use of multiple subtests to produce an
"averaged" score and (2) the introduction of the
12. concept of "mental age" (Dearborn 65-67). The
child's average score, termed <u>mental age</u> (MA), and
age in years, termed <u>chronological age</u> (CA), were

13. An equation (or table, diagram, or other kind of visual support material) is presented within the paper, where it has the most impact, not at the end of the paper. A parenthetical note is placed at the lower right side, but within the regular one-inch margin. The note includes the author, a comma, and a brief title followed by the page reference to distinguish this source from another by Eysenck and Kamin also cited in the paper.

14. The numbers, computation, and IQ scores incorporated here are not documented. Using the equation cited above, Michele compiled these figures herself.

15. Rather than redraw the curve of test scores, Michele photocopied the original and used rubber cement to insert it into her text. Below the insert, she typed the parenthetical citation. (Large-scale drawings, graphs, and so on, can be reduced to a convenient size using a photocopy machine.)

Newton 4

employed in the equation shown below to produce the

child's <u>intelligence quotient</u> (IQ).

13.
$$IQ = \frac{\text{Mental Age (MA)}}{\text{Chronological Age (CA)}} \times 100$$

(Eysenck and Kamin, <u>Controversy</u> 16)

(To avoid decimals, the result of division is multi-

plied by 100.) For example, a child with an MA of 7

14. and a CA of 7 would have an IQ of 100, the average

score; a child with an MA of 9 and a CA of 7 would

have an IQ of 128, an above-average score; a child

with an MA of 7 and a CA of 9 would have an IQ of 77,

a below-average score. The general interpretation of

the scores follows this pattern:

15.

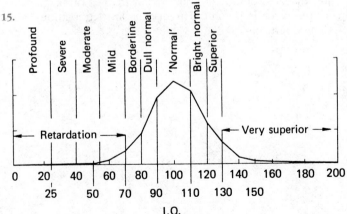

(Eysenck and Kamin, <u>Structure</u> 58)

16. In this section, Michele comments on the material she cites. She does not merely present the source material and expect readers to interpret it. This active, thoughtful summation helps Michele to help her readers understand her topic.

17. This transition paragraph establishes the link between the Binet-Simon test and its revised version, the Stanford-Binet. The transition makes the paper's structure clear for readers and adds interesting information.

18. Because Terman's name is indicated in the introductory phrase, it is not required in the parenthetical note. Notice as well the use of *sic,* without italics, within the quotation; *sic,* which means "thus," indicates that a grammatical, mechanical, or logical error exists in the original. In this instance, *sic* reassures readers that Michele knows that *less* should be in the comparative form: *lesser.*

19. Incorporating Terman's explanation of what supplemental information is useful in determining intelligence allows Michele to establish balance in her discussion, acknowledging that test designers knew that variables other than test scores were important. This list, a direct quotation, is indented ten spaces.

16. This clear mathematical expression of discrepancies between ability and age as a seemingly scientific, objective numbered score made the Binet-Simon Intelligence Scale widely popular.

17.   Binet and Simon's work prompted others to explore IQ tests, most notably Lewis M. Terman, an American psychologist working at Stanford University. In 1916, Terman adapted the Binet-Simon test, creating the Stanford-Binet Intelligence Scale.

        Terman's test, designed for American school children, evaluated primarily arithmetical and verbal skills, though Terman claimed to treat test results within a broad context. In The Measurement of

18. Intelligence he wrote, "There are no tests which are absolutely pure tests of intelligence. All are influenced to a greater or less [sic] degree also by training and by social environment" (135). Terman suggested gathering this supplemental information:

19.   1.   Social status

                2.   The teacher's estimate of the child's intelligence

                3.   School opportunities, including years in attendance, regularity, retardation

20. Michele points to a gap between Terman's theory and his practice, allowing her ideas to emerge in her use of sources.

21. Michele uses the subject headings in one of Terman's chapters to help her to summarize the points he made in a lengthy discussion without taking up too much space.

> > [working below grade level], or
> >
> > acceleration, etc.
> >
> > 4. Quality of school work
> >
> > 5. Physical handicaps, if any (135)

20. But Terman's acknowledgment of these variables did

    not guarantee that of test administrators or inter-

    preters. Further, Terman's questions, following the

    Binet-Simon pattern closely, did not incorporate the

    variables in the scale itself. Consider the skills

    required of a three-year-old on the Stanford-Binet:

    > 1. Name parts of body.
    >
    > 2. Name familiar objects.
    >
    > 3. Name objects in pictures.
    >
    > 4. Classify self as boy or girl.
    >
    > 5. State family name.
    >
    > 6. Repeat 6-7 syllables (sentences).
    >
    > 7. Repeat 3-digit sequences. (Terman
    >
    >   142-50)

    Although it followed the Binet-Simon model, the

21. Stanford-Binet claimed a larger purpose. Terman

    suggested, in a chapter called "The Uses of

    Intelligence Tests," that the Stanford-Binet be used

    to identify retarded children and children of superi-

    or ability, to assess the feeble-mindedness of

22. Another careful transition moves forward Michele's discussion of the historical development of testing. Such transitions help to hold together lengthy discussions.

23. The dates for Wechsler's tests may be considered common knowledge. Because Michele reasoned that the specific names for his tests are not common knowledge, she documented them.

24. In presenting charts or lists, reproduce the format of the original as exactly as possible, as Michele has done here.

those with mental defects (morons, imbeciles, etc.)
and of delinquents and criminals, to place students
into classes by ability, and to determine the voca-
tional fitness of people of all ages (3-21). With
such broad claims for a single test, it is no wonder
that the Stanford-Binet was seen as a panacea for
what ailed American education, the legal system, and
business.

22.   From the 1940s, the most widely used tests have
been David Wechsler's Wechsler-Bellevue Intelligence
Scale (WBIS), designed in 1939 for adults, and the
Wechsler Intelligence Scale for Children (WISC)

23. developed in 1949 (Guilford 8-9). Wechsler's tests,
administered in groups, emphasized verbal skills but
also assessed performance skills, as shown in this
list of subtests:

24.   Verbal Tests:

           Information

           Comprehension (to measure judgment or

               common sense)

           Arithmetic

           Digits Forward and Backward

           Similarities (state how two given things

               are alike)

25. Michele summarizes the ideas presented in this passage:

Durost   *Wechsler Tests*

"Intelligence Testing"
"[The Wechsler tests] were easier to administer and
provided three distinct IQ's (intelligence
quotients)—one for the entire test and one each for
two groups of subtests, one group consisting of
verbal tests, the other of performance tests. The
Wechsler tests were also supposed to yield insights
concerning emotional problems."

---

26. Having conducted an interview, Michele quotes Jill Lowery after first providing her name and credentials. Because an interview is a nonprint source (which will not have page numbers) and because the source is identified in the text, no note is required.

Vocabulary

Performance Tests:

Picture Completion (state what is missing
in each picture)

Picture Arrangement (put four pictures from
a comic strip in correct temporal order)

Object Assembly (jigsaw puzzles)

Block Design (construct color-pattern
designs in duplication of given patterns)

Digit Symbol (code substitutions, each of
nine simple symbols to be substituted
for its digit mate)

(Guilford 9)

25. Three scores were tabulated--an average of both tests
and individual scores for each part--and, at least in
theory, the test was thought to give insight into the
emotional stability of the person taking the test

26. (Durost). According to Jill Lowery, a fourth-year
doctoral student in clinical psychology and instructor at Indiana State University, the Wechsler Scales

27. Michele uses an effective transition to move from the first section of her paper — the historical overview — to the second section — the uses and misuses of intelligence tests.

28. Michele prepares to cite an example of the potential misuse of intelligence tests by providing readers with pertinent information about the case study.

29. Michele chooses to begin a quotation in midsentence, merging the quotation with her own introductory comment. Notice that within the material she quotes (identified by double quotation marks) Michele places single quotation marks around the words that were quoted in the original. Michele also inserts *and* to make the sentence read smoothly. Brackets show that the addition is hers.

are the most generally accepted tests because they
"have a very rich research history which supports
their validity and reliability."

27.   Psychologists and educators continue to revise
standard intelligence tests and to research their
effectiveness, but this is only one area of inquiry.
Of equal importance is how the tests are to be
used--and how to avoid the misuses of the past.

One fundamental error in the use of IQ scores
has been using them outside a context. As part of an
extensive study, Jane R. Mercer, a sociology professor at the University of California, examined the

28. case of a five-year-old Mexican-American boy,
Anthony, who scored 105 on the Wechsler Scale for
Children. His score, only slightly above average in
a general test group, is twenty-one points above
average if compared to the scores of other children
from Spanish-speaking homes. Considered out of his
socio-linguistic context, Anthony would move along

29. the same "relatively slow path of the tens of millions of 'ordinary' children, perhaps never realize
his abilities, [and] probably never go to college"
(Krasner 1). Considered within his context, however,

30. Although Alan Coulter is credited with the comment quoted here, his remarks appeared in an article by another author. Consequently, the parenthetical note must include the last name of the author of the article, plus the page number.

Anthony ranks among the top five percent in intelligence.

For so many children like Anthony, raw scores do
not give a complete picture of the child's potential.
By relying on scores alone, schools and society cheat
themselves and their children out of hope for the
30. future. Alan Coulter, acting director for special
education in the New Orleans School District, com-
menting on one-dimensional uses of IQ scores, says,
"IQ tests are just labeling people without leading to
achievement" (Levine 55).

An IQ label has little to do with a person's
general behavior or productivity. Nevertheless, low
scorers are often labeled slow and placed in special
classes, even if outside school they function as well
as other, so-called average children their age.
Children labeled slow may find it difficult to move
into regular classes because the expectations of
parents, peers, and teachers are fixed by the label
(Krasner 1). High scorers are also labeled on the
basis of a single test score, even though high scores
do not always predict success in school, college, or

31. Here, Michele introduces another section of her paper — the judicial misuses of intelligence tests — and illustrates her point by using an interesting case in which the Supreme Court upheld sterilization laws.

the workplace. R. J. Herrnstein, psychology professor at Harvard University, notes in IQ in the
Meritocracy, "A low IQ predicts poor performance more
reliably than a high one predicts good performance"
(113). In an ironic reversal of the harmfully low
expectations of children with low scores, parents'
and teachers' expectations for academic and other
achievement from children with high scores may be too
great (Roberts 94).

31.   Society seems to follow the lead of the schools.
At one time, even the judicial system misused IQ
scores. In 1927, the Supreme Court upheld sterilization laws in Virginia, using intelligence test scores
for justification. The case, Buck v. Bell, centered
on Carrie Buck, a young mother who had scored a
mental age of nine on the Stanford-Binet Intelligence
Scale; her mother, then fifty-two, had scored a
mental age of seven; Carrie's child, though apparently untested, was also considered "feeble-minded"
(Gould 335). Oliver Wendell Holmes, Jr., wrote the
majority opinion:

> We have seen more than once that the public
> welfare may call upon the best citizens for
> their lives. It would be strange if it

32. Rather than quote a passage that would have contained a quotation, Michele selected isolated information from this passage:

Gould   *Supreme Court Ruling*

Mismeasure, p. 335
" 'Over 7,500 sterilized in Virginia,' the headline read. The
law that Holmes upheld had been implemented for forty-eight
years, from 1924 to 1972."

---

33. Michele introduces the last section of her paper — new directions in the use of intelligence tests — smoothly and clearly.

would not call upon those who already sap
the strength of the state for these lesser
sacrifices. . . . Three generations of
imbeciles are enough. (Gould 335)

Carrie Buck was sterilized under Virginia law, although she would not be considered mentally retarded
by standards set today. This shocking story becomes
even more so when one considers that the law that
justified Carrie Buck's sterilization, and the ster-

32. ilizations of some 7,500 others, was not overturned
until 1972 (Gould 335-36).

33.   Today, theoretical, clinical, and educational
psychologists are searching for alternatives to
existing intelligence tests and for more holistic
ways to interpret their findings. Art Levine, in
"Getting Smart About IQ," noted that school psychologists are looking for "alternatives to IQ tests for
children in need of special help. They're using a
bewildering variety of academic and sensory tests,
interviewing parents and even analyzing how students
conduct themselves on the playground with friends"
(55). Katherine Lindenauer, a psychologist with the
Los Angeles School District, offered this comment on
the new method of assessment: "It's more challenging.

It's more complex. But you learn a good deal about the youngsters" (Levine 55). Psychologists are learning to look at the child as an individual and not as an intelligence test score. Dr. Francis Roberts, columnist for Parents magazine, gave the mother of a two-year-old exhibiting above-average intelligence this advice:

> Rather than focusing on test scores, center attention on your child. If you plan on nursery school for your very bright child, look for a staff that values differences among children, as well as a program that does not uniformly press for early academics, that encourages children to explore varying activities and interests, and that allows able children to pursue a specific interest or project in some depth. (94)

Reuven Feuerstein, an Israeli psychologist whose methods are being used in Detroit's special education classes, gives similar advice. Refusing to evaluate children on timed, pressured IQ tests, Feuerstein observes them completing tasks at their own pace. The child's educational future is thus determined not

34. A reference to a source by two authors must include the names of both authors, without additional punctuation. If a third author were included, commas would separate the first two names but would not appear between the last author's name and the page number.

by a test score but by close observation of individual learning patterns. The psychologist-observer diagnoses problems and recommends educational "treatments." During a one-year period, eight children out of eleven labeled mildly retarded had been promoted to a more advanced class (Levine 55). Linda Roland, the special education teacher in charge of the Detroit classroom, said, "I felt I was failing my students and they were failing me. [Now,] they have a future" (Levine 55).

Many intelligence researchers concur that intelligence can no longer be considered a single, universal concept accurately defined by a single test. Psychologists talk not about intelligence but about intelligences (Goleman 24). In 1983, Howard Gardner published Frames of Mind, describing the major intelligences. He includes standard academic skills such as linguistic and logical-mathematical skills, but he extends the traditional definition by including spatial skills, bodily grace, musical gifts, social

34. skills, and interpersonal skills (Walters and Gardner 5-12). More recently, Gardner expanded the seven categories into twenty (Goleman 24).

35. Although Michele had written down Sternberg's exact words, she decided that the quotation did not merit inclusion and chose to paraphrase it. The original quotation is shown below:

Levine   *Applied Intelligence*

"Getting Smart," p. 53
Robert Sternberg, Yale University psychologist, says:
"There are a lot of successful people who didn't do well on IQ tests. The tests put too little emphasis on practical and creative skills."

---

36. Michele begins her concluding paragraphs with a transition sentence that returns to Binet and Simon, allowing her to stress the connections among ideas in her paper.

Another innovator in the search for alternatives
to traditional IQ testing is psychologist Robert
Sternberg of Yale University. Sternberg has found
35. that many successful people did not score well on
intelligence tests; in fact, one-third of the professionals Sternberg interviewed scored below average on
intelligence tests administered in childhood (Levine
53-54). In place of traditional tests, Sternberg
suggests three types of thinking ability as criteria
to assess intelligence: the ability to learn from
context, rather than from specific instruction;
mental flexibility, the ability to adapt to new or
unusual ideas; and insight (Goleman 25). Gardner,
Sternberg, and others in the field argue that traditional IQ tests define intelligence too narrowly and
that narrow concepts encourage misapplication of test
results. Psychologists, educators, and parents, they
maintain, should focus on determining an individual
child's strengths (through a wide range of tests,
observations, and interviews) and not on one-
dimensional labels (Goleman 27).

36.   Definitions of intelligence have changed enor-
mously since the time of Alfred Binet and Theodore
Simon. Efforts continue to refine and redefine the

37. Continue page numbering, using last name and page number, through the works cited list.

38. Michele returns to Walter Lippmann for another quotation to "frame" her paper.

37.

concept of intelligence and to find ways to use

individual assessments wisely--to help people reach

their potentials, not burden them with labels.

   In a response to a 1922 article written by Lewis

38. B. Terman, Walter Lippmann said:

> I hate the impudence of a claim that in
>
> fifty minutes you can judge and classify a
>
> human being's predestined fitness for life.
>
> I hate the pretentiousness of that claim.
>
> I hate the abuse of scientific method which
>
> it involves. I hate the sense of superior-
>
> ity which it creates, and the sense of in-
>
> feriority which it imposes. (Lippmann 42)

Although Lippmann's comment was very bold in 1922, in

the more than sixty years that have passed, psycholo-

gists have come to agree that intelligence is not

one-dimensional and cannot be judged adequately by

traditional intelligence tests alone.

39. Center the title "Works Cited." Include in the list only sources providing material actually incorporated in the paper. (A works consulted page would include not only sources cited in the paper itself but also any sources read during the process of research.)

40. Alphabetize the list of sources by the first word of each entry, not including *a, an,* and *the.* Provide complete information for each entry, following exact patterns of organization and punctuation (see pages 506–19). Begin the first line of each entry at the normal left margin and indent second and subsequent lines five spaces. Double-space the entire list.

41. List multiple sources by the same author separately. Alphabetize them by title. In second and subsequent entries, omit the author's name, replacing it with three hyphens followed by a period.

39.   Works Cited

40. Dearborn, Walter Fenno. <u>Intelligence Tests: Their</u>
<u>Significance for School and Society</u>. Boston:
Houghton, 1928.

Durost, Walter N. "Intelligence Testing."
<u>Encyclopedia Americana</u>. 1985 ed.

Eysenck, H. J., and Leon Kamin. <u>The Intelligence</u>
<u>Controversy</u>. New York: Wiley, 1981.

41. ---. <u>The Structure and Measure of Intelligence</u>. New
York: Springer-Verlag, 1979.

Goleman, Daniel. "Rethinking the Value of
Intelligence Tests." <u>New York Times</u> 9 Nov.
1986, sec. 12: 23-27.

Gould, Stephen Jay. <u>The Mismeasure of Man</u>. New
York: Norton, 1981.

Guilford, J. P. <u>The Nature of Human Intelligence</u>.
New York: McGraw, 1967.

Herrnstein, R. J. <u>I.Q. in the Meritocracy</u>. Boston:
Little, 1971.

Krasner, William. <u>Labeling the Children</u>.
Washington: U. S. Dept. of Health, Education,
and Welfare, 1977.

Levine, Art. "Getting Smart About IQ." U.S. News &
     World Report 23 Nov. 1987: 53-55.

Lippmann, Walter. "The Great Confusion [A Reply to
     Terman]." The IQ Controversy: Critical
     Readings. Ed. N. J. Block and Gerald Dworkin.
     New York: Pantheon, 1976. 39-42.

Lowery, Jill. Personal interview. 8 Nov. 1988.

Roberts, Francis. "Testing the Gifted Preschooler."
     Parents Nov. 1986: 94.

Terman, Lewis M. The Measurement of Intelligence:
     An Explanation of and a Complete Guide for the
     Use of the Stanford Revision and Extension of
     the "Binet-Simon Intelligence Scale." Boston:
     Houghton, 1916.

Walters, Joseph M., and Howard Gardner. "The
     Development and Education of Intelligences."
     Essays on the Intellect. Ed. Frances R. Link.
     Alexandria, VA: Assn. for Supervision and
     Curriculum Development, 1985. 1-21.

MAKING C O N N E C T I O N S

Organizing, writing, and revising a research paper is quite an undertaking, but aside from what you learn about your topic you will benefit as a writer and thinker if you analyze and learn from your research process.

- Consider your general writing skills. Which of your previously developed skills served you best as you worked on your research paper? Which skills do you need to sharpen?

- Consider your work habits during research. What did you learn about yourself as a working writer while completing your research paper? What useful habits do you hope to exploit in later writing projects? What habits do you hope to overcome?

- Consider your past research papers. Compare your work on this research paper with other researched writing that you have done — for example, in high school or for your job. What differences do you note? Do not simply isolate mechanical matters, such as locating and documenting source materials, but think of abstract matters as well, such as the evolution of your thoughts on your topic or the effectiveness of various patterns of organization that you may have tried.

- Consider how you will be able to use your research skills. Under what circumstances will you be able to use your research and writing skills? Think of both professional and personal examples.

APPENDIXES

Appendix A
Manuscript Form

Over the years, writers have developed fairly consistent methods for presenting manuscripts of any type of material and any length. These methods, although not inflexible, have become the expected standard. It is wise to adhere to them.

Accepted guidelines for typed manuscripts (on typewriters and word processors) and handwritten manuscripts are included below. **▶▶▶** *Before submitting handwritten work, always check with your instructor to be sure that it is acceptable.* **◀◀◀**

Paper

Typed Manuscript. Use white, medium-weight, $8\frac{1}{2}$-by-11-inch paper. Avoid onion-skin paper and erasable paper. (If you must type on erasable paper, submit a high-quality photocopy on medium-weight paper.) When using a word processor, use letter-quality (not draft-quality) paper, or submit a photocopy on medium-weight paper.

Handwritten Manuscript. Use good, white, standard $8\frac{1}{2}$-by-11-inch paper, preferably with lines. Never submit work on torn-out spiral-notebook paper without first trimming the edges.

Ribbons and Pens

Typed Manuscript. Use a black ribbon and remember to clean your typewriter keys periodically. With word processors, use a letter-quality printer or use the correspondence-quality mode on a dot-matrix printer.

Handwritten Manuscript. Use a blue or black pen for handwritten work unless advised otherwise. Make sure that your pen does not blob or skip.

Typing and Handwriting Formats

Typed Manuscript. Double-space throughout to make papers easy to read and to allow space for corrections and additions. Use only one side of each page.

Handwritten Manuscript. Write on every other line unless given other advice. Write on only one side of each page, clearly and carefully forming letters.

Margins

Typed Manuscript. Leave one-inch margins *on all sides* of the page. Word-processing programs automatically establish "default" margins; if they are not wide enough, reset them.

Handwritten Manuscript. Leave one-inch margins *on all sides* of the page.

Indentions

Typed Manuscript. Indent the first word of a paragraph five spaces from the left margin. Do not skip extra lines before beginning a new paragraph.

Handwritten Manuscript. Indent the first word of a paragraph one inch from the left margin.

Headings and Title

Typed Manuscript. In the upper left corner of your paper, within the one-inch margins, type your name, the course number, the instructor's name, and the date. (Your instructor may also require section or assignment numbers.) Then double-space and type the paper's title, centered. Capitalize all important words in the title, but do not italicize it or place it in quotation marks. Double-space again and begin the first paragraph.

Handwritten Manuscript. Include the same information on handwritten as on typed work. Begin writing your name on the top line of your paper in the upper left corner.

Paging

Typed Manuscript. In the upper right corner of each page, one-half inch from the top, type your last name and the page number, separated by a space. Then double-space and continue the text of the paper. If you are using a word-processing program that automatically places page numbers at the bottoms of pages, insert additional commands to position your last name and the page number at the top. (Check your program's instructions for adding "headers.")

Handwritten Manuscript. On the top line, in the upper right corner of each page, write your last name and the page number.

Proofreading

Typed Manuscript. Proofread typed manuscripts for grammar, usage, and mechanics. Use this handbook. Check carefully for typing errors.

Handwritten Manuscript. Proofread handwritten manuscripts for grammar, usage, and mechanics and to check legibility. Re-form any unclear letters.

Corrections

Typed Manuscript. Make corrections neatly. Use correction fluid or tape. Draw a single line through words you delete at the last minute. Words accidentally omitted may be inserted *above the line.* Use a caret (∧) to indicate where they belong. Whenever possible, type corrections; otherwise insert them neatly by hand using black ink. If you are using a word processor, reopen the file, make all revisions, and then print a clean copy to submit.

½ Davis 1

Ronald Davis

1" English 231

Dr. L. C. Nichols

6 September 1990

Title of the Paper

_____

_____

_____

_____

_____

_____

_____

_____

_____

_____

_____

_____

_____

1"

1" ½" Davis 2

1"
_____

_____

Handwritten Manuscript. Follow the guidelines given above, inserting corrections by hand. **》》》** *More than two or three corrections on a page makes the writer look careless and the page messy. Retype such pages. Also, check with your instructor to see if he or she places a limit on the number of corrections permissible.* **《《《**

Submitting the Manuscript

Typed Manuscript. Submit manuscripts according to your instructor's guidelines. If you receive no specific guidelines, secure the pages with a paper clip in the upper left corner. Place lengthy papers in a 9-by-12-inch manila envelope with your name and course information typed or written on the outside. Always make and keep a photocopy of your paper before submitting it.

Handwritten Manuscript. Follow the guidelines given above for typed manuscripts.

A Final Word on Manuscript Form

If you have difficulty following these guidelines or those presented by your instructor, see him or her before you prepare the final copy of a paper.

Appendix B
APA Documentation Style

In fields such as psychology, education, public health, and criminology, researchers follow the guidelines given in the *Publication Manual of the American Psychological Association,* third edition (Washington, DC: APA, 1984), to document their work. Like MLA style (see pages 501–91), APA style encourages brevity in documentation, uses in-text parenthetical citations of sources, and limits the use of numbered notes and appended materials. The two styles, however, vary in their requirements for the organization of manuscripts and the forms for some notes.

The information that follows is an overview of APA style. If your major or minor requires APA style, you should acquire the APA manual, study it thoroughly, and follow its guidelines carefully.

Paper Format

MLA

No separate title page: Identification and title placed on the first page of the paper.

APA

Separate title page: Includes a descriptive title, author's name and affiliation, and running head. The running head is a shortened version of the paper's title. Center it at the bottom of the title page. In the upper right corner, put the first two or three words of the paper's title. Below that short title, flush against the right margin, put the page number. The title page is always page one.

Paper Format

MLA	*APA*
No abstract.	*Abstract:* On a separate page following the title page, a 75-to-150-word paragraph describing the major ideas in the paper.
Introduction: A paragraph or series of paragraphs used to present and interest readers in the topic of the paper.	*Introduction:* A paragraph or series of paragraphs used to define the topic, present the hypothesis (or thesis), explain the method of investigation, and state the theoretical implications (or context.)
Body: A series of logically connected paragraphs that explore the main idea through various patterns of description, illustration, and argument.	*Body:* A series of paragraphs that describe study procedures, the results obtained, and interpretations of the findings.
In-text parenthetical documentation: Author and page number, unless title is necessary to distinguish among multiple works by one author.	*In-text parenthetical documentation:* Author and date for summaries and paraphrases; author, date, and page number for quotations.

Paper Format

MLA

List of sources: Cited sources fully identified in a listing entitled "Works Cited."

Appendix: Seldom included.

APA

List of sources: Cited sources fully identified in a listing entitled "References."

Appendix: Included when related materials (charts, graphs, illustrations, and so on) cannot be incorporated in the body of the paper.

Manuscript Format

MLA

Type: Any standard typeface — typewriter or printer.

Margins: One-inch margins at top and bottom and on left and right. Right-justified margins are acceptable.

Paging: Author's last name and page number placed in the upper right corner.

APA

Type: Any standard typeface — typewriter or printer. Dot-matrix type without descending letters is unacceptable.

Margins: One-and-one-half-inch margins at top and bottom and on left and right. Right-justified margins are unacceptable.

Paging: The first two or three words of the title placed in the upper right corner. Two lines below the short title, put the page number. Omit the author's name.

Manuscript Format

<table>
<tr><td>MLA</td><td>APA</td></tr>
<tr><td>In-text headings: Not recommended except in very long papers.</td><td>Headings: Recommended for divisions and subdivisions of the paper.</td></tr>
<tr><td>Corrections: Neat handwritten corrections acceptable; typed corrections preferred.</td><td>Corrections: Must be typed; handwritten corrections unacceptable.</td></tr>
</table>

Citation Format

APA formats for citations in lists of references and in the text differ from MLA formats. Below are listed several basic APA forms. Differences from MLA format are noted and cross references to the MLA model in Chapter 33 are provided.

Reference List Format

A Book by One Author

```
Sullivan, M.  (1976).  International relations: Theo-
    ries and evidence.  Englewood Cliffs, NJ:
    Prentice-Hall.
```

(Use initials for the author's first name. After the author's name, place the publication date in parentheses, followed by a period. Capitalize only the first word of the title and of the subtitle and any proper nouns and proper adjectives. For MLA form, see page 506.)

A Book by More Than One Author

Vidich, A. J., & Bensman, J. (1968). <u>Small town in</u>

<u>mass society: Class, power and religion in a rural</u>

<u>community</u>. Princeton: Princeton University Press.

(Invert the names of all authors. Insert an ampersand [&] before the last author. Spell out the names of university presses. For MLA form, see page 506.)

A Book by a Corporate Author

Council on Environmental Quality. (1981). <u>The global</u>

<u>2000 report to the president</u>. Washington, DC: Gov-

ernment Printing Office.

A Work in a Collection by Different Authors

Dingwall, R., & Eekelaar, J. (1986). Judgments of

Solomon: Psychology and family law. In Martin

Richards and Paul Light (Eds.), <u>Children of social</u>

<u>worlds: Development in a social context</u> (pp. 55-73).

Cambridge: Harvard University Press.

(Do not enclose the title of a short work in quotation marks. *In* introduces its source. The editor's name, the abbreviation *Eds.* [capitalized
and placed in parentheses] followed by a comma, the collection title,
and inclusive page numbers for the short work [given in parentheses]
are provided. Abbreviate *pages*. For MLA form, see page 508.)

An Article in a Monthly Magazine

Angier, N. (1981, Nov.). How fast? How high? How far?

<u>Discover</u>, pp. 24-30.

(Give the year of publication followed by a comma and the month and day [if any]. Abbreviate *pages*. For MLA form, see page 512.)

An Article in a Journal with Separate Paging in Each Issue

```
Sills, T.  (1981).  Socrates was executed for being

    innovative.  English Journal, 70(7), 41-42.
```

(Italicize the name of the journal [but not the comma following it] and the volume number. The issue number in parentheses immediately follows the volume number; no space separates them. No abbreviation for *pages* accompanies the inclusive page numbers. For MLA form, see page 513.)

An Article in a Daily Newspaper

```
Oppenheim, C.  (1982, Mar. 19).  San Francisco transit

    running in the red.  Chicago Tribune, p. 4.
```

(Invert the date. Do not include information on the edition or section. For MLA form, see page 513.)

A Lecture or Speech

```
Brent, H.  (1981, Nov. 21).  Teaching composition

    theory in the People's Republic of China.  Paper

    presented at the meeting of the National Council of

    Teachers of English, Boston, MA.
```

(Italicize the title of the speech. Follow the title with the name of the sponsoring organization and the location, separated by commas. For MLA form, see page 515.)

Nonprint Materials

```
Fosse, B. (Director).  (1972).  Cabaret [Film].  Los
    Angeles: Allied Artists.
```

(List entries by the name of the most important contributor [director, producer, speaker, and so on]; note the specific role in full in parentheses following the name. Identify the medium [film, filmstrip, slide show, tape recording] in brackets after the title. The place of production precedes the name of the production company. For MLA form, see page 516.)

Text Citation Format

One Author

```
   Greybowski (1985) noted that . . .
```

Or:

```
In a recent study at USC (Greybowski, 1985), partici-
pants were asked to . . .
```

Multiple Authors: First Citation

```
Calendrillo, Thurgood, Johnson, and Lawrence (1967)
found in their evaluation . . .
```

Multiple Authors: Subsequent Citations

```
Calendrillo et al. (1967) also discovered . . .
```

Corporate Authors: First Citation

```
. . . a close connection between political interests
and environmental issues (Council on Environmental
Quality [CEQ], 1981).
```

Corporate Authors: Subsequent Citations

```
. . . in their additional work (CEQ, 1981).
```

Quotations Within the Text

First Option

```
She stated, "The cultural awareness of a student de-
pends, by implication, on the cultural awareness of the
parents" (Hermann, 1984, p. 219).
```

Second Option

```
Hermann (1984) added that "enrichment in our schools is
costly and has little bearing on the later lives of the
students" (pp. 230-231).
```

Third Option

```
"A school's responsibility rests with providing solid
educational skills, not with supplementing the cultural
education of the uninterested," stated Hermann (1984)
in her summary (p. 236).
```

1. APA form requires a separate title page. (For MLA form, see page 557.)

2. In the upper right corner of every page, APA style requires a short title consisting of the first two or three words of the paper's title. The short title (which does not necessarily have the same wording as the running head; see item 4 below) identifies each page in the event that any pages go astray. The page number appears on the line below the short title, aligned on the right. (For MLA form, see page 557.)

3. The title, subtitle (if any), and the author's name and affiliation are centered on the page. If a title runs over to a second line, the runover line is also centered. (For MLA form, see page 557.)

4. Near the bottom of the title page, center and type the label "Running head," followed by a colon and a shortened form of the title.

1.   Intelligence Testing

2.   1

3.   Intelligence Testing:
                     Avoiding the Sargasso Sea
                          Michele Newton
                      Indiana State University

4.   Running head: INTELLIGENCE TESTING

5. The second page of a manuscript prepared in APA style is an abstract, a 75-to-150-word paragraph describing the major ideas presented in the paper. The page is titled "Abstract." (In MLA form, there is no equivalent to the abstract.)

5.

Abstract

Since 1905, when Binet and Simon produced their well-known intelligence test, the underlying concepts of testing have changed. Terman's revised test (1916) assessed children of all levels of ability, and Wechshler's tests (1939 and 1949) assessed multiple abilities in a physical, social, and environmental context. Intelligence tests are no longer used merely to identify the mentally deficient (whether for remediation or, as sometimes happened, sterilization); students of all ability levels are now tested on many life and academic skills within a social context. The concept of intelligence, too, has been constantly challenged, refined, and redefined: it now incorporates multiple intelligences, from problem solving to creativity. Intelligence tests are no longer used to limit and label people but to help them overcome weaknesses and build on strengths.

6. The text of the paper begins on page three. (For MLA form, see page 557.)

7. Repeat the title and subtitle at the top of the third page, centered and worded as on the title page. Double-space and begin the body of the paper. (For MLA form, see page 557.)

8. Indent long quotations five spaces from the left margin. Double-space them. (For MLA form, see page 557.)

9. Parenthetical notes for long quotations follow the closing punctuation. This reference to a source by two authors shows their last names joined by an ampersand (&). The publication date, preceded and followed by commas, follows the authors' names. The page number, with the abbreviation *p.,* appears last. (For MLA form, see page 557.)

Intelligence Testing:

Avoiding the Sargasso Sea

If . . . the impression takes root that
these tests really measure intelligence,
that they constitute a sort of last
judgment on the child's capacity, that they
reveal "scientifically" his predestined
ability, then it would be a thousand times
better if all the intelligence testers and
all their questionnaires were sunk without
warning in the Sargasso Sea. (Eysenck &
Kamin, 1981, p. 90)

Walter Lippmann, a prominent columnist and
social philosopher of the first half of the
twentieth century, wrote this provocative statement in 1922. But during their eighty years of
use, intelligence tests have always generated
controversy. Today, psychologists and educators
continue to debate what the tests can measure,
how they should be designed, and how their
results should be used—and not misused.

At the turn of the century, when the first
intelligence tests were administered in large

10. If an author's name is mentioned in the text, only the publication date of the source, in parentheses, is required. In parentheses at the end of the quotation, but before the closing punctuation, indicate the page on which the information appears. (For MLA form, see page 577.)

11. Parenthetical notes for brief quotations follow the closing quotation mark but precede the end punctuation. (For MLA form, see page 577.)

12. When an author's name is not given in the text, include the author's name, the publication date of the source, and a page citation (if needed) in parentheses. (For MLA form, see page 577.)

10. the workplace. R. J. Herrnstein (1971), psychology professor at Harvard University, notes in <u>IQ in the Meritocracy</u>, "A low IQ predicts poor performance more reliably than a high one predicts good performance"

11. (113). In an ironic reversal of the harmfully low expectations of children with low scores, parents' and teachers' expectations for academic and other achievement from children with high scores may be too

12. great (Roberts, 1986, p. 94).

    Society seems to follow the lead of the schools. At one time, even the judicial system misused IQ scores. In 1927, the Supreme Court upheld steriliza- tion laws in Virginia, using intelligence test scores for justification. The case, <u>Buck v. Bell</u>, centered on Carrie Buck, a young mother who had scored a mental age of nine on the Stanford-Binet Intelligence Scale; her mother, then fifty-two, had scored a mental age of seven; Carrie's child, though appar- ently untested, was also considered "feeble-minded" (Gould, 1981, p. 335). Oliver Wendell Holmes, Jr., wrote the majority opinion:

        We have seen more than once that the public welfare may call upon the best citizens for

13. The short title and page number appear on all pages of the reference list and on any appendix pages. (For MLA form, see page 589.)

14. Center and type the title "References" at the beginning of the list of sources. APA requires that all sources included on the reference list be cited in the text. (For MLA form, see page 589.)

15. For a book by a single author, list the author's name first, inverted and followed by a period. Include the publication date in parentheses, followed by a period. Italicize (under-line) book titles but capitalize only the first word of the title and of the subtitle and any proper nouns or proper adjectives. (For MLA form, see page 589.)

16. A citation for an article in a book (in this case a reference book) begins with the author's name, followed by the publication date in parentheses. (If an article has no author, begin the entry with the article title, not enclosed in quotation marks, followed by the publication date in parentheses.) Use the word *In* before the title of the complete source. (For MLA form, see page 589.)

17. When a source has more than one author, invert the names of all the authors, not just the first. Use commas to separate the names, and place an ampersand (&) before the name of the last author. (For MLA form, see page 589.)

18. For an article in a periodical, the author's name is followed by the year, month and day (if any) of publication. The article title is not placed in quotation marks, and only the first word of the title, proper nouns, and proper adjectives are capitalized. The name of the periodical is both italicized and capitalized. Inclusive page numbers are listed with the abbreviation *pp*. (For MLA form, see page 589.)

13.   Intelligence Testing

                                                          17

14.   References

15. Dearborn, W. F. (1928). <u>Intelligence tests: Their</u>
     <u>significance for schools and society</u>. Boston:
     Houghton Mifflin.

16. Durost, W. N. (1985). Intelligence testing. In
     <u>Encyclopedia Americana</u>.

17. Eysenck, H. J., & Kamin, L. (1981). <u>The intelli-</u>
     <u>gence controversy</u>. New York: Wiley.

    Eysenck, H. J., & Kamin, L. (1979). <u>The structure</u>
     <u>and measure of intelligence</u>. New York: Springer-
     Verlag.

18. Goleman, D. (1986, Nov. 9). Rethinking the value of
     intelligence tests. <u>New York Times,</u> pp. 23-27.

    Gould, S. J. (1981). <u>The mismeasure of man</u>. New
     York: Norton.

    Guilford, J. P. (1967). <u>The nature of human intel-</u>
     <u>ligence</u>. New York: McGraw-Hill.

    Herrnstein, R. J. (1971). <u>I.Q. in the meritocracy</u>.
     Boston: Little, Brown.

    Krasner, W. (1977). <u>Labeling the children</u>. Wash-
     ington, DC: U.S. Dept. of Health, Education, and
     Welfare.

Appendix C
Writing Essay Exams

To study for an essay exam, reread course materials (books, articles, classroom notes), review important concepts, and memorize specific information related to major topics. This work is best done over a period of days or weeks.

When confronted by the exam, consider the following strategies for writing effective responses.

Point Values

Apportion your writing on each question according to its point value. For instance, if a question is worth ten points out of a possible one hundred, devote no more than ten percent of the total exam time to your response; if a question is worth fifty points out of one hundred, spend approximately half of the exam time writing your response. Spending disproportionate time on one question may leave you little time for other parts of the exam.

Multiple Questions

To respond to two or more essay questions, pace your writing. Decide, on the basis of point values, how much time each question deserves and write accordingly. An extended response to one question worth ten points and a brief, superficial response to another worth ten points may yield only fifteen points, whereas balanced discussions of both questions would probably yield more points.

Optional Topics

When given alternative questions, construct a brief topic outline for each choice, to see which essay would be most substantial. A few moments spent outlining will help you to select the questions to which you can respond most completely and effectively.

Careful Reading

Many essay questions provide an implied topic sentence for a paragraph essay or thesis statement for a longer essay. Focus your work by developing the idea presented in the question. Follow instructions carefully. Describe, illustrate, compare, contrast, evaluate, analyze, and so on according to instructions.

Style and Technical Matters

To guarantee that responses are grammatically correct, well worded, complete, and free from errors in punctuation and mechanics, adjust your writing strategies. Either write slowly, to make your sentences clear, complete, and free from errors in a first draft, or allow time to make corrections and revisions after you have written your response. For either approach, pacing is crucial.

Organization and Development

A response to an essay question is like a brief paper: It requires an introduction, a body, and a conclusion, although the development and length of each part will depend on the type of question and its point value. A ten-point and a fifty-point essay on the same question will require very different degrees of development, but the structure of each response will be similar. Before an essay exam, quickly review the patterns of development in Chapter 4 (description, examples, facts, comparison and contrast, analogy, cause and effect, process analysis, classification, and definition); you will then be able to organize your responses appropriately according to the pattern explicitly or implicitly required by the question.

Varied Organization

For an illustration of how the organizational pattern of an essay question response varies with the form of the question, examine the topic outlines below, which clearly show the differences in structure required by the two questions. The first question implicitly requires a comparison and contrast structure. The second explicitly requires an analysis structure. The full essay responses would also require appropriate support.

QUESTION

Which is more effective: the impromptu or the extemporaneous speech?

Introduction (thesis): Though both impromptu and extemporaneous speeches are flexible, the planning required for extemporaneous speeches makes them more coherent, more fully developed, and more effective.

I. Impromptu

   A. No written manuscript

   B. Words chosen while speaking

   C. Minimal preparation

   D. Unrehearsed

II. Extemporaneous

   A. No written manuscript

   B. Words chosen while speaking

   C. Substantial preparation

   D. Rehearsed

Conclusion: Extemporaneous speeches are generally more effective because they are more organized and substantive.

QUESTION
Of the four speech-making techniques, choose the one you believe is the most useful and analyze the factors contributing to its effectiveness.

Introduction (thesis): Because they are at once organized but flexible, extemporaneous speeches are the most effective.

   I. Preparation

      A. Reading

      B. Thinking

      C. Selecting

      D. Organizing

  II. Presentation

      A. Flexible

         1. Change examples

         2. Adjust to audience

         3. Add or drop material

      B. Personal

         1. Suited to audience's needs

         2. Suited to speaker's needs

         3. Not manuscript bound

         4. Better contact with audience

Conclusion: Because of advantages in planning and presentation, extemporaneous speaking is generally the most effective.

621

Degree of Development

For an illustration of the similar structures but different degree of development of essay responses with different point values, examine the samples below, prepared as part of an hour-long exam.

QUESTION

What are the four speech-making strategies and how do they differ?

Ten-point response

> There are four basic speech-making strategies. Impromptu speeches are presented on the "spur of the moment"; the speaker has no time to organize or rehearse. Extemporaneous speeches are organized in outline form but are not written word for word. Manuscript speeches are written in advance and then read from a written or typed copy. Memorized speeches are written in advance and then learned word for word, to be presented without a written copy. These four strategies allow speakers to suit their presentations to their speaking situations.

Fifty-point response

> Situations for speech making vary and speakers, as a result, choose among four different speech-making strategies to present their ideas most effectively.
>
> Impromptu speeches are given on the "spur of the moment"; the speaker has no chance to organize or rehearse. These highly informal speeches are often unfocused (because they are unplanned) and ineffective (because they were not rehearsed), but they are the usual kinds of speeches given at organization meetings and in class discussions.
>
> Extemporaneous speeches are given from prepared outlines, but they are not completely written. Rather, speakers decide what to discuss and what details or examples to use, and then they

choose words as they speak. Extemporaneous speeches have the advantage of being organized, but at the same time they are flexible, allowing speakers to modify what they say to suit the needs of their audiences. For this reason, they are often the most effective speeches at informal meetings.

Manuscript speeches are written in complete form and then read, much like a newscast. Because they are prepared in advance, manuscript speeches are well organized and carefully worded. If they are also well rehearsed, manuscript speeches are effective in formal speaking situations because they present an exact, well-worded version of the speaker's ideas.

Memorized speeches are written in complete form and then committed to memory. Because they are carefully prepared, they often present solid content, but few speakers can memorize a lengthy speech and deliver it well. In addition, memorized speeches are not flexible and only work in highly formal circumstances, like awards ceremonies and formal banquets.

Because of the differences among these four speech-making strategies — in organization, presentation, and flexibility — they provide speakers with a number of ways to share ideas with audiences.

Timed Practice

Before writing an essay exam, practice composing under time pressure. Using notes from class, write and respond to sample essay questions. Use a timer and write several practice responses over several days' time. If necessary, allow yourself extra time to respond to a question, gradually reducing the time until it approximates the time available for the exam. Practice will quicken your writing pace while helping you to study for the exam.

Appendix D
Business Writing

Business Letters

Like a good paper, a business letter should be clearly organized and carefully written in support of a stated or implied thesis. Business letters differ from papers, however, in format and purpose.

When writing business letters, be sensitive to tone. In most instances, you will be writing to solve a problem or to ask for help. A moderate tone, formal but friendly, will work best. Do not be harsh or demanding in an initial letter, but if a problem continues, use a firmer tone in later correspondence.

The following guidelines and example (see page 627) describe a modified block-form letter, which is appropriate for most purposes.

General Guidelines

Use high-quality, white 8½-by-11-inch paper.

Type the letter, using a fresh black ribbon. If your are using a word processor, use a letter-quality printer.

Maintain wide margins on all sides.

Single-space within paragraphs. Double-space between paragraphs. Do not indent the first words of paragraphs; position them flush with the left margin.

Proofread the final copy carefully for spelling, punctuation, mechanics, grammar, and typing errors.

Fold the letter in thirds and place it in a legal-size envelope.

Letter Format

Your Address. Use the address at which you wish to receive follow-up correspondence. Do not include your name with the address; type it beneath your signature at the end of the letter.

The Date. Use the date on which you plan to mail the letter.

Inside Address. Name the person to whom you are writing and include his or her title if you know it. If the letter is addressed to a company, begin this section with the name of the company and then use the complete business address.

Salutation. This greeting should be specific rather than general. Begin with *Dear,* followed by the name of the person and a colon (not a comma). Use general titles (*Mr., Ms.,* or *Dr.*) with the person's name. Use *Mrs.* or *Miss* only when you know that a woman prefers to be addressed in one of those ways. When you do not know the name of the person to whom you are writing, use "Dear Madam or Sir"; avoid "To Whom It May Concern."

Introductory Paragraph. Like a paper, a business letter needs an introductory paragraph. The first paragraph should establish the context for the letter. Be concise but specific. Include answers to the important questions that your correspondent might ask: What do you want to discuss? When did it take place?

Body Paragraph or Paragraphs. Middle paragraphs should provide a description of the problem. They should be clearly written, with careful word choices and specific details. Essentially, these paragraphs give you a chance to present your case, and they must therefore be precise and convincing. If you have tried to solve the problem, describe the strategies you have used, again supplying detailed information and descriptions.

Request for Action. The closing paragraph should ask for help in solving the problem. Be reasonable. If alternative solutions are acceptable, explain them.

Closing. Use a reasonably formal, standard closing, such as *Sincerely, Sincerely yours,* or *Yours truly.* (Align the closing with your address.)

Signature. Sign your name in ink in a space that is at least four lines deep, so that it does not look cramped.

Typed Name. Aligned under the closing, type your name as you wish it to appear in return correspondence.

Envelope Format

Return Address. Include your full return address in the upper left corner of the envelope.

Mailing Address. Address the envelope fully. Include the person's name and title (if applicable) and the full business address, including zip code.

Postage. Be sure to use sufficient postage.

The Résumé

A résumé is a brief listing of important information about your academic credentials, work experience, and personal achievements. The title "Résumé," "Curriculum Vitae," or simply "Vita" in

```
Alicia Hudson
1627 Lafayette Avenue                                    stamp
Topeka, KS  66603




            Aaron Steinmann, Service Director
            Museum Reproductions, Incorporated
            392 Hazelwood Drive
            Chicago, IL  60607
```

1627 Lafayette Avenue
Topeka, Kansas 66603
February 27, 1990

Aaron Steinmann, Service Director
Museum Reproductions, Incorporated
392 Hazelwood Drive
Chicago, Illinois 60607

Dear Mr. Steinmann:

On November 16, 1989, I ordered several small pieces of
statuary from your Fall 1989 sale catalog: <u>Child with
Rabbit</u> (#097444), <u>Sleeping Cat</u> (#097118), and <u>Swan</u>
(#097203).

On December 3, 1989, my insured package was delivered by
UPS, and I excitedly opened the cartons to examine my
newest collector's items. Two of the statues were in
excellent condition, but the third, <u>Child with Rabbit</u>, was
not. The glaze on the rabbit and the base was streaked
and irregularly colored. These flaws in the finish
disappointed me greatly, especially since that piece alone
had cost $54.

I immediately called the service number listed on the
invoice. Your representative instructed me to repack the
statue and return it for a replacement. I did so the next
day--December 4, 1989--enclosing a photocopy of the
invoice (#1784229). More than two months have passed, and
I have yet to receive my new <u>Child with Rabbit</u> statue.

I would appreciate receiving my statue soon (since I have
already paid for it), or I would like to know the reason
for the delay. If you are unable to send me the statue, I
would appreciate your crediting my account for $54. Thank
you for your help in solving my problem.

Sincerely,

Alicia Hudson

Alicia Hudson

academic work, or the general designation "Data Sheet" in almost any context, sometimes appears as a heading at the top of the page. Such a title is probably unnecessary, however, because employers are familiar with this form. A résumé is commonly submitted with a job application letter to obtain an interview and sometimes submitted with admissions or scholarship applications, funding requests, project proposals, and annual personnel reports, and in other situations when you need to document your accomplishments.

Because a résumé must make a strong, favorable impression — suggesting the caliber of employee or student you are — you should prepare it carefully. Start by analyzing your goals and background; then gather together pertinent information. Consider the following discussion and modify the format and content of the samples on pages 633 and 634 to emphasize your individual strengths and fit your own needs. Do not be too "creative" or "artistic" with your résumé unless your job objective is in a field like advertising, graphic design, or art education.

Sections

Heading.   Center your name at the top of the page. Use capitals, underlining, italics, boldface, or special lettering to make your name stand out.

Address.   List your current mailing address in standard postal form, including zip code, and your full phone number, including area code. If you expect to change addresses soon, or if you spend time in two places (such as at college and at home), include both addresses, and indicate when you use each.

Personal Information.   Include information on age, marital status, health, height, weight, and so on, *only* if it in some way is pertinent to your objective (for example, if the job has requirements about physical size, such as for a police officer or flight attendant). Employers and agencies can no longer demand such information and may not legally use it when assessing applications. Provide a photograph only if you are asked to do so.

Statement of Objectives. If you are applying for a specific position or purpose, state your immediate objectives and long-range goals. This statement is important because it serves as the controlling thesis for the description of your qualifications. Everything in the résumé should be relevant to your objective. Your statement of objectives should include the job title(s) of the position(s) you are seeking, the types of skills you possess or the types of duties you can perform, and your career goals. If the résumé is a general data sheet and its purpose is simply to list information, the career objective statement may be omitted.

Education. Students or recent students who have little work experience generally describe education before experience. Specify degrees, majors, minors, names and locations of schools, month and year of graduation (your anticipated date of graduation is acceptable), and grade point average (overall, major, or junior/senior). If specific schoolwork — important courses, term projects, or research papers — is relevant to your objective, briefly note it. If you have a college degree, you need not mention high school unless you did exceptionally well (such as being class valedictorian) or the school is prestigious or might interest the employer for some other reason (because it is in the same city, for instance). List honors and awards with education, or list them in a separate section for emphasis if they are numerous and impressive. Extracurricular activities are sometimes included here, but they too can be developed into another section if they warrant such treatment. Internships, co-op training, observation programs, conference workshops, and so on might be described as part of your education or considered as professional experience and listed in that section. The latter is a good idea if you have little relevant work experience.

Experience. Experience may appear after education, if it is not impressive or extensive, or before education, if it is impressive or recent. Arrange experience either chronologically (to show progress or promotion) or in descending order of importance, and list job titles, names of businesses or organizations (including the military), locations (not necessarily full addresses), dates of employment, and duties. Using active verb phrases, provide specific details about relevant skills employed, including technical skills, such as methods (double-entry accounting) and equipment (computers) used, and note improvements or suggestions that you contributed. If your work experience is not directly relevant to the objective of your application, mention responsibilities and accomplishments involving such general skills as communication, leadership, organization, problem solving, and money handling. Do not fail to mention volunteer work, internships, and other nonpaying experience.

Activities, Interests, and Hobbies.   List activities specifically related to your objective, such as memberships in professional, fraternal, and community organizations. Mention special participation, contributions, and official positions. Other interesting activities (such as participation in organized sports, challenging hobbies, reading preferences, and cultural interests) may be included to show your habits and character.

References.   List two to four recent employers and teachers who are willing to describe your qualifications and recommend your work. Supply their full names, titles, and work addresses and phone numbers. Be sure to contact them for permission before using them as references.

If you do not want to list your references on the résumé (perhaps because of limited space), note that references are available upon request. Use your college's career development and placement service, which will maintain a placement file that includes your letters of reference, transcripts, and data sheets. If you use your school's placement service, list the full address and phone number of the office at the bottom of your résumé.

Format

Length. Unless you have an exceptional amount of experience and education, limit your résumé to one page. If you must go to a second page, arrange the information so that you have two full and evenly balanced pages, not a page and a third. Do not split a major section between pages.

General Appearance. Make the résumé attractive, balanced, and scannable. Do not cramp information in dense blocks. Rather, divide information into discrete, parallel sections. Be consistent in your use of indentation, alignment, capitalization, boldface, underlining, parentheses, and other devices that identify similar kinds and levels of information. Use lists and columns, but make minimal use of patterns that create obvious vertical lines. Leave at least one-inch margins and double-space between sections, but avoid blocks of "white space" (large, unused areas).

Headings. Use headings that clearly describe the information in each section. Position the main headings at the left margin or center them. Headings positioned at the left margin are very noticeable, but they can create a wide strip of white space down the side and make the résumé look imbalanced. Centered headings create a better balanced design and allow more efficient use of space, and they show up clearly if they are set off in some way (underlined, boldfaced) and if adequate space is left between sections. Subheadings can further indicate and emphasize areas of special interest, but too many levels of headings will make the résumé look choppy.

Arrangement. Arrange the sections and the items within each section so that the information flows in a logical and emphatic order. One way is to start with the most relevant and impressive accomplishments and follow a descending order of importance throughout. Chronological order is appropriate when you have only a few items to mention (two part-time jobs, for instance). Reverse chronological order is effective when you have many degrees, experiences, and activities to present — especially if the most recent ones are the most important. Alphabetical order might be useful for listing references, organizations, and courses, but usually even these are best presented in order of importance.

Style. Abbreviate sparingly, using only standard abbreviations (such as for state names in addresses) and acronyms (such as professional organizations). Avoid first-person pronouns and complete sentences. Use active verb phrases. Instead of saying, "I was responsible for training new crew members," you need only write, "Trained new crew members."

Typing

Print Quality. Use standard elite or pica type, not an unusual typeface, such as italic. If you use a word processor, print the final résumé on a letter-quality (not a dot-matrix) printer.

Type with a fresh, black ribbon on heavy bond paper to produce a clear and attractive copy. Single-space within and double-space between sections.

Corrections. Use correction fluid or tape when you make changes. When you make photocopies to submit, these corrections will not show on the copy, whereas smudges on erasable paper will.

Proofreading. Proofread carefully to make sure that your résumé is free of spelling and typing errors. It represents you, so it must be "letter perfect."

Photocopying

Have high-quality photocopies made at a reliable copy shop. Consider having your résumé copied on fluorescent white bond paper, "parchment" paper, or some other special-purpose paper so that it will be distinctive. Spending a little extra money might be worth the investment.

Figure 1   Standard résumé

SANDRA K. BOYER

Present Address   After May 15, 1990
363 Maehling Terrace   431 N. Seventh St.
Alton, IL 62002   Waterloo, IL   62298
(618)465-7061   (618)686-2324

CAREER OBJECTIVE

Music teacher and orchestra director, eventually
leading to work as a Music Program Coordinator for a
school district.

EDUCATION

Bachelor of Science in Education: May 1990. Freemont
College, Alton, IL. Major: Music education. Minors:
Music theory and business. G.P.A.: 3.87 on a 4.0 scale.
Alpha Alpha Alpha, music honorary society (secretary,
1984-1985). Division 1 Ratings: violin, viola,
clarinet; Division 2 Ratings: cello, oboe

MUSICAL EXPERIENCE

Waterloo Community Orchestra (1983-1986): first violin,
1986; 10-17 performances each year, Waterloo Arts
Festival; classical and popular music
Waterloo Community String Ensemble (1986): coordinator;
8 performances each year, Waterloo Arts Festival;
classical music
Freemont College Orchestra (1987-present): second
violin, 1987-1988; first violin, 1988-present; student
conductor, 1989; 10-20 performances each year;
conducted 3 concerts; classical and popular music

WORK EXPERIENCE

Appointment secretary and sales clerk. Carter's Music
Shop, Waterloo, IL (1984-1986): coordinated 65 lessons
each week; demonstrated and sold instruments and music
Sales clerk. Hampton Music, Alton, IL (1987-present):
demonstrated and sold instruments and music

REFERENCES

Available upon request from the Placement Center,
Freemont College, Alton, IL 62002   (618)461-6299,
extension 1164; file #39261

Figure 2   Alternate résumé

RÉSUMÉ
Sandra K. Boyer

ADDRESS

School: 363 Maehling Terrace   Home: 431 N. Seventh St.
        Alton, IL 62002   Waterloo, IL 62298
School phone: (618)465-7061   Home phone: (618)686-2324

EDUCATION

1982-1986:   Benjamin Thomas High School, Waterloo, IL
1987-   :   Freemont College, Alton, IL; will graduate May 1990.
              Major: Music education. Minors: Music theory and
              business

EXTRACURRICULAR ACTIVITIES

1982-1986:   Benjamin Thomas High School Orchestra (1st violin,
              1981-1983)
              Benjamin Thomas High School String Ensemble (student
              coordinator, 1982-1983)
1987-   :   Freemont College Orchestra (2nd violin, 1987-1988; 1st
              violin, 1988-present; student conductor, 1989)
              Alpha Alpha Alpha, music honorary society (secretary,
              1984-1985)

WORK EXPERIENCE

1982-1983:   Carter's Music Shop, Waterloo, IL 62298; part-time
              appointment secretary and sales clerk
1983-   :   Hampton Music, Alton, IL 62002 (837 Telegraph and
              Alton Square shops); sales clerk

REFERENCES

Dr. Glendora Kramer, Professor of Music and Orchestra Director,
    Freemont College, Alton, IL 62002, (618)461-6299, extension
    2110
Mr. Philip Sheldon, Manager, Hampton Music, 837 Telegraph, Alton, IL
    62002, (618)466-6311
Mrs. Rhonda Travis, Music Instructor, Benjamin Thomas High School,
    Waterloo, IL 62298, (618)686-5534

Glossary of Usage

This brief glossary explains the usage of potentially confusing words and phrases. Samples illustrate how the words and phrases are used. To check words or phrases not included here, consult a dictionary.

A, An   Use *a* before a consonant sound; use *an* before a vowel sound. For words beginning with *h,* use *a* when the *h* is voiced and *an* when it is unvoiced. (Sound out the following examples carefully.)

a locket	**a** historical novel
an oration	**an** honest mistake

Accept, Except   *Accept* means "willing to receive"; *except* means "all but."

Hoover rightfully would not **accept** the blame for the Stock Market Crash of 1929.

No elected official in the United States earns more than $200,000, **except** the president.

Accidentally, Accidently   Use *accidentally,* the correct word form. The root word is *accidental,* not *accident.*

The curator **accidentally** mislabeled the painting.

Advice, Advise   *Advice,* a noun, means "a suggestion or suggestions"; *advise,* a verb, means "to offer ideas" or "to recommend."

Lord Chesterfield's **advice** to his son, though written in 1747, retains its value today.

Physicians frequently **advise** their cardiac patients to get moderate exercise and eat wisely.

Affect, Effect   *Affect,* a verb, means "to influence"; *effect,* a noun, means "the product or result of an action;" *effect,* a verb, means "to bring about, to cause to occur."

The smallness of the audience did not **affect** the speaker's presentation.

One **effect** of decontrol will be stronger competition.

To **effect** behavioral changes in some house pets is no small task.

Agree to, Agree with   *Agree to* means "to accept" a plan or proposal; *agree with* means "to share beliefs" with a person or group.

Members of the Writers' Guild would not **agree to** the contract's terms.

Although I **agree with** the protesters' position, I cannot approve of their methods.

All ready, Already   *All ready* means "all are prepared"; *already* means "pre-existing" or "previous."

Ten minutes before curtain time, the performers were **all ready.**

Volumes A through M of the *Middle English Dictionary* are **already** in print.

All right, Alright   Use *all right,* the correct form.

The Roosevelts clearly felt that it was **all right** for their children to be heard as well as seen.

All together, Altogether   *All together* means "all acting in unison"; *altogether* means "totally" or "entirely."

Synchronized swimming requires participants to swim **all together.**

Life in a small town is **altogether** too peaceful for some city dwellers.

Alot, A lot   Use *a lot,* the correct form. Generally, however, use more specific words: *a great deal, many,* or *much.*

The senator's inflammatory comments shocked **a lot** of his constituents.

The senator's inflammatory comments shocked **many** of his constituents.

Among, Between   Use *among* to describe the relationship of three or more people or things; use *between* for two.

Disagreements **among** the lawyers disrupted the proceedings.

Zoning laws usually require at least forty feet **between** houses.

Amount, Number   Use *amount* for quantities that cannot be counted separately; use *number* for items that can be counted. Some concepts, like time, use both forms, depending on how elements are described.

The **amount** of money needed to restore Ellis Island was surprising.

The contractor could not estimate the **amount** of time needed to complete the renovations.

We will need a **number** of hours to coordinate our presentations.

In the 1960s, a large **number** of American elm trees were killed by Dutch elm disease.

An   See **A.**

And/or   Generally, avoid this construction. Instead, use either *and* or *or.*

Anxious, Eager   *Anxious* means "apprehensive" or "worried" and consequently describes negative feelings; *eager* means "to anticipate enthusiastically" and consequently describes positive feelings.

For four weeks, Angie was **anxious** about her qualifying exams.

Lew was **eager** to see the restaging of *La Bohème.*

As, As if, Like   Use *as* or *as if,* subordinating conjunctions, to introduce a clause; use *like,* a preposition, to introduce a noun or phrase.

Walt talked to his cocker spaniel **as if** the dog understood every word.

Virginia Woolf's prose style is a great deal **like** that of her father, Leslie Stephens.

As, Because, Since   *As*, a subordinating conjunction, establishes a time relationship; it is interchangeable with *when* or *while. Because* and *since* describe causes and effects.

As the train pulled out of the station, it began to rain.

Because (**Since**) the population density is high, housing is difficult to find in Tokyo.

Awful   Generally avoid using this word, which really means "full of awe," as a negative description. Instead, use *bad, terrible, unfortunate,* or other similar, more precise words.

Bad, Badly   Use *bad,* an adjective, to modify a noun; use *badly,* an adverb, to modify a verb.

Napoleon's winter assault on Russia was, quite simply, a **bad** plan.

Although Grandma Moses painted **badly** by conventional standards, her work had charm and innocence.

Because, Due to the fact that, Since   Use *because* or *since; due to the fact that* is merely a wordier way of saying the same thing.

Beef prices will rise **because** ranchers have reduced the size of their herds.

Before, Prior to   Use *before* in almost all cases. Use *prior to* only when the sequence of events is drawn out, important, and legalistic.

Always check your appointment book **before** scheduling a meeting.

Prior to receiving the cash settlement, the Jacobsons had filed four complaints with the Better Business Bureau.

Being as, Being that, Seeing as   Use *because* or *since* instead of these nonstandard forms.

Beside, Besides   *Beside* means "next to"; *besides* means "except."

In Congress, the vice president sits **beside** the Speaker of the House.

Few of Georgia O'Keeffe's paintings are well known **besides** those of flowers.

Between   See **Among.**

Borrow, Lend, Loan   *Borrow* means "to take something for temporary use"; *lend* means "to give something for temporary use"; *loan* is primarily a noun and refers to the thing lent or borrowed.

People seldom **borrow** expensive items like cars, furs, or electronic equipment.

Many public libraries now **lend** compact discs and video tapes.

The **loan** of $5,000 was never repaid.

Bring, Take   *Bring* means "to transport from a distant to a nearby location"; *take* reverses the pattern and means "to transport from a nearby location to a distant one."

Soviet dissidents **bring** to the United States tales of harsh treatment and inequity.

American scholars working in Europe must **take** computers with them because the machines are not readily available at many European universities.

Can, May   *Can* means "is able to"; *may* means "has permission to." *May* is also used with a verb to suggest a possible or conditional action.

Almost anyone **can** learn to cook well.

Foreign diplomats **may** travel freely in the United States.

I **may** learn to like escargot, but I doubt it.

Can't help but   Avoid this phrase, which contains two negatives, *can't* and *but;* instead rewrite the sentence, omitting *but.*

We **can't help** wondering whether the new curriculum will help or hinder students.

Center around, Center on   Use *center on. Center around* is contradictory because *center* identifies one position and *around* suggests many possible positions.

If we can **center** our discussions **on** one topic at a time, we will use our time productively.

Compare to, Compare with   *Compare to* stresses similarities; *compare with* stresses both similarities and differences.

Jean Toomer's novel *Cane* has been **compared to** free verse.

In reviews, most critics **compared** the film version of *Amadeus* **with** the original play by Peter Shaffer.

Complement, Compliment   *Complement,* normally a noun, means "that which completes"; *compliment,* either a noun or a verb, means "a statement of praise" or "to praise."

A direct object is one kind of **complement.**

One of the highest forms of **compliment** is imitation.

The renovators of the Washington, D.C., train station should be **complimented** for their restraint, good taste, and attention to detail.

Continual, Continuous   *Continual* means "repeated often"; *continuous* means "without stopping."

In most industries, orienting new workers is a **continual** activity.

A **continuous** stream of water rushed down the slope.

Could of, Should of, Would of   Use the correct forms: *could have, should have,* and *would have.*

The athletic director **should have** taken a firm stand against drug use by athletes.

Council, Counsel   *Council,* a noun, means "a group of people who consult and offer advice"; *counsel,* a noun or a verb, means "advice" or "to advise."

The members of the **council** met in the conference room of the city hall.

Following the meeting, they offered their **counsel** to the mayor.

Ms. Reichmann **counsels** the unemployed at the Eighth Avenue Shelter.

Different from, Different than   Use *different from* with single complements and clauses; use *different than* only with clauses.

Most people's life styles are **different from** those of their parents.

Our stay in New Orleans was **different than** we had expected.

Disinterested, Uninterested   *Disinterested* means "impartial" or "unbiased"; *uninterested* means "indifferent" or "unconcerned about."

Olympic judges are supposed to be **disinterested** evaluators, but most are not.

Unfortunately, many people are **uninterested** in classical music.

Due to the fact that   See **Because.**

Each and every   Generally, avoid this repetitious usage. Use *each* or *every,* not both.

Eager   See **Anxious.**

Effect   See **Affect.**

Enthusiastic, Enthused   Use *enthusiastic,* the preferred form.

William was **enthusiastic** about his volunteer work for the Special Olympics.

Etc.   Except in rare instances, avoid the use of *etc.,* which means "and so forth." Normally, either continue a discussion or stop.

Every day, Everyday   *Every day,* an adjective-and-noun combination, means "each day"; *everyday,* an adjective, means "typical" or "ordinary."

Nutritionists suggest that people eat three balanced meals **every day.**

Congested traffic is an **everyday** problem in major cities.

Exam, Examination   *Exam,* a conversational form, and *examination,* a formal variation, are interchangeable.

The CPA **exam** (**examination**) is given three times a year.

Except   See **Accept.**

Farther, Further   *Farther* describes physical distances; *further* describes degree, quality, or time.

Most people know that it is **farther** to Mars than to Venus.

The subject of teen-age pregnancy needs **further** study if we intend to solve the financial and social problems that it creates.

Fewer, Less   Use *fewer* to describe physically separate units; use *less* for things that cannot be counted.

Fewer than ten American companies have more than one million shareholders.

Because the cost-of-living raise was **less** than we had anticipated, we had to revise our budget.

Finalize, Finish   Generally, use *finish* or *complete,* less pretentious ways of expressing the same idea.

Fun   As an adjective, *fun* should be used in the predicate-adjective position, not before a noun.

White-water rafting is dangerous but **fun.**

Further   See **Farther.**

Good, Well   Use the adjective *good* to describe someone or something; use the adverb *well* to describe an action or condition.

A **good** debater must be knowledgeable, logical, and forceful.

We work **well** together because we think alike.

Has got, Have got   Simply use *has* or *have.*

Major networks **have** to rethink their programming, especially with the challenge of cable networks.

He or she, Him or her, His or hers, Himself or herself   Use these paired pronouns with indefinite but singular antecedents; avoid awkward constructions like *he/she* or *s/he.* Generally, however, use plurals or specific nouns and pronouns when possible.

Each person is responsible for **his or her** own actions.

People are responsible for **their** own actions.

President Bush is responsible for **his** and **his staff's** actions.

Hopefully, I Hope   Use *hopefully,* an adverb, to describe the *hopeful* way in which something is done; use *I hope* to describe wishes.

Marsha **hopefully** opened the envelope, expecting to find a letter of acceptance.

I hope the EPA takes stronger steps to preserve our wildlife.

Imply, Infer *Imply* means "to suggest without stating"; *infer* means "to reach a conclusion based on unstated evidence." They describe two sides of a process.

Chancellor Michaelson's awkward movements and tentative comments **implied** that he was uncomfortable during the interview.

We **infer,** from your tone of voice, that you are displeased.

In, Into *In* means "positioned within"; *into* means "moving from the outside to the inside." Avoid using *into* to mean "enjoys," an especially nonsensical colloquialism.

Investments **in** the bond market are often safer than those **in** the stock market.

As the tenor walked **into** the reception room, he was greeted by a chorus of "bravos."

Infer See **Imply.**

Irregardless, Regardless Use *regardless,* the accepted form.

Child custody is usually awarded to the mother, **regardless** of the father's competence.

Its, It's, Its' *Its,* a possessive pronoun, means "belonging to it"; *it's,* a contraction, means "it is"; *its'* is nonstandard.

After the accident, the quarter horse favored **its** right front leg.

It's unlikely that the government will increase educational spending.

Kind of, Sort of Use *rather, somewhat,* or *to some extent* instead.

Lay, Lie *Lay* means "to place something"; *lie* means "to recline." Some confusion is typical because *lay* is also the past tense of *lie.*

In hand-treating leather, a tanner will **lay** the skins on a large, flat surface.

People with migraine headaches generally **lie** down and stoically wait for the pain to subside.

Lead, Led *Lead* is the present-tense verb; *led* is the past-tense form.

The clergy used to **lead** quiet lives.

Montresor **led** the unsuspecting Fortunato into the catacombs.

Learn, Teach *Learn* means "to acquire knowledge"; *teach* means "to give instruction." These are two sides of the same process.

Children **learn** best in enriched environments.

Experience **teaches** us that hard work is often the key to success.

Less See **Fewer.**

Lie See **Lay.**

Like See **As.**

Loan See **Borrow.**

Loose, Lose *Loose,* an adjective, means "not tight or binding"; *lose,* a verb, means "to misplace."

In tropical climates, people typically wear **loose,** lightweight garments.

Overcooked vegetables **lose** vitamins, minerals, texture, and color.

May See **Can.**

May be, Maybe *May be,* a verb, means "could be"; *maybe* means "perhaps."

The use of animals in research **may be** legal, but it raises ethical questions.

Maybe Van Gogh was mad; if so, his work is the result of an inspired madness.

645

Number   See **Amount.**

Off of   Use *off* by itself; it is perfectly clear.

During re-entry, a number of tiles came **off** the first space shuttle.

On account of   Use *because* or *since,* briefer ways of saying the same thing.

Passed, Past   Use *passed* as a verb; use *past* as a noun, adjective, or preposition.

Malcolm X **passed** through a period of pessimism to reach a time of optimism in his last months.

The **past,** as the saying goes, helps to determine the present.

Thoughtful people often reflect on their **past** actions and inactions.

The ambulance raced **past** the cars, hurrying from the fire site to the hospital.

People, Persons   Use *people* when referring to a group, emphasizing anonymity; use *persons* to emphasize unnamed individuals within the group.

People who lobby for special-interest groups must register their affiliations with Congress.

Several **persons** at the hearing criticized the company's environmental record.

Percent, Percentage   Use *percent* with a number; use percentage with a modifier.

Over fifty **percent** of the government's money is spent on Social Security and defense.

A large **percentage** of divorced people remarry.

Persons   See **People.**

Pretty   *Pretty* means "attractive" or "pleasant looking"; do not use it to mean "rather" or "somewhat."

Principal, Principle *Principal,* an adjective, means "main" or "highest in importance"; *principal,* a noun, means "the head of a school"; *principle,* a noun, means "a fundamental truth or law."

The **principal** difficulty of reading the novels of Henry James is sorting out his syntax.

The **principal** in the satiric novel *Up the Down Staircase* seems oblivious to the needs of his students.

The **principle** of free speech is vital to American interests.

Prior to See **Before.**

Quotation, Quote *Quotation,* the noun, means "someone else's material used word for word"; *quote,* the verb, means "to use a quotation." In conversation, *quote* is often used as a noun; in formal writing, however, distinguish between these two forms.

In his speeches and essays, Martin Luther King, Jr., frequently incorporated **quotations** from the Bible.

In his poem "The Hollow Men," T. S. Eliot **quotes** from *The Heart of Darkness,* a brief novel by Joseph Conrad.

Reason, Reason why, Reason is because *Reason,* used by itself, is sometimes unclear; *reason why,* a more complete expression, is generally preferred. *Reason is because* is repetitive, because *reason* itself implies a connection.

Literature about AIDS often explores the **reasons why** the general public reacts so irrationally to the disease.

Respectfully, Respectively *Respectfully* means "showing respect" or "full of respect"; *respectively* means "in the given order."

George Washington **respectfully** declined to be named king of the newly independent colonies.

These cited passages were submitted by Joshua Blaney, Andreas Church, and Joanna Meredith, **respectively.**

Seeing as   See **Being as.**

Set, Sit   *Set* means "to place or position something"; *sit* means "to be seated."

The photographer **set** the shutter speed at 1/100th of a second.

Many civil rights demonstrators refused to **sit** in segregated sections of buses, theaters, and government buildings.

Shall, Will   *Shall,* which indicates determination in the future tense, was once clearly distinguished from *will,* which merely describes future actions or conditions. Past distinctions between these forms are disappearing, and *will* is used in almost all cases. *Shall* remains standard, however, for questions using the first person.

Many animals raised in captivity **will** die if released into the wild.

"**Shall** I compare thee to a summer's day?" — Sonnet 18, William Shakespeare

Should, Would   Use *should* to explain a condition or obligation; use *would* to explain a customary action or wish.

Universities **should** not invest funds in companies whose policies conflict with their own.

When asked a pointed question, John Kennedy **would** often begin his response with a humorous remark to ease the tension.

Should of   See **Could of.**

Since   See **As, Because.**

Sit   See **Set.**

Sort of   See **Kind of.**

Suppose to, Supposed to   Use *supposed to,* the standard form.

Affirmative Action policies are **supposed to** ensure fair hiring practices nationwide.

Take   See **Bring.**

Teach   See **Learn.**

That, Which, Who   Use *that* to refer to people or things, but usually to things; use *which* to refer to things; use *who* to refer to people.

The musical work **that** set the standard for CD size was Beethoven's *Ninth Symphony.*

O'Neill's *Long Day's Journey into Night,* **which** won the 1957 Pulitzer Prize, was published posthumously.

People **who** cannot control their tempers are irritating and sometimes dangerous.

Their, There, They're   *Their,* a possessive pronoun, means "belonging to them"; *there,* usually an adverb, indicates placement; *they're,* a contraction, means "they are."

Legislation is pending to give artists royalties whenever **their** work is sold for profit.

Put the boxes over **there,** and I will open them later.

Investment banks should monitor **their** loan-granting policies more carefully.

Theirself, Theirselves   Use *themselves,* the standard form.

The members of Congress hesitated to vote **themselves** a raise.

There   See **Their.**

They're   See **Their.**

Threw, Through, Thru   *Threw,* the past tense of the verb *throw,* means "hurled an object"; *through* means "by way of" or "to reach an end"; *thru* is a nonstandard spelling of *through.*

In a pivotal scene in *Hedda Gabler,* Hedda **threw** Lovborg's manuscript into the fire.

Blue Highways is a picaresque account of William Least Heat Moon's travels **through** the United States.

Till, Until, 'Til   Both *till* and *until* are acceptable; *'til,* though slightly archaic, is also admissible; watch spellings and punctuation.

There will be no peace in the Middle East **till** (**until**) religious groups there become more tolerant of each other.

To, Too, Two   *To* is a preposition or part of an infinitive; *too* is a modifier meaning "in extreme" or "also"; *two* is the number.

In Cold Blood was Truman Capote's attempt **to** create what he called a nonfiction novel.

James Joyce's *Finnegan's Wake* is **too** idiosyncratic for many readers.

China gave the Washington Zoo **two** pandas who were promptly named Yin and Yang.

Try and   Use *try to,* the accepted form.

Producers of music videos **try to** recreate the essence of a song in visual form, with mixed success.

Uninterested   See **Disinterested.**

Until   See **Till.**

Use to, Used to   Use *used to,* the standard form.

Painters **used to** mix their own paints from pigments, oils, and bonding agents.

Utilize, Utilization   Generally use *use,* a shorter, simpler way of expressing the same idea.

Wait for, Wait on   *Wait for* means "to stay and expect"; *wait on* means "to serve."

In Beckett's famous play, Vladimir and Estragon **wait for** Godot.

Because of severe bouts of asthma and allergies, Marcel Proust was frequently bedridden and had to be **waited on** most of his life.

Weather, Whether   *Weather* means "conditions of the climate"; *whether* means "if."

In the South, rapid changes in the **weather** can often be attributed to shifts in the Gulf Stream.

Citizens must pay taxes **whether** they like it or not.

Well   See **Good.**

Whether   See **Weather.**

Which   See **That.**

Who   See **That.**

Who/Whom, Whoever/Whomever   Use *who* and *whoever* as subjects; use *whom* and *whomever* as objects.

Doctors **who** cannot relate well to patients should go into research work.

Whoever designed the conference program did a splendid job.

To **whom** should we submit our report?

Contact **whomever** you wish. I doubt that you will get a clear response.

Who's, Whose   *Who's,* a contraction, means "who is" or "who has"; *whose,* a possessive pronoun, means "belonging to someone unknown."

We need to find out **who's** scribbling graffiti on the walls.

A spelunker is someone **whose** hobby is exploring caves.

Will   See **Shall.**

Would   See **Should.**

Would of   See **Could of.**

Glossary of Grammatical Terms

Absolute Phrase   See **Phrase.**

Abstract Noun   See **Noun.**

Active Voice   See **Voice.**

Adjective   A word that modifies or limits a noun or pronoun by answering one of these questions: *what kind, which one, how many, whose.*

> **Distilled** water makes the best ice cubes.

A **regular adjective** precedes the word it modifies:

> The **velvet** dress cost two hundred dollars.

A **predicate adjective** follows a linking verb but modifies the subject of the sentence or clause:

> Ladders should be **sturdy** and **light-weight.**

An **article** (*a, an, the*) is considered an adjective:

> **A** good friend is **a** good listener.

A **demonstrative adjective** can show closeness (*this, these*) or distance (*that, those*) and singularity (*this, that*) or plurality (*these, those*):

> All of **these** books will not fit in **that** bookcase.

A **pronoun-adjective** is a pronoun that modifies a noun:

> **Somebody's** car is parked in **my** space.

Adjective Clause   See **Clause.**

Adjective Phrase   See **Phrase.**

Adverb   A word that modifies a verb, adjective, adverb, clause, phrase, or whole sentence by answering one of these questions: *how, when, where, how often, to what extent.*

Roberto enunciates **carefully.** (*Carefully* modifies *enunciates,* telling how.)

He is **usually** soft-spoken. (*Usually* modifies *soft-spoken,* telling when.)

He sometimes speaks **too** softly. (*Too* modifies *softly,* telling to what extent.)

Frequently, he has to repeat comments. (*Frequently* modifies the whole sentence, telling how often.)

Adverb Clause   See **Clause.**

Adverbial Conjunction   See **Conjunctive Adverb.**

Agreement   The matching of words according to number (singular and plural) and gender (masculine, feminine, and neuter). A verb takes a singular or plural form depending on whether its subject is singular or plural. A pronoun must match its antecedent (the word it refers to) in gender as well as number. A demonstrative adjective must match the number of the word it modifies (*this* and *that* for singular, *these* and *those* for plural).

Antecedent   The word to which a pronoun refers.

Rachel changed the tire herself. (*Rachel* is the antecedent of the reflexive pronoun *herself.*)

Appositive   A word or group of words that restates or defines a noun or pronoun. An appositive is positioned immediately after the word it explains.

Nonrestrictive appositives clarify proper nouns and are set off by commas:

Crest, **the best-selling toothpaste,** is recommended by many dentists.

Restrictive appositives are themselves proper nouns and require no commas:

The toothpaste **Crest** is advertised heavily on television.

Article See **Adjective.**

Auxiliary Verb Same as Helping Verb. See **Verb.**

Balanced Sentence See **Sentence.**

Case The form that a noun or pronoun takes according to its grammatical role in a sentence.

> **Subjective case** describes a word used as a subject or predicate noun:
>
> > **She** drives a Mazda 626.
>
> **Objective case** describes a word used as a direct object, indirect object, or object of a preposition:
>
> > The small size is just right for **her.**
>
> **Possessive case** describes a word used to show ownership:
>
> > **Her** Mazda is cherry red.
>
> Most nouns and pronouns change only to form the possessive case (by adding an apostrophe and *s: cat's, someone's*). Personal, relative, and interrogative pronouns, however, change form for all three cases.

Clause A group of words that has a subject and predicate.

> An **independent clause** is grammatically complete; when used separately, it is indistinguishable from a simple sentence:
>
> > **Dinosaurs had small brains.**
>
> An independent clause can be joined to another clause with a coordinating conjunction, a subordinating conjunction, or a semicolon.
>
> A **subordinate clause** also has a subject and predicate, but it is not grammatically complete; it must be joined to an independent clause:

Although dinosaurs had enormous bodies, they had small brains.

A subordinate clause can function as an adjective, an adverb, or a noun.

An **adjective clause** modifies a noun or pronoun:

We want a television **that has remote control.**

An **adverb clause** modifies a verb, an adjective, another adverb, a clause, a phrase, or a whole sentence:

Jason gets up earlier **than I usually do.**

A **noun clause** functions as a noun:

Whoever finds the wallet will probably return it.

Collective Noun   See **Noun.**

Comma Fault   See **Comma Splice.**

Comma Splice   Independent clauses incorrectly joined by a comma:

Einstein's brain has been preserved since his death, the formaldehyde has damaged the tissue.

Common Noun   See **Noun.**

Comparative Degree   See **Degree.**

Complement   Words or groups of words that complete the meaning of a sentence.

A **direct object** follows a transitive verb and answers these questions: *what, whom:*

Jason rented some **skis.**

An **indirect object** follows a transitive verb, is used with a direct object, and answers these questions: *to what, to whom:*

Jason gave **me** skiing lessons.

A **predicate noun** follows a linking verb and restates the subject of the sentence or clause:

Jason is a patient **instructor.**

A **predicate adjective** follows a linking verb and modifies the subject of the sentence or clause:

Nevertheless, the lessons were **frustrating.**

Complete Predicate   See **Predicate.**

Complete Subject   See **Subject.**

Complex Sentence   See **Sentence.**

Compound   Two or more words, phrases, or clauses that work together as one unit.

Compound words:

dining room, razzle dazzle.

Compound subject:

Shimita and **Amir** were married on Tuesday.

Compound predicate:

We **attended** the wedding but **skipped** the reception.

Compound-Complex Sentence   See **Sentence.**

Compound Predicate   See **Compound.**

Compound Sentence   See **Sentence.**

Compound Subject   See **Compound.**

Concrete Noun   See **Noun.**

Conjunction   Words that join words, phrases, and clauses. Conjunctions link compound words, explain alternatives, show contrast, clarify chronology, and explain causal relationships.

A **coordinating conjunction** (*and, but, for, nor, or, so,* or *yet*) links equivalent sentence parts:

> Stenographic **and** typing skills are required for the job.

A **subordinate conjunction** (*although, because, until,* and others) introduces a subordinate clause in a sentence:

> **Although** Todd could type, he could not take shorthand.

A **correlative conjunction** (*either . . . or, neither . . . nor,* and others) links equivalent sentence parts and provides additional emphasis:

> He will **either** learn shorthand **or** look for other work.

Conjunctive Adverb   An adverb used to link ideas logically; it does not make a grammatical connection as a traditional conjunction does and must therefore be used in an independent clause:

The experiment lasted two years; **however,** the results were inconclusive.

Coordinating Conjunction   See **Conjunction.**

Correlative Conjunction   See **Conjunction.**

Dangling Modifier   An introductory modifier that does not logically modify the subject of the sentence:

Charred from overcooking, we could not eat the steaks.

Degree   The form that adjectives and adverbs take to show degrees of comparison. **Positive degree** is a direct form, with no comparison: *simple.* **Comparative degree** compares two items: *simpler.* **Superlative degree** compares three or more items: *simplest.*

Demonstrative Adjective   See **Adjective.**

Demonstrative Pronoun   See **Pronoun.**

Dependent Clause   Same as Subordinate Clause. See **Clause.**

Direct Address   The use of a noun to identify the person or people spoken to; the noun is set off by commas and restricted to speech or writing that approximates speech:

Friends, it is time for us to voice our opinions.

Direct Object   See **Complement.**

Direct Quotation   Repeating someone's exact words, taken from speech or writing and used in speech or writing. Quotation marks indicate where the quoted material begins and ends:

Jim often says, **"Writing is never finished; it is only abandoned."**

An **indirect quotation** reports what people say without using direct wording; an indirect quotation is often introduced with *that* for statements and *if* for questions:

Jim asked **if I understood what he meant.**

Elliptical Construction   A construction that omits words (usually verbs and modifiers) that are considered understood:

Gorillas are more intelligent than chimpanzees [are].

Expletive Construction   A construction (*here is, it is, there are,* and *there is*) that functions as the subject and verb of a sentence or clause but depends on a complement to create meaning:

There are too many desks in this office.

Fragment   A group of words improperly presented as a sentence, with a capital letter at the beginning and with end punctuation. A fragment can lack a subject or a verb:

Left her baggage in the terminal.

It can be an unattached subordinate clause:

> Although the clerk had said the bags were ready.

It can be an unattached phrase:

> Stood at the baggage claim area for ten minutes.

Fused Sentence   Two or more independent clauses placed one after the other with no separating punctuation:

The vegetables at Trotski's Market are always fresh those at Wilkerson's are not.

Future Perfect Tense   See **Tense.**

Future Tense   See **Tense.**

Gender   Three classes of nouns and pronouns based on sex: masculine (*Roger, he*), feminine (*Blair, she*), and neuter (*tractor, it*).

Gerund   See **Verbal.**

Gerund Phrase   See **Phrase.**

Helping Verb   Same as Auxiliary Verb. See **Verb.**

Imperative Mood   See **Mood.**

Indefinite Pronoun   See **Pronoun.**

Independent Clause   Same as Main Clause. See **Clause.**

Indicative Mood   See **Mood.**

Indirect Object   See **Complement.**

Indirect Quotation   See **Direct Quotation.**

Infinitive See **Verbal.**

Infinitive Phrase See **Phrase.**

Intensive Pronoun Same as Reflexive Pronoun. See **Pronoun.**

Interjection A word that expresses surprise or emotion or that provides a conversational transition:

Well, I don't want to go either.

Interrogative Pronoun See **Pronoun.**

Intransitive Verb See **Verb.**

Irregular Verb See **Verb.**

Linking Verb See **Verb.**

Loose Sentence See **Sentence.**

Main Clause Same as Independent Clause. See **Clause.**

Misplaced Modifier A modifier incorrectly placed in a sentence; the word, phrase, or clause it modifies is not clear:

Jason said before midnight he would have his paper done.

Modifier A word, phrase, or clause used as an adjective or adverb to limit, clarify, qualify, or in some way restrict the meaning of another part of the sentence.

Mood A verb form that allows writers to present ideas with proper meaning.

Indicative mood presents a fact, offers an opinion, or asks a question:

The baby **has** a fever.

Imperative mood presents commands or directions:

Call the doctor.

Subjunctive mood presents a conditional situation or one contrary to fact:

I wish she **were feeling** better.

Nominative Case   Same as Subjective Case. See **Case.**

Nonrestrictive Element   An appositive, phrase, or clause that supplies information that is not essential to the meaning of a sentence. A nonrestrictive element is separated from the rest of the sentence by commas:

Cabaret, **my favorite film,** is on Cinemax next week.   (appositive)

Michael York, **with charm and humor,** played the leading male role. (phrase)

Marisa Berenson, **who is better known for her modeling than for her acting,** played the wealthy Jewish woman who came for English lessons.   (clause)

Noun   A word that names a person, place, thing, idea, quality, or condition. A **proper noun** names a specific person, place, or thing: *Elijah P. Lovejoy, Versailles, the Hope Diamond.* A **common noun** names a person, place, or thing by general type: *abolitionist, palace, jewel.* A **collective noun** names a group of people or things: *team, herd.* A **concrete noun,** either common or proper, names something tangible: *Mrs. Mastrioni, clinic, credit card.* An **abstract noun** names an intangible quality or condition: *honesty, nervousness.*

Noun Clause   See **Clause.**

Noun Marker   Same as Article. See **Adjective.**

Number   Two classes of nouns, pronouns, and verbs: singular (one) and plural (two or more). A noun in the plural form usually ends with *s: problem* (singular), *problems* (plural); a verb in the third-person singular form ends with *s: she cares* (singular), *they care* (plural); a demonstrative pronoun in the plural form ends with *se: this rabbit* (singular), *these rabbits* (plural).

Objective Case   See **Case.**

Object of a Preposition   A noun or pronoun that a preposition links to the rest of the sentence:

The electrical outlet is behind the **couch.**   (*Couch* is linked to *is,* telling *where.*)

Parallelism   The use of the same form for equivalent verbs in the same tense, a series of similar verbals or predicate nouns, and so on:

Congressman Abernathe **denied** the charges, **questioned** the evidence, **produced** full records, and **received** a formal apology.   (all past-tense verbs)

Parenthetical Expression   A word or group of words that interrupts the pattern of a sentence, separating elements and adding secondary information. Such expressions are separated by parentheses or dashes:

Seeing *Cats* on Broadway was expensive — **the tickets were thirty-five dollars each** — but worthwhile.

Participial Phrase   See **Phrase.**

Participle   See **Verbal.**

Parts of Speech   The classification of words into eight categories according to their use in sentences: noun, pronoun, verb, adjective, adverb, conjunction, preposition, and interjection. Each part of speech is separately defined in this glossary.

Passive Voice   See **Voice.**

Past Participle   See **Verbal.**

Past Perfect Tense   See **Tense.**

Perfect Tenses   See **Tense.**

Periodic Sentence   See **Sentence.**

Person   Three classes of nouns, pronouns, and verbs that indicate the relationship between the writer and the subject. **First person** (*I am, we are*) indicates that the writer writes about himself or herself; **second person** indicates that the writer writes about and to the same people (*you are*); **third person** indicates that the writer is writing to an audience *about* someone else (*she is, they are, Mitch is, the researchers are*).

Personal Pronoun   See **Pronoun.**

Phrase   A group of words that cannot function independently as a sentence but must be part of a sentence. A whole phrase often functions as a noun, adjective, or adverb.

A **prepositional phrase** consists of a preposition (*above, during, under,* and others), its object, and any modifiers: *above the front doorway, during the thunder storm, under the subject heading.* A prepositional phrase can function as an adjective or adverb:

The woman **next to me** read **during the entire flight.**   (*Next to me* is adjectival, modifying *woman*; *during the entire flight* is adverbial, modifying *read.*)

A **gerund phrase** combines a gerund and its complements and modifiers; it functions as a noun:

Conducting an orchestra requires skill, patience, and inspiration. (*Conducting an orchestra* is the subject of the sentence.)

A **participial phrase** combines a participle and its modifiers; it functions as an adjective:

From her window, Mrs. Bradshaw watched the children **playing under her maple tree.** (*Playing under her maple tree* modifies *children.*)

An **infinitive phrase** combines an infinitive and its complements and modifiers; it functions as a noun, an adjective, or an adverb:

To succeed as a free-lance artist is difficult. (noun)

Supplies **to use in art classes** are costly unless I get them wholesale. (adverb).

To make ends meet, I work part time at a bank. (adjective)

An **absolute phrase** modifies a whole sentence or clause. It contains a noun and a participle and is separated from the rest of the sentence by a comma:

All things considered, the recital was a success.

Positive Degree   See **Degree.**

Possessive Case   See **Case.**

Predicate   A word or group of words that expresses action or state of being in sentences; it consists of one or more verbs, plus any complements or modifiers.

A **simple predicate** is the single verb and its auxiliaries, if any:

Iago mercilessly **destroyed** the lives of Othello and Desdemona.

A **complete predicate** is the simple predicate, plus any complements or modifiers:

Iago **mercilessly destroyed the lives of Othello and Desdemona.**

Predicate Adjective   See **Complement.**

Predicate Noun   See **Complement.**

Preposition   A word that establishes a relationship between a noun or pronoun (the object of the preposition) and some other word in the sentence:

After his term **in** office, Jimmy Carter returned **to** Plains, Georgia. (*Term* is linked to *Carter; office* is linked to *term; Plains, Georgia* is linked to *returned.*)

Prepositional Phrase   See **Phrase.**

Present Participle   See **Verbal.**

Present Perfect Tense   See **Tense.**

Present Tense   See **Tense.**

Progressive Tense   See **Tense.**

Pronoun   A word that substitutes for a noun (its antecedent). A **personal pronoun** refers to people or things: *I, me, you, he, him, she, her, it, we, us, you, they, them.* A **possessive pronoun** shows ownership. Some possessive pronouns function independently: *mine, yours, his, hers, its, ours, yours, theirs*; some must be used with nouns: *my, your, his, her, our, your, their.* A **reflexive pronoun** shows that someone or something is acting for itself or on itself: *myself, yourself, himself, herself, itself, ourselves, yourselves, themselves.* An **interrogative pronoun** is used to ask a question:

who, whom, whoever, whomever, what, which, whose. A **demonstrative pronoun** is used alone: *this, that, these, those.* An **indefinite pronoun** has no particular antecedent but serves as a general subject or object in a sentence: *another, everything, most, somebody,* and others. A **relative pronoun** introduces an adjective or noun clause: *that, what, which, who, whom, whoever, whomever, whose.*

Proper Adjective   An adjective derived from a proper noun:

Belgian lace, Elizabethan sonnet.

Proper Noun   See **Noun.**

Quotation   See **Direct Quotation.**

Reflexive Pronoun   Same as Intensive Pronoun. See **Pronoun.**

Regular Verb   See **Verb.**

Relative Pronoun   See **Pronoun.**

Restrictive Element   An appositive, phrase, or clause that supplies information necessary to the meaning of a sentence. A restrictive element is not set off by commas:

The police show ***Cagney and Lacey*** was critically successful but only moderately popular. The problems **that two female detectives might face** were dealt with honestly.

Run-on Sentence   See **Fused Sentence.**

Sentence   An independent group of words with a subject and predicate, with a capital at the beginning, and with end punctuation. It expresses a grammatically complete thought. For most purposes, sentences are classified by their structure.

A **simple sentence** contains one independent clause and expresses one relationship between a subject and predicate:

The test flight was a success.

A **compound sentence** contains two or more independent clauses joined by a comma and a coordinating conjunction or by a semicolon:

The test flight was a success, and we began production on the jet.

A **complex sentence** contains one independent clause and one or more subordinate clauses:

Although there were some problems, the test flight was a success.

A **compound-complex sentence** contains at least two independent clauses and one subordinate clause:

Although there were some problems, the test flight was a success, and we began production on the jet.

In addition, a sentence can be classified by the arrangement of its ideas. A **loose sentence** presents major ideas first and then adds clarifications:

The bus was crowded with students, shoppers, and commuters.

A **periodic sentence** places the major idea or some part of it at the end:

Although we wanted a car with power steering, power brakes, power windows, automatic transmission, air conditioning, and quadraphonic sound, we couldn't afford one.

A **balanced sentence** contains parallel words, phrases, or clauses:

Jeremy was irresponsible, undisciplined, and rowdy, but his brother Jerod was responsible, disciplined, and reserved.

Sentence Fragment　See **Fragment.**

Simple Predicate　See **Predicate.**

Simple Sentence　See **Sentence.**

Simple Subject　See **Subject.**

Simple Tenses　See **Tense.**

Subject　The people, places, things, ideas, qualities, or conditions that act or are described in an active sentence or that are acted upon in a passive sentence.

A **simple subject** is the single word or essential group of words that controls the focus of the sentence:

Oppenheimer and Teller, participants in the Manhattan Project, disagreed about the development of the hydrogen bomb.

A **complete subject** is the simple subject, plus all related modifiers, phrases, and clauses:

Oppenheimer and Teller, participants in the Manhattan Project, disagreed about the development of the hydrogen bomb.

Subjective Case　Same as Nominative Case. See **Case.**

Subjunctive Mood　See **Mood.**

Subordinate Clause　See **Clause.**

Subordinating Conjunction　See **Conjunction.**

Superlative Degree　See **Degree.**

Tense　The modification of main verbs to indicate when an action occurred or when a state of being existed. **Simple**

tenses include the **present** (*he plans, they plan*), **past** (*he planned, they planned*), and **future** (*he will plan, they will plan*). **Perfect tenses** include the **present perfect** (*he has planned, they have planned*), **past perfect** (*he had planned, they had planned*), and **future perfect** (*he will have planned, they will have planned*). The **progressive tenses** indicate habitual or future action (*he is planning, he was planning, he will be planning, he had been planning, they are planning, they were planning, they had been planning, they will have been planning*).

Transitive Verb   See **Verb.**

Verb   A word or group of words that expresses action or a
state of being. For most purposes, verbs are classified by
their function. An **action verb** expresses physical or mental
action:

The cat **pounced** on the mouse. I **thought** it was cruel.

A **linking verb** expresses a state of being or condition and
joins the subject with a complement:

The cat **seemed** indifferent to my reaction. Cats **are** skillful predators.

An **auxiliary verb** is used with a main verb to form a verb
phrase, commonly used to clarify time references, explain
states of being, or ask questions:

We **will** stay on schedule.

Things **could** be worse.

Can you play the harpsichord?

All verbs are classified by the way they form basic verb parts. A **regular verb** forms the past tense by adding *-ed* or *-d* and maintains that form for the past participle: *talk, talked, had talked; close, closed, has closed.* An **irregular verb** follows varied patterns and may change for each form: *go, went, has gone; sing, sang, had sung.*

Verbal A verb form used as a noun, adjective, or adverb. A **gerund** is an *-ing* verb form that functions as a noun; the form of a gerund is the same as the present participle:

Hiking is my favorite sport.

An **infinitive** is a verb form that uses *to;* it functions as a noun, adjective, or adverb:

To open his own shop is Gerhardt's dream.   (noun)

Raising enough money is his biggest obstacle to overcome.   (adjective)

Gerhardt is too committed **to give up.**   (adverb)

A **participle** is a verb form that uses *-ing, -ed, -d, -n,* or *-t;* it functions as an adjective or adverb. A **present participle** ends in *-ing:*

Beaming, Clancey accepted the first-place trophy.

A **past participle** ends in *-ed, -d, -n,* or *-t;* a past participle can also help form a verb phrase:

The window pane, **broken** by a baseball, must be replaced.   (adjective)

We have **broken** that window many times.   (part of main verb)

See also **Phrase.**

Verb Phrase   See **Phrase.**

Voice   The form of a transitive verb that illustrates whether the subject *does* something or has something *done to it.*

Active voice indicates that the subject acts:

Roy Hobbs **hit** the winning home run.

Passive voice indicates that the subject completes no action but is instead acted upon:

The winning home run **was hit** by Roy Hobbs.

Word-Processing Index

673

General Index

Boldface numbers refer to section numbers; other numbers refer to pages.

679

General Index

General Index

Expressive writing, 24
    purpose of, 111

Facts
    assertions of, **5c:** 118
    as common knowledge, **32g:**
        493–494
    definition of, 120
    documentation of, 121
    as evidence, **5d:** 120–121
    paragraph development and, **4d:**
        98
    use of, **2d:** 49–50, 53
Facts of publication, 483, 504
Fallacies, *see* Logical fallacies
False analogy, **5e:** 130
Farther, Further, 642
Fewer, Less, 642
Figures, use of, **2d:** 49–50, 53
Figures of speech, use of, **14d:**
        274–276
Films
    capitalization for titles of, 418
    citation form for, **33e:** 516
    italics for titles of, 423
Finalize, Finish, 643
Final manuscript
    page numbers for, 556, 586, 597
    preparing and submitting, **3f:**
        72–73; 421; **34f:** 545–546;
        595–599
    word processor and, 73, 546
Final thesis, 26
First person, definition of, 664
Footnotes, 536
For
    meaning implied by, 213
    parallelism and, 232–233
Foreign words, italics for, **28c:** 425
Foreword, citation of, **33c:** 511
Formal diction, 256
Formal outline, **2b:** 36, 38–41
    preparing, 40; **34a:** 526
    sample of, 548–555
Format
    for business letters, 625–626

for citations, *see* Parenthetical
        notes; Works cited
    for envelopes, 626
    for manuscript, 602–603
    paper, 600–602
    for reference list, 603–606
    word processor and, 249, 370, 379
Fragments, **15:** 284–289
    clauses as, **15b:** 286–287
    definition of, 660
    lacking subjects, **15a:** 285
    lacking verbs, **15a:** 285–286
    phrases as, **15a:** 284–286
    use for special effect, **15c:** 287–288
Framing pattern, use of, **2d:** 54–55
Freewriting, **1b:** 7, 9–10
    dimming screen for, 10, 14, 24
    looping and, 13
    unfocused and focused, 7, 9
Fun, 643
Further, Farther, 642
Fused (run-on) sentences, **16:**
        290–296
    conjunctive adverbs in, **16d:**
        292–294
    definition of, 660
    forming compound or complex
        sentence from, **16c:** 291–292
    joining independent clauses in,
        16b: 291
    revising with word processor, 295
    separating independent clauses in,
        16a: 290–291
Future perfect tense, **6c:** 161; **19b:**
        328
    definition of, 670
    in subordinate clauses, **19d:**
        330–331
Future tense, **6c:** 160; **19a:** 327
    definition of, 670
    in subordinate clauses, **19d:**
        330–331

Gender
    definition of, 660
    See also Sexist language

General Index

Predicate adjectives, **6d:** 164–165; **7a:** 183, 184
  definition of, 653, 657
  linking verbs with, 153
Predicate nouns, **7a:** 183, 184
  definition of, 657
  linking verbs with, 152
  pronouns used as, **18a:** 315–316
Predicates, **7a:** 181–183
  complete, **7a:** 182–183; 666
  compound, **7a:** 181–182; 657
  definition of, 665–666
  simple, **7a:** 181
Prediction, use of, **2d:** 55–56
Preface, citation of, **33c:** 511
Prefixes
  hyphens to link to words, **26b:** 402–403
  spelling and, **31a:** 444
Prepositional phrases, 172, 173–174; **7a:** 186–187
  beginning sentences with, **8c:** 210
  commas to separate from rest of sentence, 361; **22d:** 364
  definition of, 664
  nouns and pronouns in, 179
  positioning, **12a:** 245
Prepositions, **6g:** 172–174
  caution against using colons between objects and, **24f:** 386–387
  with compound object, 316
  definition of, 666
  objects of, 186; **18b:** 316; 663
  pronouns as objects of, **18b:** 316
Present participles, 187; **19d:** 329
  definition of, 671
Present perfect tense, **19b:** 327
  definition of, 670
  in subordinate clauses, **19d:** 330–331
Present tense, **19a:** 325–326
  definition of, 670
  for descriptions of works of art, **19a:** 326
  for general beliefs and scientific

principles, **19a:** 326
  for repeated or habitual actions, **19a:** 326
  in subordinate clauses, **19d:** 330–331
Pretentious language, avoiding, **14b:** 272–273
Pretty, 646
Primary evidence, 121
Principal, Principle, 647
Print quality
  documentation style and, 602
  for résumé, 632
Prior to, Before, 638–639
Process analysis, paragraph development and, **4d:** 101
Professional degrees
  capitalization of, 416, 417
  commas to set off, **22g:** 368
Progressive tenses, **6c:** 161; **19c:** 328
  definition of, 670
Pronoun adjectives, 144, 317
  definition of, 653
Pronoun-antecedent agreement, **17b:** 304–310
  collective nouns and, **17b:** 308
  compound antecedents joined by *and* and, 306–307
  compound antecedents joined by *or, nor, either . . . or,* or *neither . . . nor* and, **17b:** 307–308
  indefinite pronouns and, **17b:** 308
  maintaining with word processor, 311
  sexist language and, **17b:** 305–306
Pronoun case, **18:** 313–322
  in appositives, with nouns, and in elliptical constructions and, **18d:** 318–320
  direct objects, indirect objects, or objects of prepositions and, **18b:** 316
  objective, 314
  pronouns showing ownership or modifying a gerund and, **18c:**

General Index

General Index

707

General Index

708

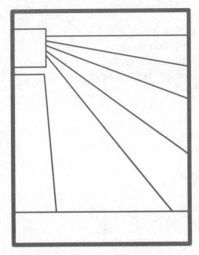

THE
BEACON
HANDBOOK SECOND EDITION

INSTRUCTOR'S MANUAL

Contents

Preface

Writing is thinking and thinking evolves with experience, so learning to write well is a lifelong endeavor. In the writing classroom, where the serious study of writing to communicate often begins, learning to write is best accomplished as an apprenticeship during which students acquire information and attitudes and practice skills and techniques with the help of an active practitioner of the craft and art of writing.

Teachers in such classrooms pursue their own writing and share with their student-apprentices the strategies and methods learned through this work. Those of us who teach writing in this way know that reading others' writing or reading and talking *about* writing is no substitute *for* writing, and consequently we provide students with numerous opportunities to write. We know that learning the terminology of writing and grammar — *thesis statement, noun, verb, clause,* and so on — helps students to analyze and improve their writing. We know that fostering experimentation and exploration allows students to develop their voices and skills more effectively than does rigidly sequenced instruction or overemphasis on disinterested judgments of a final product. We know that writing teachers must balance negative with positive comments, encouraging students to learn to express themselves as clearly and completely as possible. And we know from experience that writing is difficult to master, and hence we remain realistic in our assessments of students' progress, encouraging in our responses to their writing, and advisory in our daily teaching.

The principles articulated above have guided my teaching of writing, my training of new teachers, and my writing of *The Beacon Handbook* and of this instructor's manual. The discussions that follow describe approaches, activities, recommendations, and hints derived from eighteen years of active learning, teaching, and writing.

R.P.

I   Advice to the New Instructor

Because writing involves the application to almost any topic of so many different skills — generating ideas, organizing them, expressing them coherently and completely, and thinking critically — teaching writing is challenging; it makes no sense to say otherwise. But although it is demanding, helping students to develop strategies for expressing their ideas effectively in writing is also rewarding.

As you prepare for your first writing class, it will be helpful for you to formalize your thoughts on what writing is, what the teaching of writing should be, what students should learn through writing, and how they can best learn it. Reading the research on the theories and teaching of composition is a good way to begin to find your own answers, and the following articles and books provide a useful place to begin:

Diederich, Paul B. *Measuring Growth in English.* Urbana: NCTE, 1974.

Donovan, Timothy R., and Ben W. McClelland, eds. *Eight Approaches to Teaching Composition.* Urbana: NCTE, 1980. Particularly useful are the articles by Thomas Carnicelli, Paul Eschholz, and Donald Murray.

Hillocks, George. *Research on Written Composition: New Directions for Teaching.* Urbana: National Conference on Research in English, 1986.

Shaughnessy, Mina P. *Errors and Expectations: A Guide for the Teacher of Basic Writing.* New York: Oxford UP, 1977.

Tate, Gary, and Edward P. J. Corbett, eds. *The Writing Teacher's Sourcebook.* 2nd ed. New York: Oxford UP, 1988. Particularly useful are the articles by David Bartholomae, James Berlin, Wayne Booth, Peter Elbow, Janet Emig, Lee Odell, Douglas

Park, William Riley Parker, Mina Shaughnessy, Nancy Sommers, and Harvey Weiner.

Even before you have read these and other books and articles on composition, you can begin to clarify your thinking about writing and the teaching of writing by reflecting on your own experiences and the experiences of others. What kinds of writing do you do? How do you approach different kinds of writing? Are you better at one kind than another? Do all stages of composing proceed smoothly? Or are some — or all — difficult or challenging? Do you write slowly or quickly? After answering these and similar questions for yourself, consider how other writers you know or have read about might answer them. The specificity and variety of these responses will confirm several principles useful for guiding your planning and teaching of a writing course.

Composing is fluid, unpredictable, and often complex.

Different writing tasks require different approaches.

Different writers respond to similar challenges in different ways.

Some writing strategies are reliably helpful for many writers and can be shared.

Remembering these principles will help you to remain honest, helpful, and realistic when you work with your own apprentice writers.

It is useful to reflect, as well, on the formal and informal writing instruction you have received. Consider the approaches and activities used by your classroom teachers of writing; you will no doubt quickly accumulate many that you will want to try in your class. Consider as well techniques and projects that as a student writer you found ineffective; you may want to avoid these, but try to mine them for anything useful for particular writing situations or particular students. Analyze the informal writing instruction you received from friends, teachers in nonwriting classes, and others. What makes you remember their help? How did their help differ from that in a traditional writing class? Could that kind of help be replicated in the writing classroom? Should it be?

Finally, give some thought to how your papers were evaluated and graded and how you responded. What kinds of notations proved most helpful? What seemed counterproductive? What did you learn from the corrections and comments on your papers? Depending on the writer, the paper, and the problems, excessive marking can be discouraging, and superficial marking can be frustrating. Remembering your responses to various forms of evaluations and grades will help you to make your evaluation and grading of your students' work as apt and useful as possible.

Remembering this variety of circumstances, challenges, problems, and responses will help you to remain flexible, exploring and experimenting with ways to help your students learn to communicate effectively in writing.

Writing and Teaching in a Context

As you begin planning your writing course, consider the context in which your students will write and you will teach. Full understanding of the complex interrelationship of courses, programs, schools, and students — all subject to variety and change — may take years to develop. But considering the questions below is a good way to begin. Do your best to discover answers, even tentative ones. (If you are teaching in a highly structured writing program, the answers to some of these questions will be supplied for you.)

- *What is the purpose of the course you will teach?* Should the course provide experience in writing personal experience papers, arguments, researched writing, or a combination of these?
- *How does the course fit into the department's curriculum?* Is the course part of a sequence or is it the only writing requirement? Is the course a service course where students learn crucial skills to be applied in other courses?

- *What kinds of and how much writing should students complete?*
  Should students keep journals? Should they write papers in the
  various modes? Should they complete a brief documented paper? Should they write a specific number of papers or a specific
  total number of pages?

- *What kinds of students will you teach?* Will you be teaching
  mostly eighteen-year-old students direct from high school? Or
  will you be teaching, as most people currently are, a group including many older, returning students? Will the backgrounds
  and experiences of your students be homogeneous or varied?
  Will all of your students speak and write English as their primary language?

- *What texts are you expected to use?* Are you free to choose any
  text but required to use certain types — for example, a rhetoric,
  reader, or handbook? Has your department adopted texts that
  you are required to use?

With responses to these questions in mind, your goals for your
students as well as tentative ideas for meeting those goals should
start to fall into place.

Special Aspects of the Writing Course

Assessing Your Students' Writing Ability

Often, a diagnostic paper is the most useful way to discover how
well your students write. At many schools, SAT or ACT scores are
used to place students in appropriate composition courses; at
other schools, students are assigned to writing courses after
completing a writing sample that is scored by a department
group. Although such placement procedures will give you some
idea of your students' general skills, nothing can tell you what
their specific writing strengths and weaknesses are except their
writing. Unless writing samples are made available to you, have

students write an in-class diagnostic paper during the second class session.

Design the assignment carefully. Students will have only one class period, approximately fifty minutes, to complete the paper, so the topic should be one for which they can easily use personal experience to illustrate their points. Provide more than one topic and explain on the assignment sheet what you expect and how the paper will be evaluated. Sample topics and assignment sheets are included in the Instructor's Support Package.

Evaluate the completed diagnostic papers quickly but completely. Since the purpose of the diagnostic paper is to discover what students know and do not know about writing, do not spend too much time evaluating content and style. Focus on basic principles of effective written communication. The evaluation sheet in the ISP identifies seven primary traits useful for describing student work; grade ranges rather than specific grades give students a general sense of where they stand. Comment on special strengths or weaknesses at the bottom of the evaluation sheet.

Return the diagnostic paper as soon as possible. The evaluation sheets will make this easier. Returning papers quickly is a good idea for a number of reasons. First, you will know immediately if your plans are appropriate and how to teach the class. Second, your students will have a clear statement of your opinion of their work. Third, you will establish a context for your evaluation and more specific grading of later work.

Writing Assignments

Designing assignments involves more than announcing the kind of paper students are to write and the due date. Equally important are establishing the context for the assignment, identifying its goal, and articulating the criteria by which it will be evaluated.

A well-planned and clearly presented assignment will improve your students' chances of learning from and successfully completing the assignment — and make your evaluation of their writing more enjoyable. Here are some guidelines to help you design and present assignments effectively.

- *Provide written instructions for major assignments.* Your students will benefit from clear written instructions to which they can refer as they write. (A sample assignment sheet is included in the ISP.)
- *Provide identifying information.* An assignment or activity sequence number or a designation by type of paper will minimize confusion among assignments.
- *Establish a context for the work.* On the assignment sheet, briefly describe situations in which the assigned type of writing is commonly used; such contextual notes help students to see the value of the work.
- *Allow students to choose their own topics.* Although all students should complete the same kind of work — a classification paper, for example — specific topics should be of the students' choosing. They will be more engaged by the work, and you will appreciate having papers on different topics. Be ready with a variety of examples of appropriate topics to discuss in class.
- *Clarify any special requirements.* If you expect to see intermediate stages in addition to the final paper — a rough draft, for example — state that clearly on the assignment sheet.
- *Refer students to text pages and examples.* List on the assignment sheet text pages of relevant discussions and examples, even if you have just covered that section of the text. Provide handouts or discuss additional examples if necessary.
- *Offer useful hints for completing the assignment.* In class or briefly on the assignment sheet, describe any strategies you as a writer have discovered or developed that are specifically relevant to the problems of the particular assignment.
- *Specify the primary emphases of your evaluation.* If you will focus in your evaluation on particular writing skills or aspects of

the assignment, state your intention on the assignment sheet and in class. Knowing these criteria — for instance, that thesis statements and topic sentences will receive special attention — will help students to learn to focus on and revise for the effectiveness of these elements.

■ *Schedule time for peer editing.* On the assignment sheet, state the date on which rough drafts are due for peer editing; also state whether a handwritten or typed version is required.

■ *Specify the day the final assignment is due.* State the due date on the assignment sheet. Make sure that you will be able to evaluate the papers shortly after they are submitted. It is unproductive to hold students to rigid deadlines for submission, only to have the papers sit on your desk while you attend a conference.

■ *Take class time to discuss the assignment and to answer questions.* Take a few minutes of class time to review the assignment and to clear up any questions.

Preparing a complete assignment sheet, especially when an assignment is a variation of one presented in a text, may seem time consuming. It is. But the time spent in making the meaning and importance of assignments clear to inexperienced writers will clarify your thinking about the requirements and benefits of the specific writing tasks in your course.

Peer Editing

Peer editing involves having students in pairs or small groups exchange papers and read, evaluate, and edit each other's work. Using peer editing in the classroom creates a support group for students, emphasizing writing as an effort to communicate rather than to convince — or fool — an audience of one, the instructor. To use peer editing successfully, establish clear, appropriate guidelines for students. I have found the following useful:

■ *Make peer editing part of your class routine.* It takes some time for students to develop peer editing skills, and practice is the only way to ensure that their comments will be specific and helpful. Schedule a peer editing session for every major assignment, usually at least one session before it is due. Establish a routine for editing sessions — distribution of evaluation sheets, formation of groups, silent reading of papers, discussion, and so on — and follow it consistently. Students will soon be familiar with the pattern and will get started smoothly without wasting class time.

- *Provide criteria for students' judgments.* Use peer evaluation sheets with specific questions or write questions on the board. The evaluation standards you describe on assignment sheets can also be used to focus peer evaluation. Sample peer editing sheets are included in the ISP, but you should tailor your questions to meet the individual needs of your students and to match individual assignments.

- *Be involved with the editing but stay in the background.* For peer editors to gain confidence in their judgments and to feel they are helping another writer, they must feel autonomous. You should be ready to take a secondary role during these sessions (a challenge for many teachers) and allow students to interact directly with each other. Move around the room, pausing briefly at each group, but resist the temptation to talk with them or add your judgments. (There will be time for that later.)

- *Keep students "on task."* Move around the classroom, monitoring students' work. Your interest in their activity (but not your interference) is usually enough to keep students focused on their task, but do not hesitate to redirect students' attention if they have strayed from editing.

- *Serve as a "referee."* When peer editors disagree (or when an editor and writer disagree), take an active role as referee. If students seem too dependent on this help, limit your involvement to only one question or comment per paper; that way, students will have to select the most important element to refer to you and handle other disagreements themselves. Do not allow students to relinquish their editing responsibilities.

- *Limit the time devoted to peer editing.* If editing time is longer than needed, students will drift into unrelated conversations. Unless the written work is long — a researched paper, for example — fifteen to twenty minutes is usually enough time to read a paper and offer specific, focused comments. If you follow the three-stage revision pattern in *Beacon* — first content, then style, and last grammar, punctuation, and mechanics — ten minutes for each would be in order. Brief, directed editing sessions are more productive than long, unfocused ones.

- *Vary the makeup of the editing groups.* Be flexible. Sometimes have students work in pairs, at other times in trios. Mix up the groups so that students have the benefit of comments and responses from many different classmates, not just those who sit near them. Consider a number of alternatives for determining the makeup of the groups: number of students, majors and minors, related paper topics, and so on.

- *Encourage honest evaluation.* When they begin peer editing, students often hedge on their comments because they feel it is impolite or mean-spirited to offer negative criticism. Stress that only candid responses help writers to improve their work substantively. Some teachers require that for each paper they evaluate editors describe two strengths and two weaknesses.

- *Encourage editors to pose questions, not make changes.* Peer editors should comment on papers, offering the writer guidance and advice; they should not revise the paper. Encourage students to pose questions about papers or to provide summary evaluations (using peer editing sheets), rather than making corrections on the paper itself, which sometimes leads to a focus on technical matters only. Some teachers insist that editors make no interlinear marks on the paper, only marginal notes.

Peer editing helps to emphasize the importance of revision to a successful final paper and show that revision is meant to improve a paper, not just to change it. Managed well, peer editing ensures higher quality papers and increases students' learning and satisfaction with their writing.

Student Conferences

Having individual conferences with students allows you to give students help with specific writing problems. To make the most effective use of conference time, establish guidelines. I have found the following useful:

- *Limit the time for each conference.* Restrict the time you spend in a single session; ten to twenty minutes is generally sufficient. If students have severe problems, a series of brief conferences, each addressing a single problem, will be more productive than one long one.
- *Have students prepare for the conference.* Before coming to your office, have a student read a section of the text, complete an exercise, review and classify markings on papers, gather samples of their own or others' writing, jot down specific questions, or do whatever is appropriate to the situation. Having students actively prepare for the conference helps to ensure that your time will be well spent.
- *Concentrate on a limited number of topics.* Discussing many features of a paper or many aspects of a student's progress in the course can make a conference seem fragmented and superficial. Instead, concentrate on one or two crucial elements and give them thorough attention.
- *Talk about writing, not about grades.* Although a student's concern with grades may be justified, spending conference time quibbling about them is not. Instead, insist that your conference time be spent solving writing problems; stress that

solving the problems will result in better writing and ultimately better grades. (Students wishing to discuss grades should make an appointment specifically to do so; they must understand that writing conferences will be devoted to the discussion of writing.)

Planning the Course

If you are working in a department with a highly structured writing program, a recommended course plan may be provided for you, one developed by experienced teachers of the course. In other, less standardized departments, you may not receive such firm guidance, but the program director, mentors, or teaching advisers will offer you assistance as you plan your course.

Whichever kind of program you will be teaching in, the daily conduct of the class is your decision and responsibility. Remember that planning a composition course is very much like planning a paper. You must keep your general purpose in mind; you must begin to establish your role as the teacher of the course; and you must keep your audience — your students — very much in mind. As with planning a paper, you must establish a logical, coherent sequence of information, but you must remain flexible, allowing the needs and responses of your audience to influence and if necessary radically alter the plans that you have made.

Begin your planning by blocking out a schedule. Use a planning book, calendar, or photocopies of the sample planning pages in the ISP and note the important days of the term: the first day's meeting, a diagnostic paper if you will require one, the midterm and final exams, holidays and professional conference days on which the class will not meet, and so on. This visual representation of the term will allow you to pace class activities realistically. After you have delimited the term, you can begin to plan specifically for writing assignments, days for peer editing, student conferences and discussion of readings, and so on. Try working on loose pages placed side by side for an overview of sequenced activities such as writing successive drafts or a research assignment.

Major Writing Assignments

Determine how many and what kinds of papers you or your department will require from students. Each phase of an assignment, whether rough drafts for peer editing, revisions, or final versions, should be tentatively scheduled. Students usually require a week to write a 500- to 700-word paper once they learn how to develop writing through the stages of planning, drafting, and revising. Pace the major assignments so that they are due no closer than one or one and a half weeks apart; to cluster them more closely will not allow students sufficient time to write or you sufficient time to evaluate, grade, and return the work before the next assignment is due. (See "Evaluation and Grading," pages IM-17–22.) Remember to schedule time to explain fully the assignments and the skills necessary to complete them. If your department does not recommend a specific sequence for types of assignments, follow the order in which materials appear in your text or ask an experienced teacher for advice.

Using Textbooks

Read through your textbooks carefully, and begin deciding, if only tentatively, what you will cover and in what order. Textbooks generally include much more information and many more assignments and activities than can be accommodated in a single term, so knowing your goals, those of your department, and your students' needs will help you to use the texts to best advantage. If your course will include readings, consider what readings you will assign and block in days for discussion of reading assignments.

Peer Editing Sessions

If you plan to use the advantage that peer editing gives in improving students' work and increasing their autonomy as writers, block in editing sessions for one or two class sessions preceding due dates for drafts or final papers. That way, students will have time to revise their drafts, using comments from their peers and you and prepare their final drafts.

Conference Days

Reserve one or two class sessions to schedule individual conferences with each of your students. During the first two months of the course, but certainly by midterm, you should spend ten to fifteen minutes discussing each student's progress in the course (see "Student Conferences," page IM-10–11); the importance of these conferences justifies canceling class. You should also expect to have individual conferences with students who need special attention.

Research Activities

If your course requires researched writing, schedule the stages of this work so that the sequence is intense enough to keep students focused and interested but sufficiently drawn out to allow students time to research, read, and synthesize materials before writing the paper. An orientation to your library is generally a good idea; if you want a library staff member to provide the orientation, make your request early in the term.

(See Part III of this instructor's manual for additional information on teaching the research paper.)

Unscheduled Days

To remain flexible enough to address your students' special writing needs as you discover them, leave approximately one hour open for every six available, or approximately one hour every two weeks. After you have evaluated your students' diagnostic papers or their first major paper, you will be able to select appropriate activities for the open days. Leaving a few days open until you get to know the strengths, weaknesses, and interests of your students will save you from having to overhaul your schedule.

First-day Handouts

The materials you distribute on the first day of class should be specific and clear — providing necessary information, describing basic procedures and policies, and stating goals for the course.

Course Information Sheet

A first-day information sheet is a contract for the course, explaining to students what you will expect of them. As you prepare this handout, your expectations and basic requirements and policies will become clear. (A sample information sheet is included in the ISP.)

Include the following for a comprehensive course information sheet.

- Course number, descriptive title, and section number
- Class time, meeting days, and room assignment
- Information about you: office address and telephone number and regular office hours
- Required texts and materials
- Policies for completing the course
- Policies for submitting assignments (late policies, policies for extensions, and so on)
- Information about conferences
- Attendance policies
- Format specifications for typed and handwritten papers
- Advice for seeking additional help (tutoring, writing center, and so on)

Specifications for Typed and Handwritten Manuscripts

A one-page handout describing basic requirements for preparing typed and handwritten manuscripts will be helpful to your students, especially when completing in-class work. The handout should describe briefly your requirements for headings, margins, spacing, correction of errors and so on. Appendix A in *The Beacon Handbook* offers a complete description of a standard format. (See the ISP for a sample handout.)

Schedule of Major Assignments

To give students a clear understanding of the kind and amount of writing they will be doing during the term, but to avoid the constraints of a day-by-day syllabus that may have to be modified later, consider offering a list of major assignments. A simple list of the assignment sequence, with a brief description of each assignment but without dates, gives you the most flexibility. A list with assignments, descriptions, and due dates gives students more specific information about their work load; you can, of course, change due dates later if necessary.

The First Session

The first class session is, inevitably, largely administrative. But you can also use it to set the tone of the course and to demonstrate for your students its general pace. Be organized, clear, and professional. To establish a professional yet comfortable atmosphere, consider these suggestions.

Careful Preparation and Arrangements

Careful preparation and arrangements for the first class session will give you a feeling of control and your students a feeling of serious purpose. It will set the stage for effective teaching and learning. So be organized for the first day of class.

■ *Prepare your handouts early.* Review your materials for completeness and accuracy. Have copies made for each student registered for the course, along with at least ten extra copies for late-enrolling students.

■ *Collect samples of all materials that you will want to show your students.* Gather textbooks, a collegiate dictionary, a spelling dictionary, recommended paper or typing correction fluid, and so on. Showing is always better than telling, so collect and bring to class the materials you want to show students on the first day.

- *Bring a packet of index cards.* You will probably want to collect some information about your students during the first class meeting (see below); 3-by-5-inch or 4-by-6-inch index cards are ideal for this purpose, so bring a good supply to class.
- *Review your class list.* Review your students' names. You will not be able to pronounce all the names correctly (even phonetics will not always help!), but getting most names correct will make you and your students more comfortable.

Techniques for the First Class

Use the first class session to establish the rhythm of your course, demonstrating to students its emphasis and pace. To achieve those goals, focus your activities.

- *Arrive early and arrange your materials.* Unpack and arrange your materials on the desk or table; they will be easy to get to and thus to use comfortably and smoothly.
- *Write identifying information on the board.* Your name, the course title and number and any section number are usually all that are required so that students may check to see if they are in the correct course.
- *Begin class on time.* Although you should expect a few stragglers, you should begin class on time, an important signal that you intend to be businesslike in your teaching.
- *Take attendance.* Use the class list and note who is present and who is not. Do not use your grade book yet because the enrollment will undoubtedly change as students drop and add.
- *Pass out and review the first-day handouts.* Reiterate (but do not read) major points on the handouts and ask whether students have questions.

- *Explain the diagnostic paper.* If you intend to assign a diagnostic paper during the second class session, briefly describe its purpose, nature, and evaluation; remind students to bring paper, pens, dictionaries, and the manuscript guidelines.
- *Find out something about your students.* On index cards, have students write their names, the course number (and time or section number if you have several sections), and their majors and minors. Ask them other questions that will reveal their backgrounds or relate, if only tangentially, to their interest in or preparation for the course: other writing courses or experiences, special interests, hobbies, work experience, favorite writers, favorite kinds of reading, and so on.
- *Have students write.* On the back of the information card, ask students to write. One useful and relevant subject for this is a description of their previous writing experiences (the number of writing classes they have taken, their favorite kinds of writing, their strengths as writers, and so on). Or ask students to write brief comments on a topic of current interest of your choosing. These brief writing samples, along with the other information on the card, will help you begin to see your students as people and as writers. And writing, however, briefly, during the first class session signals that communicating ideas will be central to the course.
- *Conclude the session.* Dismiss your students on time, but be prepared for a few individual questions.

Evaluation and Grading

Evaluation and grading are basic, necessary aspects of teaching composition. Students rightly expect evaluation that is advisory, clear, and consistent; they also expect grading that is fair and realistic. You should expect your students to respond to your evaluations and grades seriously by working to improve their subsequent papers.

Many composition teachers become weighed down by the responsibility and amount of evaluation and grading. You can avoid this by developing specific strategies that will help you to evaluate and grade papers efficiently and with no sacrifice of clarity or usefulness.

Effective, Efficient Grading

Evaluation, the marking of the paper itself, gives teachers the chance to comment, praise, question, challenge, and generally respond to students' work. Evaluation must ultimately be global, responding to students' work in its every aspect. Pragmatically, a variety of markings are used to comment on the various levels of the work.

- *Interlinear comments.* Within lines of text, point out technical problems with punctuation, grammar, mechanics, sentence structure, diction, and so on.
- *Marginal comments.* In the margins, comment on larger issues like paragraph organization and transitions, sentence variety, and effective or ineffective examples.
- *Terminal comments.* At the end of the paper, respond to the largest issues of content and style: overall arrangement, unity of ideas, consistency of tone, clarity of thesis statement and its application in the paper, and so on.

An effective evaluation uses all three marking strategies, neither overemphasizing nor overlooking any significant element from the specific to very general.

Yet despite the desire to do this thorough an evaluation and thus provide the maximum benefit to students, many instructors find the paper load prohibitive. To provide thorough evaluation within the available time, teachers have developed specific strategies for coping. Consider the strategies listed below and select those that best suit your teaching style and best serve your students:

- *Correction Symbols.* Rather than write out comments like "you have problems with subject-verb agreement throughout this paragraph" use correction symbols such as those on the endpapers of *Beacon,* in this case noting only "agr." Students can then refer to the correction symbol chart and find the symbol's explanation. (The chart in *Beacon* also includes a text reference.) For serious or recurrent errors, place the symbol in the margin and circle or underline samples in the paper.

- *Grading Sheets.* Use a dittoed or photocopied evaluation sheet to comment on each student's work. Grading sheets tailored to specific assignments allow you to focus your evaluation on the paper's most significant features. (Several samples are included in the ISP.)

- *Primary and selected features.* Teachers need not mark every element of a paper, at least not every time. Rather, mark the most significant and relevant, and at times selectively review a paper looking only for the application of a major principle, such as diction, that has been the focus of recent class work.

- *Time limit for grading each paper.* Allow yourself a fixed period of time to grade each paper — for instance, ten or fifteen minutes — and no more. Resist the urge to labor longer over papers, unless they are especially long or complex, such as a research paper. Returning helpfully marked papers after a reasonable time, even if every feature is not marked, is more important than returning papers, however fully marked, too late to be of use on the next paper.

- *Small batches.* Avoid marking papers in long sittings. Rather, begin grading papers in small batches the day you receive them. You'll find that your marking time will be better spent when you don't feel shackled to thirty papers in one evening.

■ *Realistic planning.* You do have a life outside teaching and evaluating papers, so remember to give yourself a break. Avoiding martyrdom will help you to keep your enthusiasm for the course, which will have greater impact on students and their writing than exhaustive markings by an exhausted teacher.

The evaluation of students' papers should strike a balance between completeness and common sense. Don't overestimate what the markings on one paper can or should do. Rely on an accumulation of clear, helpful comments throughout the term to help students improve their writing.

Realistic, Consistent Evaluation Criteria

Assigning grades to students' work is one of the most difficult aspects of teaching writing. To prepare yourself to assign grades, establish your standards for *A* through *F* and unacceptable.

I have found the following grading criteria useful. Consider making descriptions of your grading criteria available to your students.

A Artistic and challenging. Written with style and with a forceful thesis; clear, compelling sense of role, audience, and purpose; discriminating arrangement of material in paragraphs, sentences, and phrases; original, insightful supporting material; artful, surprising choices of nouns, verbs, adjectives, and adverbs; sentences widely varied in length and type; free from technical inconsistencies, polished and carefully proofread.

B Appealing and stimulating. Effectively written, with a forceful thesis; skillful, clear use of role, audience, and purpose; effective arrangement of material in paragraphs, sentences, and phrases; interesting, insightful use of supporting material; skillful, appealing choices of nouns, verbs, adjectives, and adverbs; sentences varied in length and type; free from most technical errors, fairly well polished and proofread.

C *Competent and clear.* Clearly written, with an effective thesis; clear use of role, audience, and purpose; suitable arrangement of material in paragraphs and sentences; clear, sufficient use of supporting material; satisfactory, clear choices of nouns, verbs, adjectives, and adverbs; sentences somewhat varied in length and type; free from most technical errors, somewhat polished and superficially proofread.

D *Unfocused and confusing.* Awkwardly written, with an ineffective thesis; unclear use of role, audience, and purpose; acceptable, though mechanical, organization at the paragraph level; inadequate, incomplete use of supporting material; questionable, confusing, and sometimes unclear choices of nouns, verbs, adjectives, and adverbs; sentences repetitious in both length and type; cluttered by technical errors, unpolished and inadequately proofread.

F *Unacceptable.* Poorly written, without a thesis; no sense of role, audience, or purpose; lack of organization; irrelevant, inadequate, or nonexistent supporting material; inaccurate and inappropriate word choices; many monotonous, flawed, ungrammatical sentences; an excessive number of technical errors, neither polished nor proofread.

These guidelines, especially used in conjunction with a detailed, specific evaluation sheet, will allow you to assign grades fairly and consistently.

Several other principles should guide your grading of papers:

■ Do not let a single feature of a paper influence the grade too strongly. Remember that a paper's grade should reflect its overall achievement. Failing a paper solely because it contains comma splices is as unfair as giving an *A* to a paper just because it is interesting.

■ Remember that you can assign more weight to grades in the last half of the term. Allow for an uncertain start and assume that steady progress will follow. The following are among the strategies you might try for giving proportionally greater credit for papers written later in the term: Establish differing point values to papers by multiplying early grades by *1* and later grades by *2* or *3;* evaluate but do not grade the first few papers, using only later assignments to determine students' course grades; drop the grade for one assignment before you average students' course grades, either allowing students to choose the assignment to be discounted or choosing it yourself for each student individually or for the class as a whole. These strategies for weighting grades will allow you to reward improvement while relieving students' anxieties over grades as they grapple with the challenging task of learning to write.

- Avoid the tendency to inflate grades. Students want good grades, as well they should. But that desire should not translate into high grades on average work. So rather than inflate early grades to boost students' confidence or to win them over, remind students — and yourself — that grades on later, more accomplished papers will be worth more.

》》》 *Evaluation and grading are crucial aspects of any course, but they are especially important in writing courses, where students' progress depends on skills developed through practice. Be sure to return evaluated and graded papers before the next assignment is due, preferably before its peer editing session, so that students will have the chance to learn from your comments and improve their next paper.* **《《《**

The following suggestions for using *The Beacon Handbook,* though practical and complete, offer only one view of how to use *Beacon* — my own view. You will discover other approaches to these materials that will work better for you. I am pleased when teachers adapt my materials to suit their needs or the needs of their students, for that demonstrates the sensitivity to audience that is integral to today's teaching of writing and research. I do hope, however, that the following materials will provide a useful place to begin.

Introduce Students to *Beacon*

Handbooks can be intimidating to students, especially to those who have not used one before. These small but densely packed books may overwhelm students with lists of correction symbols, many numbered and lettered subdivisions, precepts, compressed explanations, annotated examples, exercises, tabbed headings, lengthy indexes — all the features that are planned, in fact, to make the handbook an accessible reference tool. We can hardly blame students for being overwhelmed by the complexities of handbooks.

To help students become familiar with and adept at using their handbook, take time to show them its organization and contents and offer advice about and practice in finding the information they need. Take a class session — or a portion of a class session — to introduce students formally to *Beacon*. Begin with a general introduction to its basic features, making comments on them as you look through the book with students. The following list includes the important features of *Beacon*.

- *The endpapers*. Point out that the endpapers include a brief guide to the book and provide the most compact reference to its contents.

Introduce Students to *Beacon*

- *The list of correction symbols.* Describe how the standard abbreviations and symbols, which appear on the back endpapers, correspond to key descriptive words and precept numbers, directing students to the relevant text section.

- *The table of contents.* Explain that the table of contents (pp. v–xv) outlines fully the materials in the entire text.

- *"How to Use This Book."* Discuss with students this portion of the preface, written expressly for them and describing briefly the text's basic features. Remind them to turn to this section when they have questions about working with *Beacon*.

- *The coded format of the book.* Show students how the coding system works, stressing that the coding in each section of the book follows a uniform format to aid them in their search for information. Explain the use of (1) numbered divisions, indicating division into chapters covering large topics; (2) numbers with letters, indicating precepts for writing, grammar, and usage; (3) three levels of headings, indicating the organization of discussions within the precept sections. (The sections on fragments, comma splices, and fused sentences are especially good ones to use as class examples.)

- *The presentation of examples.* Point out that examples illustrate almost every topic treated in the text and that multiple examples appear in especially complicated sections. Show students how examples are generally labeled and how parenthetical explanations describe problems and possible solutions.

- *"Connections."* Note that major sections of the book — Part 1, "Composing," Part 2, "Understanding Sentences," and so on — and some chapters are introduced by brief essays that place the part or chapter topic in a rhetorical context, suggesting how the materials relate to writing.

- *"Quick Reference" sections.* Stress that each chapter or numbered division of *Beacon* includes a "Quick Reference" near the beginning. Point out that these "Quick References," clearly separated from the primary text, provide an abstract of the most crucial elements in the section.

- *Computer notes and boxes.* Point out that these portions of the text, marked with a special symbol (▐), offer advice on how to write using a word processor. Note that in some sections — "Composing," for instance — computer notes appear throughout the text; in other sections, computer boxes may summarize suggestions and appear at the ends of chapters.

- *"Making Connections."* Show students that at the ends of chapters, a section called "Making Connections" provides them with activities and questions that ask them to analyze their writing habits or to apply what they have learned in a chapter to their general writing.

- *Special notes.* Point out that special notes, marked by the symbols ▶▶▶ ◀◀◀ , describe exceptions to general rules or offer hints for applying specific principles of writing.

- *Tables, charts, and lists.* Explain how tables, charts, and lists, set off by a distinct design, present information succinctly in an easily accessible format.

- *Appendixes.* Direct students to the appended material. Reference sections on manuscript preparation, business writing, APA style, and writing essay exams provide concise discussions of topics related to the classroom writing students will occasionally do.

- *"Glossary of Usage."* Draw attention to the "Glossary of Usage," which provides definitions of troublesome words and often-confused words; point out that brief examples illustrate correct usage.

- *"Glossary of Grammatical Terms."* Point out that the "Glossary of Grammatical Terms" is an alphabetically arranged mini-handbook that briefly defines the terms discussed fully in the text itself. Also note that samples illustrate each definition.

- *Indexes.* Have students look at the indexes to *Beacon*. The general index is the most complete reference (and cross reference) to topics and discussions within the text. The index of computer notes and boxes will provide students working on word processors with a quick listing of this advice.

- *Exercises.* Direct students to the sentence and paragraph exercises throughout each chapter. They provide students with opportunities to practice applying the principles covered. Also mention that ASCII exercises are available for completion on a computer.

- *Sample papers with annotations.* Point out the sample student papers that illustrate the writing processes discussed in the "Composing" and "Research" sections; a professional sample appears in the "Critical Thinking" section. Emphasize that annotations on facing pages discuss both the technical and the rhetorical principles illustrated.

- *The use of color.* Draw attention to the way in which color is used in *Beacon* to distinguish elements of the text: blue indicates precept numbers, headings, "Connections," and "Making Connections"; green indicates computer notes and boxes and ASCII exercises; red indicates "Quick References," tables and charts, special notes, labels for examples, and other emphasized instruction.

Have Students Practice Using *Beacon*

To give students practice in using *Beacon,* have them complete the activity sheet included in the ISP. The activity sheet asks students to "scavenger hunt" for answers to twenty questions, to be found by using the indexes, the "Brief Guide," the table of contents, and the correction chart. Stress that the purpose of the search is not only to find the right answers but to learn *how* to find the right answers.

Finding Information in Beacon

Use the general index to begin your search for answers to these questions:

1. Is *should of* acceptable usage?

2. What punctuation follows "Dear _____" in a business letter?

3. Is the same heading used for a research paper as for other papers?

4. Should neologisms be used in current writing?

5. What verb is fully conjugated in *Beacon?*

Use the "Brief Guide" to begin your search for answers to these questions:

6. Are names of statues capitalized?

7. How can a writer correct a fragment that is a subordinate clause?

8. When should writers use British spellings of words?

9. Does APA style require a title page for a researched paper?

10. What are the three cases of pronouns?

Use the table of contents to begin your search for answers to these questions:

11. What are the three kinds of revision?

12. What four subjects are treated in the appendixes?

13. Is double-spacing or single-spacing required in typed manuscripts?

14. Do song titles appear in italics, with quotation marks, or with no marks?

15. Which relative pronoun can describe either people or things?

Use the correction chart to begin your search for answers to these questions:

16. What are the two kinds of agreement?

17. What does ¶ stand for?

18. What does the apostrophe indicate in a contraction?

19. If a *d* appears in the markings on a paper, what problem is the teacher pointing out?

20. What are three of the many ways to achieve variety in sentences?

After students complete the exercise, discuss their strategies for finding answers. Stress the value of using different searching strategies to find different kinds of information.

Using *Beacon* for Class Work

Beacon can support your teaching in a variety of ways: it can serve as your primary text for a course; it can serve as a supplementary text for students with individual problems; its samples can serve as models and as the basis for discussion; its exercise sentences and paragraphs can provide your students with practice in applying principles of writing; its special features — "Connections," "Quick References," computer notes and boxes, and "Making Connections" — can direct students' work in unique ways. With its wide range of textual material, exercises, and special features, *Beacon* can fit into your unique classroom context.

Written Work Using *Beacon*

One of the most effective uses of *Beacon* is to have students complete exercises in writing and then to review their work in class.

Their written work can be graded as practice or as quizzes or used as the basis for discussion. Because many exercises ask for revisions, not for "correct" answers, each student will revise sentences and paragraphs differently. Discussing these varied solutions, stressing that alternatives almost always exist for solving writing problems, can be fruitful.

Oral Work Using *Beacon*

Completing exercises orally can be useful because students must think and apply principles quickly. Oral work varies the rhythm of class meetings and the types of responses and participation expected of students. Because oral work moves quickly, without opportunity for students to double-check their responses, they will answer incorrectly more often than in written work. But discussions of incorrect answers and how students produced them can be very useful when they are conducted in a positive atmosphere.

Evaluating Writing Using *Beacon*

Two features in particular make *Beacon* ideal to use when evaluating students' writing: correction symbols and corresponding precept codes.

Using the correction symbols listed on the back endpapers and on the correction chart will simplify your marking of papers. Why write "You need a new paragraph here" when the symbol ¶ makes that idea clear neatly, simply, and briefly? Explaining to students that you will be using correction symbols is crucial, however, so that they will be able to interpret your markings easily and accurately.

It is unnecessary to memorize the full set of codes used to describe the precepts in *Beacon,* but learning the ones that correspond to your students' most frequent errors (15 for fragment or 17a for subject-verb agreement, for instance) can save you time and help you to direct students efficiently to sections of the book where they can receive needed help.

Individual Work Using *Beacon*

If you are using a rhetoric and perhaps a reader with your classes, *Beacon* will be essentially a reference book. As you discover students' individual problems, refer them to appropriate sections of the book to find explanations, examples, and practice. By asking students to complete the exercises in sections corresponding to their areas of weakness, you can confirm that they have understood and applied the principles accurately.

Computer Writing Using *Beacon*

If your school has a computer center or computer-equipped classrooms, *Beacon* will provide additional instructional support through its computer boxes and notes.

In "The Composing Process" and "Research," recommendations for using word processors appear throughout each chapter, offering advice for using computers during planning, drafting, revision, and preparing final manuscripts. Such advice, focused on students' active involvement with writing and computers, is presented with a minimum of computer jargon. You may have to offer further support — sometimes technical, sometimes practical, and sometimes emotional — as students, perhaps for the first time, use word processors to compose papers.

In almost every chapter of *Beacon,* students will find specific advice on how to use a word processor's capabilities to solve specialized writing problems. Not every student will need to employ these strategies; however, when students have repeated problems with a specific aspect of their writing — pronoun-antecedent agreement, for instance — they can usefully follow the advice in the relevant specific note.

As with your other teaching, share the knowledge you have gained from your own active work at the keyboard. Sharing the fears and frustrations you felt when you faced a monitor for the first time, sharing the strategies and techniques that you have developed for various writing tasks and contexts, and sharing the enthusiasm that you feel for the computer as a writing tool are the most critical aspects of helping students begin active, effective writing with a word processor.

Computer-based Classrooms Using *Beacon*

If you choose to teach your writing class in your school's computer center, *Beacon* and its support materials will prove helpful.

At least one exercise in each chapter is available in ASCII form; completing these exercises at computer terminals will provide students with practice in writing, revising, and word processing. In addition, notes and boxed discussions throughout *Beacon* provide specific advice about using computers to prepare and revise drafts.

When planning classes in a computer center, consider taking these useful steps:

- *Schedule your class in the center before the term begins.* Because most computer centers have limited facilities, you will need to arrange in advance for an adequate number of terminals for your students during your scheduled class time. Also make sure that the person who assigns rooms knows that you will meet regularly in the center.

- *Preview available word-processing programs.* Most computer centers make a number of word-processing programs available for class use. Try them all and then choose the one that will best suit your students. Keep in mind that many of them will not be "computer literate" and that an excellent program for an experienced computer user may be a poor choice for classroom use.

- *Plan an introduction to using the word processor.* You will need two or three class sessions to introduce students to terminals, diskettes, access codes, control codes, and so on. Prepare your own set of instructions unless you are lucky enough to have a computer-center staff member who is a capable instructor as well as a computer technician.

- *Provide for simple but active practice that will produce a piece of computer-generated writing.* Many word-processing programs provide training exercises, but they often involve typing, revising, and formatting artificial samples. Rather than use those exercises, have students write letters or journal entries so that they compose, not merely type.
- *Make sure that necessary supplies are available.* Check with your school's bookstore to be sure diskettes and diskette carriers will be available.

Learning to use a word processor requires patience and practice, just as writing does, but with sufficient encouragement and advice most of your students will learn quickly.

Revision Using *Beacon*

Beacon's approach to writing instruction encourages careful re-reading and rewriting, guided by explicit instruction and revision checklists in Chapter 3, "Revising," and supported by a comprehensive reference text covering the essentials of effective written communication.

Although experienced writers complete simultaneous revisions for content, style, and technical correctness, students learn revision more easily when these three techniques are practiced discretely. To help students begin their work with revision, therefore, *Beacon* explains, illustrates, and provides checklists for each type of revision separately.

This approach to revision mirrors the organization of *Beacon,* so it will be a simple matter to direct students to discussions of issues relevant to the specific aspect of revision with which they are engaged or with which they are having problems. Use parts and chapters of *Beacon* to instruct students in the details of revision and to guide and reinforce their efforts at revision throughout the course.

- *Content revision.* The content revision checklist appears on page 60 and on the inside back cover. Have students consult

Chapter 1, "Planning," Chapter 2, "Drafting," Chapter 4, "Paragraphs," Chapter 5, "Critical Thinking and Writing," Chapter 32, "Choosing and Researching a Topic and Taking Notes," and so on, for help with problems relating to content.

- *Style revision.* The style revision checklist appears on pages 64–65 and on the inside back cover. Students can consult Chapter 4, "Paragraphs," Part 2, "Effective Sentences," Part 3, "Diction," Part 4, "Grammar," Part 5, "Punctuation," Chapter 34, "Organizing, Writing, and Documenting the Research Paper," and so on, for help with their writing style.

- *Technical revision.* The technical revision checklist appears on pages 66–68 and on the inside back cover. Students will find help with technical matters in Part 2, "Effective Sentences," Part 4, "Grammar," Part 5, "Punctuation," Part 6, "Mechanics," Part 7, "Research," and so on.

The "Connections" boxes at the beginning of each part and of some chapters further reinforce the techniques and benefits of revision by drawing students' attention to the relation between the content, style, and technical issues discussed in that part and the means through which students can achieve overall clarity, control, and expressiveness in their writing. These various options should help you emphasize to your students not only the importance of revision but also their ability to perform this seemingly complex and alien aspect of writing.

Teaching Research

The value of writing a research paper is apparent to us but sometimes not to our students. Often, memories of unproductive,
tedious high school research projects interfere with students' ability to enter into the challenge and excitement research can provide. The teacher of the research paper must provide opportunities for our students to learn the value of researching techniques in
the classroom and beyond.

Explain Your Assumptions About Research

Often, students misconstrue the purpose of writing a research paper. They find the project long and burdensome because their
teachers seem to emphasize technical skills and accuracy in documentation without articulating the larger goals of exploring a
subject and reconciling a variety of sources and without helping
students to connect the research process with other, more familiar
writing and thinking processes. By making explicit your assumptions about and goals for students' research, you will help to make
their efforts more effective. Providing clear evaluation criteria for
each stage of the research process can help students both to understand their goals and to chart their progress.

Some Assumptions About Student Research Projects

- *Researching is not easy.* If you acknowledge that the process of
  researching is rewarding but also complex and challenging,
  you will help to prepare students for possible problems and set-
  backs. With this preparation, students will realize that all researchers discover and then solve problems.
- *Research papers develop in stages, just as other papers do.* Much
  about researching will be unfamiliar to students, but we should
  stress that many stages of the work — planning, drafting, revising, and preparing the final manuscript — *are* familiar. Students should realize that although research is complex, with

some problems exacerbated by the length and depth of effort expected and required, the many familiar stages will help them on their way.

■ *Researching skills are learned through practice.* If you emphasize the process of research, rather than the final product, by organizing students work into discrete stages (for example, requiring submission of a working thesis, a preliminary bibliography, a rough outline, and a rough draft), your students will discover that techniques and formats can be learned, practiced, and refined incrementally.

■ *Researching means gathering materials to reach a judgment, not merely repeating others' findings or replicating technical formats.* At the center of researching should be the goals of finding and evaluating sources in order to learn about a topic and express a viewpoint on that topic. With these goals, students should more easily learn to emphasize the content-centered, rather than the mechanical, aspects of research.

■ *Research as a way of gathering information has broader applications than producing a researched paper.* Take some time to explain that researching has uses in contexts beyond the classroom, both in one's personal life, for example, comparative shopping and finding out about a potential employer, and in one's professional life, for example, when a personnel manager must research benefits packages in his or her industry or a librarian must determine which of several competing databases would be best for his or her particular patrons. Pointing out these nonacademic uses of research can help motivate students to develop the necessary skills by writing the assigned documented paper.

■ *Accurate documentation is a form of intellectual honesty, not simply a set of complicated typing requirements.* Documentation *is* complicated, and many students' mistaken belief that it is an end in itself does not increase their enthusiasm for learning it. The importance of careful use, accurate representation, and complete acknowledgment of sources becomes much clearer and more valuable when students understand the underlying principles of fairness and intellectual honesty rather than seeing the process as another set of hoops to jump through.

Teach Researching Skills Through Monitored Practice

Students often come to us with only limited research experience. Many have done research in small libraries with few sources; many have used writing texts that present dated and unnecessarily complicated documentation forms; and many have been required to apply dubiously restrictive guidelines (twenty-seven sources, no more, no fewer; no reference works; and so on). To move students beyond these sometimes limited and sometimes pedantic experiences, emphasize that the goal of researching is free intellectual inquiry, accomplished through the practice of specific skills that can be developed through practice.

Monitored Practice

Use the exercises in *Beacon* to practice skills such as note taking, emphasizing that researching skills take time to develop. Have students take notes and then discuss as a group the choices they made. Challenge them to analyze their work or restate its principles by asking questions: What is worth quoting and why? What in this paragraph is common knowledge? Why is paraphrasing the best strategy here? Emphasize that research offers many alternatives, that there are sometimes several "right" ways to complete research. At the same time, point out that sometimes one choice will be better than another; use your experiences as a guide.

Do not expect students to develop researching skills without practice; reading chapters and seeing samples often are not enough. Students need to apply the principles themselves by completing exercises and receiving the benefit of your comments *as* they develop skills, not *after* the research paper is complete.

Class Activities

Because active learning is more productive than passive, plan activities in which students participate. Have students evaluate each other's preliminary bibliographies using guidelines you provide. Have students write sample works cited entries on the board to use for discussions, rather than submitting them as exercises. Have students in small groups discuss the strategies and sources used in the sample research paper in the ISP (Yasuko Kawamura's paper on the internment of Japanese Americans during World War II). By involving students in evaluative work, you will enhance their learning of researching skills.

A Mini-Research Paper

To give students the chance to employ all elements of researched writing before they prepare their major research project, have them write a brief research paper (approximately three or four pages). This practice paper will give students the opportunity to apply the research principles they are learning — for example, note taking, using quotations, and documentation formats, *in a writing context*. They will be able to overcome any technical problems you discover in these brief papers before these problems affect work on their major research paper, usually an important part of their course grade. The practical benefits of a practice paper make it worth your time and your students'.

To relate the mini-research paper to students' major research projects, consider these approaches:

Topics for Mini-Research Papers

■ *The Historical Context for My Topic.* Have students do a brief but fully documented paper that explains the historical context for the topic of their major research paper. (This paper, in modified form, can be incorporated in the larger paper — an additional benefit.)

- *A Critique of My Best or Worst Source.* Using a source discovered during their research, students write a critique, fully documented using internal evidence, identifying the source's specific strengths or weaknesses of organization, content, evidence, style, currency, applicability to the student's purpose, and so on. Students should support and qualify their assessments. (Besides learning to document, students completing this project will learn to evaluate sources critically.)

- *A Comparison-Contrast Discussion of Two Sources.* Using two of their sources, students write a documented discussion and evaluation of both. (This project has the additional benefit of showing students — in a schematic way — why one source is more useful than another.)

Clear Evaluation Guidelines

As you begin planning research activities, establish in writing the criteria by which you will judge the final papers, and share those criteria when you first introduce the project. If, for example, you intend to emphasize the importance of preliminary stages of research by giving credit for materials such as working thesis statements, preliminary bibliographies, rough outlines, and rough drafts, share that information with your students. Knowing that they will be given credit for each stage of the process will lessen your students' anxiety over their final grade. If you distribute an evaluation sheet when you introduce the research project, students will have a checklist of primary concerns, such as organization, clarity, variety of sources, and effective use of quotations, through documentation. (A sample evaluation sheet is included in the ISP.)

Students Choose Their Own Topics

Students will be more engaged in their research if they have selected their own topics. Some teachers fear that if given a choice of topic, students will use one of their old papers or use someone else's. If your evaluation of a research project involves checking stages of the work and if your requirements are specific enough, students will, of necessity, produce new work — even if an old paper is the basis of the new work.

Actually, much good writing develops from old writing, but it has to be modified to meet the writer's new role, readers, and purpose. In some instances, it is even advisable to encourage students to use an old research paper as the *starting point* for more thorough research work; make sure, however, that students understand that extensive new research and substantive changes in their writing will be necessary.

Firm, Sequenced Deadlines

Students who are learning and practicing research skills seem to do so best in increments. If you require students to complete portions of their work to be checked, peer edited, or graded according to a schedule, students will be less likely to fall behind in their work. (The evaluation sheet in the ISP makes the checking of the preliminary stages part of the evaluation.)

Find Ways to Make Research Easier

There are no sure ways to guarantee students' success in researched writing, but there are ways to improve their chances of success.

Time in the Library

Near the beginning of your research unit, have your students attend an orientation to the library. After that general orientation, consider spending several class periods in the library with your students. Establish your "home base" in a central location, perhaps in the reference room, and make yourself available for consultation. By spending a few hours with students in the library, you will be able to answer questions immediately, offer researching advice, and share techniques for locating materials. Students will get a quick start on their work, with a minimum of frustration.

Problems and Concerns

As students begin their research, they will encounter problems. Some of those problems will be unique to individuals, but some will be universal, plaguing many other students as well. When a number of students raise the same questions, take class time to talk about them. Ask students to describe the problem and discuss their techniques for trying to solve it. You can then share suggestions and recommendations with the entire class and simplify or perhaps eliminate the problem for other students.

Using Students' Materials in Class Activities

The materials in *Beacon* provide clear and direct information and examples to illustrate most major issues of research; the exercises provide preliminary practice that can be carefully monitored. But after students work with the materials in *Beacon,* they can benefit from focused practice using their own materials. Consider these kinds of activities using your students' materials:

Activities Using Student Materials

- *Practice note taking.* Ask each student to bring in one source and take notes during a portion of class. Circulate through the class as students work, reviewing the format and content of their note cards, making suggestions, and answering questions. Alternately, have students take various kinds of notes on two or three paragraphs of their source and then exchange materials; after reading each other's notes and the passages they were based on, students discuss the effectiveness of their note-taking choices and strategies.
- *Selecting quotations.* Have each student bring a quotation to read aloud; ask the student to explain what criteria he or she used in selecting the quotation; follow this with general discussion of the problems of evaluating quotations.

- *Revising thesis statements.* Have each student write his or her working thesis statement written on an index card. Review the criteria for good thesis statements and then read and discuss the examples, having students make suggestions for improvement.
- *Evaluating sources.* Ask students to evaluate one of their sources and to explain to the class why the source is potentially useful or useless for further research on their topics. Have students use the criteria for evaluating sources that appear on pages 482–83.
- *Selecting nontraditional sources.* Have each student describe briefly his or her research project and explain plans for finding nontraditional sources (films, interviews, questionnaires, and so on). Have the class discuss the options and make additional suggestions to one another.

Research Conferences

At an intermediate stage of your students' research — probably after they have begun to organize their materials — schedule individual conferences to discuss each student's progress. Keep conferences very brief (ten minutes, perhaps) and highly focused; after all, you will have spent many class sessions dealing with common, general problems, so individual conferences need not be long. Here are some suggestions for a conference immediately preceding the writing of the rough draft:

Advice for a Research Conference

- *Announce what you expect to review in the conference.* Make students aware that you intend to check specific features of their work, not chat with them. List on the board or on a handout the materials they must bring with them.
- *Use check-sheets during the conference.* To ensure that you review what you want to review, use a check-sheet for each student (the sample research evaluation sheet in the ISP includes a check list). Check such things as sample citation cards (the

appropriate kind and number of sources), a brief outline (one typed on a 4-by-6-inch index card is usually sufficient), and sample note cards (uniform format and attention to detail).

- *Ask students to write down their questions.* In the intensity of a brief conference, it is easy to forget questions, so ask students to write theirs down before coming to your office.

Incorporate Special Activities in Research Classes

Beacon provides a comprehensive discussion of the process of researching, and its exercises provide substantial practice in researching techniques. Nonetheless, in classes that concentrate on researched writing, other activities can usefully complement the materials in *Beacon*.

Related Research Activities

- *Thesis statements.* Have students use photocopies of articles in magazines or journals (preferably those used in their own research) and locate their thesis statements. Have students consider the title as a modified thesis statement, skim the opening paragraphs to find a clearly stated topic and opinion, and identify special qualifications or limitations. An assignment sheet is included in the ISP.

- *Topic sentences.* Using the same, or another article, students underline the topic sentences in each paragraph and then write a topic-sentence outline of the article. An assignment sheet is included in the ISP.

- *Introductory and concluding strategies.* Using three or four of their source articles, students identify the introductory and concluding strategies that authors use to create interest in the subject (introduction) and to create a final impression (conclusion). Students then describe how these strategies help to create impressions appropriate for the authors' purposes and readers. An assignment sheet is included in the ISP.

- *Transitional devices*. Using photocopies of three or four pages from books, students underline all transitions that authors employ to create needed connections. Have students label the transitions by purpose (to present additions, similarities, examples, location, restatements, and so on) and describe why such transitions are appropriate to the passage.
- *Evaluating a source*. Have students respond to the questions included in Chapter 32 (a copy is included in the ISP) and write a brief paper that incorporates the most relevant points.
- *Analyze a source to avoid plagiarism*. Using the criteria given in *Beacon,* students analyze two of their sources, either portions of books or entire articles. In outline form, have students characterize each source's diction, sentence structures, factual information, and ideas.
- *Prepare for and conduct an interview*. Using the guidelines included in the ISP, have students prepare to conduct an interview. Require careful preparation for the interview: initial contacts, arrangements, background reading, writing questions, selecting sample materials, practice note taking, and so on.

Evaluate the Research Paper

Your evaluation and grading of your students' research papers are crucial aspects of their learning about research, since your comments on the strengths and weaknesses of students' work will serve as guidelines for their researched writing throughout their academic and professional careers.

To respond carefully to researched writing takes time, but the following strategies will help you to perform these evaluations consistently as well as efficiently.

- *Use an evaluation sheet*. Certain features of researched writing can be evaluated effectively and clearly using an evaluation sheet. (See the sample evaluation sheet in the ISP.) Evaluation sheets should list required materials and activities such as preliminary stages of research (working thesis statement, working outline, rough draft), correct manuscript form, appropriate number and kinds of sources, rough drafts to be included with the final paper, correctly formatted final outline, and so on. Use evaluation sheets to acknowledge receipt of and provide comments on these materials, saving time for rigorous evaluation of the content and presentation.

- *Expect qualities found in all good writing.* Comment on the qualities that characterize all good writing: (1) effective thesis; (2) awareness of role, reader, and purpose; (3) clear, coherent content supported by appropriate evidence; (4) logical organization at the paper, paragraph, and sentence level; (5) effective word choices; (6) varied and interesting sentences; and (7) correctness and consistency in technical matters: grammar, punctuation, and mechanics. Students should achieve correct and complete documentation, but their larger, more important goal is to achieve good researched writing.

- *Emphasize synthesis of materials.* Effective researched writing selectively uses information to make original discoveries. Granted, our students' "discoveries" may not change the scholarship in the fields they choose to write about, but students should be making their own intellectual discoveries, not creating a pastiche of source materials without thoughtful evaluation, analysis, and synthesis.

- *Emphasize improvement.* If your students have completed small research projects of the sort described on pages IM-37–38, they will have discovered any weaknesses in their research techniques and writing before turning to their major research assignment. In grading their major research projects, therefore, you can point to the improvement they have made. Such encouraging comments will reinforce their continuing efforts to master the techniques for writing research papers.

- *Be realistic in your assessments.* Researched writing is difficult and best learned over time and through practice. Do not set your expectations so high that you are disappointed in your students' papers. To prevent this, establish a standard of minimal competence at research, for example, meeting stated requirements, keeping sight of a strong, original thesis, and providing citations for all materials taken from sources. Aspects of researched writing such as varied and compelling style, original diction, creative (as opposed to competent) use of sources, will mark exceptional papers.

- *Weight the grade for the research paper proportionally.* Make sure that a student's grade for the long research paper receives no more or less than its proportional weight in figuring the student's course grade. If the research paper figures as only one element among many in your writing course, and especially if your course emphasizes another type of writing — for example, writing from personal experience — this should be reflected in the low proportional weight given the research paper. On the other hand, if your course concentrates on researched writing, and especially if students have worked through shorter, simpler preparatory writing projects, weight the grade for the long research paper heavily; in such a course, the research paper is a culminating project, which should be reflected in the final grade. A useful general strategy is to weight the grade for the research paper in proportion to the class time devoted to researched writing.

IV Using the Instructor's Support Package and Transparencies

The Instructor's Support Package and the Transparencies supplement the instruction and exercises in *The Beacon Handbook*. These materials are intended to make your work with *Beacon* and in the writing course easier and more flexible by offering, in a convenient format, classroom-tested models.

Although I originally designed the materials to suit my own teaching style and my students' needs, I have redesigned many of them to accommodate a variety of teaching styles and situations. Use the materials as created or adapt them using the ASCII versions provided on disk.

The Instructor's Support Package

The ISP is organized into three parts: Materials for Course Administration, Materials for Teaching the Composing Process, and Materials for Teaching Research. These materials are described below.

Materials for Course Administration

Materials related to the diagnostic paper. If you choose to use the diagnostic paper to learn about your students' writing skills, three sets of topics (Forms A, B, and C), all class-tested, are provided. A sheet, also included, defines and explains the criteria on which the diagnostic paper will be graded; you can hand this to students, along with topic sheets, to provide reassurance and guidance. Finally, you will find evaluation sheets (Form A and B) designed specifically for use with each set of diagnostic topics.

Writer's questionnaires. To find out something about your students and to give them a chance to begin articulating ideas and thinking freely about topics for writing and about themselves as writers, ask students to complete one of the five forms of the writer's questionnaires. Form A is abstract but asks students to begin thinking seriously about personal topics. Form B asks students to begin identifying subjects that may provide topics for later papers. Form C asks students to respond to a wide range of questions — some serious, some not; it can serve as an "ice breaker" if students use the information to introduce each other to the class. Form D asks students to think in detail about their preconceptions about writing, their writing experiences, and themselves as writers. Form E will provide you with basic information about your students' word-processing skills, should you have access to a computer-equipped classroom or writing lab.

Calendar forms. These forms can be used for planning course activities. As simple blank forms, they are disposable, enabling you to make and change plans as constraints on and opportunities for using class time emerge; you can also see several months of planning or several courses or sections side by side. Students can use them to schedule projects.

Materials for the first day of class. A number of sheets can be used during first-day discussions with students to provide course guidelines. The sample first-day handout is one useful way to articulate for your students the criteria for the course. "What Makes an *A, B, C, D,* and *F* paper" can be used to explain the criteria for assigning grades to papers. The manuscript guidelines can explain for students the requirements for preparing papers. The set of questions in "Finding Information in *Beacon*" directs students to use various features of *Beacon* to find answers. It provides students with an introduction to using the book, showing them the many methods available for finding information.

Study skills handouts. For students who are having trouble with basic college study skills, such as taking class notes, reading a text, and so on, I have provided five handouts with simple, straightforward, practical advice that has worked for my students.

Materials for Teaching the Composing Process

Most of the handouts in the ISP serve as classroom supplements to the instruction, examples, or exercises in *Beacon*. They can be used as part of class activities, or they can be assigned to students needing additional practice.

Sample introductions and conclusions. These student samples, all written on the topic of television, provide additional models of the introduction and conclusion strategies presented in *Beacon.* These samples can be used as models for discussion, analyzing how each strategy is achieved and what it does. They can also be used as exercises, by having students underline the thesis statements in the paragraphs and then describe the tone each strategy establishes and the form of development it implies.

Sample paragraphs. These student samples, written on a wide range of topics, provide additional models of paragraphs using the methods of development presented in *Beacon,* and illustrated in the text with professional examples. These can be used as additional models for class discussion or as exercises. One useful activity is to have students underline the topic sentences and then label the primary features in each pattern of development.

Writing evaluation sheets. A number of evaluation sheets are provided, one for each pattern of development discussed in *Beacon.* These sheets have corresponding peer review forms, so that you and your students can work toward the same goals. Each form can be used at any stage in the writing process to assess progress or to grade final papers. And, of course, the forms provided can be modified to suit other types of writing or assignments.

Peer review sheets. The peer review sheets correspond to each pattern of development in *Beacon* and to the evaluation sheets designed for your use. By having students use these sheets during editing sessions, you will focus the editors' work and, as a result, the writers' work as they revise their drafts. If you choose not to use peer editing, these sheets can be used by writers as guidelines and checklists for their own drafts.

Workshop A: Composition. In addition to Jacob's planning, drafting, and revising in Chapters 1 through 3 of the text, the ISP provides a second complete set of student materials for writing a paper. Samples of each stage of Gabriel's preliminary work and a draft of his personal paper on status symbols are included, as are materials for Marcus's literature paper on Shakespeare's use of contrast in two sonnets. These materials can be the basis of classroom discussion and critique, further illustrating and reinforcing principles of the writing process; or they can be used as practice, by, for example, having students evaluate, revise, or proofread the drafts.

Materials for Teaching Research

Models and activities. Numerous research models and activities have been included in the ISP; some will be useful for course administration, but most are intended for students' use. A sample research information sheet demonstrates guidelines for structuring a major research project; it spells out general and particular expectations and criteria and encourages students to begin careful, detailed plans, including a schedule. The "Library Reference Chart" shows the basics of documentation and research in a two-page format that students can easily carry to the library. Other convenient lists include guides to Dewey Decimal and Library of Congress subject listings and a "List of Short Names for Publishers," which provides students with a ready reference for abbreviations to be used in citations. A number of exercises focus on central issues in using sources — identifying an author's thesis and topic sentences; analyzing introductions, conclusions, and transitions; questioning an author's content and organization; learning to quote effectively; practicing interviewing techniques; and writing the research proposal. These can be used to supplement the research activities in *Beacon* as a class review, activity, or assignment; they can also be used to help individual students practice particular skills. A peer review sheet and evaluation sheet, specifically tailored to the research paper, are also included.

Workshop B: Research. Workshop B presents two papers: Yasuko's formal outline and final draft of a research paper about the internment of Japanese Americans during World War II and Sarah's literature research paper about *Jane Eyre*. The models can be used to provide additional examples for extending class discussion of the principles of research and the patterns of researched writing, beyond Michele's paper on intelligence testing. They can also be used with individual students having problems with the structure or writing of the research paper — for example, problems using quotations smoothly or correctly embedding parenthetical notes. Full annotations of Yasuko's paper, provided on a separate sheet, may be used to focus discussion; an alternative activity is to have students read the paper and provide their own annotations, which can be compared and discussed in class.

The Transparency Package

The Transparency Package includes copies on acetate of the tables and lists in *Beacon* most useful for general class discussion. Many of the lists appear in condensed form, providing prompts that will allow students to focus on and discuss major principles. Many of the materials illustrate grammatical concepts and can be used when covering those materials to ensure that even students who have forgotten their texts get the full benefit of the discussion.

Materials on the writing process can be used in many ways. The list of ways to think of topics can be used for in-class brainstorming sessions. The chart illustrating degrees of specificity in diction can be used first to illustrate concepts and patterns and then to guide students in exploring the concepts illustrated, encouraging them to supply examples from their own experience. The peer editing guidelines and questions can be projected for easy reference while peer editing groups are meeting.

If no transparency projector is available to you, the transparencies can be photocopied; but if you have a projector, you will find these materials a useful way to focus all students' attention simultaneously on you and on material from *Beacon*.

V Exercise Answers, Samples, and Optional Activities

The following answer key includes corrected versions of all paragraph exercises in *The Beacon Handbook*. When appropriate, sample revisions are provided, although other versions are often equally acceptable.

Comments on some exercises are also provided, describing potential problems, features to stress, and additional activities using the sample sentences and paragraphs.

EXERCISE 1.1 ❯ General subjects

Asking students to identify twenty-four potential subjects will challenge them, and typically some students will have difficulty. But if students use the questions — and model their subjects on those in the explanations — most will produce the required number of topics with relative ease.

EXERCISE 1.2 ❯ Planning strategies

Freewriting will give students some trouble because many will not believe that they are truly "free." Expect to have to encourage this work, and consider providing a sample of your own freewriting. If students see just how free you have been in your writing, they will probably feel free themselves.

Journal writing is probably familiar to your students (because it is described in most secondary writing texts), so students are less likely to have trouble with writing in a journal. If they do have problems, consider sharing a sample of your own work in a journal.

Journalists' questions provide such a clear focus that students are not likely to have problems responding to them. Encourage students to modify the questions, as Jacob did, to suit their particular topics.

Looping may be new to your students, but it will not be difficult once you have experimented with freewriting. Generally, have students move through at least three stages of looping to narrow a subject sufficiently.

1   Planning

Clustering may be totally unfamiliar to your students, who likely have worked with more structured planning strategies. Practice clustering as a group, writing information on the board, and offer your students constant reassurance that form and neatness are of little importance.

Brainstorming-grouping is a familiar activity for many students these days, although many students will try to control their work too closely, missing the freedom that effective brainstorming can provide. Most commonly, students need reinforcement as they work freely, so that they do not worry when some items in their lists seem unrelated; they also need to learn that structuring comes later in their work, at the grouping stage.

EXERCISE 1.3 ❯ A specific topic

Having produced twenty-four potential topics, students will be able to select from among many workable ideas. Some students may have trouble effectively stating the topic in a phrase or sentence, however, since such work requires concision. With practice, students will learn to describe their narrowed topics clearly and succinctly.

EXERCISE 1.4 ❯ Role, readers, and purpose

With the questions provided in the text — and with the sample in the exercise — students should be able to complete an outline of role, readers, and purpose easily. Many students, however, will need specific guidance to understand fully how responding to these three prompts will influence the planning and writing of their papers.

EXERCISE 1.5 ❯ Thesis statements

Thesis statements reproduced from text, followed by sample evaluations and suggested revisions.

1. Some critics maintain that the *Iliad* and the *Odyssey* are the foundation works on which all subsequent literature in the Western tradition are based.   Evaluation: clear topic, no opinion, effective tone, appropriate qualifications. Revise by introducing stronger, more

judgmental language: "critics rightly maintain" or "critics unjustly maintain."

2. The 1988 Winter Olympics were held in Calgary.   Evaluation: clear topic, no opinion, reasonable tone. Revise by adding opinion and qualification: "Although Calgary seemed a good city in which to hold the 1988 Winter Olympics, it did not prove to be a good choice."

3. Contrary to commonly held opinion, anti-Communist hysteria in the United States predated the rabid speeches and accusations made by Senator Joseph R. McCarthy in the early 1950s.   Evaluation: clear topic, strong opinion, extreme tone, useful qualification. Revise by adjusting the language: change *hysteria* to *activities* and *rabid* to *inflammatory*.

4. Even though a lot of people will disagree, I think that prayer is okay in public schools.   Evaluation: clear topic, stated opinion, ineffective tone, reasonably qualified. Revise by making the language more formal: "Even though many people will disagree, prayer should be permitted in public schools."

5. By encouraging managers in some U.S. corporations to play with a matchbox, some string, and a candle, cognitive psychologists are passing on important lessons in creative problem-solving.   Evaluation: clear topic, clear opinion, effective tone. Revision is unnecessary.

6. The United States government should quickly retaliate against terrorism.   Evaluation: clear topic, forceful opinion, direct tone, no qualification. Revise by adding a qualification: "Although using military force should not be an automatic response to all global problems, . . ."

7. Achieving competency in a foreign language is among the highest rewards of education.   Evaluation: clear topic, acceptable opinion, suitable tone, no qualification. Revise by adding a qualification: "Although the study of a second language is difficult, ..."

8. Women should not always be awarded custody of children in divorce settlements.   Evaluation: clear topic, clear opinion, acceptable tone, no qualification. Revise by adding a qualification: "Al-

though tradition suggests that mothers are better single parents, ..."

EXERCISE 1.6 ❯ *Thesis statements*

With the practice provided in previous exercises, most students will write their thesis statements with relative ease. Stating the topic, students will quickly discover, is simple. Introducing an opinion is simple as well, but setting the right tone (usually through word choices) is often challenging. Qualifying the thesis statement may pose problems. Encourage students to notice that a positive opinion often needs a negative qualification to make the thesis statement seem realistic; conversely, a negative thesis statement often needs a positive qualification to avoid seeming unrealistically pessimistic.

EXERCISE 2.1 ❯ *Organizing materials*

Students are often familiar with outlining procedures, although they often need to be reminded of the rhetorical — not just technical — issues involved. Sometimes, too, students have heard teachers stress the *forms* of outlining over the purposes that outlining serves. To help students move beyond this emphasis on form alone, emphasize that an organization plan must grow from the materials, not be imposed on them.

EXERCISE 2.2 ❯ *Informal outlining*

Students will be greatly relieved to discover that their idiosyncratic strategies for early planning are accepted — even encouraged. But make sure that students' strategies are coherent and consistent. Then let them work, reminding them that a more formal and conventional system can be imposed on the materials later.

EXERCISE 2.3 ❯ *Formal outlining*

Stress that formal outlining provides the chance to elaborate fully the finer details that are often omitted in informal outlining; hence, formal outlining is a logical extension of early planning, not merely a set of mechanical rules to apply. You will probably have to reemphasize complicated issues of format; consider using peer editing as a way to double-check work with formal outlining procedures.

EXERCISE 2.4 ❯ Rough draft

Preparing a rough draft under your supervision provides students with needed practice. Some — those with limited writing experience — will need to be given careful guidance. Others — especially those who have written only one draft of a paper before submitting it — will need firmer guidance to counter past habits of one-draft writing.

EXERCISE 2.5 ❯ Title and introductory paragraphs

Titles and opening paragraphs typically cause problems for students, primarily because students have been admonished to avoid certain strategies yet are given no alternatives or positive advice. The positive nature of the discussions in the text and the samples offer students techniques to try, and they will succeed with some practice.

To reinforce work with titles and introductory paragraphs, consider using samples from magazine articles. Select some yourself and have students identify the techniques that professional writers have used or have students find samples of their own.

EXERCISE 2.6 ❯ Concluding paragraphs

The principles for introductory paragraphs also apply to concluding paragraphs. Be aware, however, that concluding paragraphs are often even more difficult for students to write than are introductory ones. Provide support and encourage students to experiment freely with their strategies.

EXERCISE 3.1 ❯ Content revision

Many students see revision as a time to make minor changes rather than to reevaluate content. The specific questions in the text will give students ways to evaluate content and suggest areas that might need changes.

To reinforce work with content revision, devote class time to peer editing. Have students read each other's papers and respond to the questions, pointing out elements of the papers that already work well and those that need to be improved. Such work teaches useful reading, writing, evaluating, and revising strategies.

EXERCISE 3.2   ❯   *Style revision*

Early in the term, style revisions are especially difficult for students because such revisions depend on fairly sophisticated knowledge of sentence formation, word choice, and arrangement. The questions in the text do not address all issues of style, but they do present some simple features of style that beginning writers can manage effectively. As students' writing skills develop, and as they become more aware of language, they will begin to make more complex stylistic revisions.

EXERCISE 3.3   ❯   *Technical revision*

Technical revisions may present special problems because students must be able to recognize errors that are comprehensive and complex. Other times, of course, technical revisions depend on identifying and correcting simple errors. The questions in the text, especially with cross references to useful sections in the handbook, offer a place to begin.

Stress the need to proofread carefully and to make technical revisions — but *not* focus primarily on your comments about punctuation and mechanics. Students need to understand that this stage of revision is necessary to put ideas in their final form for an interested reader.

EXERCISE 3.4   ❯   *Peer editing*

Peer editing is a remarkably useful approach for teaching and learning, but it requires monitoring. Preparing a list of specific features to examine or using a list of specific questions like those provided in the text are useful ways to keep peer reviews focused.

Many students will come to you experienced in peer editing, but others will be unaware that fellow students can offer useful suggestions and comments. You may have to spend some class time explaining your specific goals for peer editing and how these goals will help you and your students achieve the general goals for the class.

EXERCISE 3.5 ❯ A final copy

This exercise, as part of the process of completing a paper, is left deliberately open-ended, so that you can determine the format you wish your students to use in preparing a final copy of a paper.

Manuscript guidelines are included in Appendix A.

EXERCISE 4.1 ❯ Topic sentences

The paragraph below is a revision of the paragraph in the text; new topic sentence appears in boldface and irrelevant material has been excised.

Since the early days of television, portrayals of children have become increasingly more realistic. In early television, children in major roles were represented as stereotypically childlike. Timmy, the boy on *Lassie,* was naive in a way children were only portrayed in early television. He ignored warnings, got into trouble, was rescued by his dog, and learned a new lesson each week — and the lesson always had to do with following adults' rules. Timmy, in an idealized way, always learned to like adult rules. Nobody on today's programs is like that. Certainly Kevin, the boy on *The Wonder Years,* isn't so attuned to adult expectations. Unlike Timmy, Kevin doesn't learn simple and positive lessons about adult rules. In fact, Kevin often learns to accept the stupidity but inevitability of adult rules with a wry and cynical maturity. He and Timmy may both be adorable, but Kevin shows that television's portrayals of children have become more realistic in at least one way.

By restricting the topic sentence to the portrayal of children on television, the paragraph can be clearly focused. Details about the physical appearance of the children have been removed and saved, perhaps for another paragraph.

EXERCISE 4.2 ❯ Topic sentences

Having worked with thesis statements earlier in the unit, work with topic sentences should be fairly easy for students. An important distinction between thesis statements and topic sentences — one worth stressing again — is that a topic sentence focuses specifically on only one part, or one paragraph, of a larger discussion.

Some students may work more effectively with topic sentences if they first think of a thesis statement, identify its major points of support, and then present one point in topic-sentence form.

EXERCISE 4.3 ❯ Transitions and repeated sentence elements

Paragraphs reproduced from the text; transitions noted in boldface.

One great difficulty in getting straightforward answers is that so many of the diseases in question have unpredictable courses, **and** [addition] some of them have a substantial tendency toward spontaneous remission. In rheumatoid arthritis, **for instance** [example], when such widely disparate therapeutic measures as copper bracelets, a move to Arizona, diets low in sugar **or** [alternatives] salt **or** [alternatives] meat **or** [alternatives] whatever, **and** [addition] even an inspirational book have been accepted by patients as useful, the trouble in evaluation is that approximately 35 percent of patients with this diagnosis are bound to recover no matter what they do. **But** [contrast] if you actually have rheumatoid arthritis **or** [alternatives], **for that matter** [emphasis], schizophrenia, **and** [addition] then get over it, **or** [alternatives] if you are a doctor **and** [addition] observe this happen, it is hard to be persuaded that it wasn't *something* you did that was responsible. **Hence** [result] you need very large numbers of patients **and** [addition] lots of time, **and** [addition] a cool head.

Magic is back again, **and** [addition] in full force. Laetrile cures cancer, acupuncture is useful for deafness **and** [addition] low-back pain, vitamins are good for anything, **and** [addition] meditation, yoga, dancing, biofeedback, **and** [addition] shouting one another down in crowded rooms over weekends are specifics for the human condition. Running, a good thing to be doing for its own sake, has acquired the medicinal value formerly attributed to rare herbs from Indonesia. — Lewis Thomas, "On Magic in Medicine"

Thomas's extensive use of transitions presenting additions stresses the multitude of ailments and cures, thus creating a catalog of conditions and treatments. The use of alternatives suggests that single treatments are accepted for numerous conditions or that multiple treatments are used for single ailments. The use of so many additions and alternatives helps Thomas clarify his point that much about medicine is uncertain or conditional.

EXERCISE 4.4 ❭ *Transitions and repeated sentence elements*

Assuming that students have thought about the discussion in the text, examined the list of transitional words, and selected a paragraph that is worthy of revision, this can be an enjoyable exercise. This kind of work brings to each student's writing a stylistic maturity that is pleasing for a beginning writer. Expect a few students to be overzealous, adding transitional devices at every possible point in a paragraph; such zeal is quickly moderated as students gain more experience as writers.

EXERCISE 4.5 ❭ *Complete paragraphs*

Because students will be working with topics of their choice, they should have little difficulty with this exercise.

EXERCISE 4.6 ❭ *Complete paragraphs*

Sample paragraph.

In recent years, presidents' wives have provided a useful focus on national issues. Eleanor Roosevelt, through her speeches and visits with organizations, emphasized that minorities deserved their fair share of American privileges; she also represented the United States in the General Assembly of the United Nations. Jacqueline Kennedy supported historical preservation, supervising the restoration of the White House; she organized concerts and art exhibits there as well. Lady Bird Johnson devoted her energies to environmental issues, like forestation and park preservation. Betty Ford, with great candor, acknowledged her own substance dependence and used herself as a model in her efforts to mobilize substance-abuse programs. Nancy Reagan continued efforts to end substance abuse and endorsed foster-child programs through personal appearances. Barbara Bush continues in this long tradition as she promotes literacy programs nationwide. As these women demonstrate, a president's wife can direct attention to issues of national importance.

EXERCISE 4.7 ❯ Deductive and inductive structure

Work on these two patterns of development may prove challenging. A deductive paragraph is usually easier for students to develop and control, probably because it is so straightforward. An inductive paragraph probably will be more troublesome, simply because it requires somewhat better focus and control to be effective. Practice with both methods of paragraph development, however, is important for later writing.

Analysis of paragraphs — stressing why some topics are more effectively treated with one structure than the other — will make students conscious of the choices they have when planning a paragraph.

EXERCISE 4.8 ❯ Paragraph development

Given the freedom to choose which kinds of paragraphs to write, students should have little difficulty generating paragraphs. They may, of course, have problems supplying the level of development needed to make the paragraphs effective. Encourage them to reread the text and reexamine the samples and then revise their paragraphs to make them complete and clear.

Paragraphs using *descriptions, examples,* and *facts* are probably the easiest to write. They are extremely useful methods, however, because they bolster many of the other, more complicated patterns.

Paragraphs using *comparison and contrast* will probably be a familiar strategy for most students, although they may not be aware of the varied patterns for arranging ideas (whole-to-whole and part-to-part). It is important that students understand how the two patterns of arrangement shift the focus in paragraphs. *Analogy* will be a less familiar and therefore more challenging strategy for developing a paragraph — certainly more so than the traditional comparison and contrast. Expect some problems, offer guidance, and assume that students will need practice before they can master this strategy.

Cause and effect paragraphs will challenge students because the connections among the ideas and events must be so clearly drawn. Such work requires attention to detail and skill, neither of which comes easily to most beginning writers. Expect some problems and be ready to offer advice. Writing a *process* paragraph will be less demanding than a cause and effect paragraph since it describes a series of steps that students can readily identify. Encourage students to select a process they understand well, think about the steps carefully, maintain a clear chronological order, and account for slight variations. Few problems should arise.

Paragraphs using *classification* and *definition* should challenge even the best of your students. They are, quite simply, difficult paragraphs to write because they combine classification with numerous other patterns of development. In addition, they are generally more abstract, and that can confuse students as well. Be ready for problems, perhaps plan a day of peer editing at the rough draft stage, and be ready to offer advice.

EXERCISE 5.1 ❯ *Patterns of critical thinking*

Inductive argument

Evidence

College students are involved in community projects.
College students are active in politics.
College students are responsible for their own actions.

Conclusion

College students contribute to and are responsible members of society and should be treated accordingly.

Deductive argument

Major premise

Children require good nutrition in order to concentrate and learn in school.

Minor premise

Schools have a responsibility and public mandate to ensure that students concentrate and learn.

Conclusion

Schools should provide students with nutritious food.

Warrant-based argument

Assertion

Capital punishment is immoral and should be illegal.

Evidence

Executions do not deter others from similar crimes and encourage barbaric public displays in a carnival atmosphere.

Warrant

Because executions encourage barbaric public displays in a carnival atmosphere, they are immoral and should be illegal.

EXERCISE 5.2 ❯ Warrants

Paragraph reproduced from the text; warrants identified in boldface or inserted in brackets.

Low wages and lack of job security create frustration, however. This leads to a 40 percent turnover rate among congressional staffers. There is something to be said for new blood [new staff introduce new ideas], but not when a complete transfusion is taking place about every two years. The result is not only a less efficient staff but in the long run a less effective Congress [new staff are less efficient than experienced staff] [the efficiency of support staff creates an efficient Congress]. **Without ex-**

perienced staff, there is no institutional memory [an "institutional memory" is important] — those who will recall what happened on an issue four years before. Without them, in fact, **Congress becomes more vulnerable to criticism even from the people it most benefits** [inefficiency leads to complaints from constituents]. — Jonathan Yates, "'Reality' on Capitol Hill"

EXERCISE 5.3 ❯ *Summaries*

Sample summaries.

A.   Edward O. Wilson asserts in "The Superorganism" that because tropical rain forests have their greatest percentage of organic matter in trees, not top soil or humus, the decimation of rain forests leaves behind soil that is easily depleted of nutrients and is subsequently barren in two to three years.

B.   Elisabeth Kübler-Ross notes in "On the Fear of Death" that all people — in old cultures and new — view death as the "malicious intervention" of external forces because people are unable to accept death as a natural process.

C.   In "Territorial Behavior," Desmond Morris suggests that territorial behavior is a protective reaction to class systems. Territorial behavior, in such institutions as the military and business, manifests itself in unarticulated but agreed-upon rules of conduct and in power struggles between different classes of people.

EXERCISE 5.4 ❯ *Assertions*

Sentences reproduced from the text, followed by type of assertion used and type of verification needed.

1.   Americans do have a heightened interest in health, thanks in part to Dr. Kenneth H. Cooper.   Assertion: opinion. We expect some explanation of how Cooper heightened interest or some explanation of the extent of his influence.

2. Cooper's clinic has conducted 100,000 physical examinations, generating an invaluable data base for the study of preventative and rehabilitative behavior.   Assertion: fact. No clarification necessary.

3. There is something sick about some contemporary thinking about health.   Assertion: belief. We expect clarification through examples and descriptions.

4. The modern refusal to accept material and social limits has enabled mankind to live better, materially and morally, than premodern peasants.   Assertion: opinion. We expect facts, examples, and explanations, perhaps with comparisons to earlier times.

5. Many values of modernity conflict with another value, grace in the face of the fact of death.   Assertion: opinion. We expect examples and a good deal of explanation.

EXERCISE 5.5 〉 *Evidence*

Paragraphs reproduced from the text; kind of evidence used appears in brackets.

Spurred by a scientific consensus that significant greenhouse-effect warming will occur in the early decades of the next century, delegates from 46 countries at a Conference on the Changing Atmosphere held in Toronto have called for an urgent action plan [fact, expert testimony]. The conferees, who included scientists and policymakers (but no senior U.S. Government official) [expert testimony], recommended that governments initially reduce emissions of carbon dioxide — thought to play a major role in greenhouse warming — by 20 percent before the year 2005 [statistics].

Some workers maintain that greenhouse warming, which results when trace gases prevent infrared radiation from the earth's surface from escaping to space [fact], has already set in; indeed, a scientist at the National Aeronautics and Space Administration (NASA) [expert testimony] is searching for a greenhouse "fingerprint" in existing data. The four warmest years in a century of instrumental records have fallen within the 1980s, and the first five months of 1988 were the hottest five-month period ever recorded [facts, examples].

One climate analyst, James E. Hansen of NASA's Goddard Institute for Space Studies [expert testimony], told a Senate subcommittee in Washington just before the Toronto conference that the recent warming could be ascribed "with a high degree of confidence" to the greenhouse effect. At Toronto the delegates kept an open mind about whether the greenhouse effect has contributed to the warmth of the 1980s. They agreed, however, that past emissions of greenhouse gases make significant warming inevitable [example]. Indeed the most recent computer models predict that accumulating trace gases will harm the lower atmosphere sooner than expected [example].

Carbon dioxide, which is increasing by .4 percent each year because of combustion of fossil fuels and the destruction of tropical forests, accounts for half the predicted warming [statistics, example]. Other greenhouse gases include methane, which is increasing at an even faster rate, and the synthetic refrigerants and solvents called chlorofluorocarbons (CFC's) [facts, example].

The consensus view was that a global warming of between three and nine degrees Fahrenheit is likely to occur by the middle of the next century if emissions are not curtailed [fact]. It is impossible to say what the climatic consequence for particular regions would be — the current U.S. drought, for example, cannot necessarily be blamed on the greenhouse effect [example]. Nevertheless, some studies suggest that continental interiors will become dryer as greenhouse warming occurs [example]. The sea level is expected to rise by at least 30 centimeters over the next 50 to 100 years [fact, example]. — Tim Beardsley, "Winds of Change"

EXERCISE 5.6 ❭ Logical fallacies

Sentences reproduced from the text, followed by logical fallacy exemplified.

1. Ernest Hemingway's novels should not be regarded so highly. After all, he was clearly sexist. Fallacy: ad hominem. The issue should be the quality of Hemingway's novels, not Hemingway's views on women's rights.

2. Many Nobel Prize winners in science used animals in their experiments, so using animals in research must be acceptable. Fallacy: association. The fact that a Nobel Prize has been awarded for an

experiment does not automatically justify the research methodology.

3. I saw a woman at the grocery store use food stamps to buy steaks, artichokes, and hand-packed ice cream. Food stamps allow the unemployed to eat very well.   Fallacy: hasty generalization. One extreme example does not establish a pattern.

4. If secondary schools require four years of English, writing skills will no doubt improve.   Fallacy: oversimplification. A change in requirements alone will not produce improved skills; good teaching and serious practice are also required.

5. If business people can deduct expenses for lunches, then factory workers should have the same privilege.   Fallacy: false analogy. This ignores important differences in the two situations.

6. To reduce the trade deficit, all we need to do is increase taxes. Fallacy: oversimplification. We would also need to reduce spending, lessen importation, and increase exportation of goods.

7. Unless we imprison industrial spies, all our technological secrets will end up in the hands of the Russians.   Fallacy: either/or. Other, more moderate alternatives exist.

8. Atlanta is the home of the Turner Broadcasting System and the Braves. It is a great place to raise a family.   Fallacy: non sequitur. Baseball teams and television stations do not necessarily improve the quality of family life.

9. If an actress lives long enough, she is sure to win an Academy Award.   Fallacy: oversimplification. An actress must also give a superior performance and receive the largest number of votes by academy members.

10. Since smoking marijuana is immoral, we should punish anyone caught using it.   Fallacy: begging the question. The immorality of marijuana use has not been established.

5f ❯ *A sample argument*

Though it is not an exercise, the sample argument, Norman Ornstein's "You Get What You Pay For," can be used as the basis for class discussions. Strategies are annotated the first time they appear, but it is useful to have students locate and discuss additional examples of strategies.

EXERCISE 6.1 ❯ *Nouns and pronouns*

1. Acuncture [common], a medical treatment [common], developed centuries [common] ago in China [proper].

2. The acupuncturist [common] uses extremely thin gold needles [common] to pierce the patient's skin [common].

3. Patients [common] frequently receive sedation [common] before the treatment [common] begins and the needles [common] are implanted.

4. The areas [common] where the needles [common] are inserted do not correspond to the areas [common] of discomfort [abstract] or pain [abstract].

5. Those [indefinite] who [relative] have been helped by acupuncture [common] advocate the treatment [common] most strongly.

6. Why should those [indefinite] of us [personal] who [relative] have not tried acupuncture [common] question their [possessive] satisfaction [abstract]?

7. Teams [collective] of Western scientists [common] have studied acupuncture [common] and found no physiological explanations [common] for its [possessive] success [abstract].

8. Yet success rates [common] for patients [common] who [relative] have faith [abstract] in the procedure [common] suggest that we [personal] can learn more than we [personal] already know about the psychological effects [abstract] of medical treatments [common].

9. Ironically, while acupuncture [common] has been attracting attention [common] in Europe [proper] and America [proper] in recent

years [common], its [possessive] use [abstract] in China [proper] has declined.

10. Some [indefinite] say acupuncture [common] is merely a medical hoax [common], but others [indefinite] continue to search for scientific explanations [common] for its [possessive] apparent success [abstract].

EXERCISE 6.2 ❯   Nouns and pronouns

Theodore Roosevelt, the twenty-fifth president of the United States, was an individualist. Nonetheless, **he** served the public well. Roosevelt's individualistic tendencies were illustrated first by **his** attempts at boxing, an uncommon activity for an upper-class gentleman at Harvard. After **his** graduation, Roosevelt made a trip west, where **he** experimented briefly with ranching and cowboy life. Roosevelt returned to the East to serve in the government, but in 1898 **he** resigned **his** post as secretary of the navy to organize the Rough Riders, a regiment formed to fight in the Spanish-American War. The Rough Riders found Roosevelt to be an able leader, and though **they** did not follow **him** up San Juan Hill as legend has it, **they** did fight with **him** in Cuba. Roosevelt returned to the United States a hero; **his** notoriety helped Roosevelt to win the mayoral race of New York. Two years later, **he** was elected vice-president in spite of opposition from political bosses and industrial leaders. **They** must have found **his** freewheeling individualism unsettling and certainly unpredictable. The political bosses and industrial leaders fought Roosevelt in **his** anti-trust actions when **he** became president after McKinley's assassination. Throughout **his** presidency and the rest of **his** life, Roosevelt continued to act as an individual but with the public good in mind.

EXERCISE 6.3 ❯   Verbs

1. Stoics are [linking] people who accept [action, transitive] their fate without question.

2. They have [auxiliary] learned [action] not to concern themselves with what they will [auxiliary] be [linking] unable to change [action,

intransitive] or to waste [action, transitive] time worrying about what is [linking] past.

3. Modern stoics have [action, transitive] as their model, though they may [auxiliary] not know [action, transitive] it, a fourth-century Greek philosopher.

4. Zeno and his followers believed [action, transitive] that the Fates (goddesses in Greek mythology) determine [action, transitive] people's destinies.

5. Modern-day stoics, however, must [auxiliary] grapple [action, intransitive] with Judeo-Christian beliefs that teach [action, transitive] us that we have [action, transitive] free will.

EXERCISE 6.4 ❯ Verb tenses

1. In 1947, Kenneth Arnold, a pilot, described [past] saucer-shaped objects that he saw [past] traveling [present progressive] at great speeds.

2. Since then, thousands of people around the world have reported [present perfect] similar incidents of seeing "unidentified flying objects" (UFOs).

3. During the 1950s and 1960s, Project Bluebook, a division of the U.S. Air Force, attempted [past] to explain these sightings and found [past] that most were [past] misinterpreted observations of natural phenomena.

4. By the late 1960s, Project Bluebook had served [past perfect] its purpose — to reassure military and civilian populations that the earth was not being watched or attacked [past progressive] — and was [past] consequently disbanded.

5. Today, some people still claim [present] to see bright, formless objects traveling [present progressive] at great speeds through our skies — and no doubt such claims will continue [future].

> **!**   **EXERCISE 6.5** ❯ *Verbs*

I made a small cross of two light strips of cedar, the arms so long as to reach to the four corners of a large thin silk handkerchief when extended; **I tied** the corners of the handkerchief to the extremities of the cross, so **I would** have the body of a kite; which being properly accommodated with a tail, loop, and string, **rose** into the air, like those made of paper; but this **was** silk, **was** fitter to bear the wet and wind of a thunder-gust. To the top of the upright stick of the cross **I fixed** a very sharp-pointed wire, rising a foot or more above the wood. To the end of the twine, next the hand, **I tied** a silk ribbon, and where the silk and the tie **joined**, a key **was** fastened. This kite **was** raised when a thunder-gust **appeared** to be coming on, and **I held** the string **and stood** within a door, so that the silk ribbon **would** not be wet; and **I took** care that the twine **did** not touch the frame of the door or window. . . . And when the rain **wet** the kite and twine, so that it **conducted** the electrical fire freely, **I found** it **streamed** out plentifully from the key on the approach of **my** knuckle. — Benjamin Franklin, "Letter to Peter Collinson"

EXERCISE 6.6 ❯ *Adjectives and adverbs*

1. American folklore has created a number of important national heroes, among them Abraham Lincoln.

2. Lincoln, the sixteenth president of the United States, was a man destined to become a legend.

3. His solemn, idiosyncratic appearance made him an easily recognizable figure, and his pivotal role during the Civil War clearly made him an important historical character.

4. Yet the reverential anecdotes and the blatant fabrications about him must surely seem questionable.

5. Lincoln's early life, though austere, was not backward, yet the rail-splitting Abe of the rustic log cabin in New Salem far overshadows the sophisticated lawyer that Lincoln clearly was in Springfield.

6. Lincoln belonged to no Christian church, yet he was often depicted in Christ-like terms as an always suffering, always kind, and always patient man.

7. Folklore has undoubtedly skewed the biographical facts of Lincoln's life, but it has created a fascinating — albeit false — vision of a man.

EXERCISE 6.7 ❯ *Adjectives and adverbs*

My favorite spot at Aunt Ruth and Uncle Dan's house is the small, secluded patio just outside their bedroom. Every time I quietly open the sliding doors and step outside, I know I will feel more peaceful. The eight-by-eight-foot patio is brick, meticulously set in a herringbone design. A comfortable, well-padded lounge chair provides a place to sit, and a small redwood table is a convenient spot to place my usual drink, a tall glass of Aunt Ruth's lightly spiced tea. Once comfortably seated, I always enjoy the various flowers, my favorite feature. Close to the front edge of the patio are pink, plum, red, and yellow moss roses, gently trailing their waxy green stems onto the dull red bricks. Slightly back, radiating away from the patio, are miniature yellow and orange marigolds, with their dense, round flowers set against dark green, sharp-edged leaves. Close behind those are Aunt Ruth and Uncle Dan's prize roses — white, pink, red, and yellow tea roses that are carefully pruned. The small buds, usually a darker color, contrast noticeably with the large open blossoms that always remind me of fine damask. I always love to escape from the cheerful but noisy family activities to this secluded spot where the flowers are so beautiful. Inevitably, a visit to this floral oasis makes me feel more tranquil than before.

EXERCISE 6.8 ❭ Conjunctions

1. Geography is the study of land masses. It includes **not only** the study of territorial divisions **but also** the study of bodies of water.

2. **Although** geography was once studied as a separate course in public schools, it has now been subsumed by the social studies curriculum in most schools.

3. American students today are not receiving sufficient instruction in geography, **and** they are not making the effort to learn the material.

4. College students in 1950 took a geography test sponsored by the *New York Times*. **When** college students in 1984 took the same test, the comparative scores were startling.

5. Scores in some areas dropped 50 percent, **but** that is not surprising **because** 72 percent of the 1984 sample group said they had received little instruction in geography.

EXERCISE 6.9 ❯   *Prepositions*

The dog has got more fun out of [prep.] Man [obj.] than Man has got out of [prep.] the dog [obj.], for [prep.] the clearly demonstrable reason [obj.] that Man is the more laughable of [prep.] the two animals [obj.]. The dog has long been bemused by [prep.] the singular activities [obj.] and the curious practices [obj.] of [prep.] men [obj.], cocking his head inquiringly to [prep.] one side [obj.], intently watching and listening to [prep.] the strangest goings-on [obj.] in [prep.] the world [obj.]. He has seen men sing together and fight one another in [prep.] the same evening [obj.]. He has watched them go to [prep.] bed [obj.] when it is time to get up, and get up when it is time to go to [prep.] bed [obj.]. He has observed them destroying the soil in [prep.] vast areas [obj.], and nurturing it in [prep.] small patches [obj.]. He has stood by while men built strong and solid houses for [prep.] rest [obj.] and quiet [obj.], and then filled them with [prep.] lights [obj.] and bells [obj.] and machinery [obj.]. His sensitive nose, which can detect what's cooking in [prep.] the next township [obj.], has caught at [prep.] one and the same time [obj.] the bewildering smells of [prep.] the hospital [obj.] and the munitions factory [obj.]. He has seen men raise up great cities to [prep.] heaven [obj.] and then blow them to [prep.] hell [obj.]. — James Thurber, "A Dog's Eye View of Man"

EXERCISE 6.10 ❯   *Parts of speech*

In the (1) old [adjective] days, when I (2) was writing [verb, past progressive] a great deal of (3) fiction [noun], there would come, once in a while, moments when I was (4) stymied [adjective]. (5) Suddenly [adverb], I would find I (6) had written [verb, past perfect] (7) myself [pronoun] (8) into [preposition] a hole and could see no way out. To take care of that, (9) I [pronoun] developed a (10) technique [noun] which (11) invariably [adverb] worked.

It was simply this — I (12) went [verb, past] (13) to [preposition] the movies. Not just any movie. I had to pick a movie which was loaded with action (14) but [conjunction] (15) which [pronoun] made no demands on the (16) intellect [noun]. (17) As [conjunction] I watched, I did my best to avoid any (18) conscious [adjective] thinking concerning my (19) problem [noun], and (20) when [conjunction] I came out of the movie I knew exactly what I would have to do to put the story back on track.

It never failed. — Isaac Asimov, "The Eureka Phenomenon"

EXERCISE 7.1 ❯ *Subjects*

1. The [musical], a combination of drama and music, developed as a distinctly American art form.

2. Emerging from vaudeville traditions, [productions] like George M. Cohan's *Little Johnny Jones* offered engaging tunes like "Yankee Doodle Boy" and "Give My Regards to Broadway" in very predictable plots.

3. However, in 1927, [Jerome Kern] and [Oscar Hammerstein] presented *Show Boat,* the first major musical based on a respected novel, and changed musicals forever.

4. [*Oklahoma*], [*South Pacific*], [*My Fair Lady*], and [*West Side Story*] remain the most lasting contributions of the 1940s and 1950s, the golden years of the American musical.

5. In recent decades, British [musicals] have enjoyed both critical and popular success on Broadway, while American [productions] have often seemed insipid by comparison.

EXERCISE 7.2 ❯ *Predicates*

1. Professional ice hockey associations [were] first [formed] in Canada near the beginning of the twentieth century.

2. The first major league, the National Hockey Association, [was founded] in 1910 and [included] teams only from eastern Canada.

3. The following year, the Pacific Coast League [organized] teams from western Canadian cities, cities from the American northwest, and later other American cities.

4. In 1917, the National Hockey Association [was reorganized] to form the National Hockey League.

5. Since then, teams from both Canada and the United States [have competed] throughout the regular seasons and [have vied] for the Stanley Cup, the symbol of the League championship.

EXERCISE 7.3 > Subjects and predicates

Most tarantulas [subject] live [verb] in the tropics, but several species [subject] occur [verb] in the temperate zone and a few [subject] are [verb] common in the southern U. S. Some varieties [subject] are [verb] large and have [verb] powerful fangs with which they [subject] can inflict [verb] a deep wound. These formidable looking spiders [subject] do not, however, attack [verb] man; you [subject] can hold [verb] one in your hand, if you [subject] are [verb] gentle, without being bitten. Their bite [subject] is [verb] dangerous only to insects and small mammals such as mice; for man it [subject] is [verb] no worse than a hornet's sting.

Tarantulas [subject] customarily live [verb] in deep cylindrical burrows, from which they [subject] emerge [verb] at dusk and into which they [subject] retire [verb] at dawn. Mature males [subject] wander [verb] about after dark in search of females and occasionally stray [verb] into houses.

After mating, the male [subject] dies [verb] in a few weeks, but a female [subject] lives [verb] much longer and can mate [verb] several years in succession. In a Paris museum is [verb] a tropical specimen [subject] which [subject] is said [verb] to have been living in captivity for 25 years. — Alexander Petrunkevich, "The Spider and the Wasp"

EXERCISE 7.4 ❯ Complements

1. The year 1896 was not only a tribute [pred.n.] to humanity's best but also a reflection [pred.n.] of humanity's worst characteristics.

2. At the Democratic Convention, William Jennings Bryan gave his "Cross of Gold" speech [d.o.] and sparked interest [d.o.] in an uneventful campaign.

3. The British Patent Office granted Guglielmo Marconi [ind.o.] a patent [d.o.] for the wireless telegraph.

4. When the United States Supreme Court handed down its *Plessy* v. *Ferguson* decision [d.o.], it established a "separate but equal" standard [d.o.] that institutionalized racism.

5. Athens, Greece, was the site [pred.n.] of the first modern Olympiad.

6. Alfred Nobel was the benefactor [pred. n.] of an endowment which began by awarding yearly prizes [d.o.] in peace, science, and literature.

EXERCISE 7.5 ❯ Complements and clauses

Henry Reed was class valedictorian [pred. n.]. He was a small, very black boy [pred. n.] with hooded eyes, a long, broad nose and an oddly shaped head. I had admired him [d.o.] for years because each term he and I vied for the best grades in our class. Most often he bested me [d.o.], but instead of being disappointed I was pleased that we shared top places [d.o.] between us. Like many Southern Black children, he lived with his grandmother, who was as strict as Momma and as kind as she knew how to be. He was courteous [pred. adj.], respectful [pred. adj.] and soft-spoken [pred. adj.] to elders, but on the playground he chose to play the roughest games [d.o.]. I admired him [d.o.]. Anyone, I reckoned, sufficiently afraid or sufficiently dull could be polite [pred. adj.]. But to be able to operate at a top level with both adults and children was admirable [pred. adj.]. — Maya Angelou, "Graduation"

EXERCISE 7.6 ❯ Prepositional phrases

1. (In the last three decades), the once inexact study (of weather) has become a highly complex science.

2. The National Weather Service currently uses computers to synthesize data it receives (from satellites, balloons, ground stations, and airplanes).

3. Once computers (at the National Meteorological Center) compile this information, it is relayed (by a variety) (of electronic means) (to regional weather stations) where teams evaluate the results.

4. (Of particular interest) are the findings (of the National Severe Storms Forecast Center (NSSFC) (in Kansas City), Missouri, for its team channels information (about potentially dangerous storms) (to affected areas).

5. Using <u>data</u> (from the NSSFC), local meteorologists issue a wide <u>range</u> (of <u>watches and warnings</u>), notably (for tornadoes, severe thunder storms, blizzards, and hurricanes).

6. (By providing systematically gathered and carefully organized information,) weather <u>forecasters</u> are able to <u>warn</u> people (of danger) — saving <u>millions</u> (of dollars <u>worth</u>) (of property) and saving <u>thousands</u> (of lives).

EXERCISE 7.7 ❭ *Gerund phrases*

1. <u>Learning [a second language]</u> is a complicated task, but it is a rewarding one.

2. The benefits can be as simple as <u>reading [a menu in a foreign restaurant, a book in a used book store, an untranslated quotation in a scholarly work, or a magazine in a library]</u>.

3. <u>Working [for international corporations]</u> is one career option open to people trained in a second language.

4. <u>Traveling [outside the United States]</u> is especially enjoyable when <u>reading and speaking [a country's language]</u> is possible.

5. Through <u>studying [other languages]</u>, people become sensitive to language <u>itself</u> and that sensitivity can increase their effectiveness as thinkers, readers, writers, speakers, and listeners.

EXERCISE 7.8 ❭ *Participial phrases*

1. (Challenged [past] by books like E. D. Hirsch's *Cultural Literacy* and Allan Bloom's *The Closing of the American Mind*), <u>Americans</u> have begun to reassess their educational system.

2. <u>Articles</u> have appeared in the popular media, (questioning [present], on the one hand, the assumptions of these books) and, at the same time, (criticizing [present] our educational system).

3. (Enticed [past] as they are by eye-catching but often misleading headlines and titles), <u>writers</u> have provided misleading clues about the goals of these books.

4. (Limited [past] by time and length constraints), television and print <u>journalists</u> have offered elliptical, abbreviated summaries of Hirsch's and Bloom's positions, (oversimplifying [present] their statements).

5. Talk-show <u>hosts</u>, by (sensationalizing [present] discussions of Hirsch's and Bloom's books), have failed to help viewers address important educational concerns.

6. Such <u>problems</u> in evaluating educational problems, (made [past] worse by American tendencies to oversimplify), will persist until Americans consent to read Hirsch's and Bloom's books for themselves.

EXERCISE 7.9 ❯ *Infinitive phrases*

1. It is hard <u>to believe how much wood and how many wood products Americans use without being aware of them</u> [noun].

2. <u>To start off our mornings</u> [adverb], many of us eat cereals packaged in cardboard boxes while reading newspapers made from wood pulp.

3. <u>To go about our daily routines</u> [adverb], we move between rooms built with two-by-fours, walk on hardwood floors, and open wooden doors, often oblivious to the structural uses to which wood is put.

4. We talk on the telephone — <u>to convey messages or simply to converse</u> [adverb] — without thinking that wood resins are used in the plastic casing for the phone, let alone that millions of wooden telephone poles help <u>to make such communication possible</u> [adverb].

5. Many of us use pencils to write with [adverb], paper to write on [adverb], and desks or tables to write at [adverb]— all of them products of forest-related industries.

6. To think of how many trees are necessary [noun] to support the activities of even one person [adjective] is virtually impossible.

EXERCISE 7.10 ❯ *Appositives*

Sample revisions.

1. Sporting dogs — pointers, setters, retrievers, and spaniels — hunt by smelling the air to locate game.

2. Working dogs, a group comprising twenty-eight separate breeds, serve or once served as herders, sled dogs, and guards.

3. Terriers hunt by digging, an activity for which their strong front legs seem natural.

4. Nonsporting dogs, many descended from breeds in other classifications, include nine breeds most usually kept as pets.

5. Most toy dogs, almost always kept only as pets, have been bred down from larger breeds of dogs.

EXERCISE 7.11 ❯ *Phrases*

1. Intrigued (by the history) [prepositional] (of Great Britain) [prepositional] [participial], many Anglophiles are Americans obsessed (by England and English things) [prepositional].

2. To learn (about their "adopted" country) [prepositional] [infinitive], Anglophiles often subscribe (to magazines) [prepositional] (like *British Heritage*) [prepositional].

3. They read as well materials (in books and newspapers) [prepositional] that offer insight (into the English way) [prepositional] (of life) [prepositional].

4. Many Anglophiles, their daily schedules rearranged [absolute], watched the satellite broadcasts (of the royal weddings) [prepositional] (of Charles and Diana) [prepositional] and (of Andrew and Sarah) [prepositional].

5. Anglophiles, often people who feel displaced (in the rush) [prepositional] (of American activities) [prepositional] [appositive], find pleasure in learning (about "that sceptered isle.") [prepositional] [participial]

6. Visiting England [gerund] is the lifelong dream (of most Anglophiles) [prepositional], but spending time there [gerund] often spoils illusions that have developed (through years) [prepositional] (of active fantasizing) [prepositional].

EXERCISE 7.12 ❯ *Phrases*

When (in the winter) [prepositional] (of 1845-6) [prepositional], a comet called Biela became oddly pear-shaped and then divided (into two distinct comets) [prepositional], one (of the astronomers) [prepositional] who observed them, James Challis (of Cambridge) [prepositional] [appositive], averted his gaze. A week later he took another peep and Biela was still flaunting its rude duality. He had never heard (of such a thing) [prepositional] and (for several more days) [prepositional] the cautious Challis hesitated before he announced it (to his astronomical colleagues) [prepositional]. Meanwhile American astronomers (in Washington D.C. and New Haven) [prepositional], equally surprised but possibly more confident (in their own sobriety) [prepositional] [participial], had already staked their claim (to the discovery) [prepositional]. Challis excused his slowness (in reporting the event) [prepositional] (by saying) [prepositional] that he was busy looking (for the new planet) [prepositional] (beyond Uranus) [prepositional]. When later (in the same year) [prepositional] he was needlessly beaten (to the discovery) [prepositional] (of that planet Neptune) [prepositional] (by German astronomers) [prepositional], Challis explained that he had been preoccupied (with his work) [prepositional] (on comets) [prepositional]. — Nigel Calder, "Heads and Tails"

EXERCISE 7.13 ❯ *Clauses*

1. <u>Wherever I hang my hat</u> [noun] is home.

2. Don't count your chickens <u>before they hatch</u> [adverb].

3. Absence makes <u>the heart grow fonder</u> [noun].

4. All <u>that glitters</u> [adjective] is not gold.

5. Fools rush in <u>where angels fear to tread</u> [adverb].

EXERCISE 7.14 ❯ *Clauses*

<u>When the credits run at the end of a film</u> [adverb], audience members <u>who stay to read them</u> [adjective] discover the names of people <u>whose contributions are sometimes as important to the film as the actors' are</u> [adjective]. For instance, producers control and organize the entire film production, finding people <u>who will finance the project</u> [adjective] and finding creative people <u>who will actually make the film</u> [adjective]. <u>That directors are in charge of the filming</u> [noun] is well known, but many people do not realize <u>that directors also choose and coach actors and find locations and select technicians</u> [noun]. <u>When the filming is finally completed</u> [adverb], editors begin their work. They take thousands of feet of film, select the best shots, and piece together the version of the film <u>that audiences eventually see</u> [adjective]. Besides the producers, directors, and editors, hundreds of other people are involved in the making of a film. Learning <u>who they are and what they do</u> [noun] makes audience members more appreciative of the combined efforts involved in film making.

EXERCISE 7.15 ❯ *Sentences*

Sample revisions.

1. In the early 1900s, the Palo Verde and Imperial valleys seemed ideal for development, even though at times floods washed away crops, and at other times crops withered. [compound-complex]

2. In 1918, the Bureau of Reclamation submitted a report that suggested building a dam to improve water control. [complex]

3. Water control was the primary goal for the project, but generating electricity was a secondary goal. [compound]

4. After the Bureau of Reclamation designed the dam, six companies worked on the project, making a joint venture that involved an average of 3,500 workers a day. [complex]

5. The finished dam is 726 feet high, 1,244 feet long, and contains 4,400,000 cubic yards of concrete, which is enough to pave a one-lane road from New York to San Francisco. [complex]

EXERCISE 7.16 ❭ *Sentence structures*

Rodeo, like baseball, is an American sport and has been around almost as long [simple]. While Henry Chadwick was writing his first book of rules for the fledgling ball clubs in 1858, ranch hands were paying $25 a dare to a kid who would ride five outlaw horses from the rough string in a makeshift arena of wagons and cars [complex]. The first commercial rodeo in Wyoming was held in Lander in 1895, just nineteen years after the National League was formed [complex]. Baseball was just as popular as bucking and roping contests in the West, but no one in Cooperstown, New York, was riding broncs [compound]. And that's been part of the problem [simple]. After 124 years, rodeo is still misunderstood [simple]. Unlike baseball, it's a regional sport (although they do have rodeos in New Jersey, Florida, and other eastern states); it's derived from and stands for the western way of life and the western spirit [compound]. It doesn't have the universal appeal of a sport contrived solely for the competition and winning; there is no ball bandied about between opposing players [compound]. — Gretel Ehrlich, "Rules of the Game: Rodeo"

EXERCISE 7.17 ❭ *Sentence purposes*

1. "Tell me what you eat, and I will tell you what you are." — Anthelme Brillat-Savarin. [imperative]

2. "Education is what survives when what has been learnt has been forgotten." — B. F. Skinner [declarative]

3. "One only dies once, and it's for such a long time!" — Molière [exclamatory]

4. "How can we know the dancer from the dance?" — W. B. Yeats [interrogative]

EXERCISE 8.1 ❯ Sentence length

Sample revisions.

1. Sometimes castles served as prisons, treasure houses, or seats of local governments as well because they were secure and centrally located. Because some castles, notably those in central Europe, were built on irregular terrain, access to castles was sometimes limited.

2. Because of their unusual stonework and unique design, some castles are attractive.

3. Some used drawbridges, which could be raised to restrict access, to protect inhabitants from hostile forces.

4. Battlements, also called parapets, were the tall, structural walls from which soldiers observed the countryside. During battles these same soldiers positioned themselves in these lofty places to shoot arrows or hurl rocks at the invaders below.

5. Although some travelers have visited castles, most people know of castles from films.

EXERCISE 8.2 ❯ Types of sentences

1. Almanacs, published yearly in book or pamphlet form, include calendars, citations for important dates, information about geography and weather, and a myriad of other facts. [loose]

2. Almanacs are informative and practical, yet they are also idiosyncratic and entertaining. [balanced]

3. Though generally associated with colonial American farmers and navigators, almanacs have as their precedents the works of an unsuspected group: Persian astrologers. [periodic]

4. Over the years, sailors have relied on the *Nautical Almanac,* farmers have used the *Old Farmer's Almanac,* and amateur weather forecasters have depended on the *Ford Almanac.* [balanced]

5. With its proverbs, its lists of counties and roads, its advice on planting, its selections of verse, and its astrological information, *Poor Richard's Almanac* is probably the best-known early almanac. [periodic]

6. Contemporary almanacs are best represented by works such as the *Information Please Almanac,* compendiums of widely divergent statistics on thousands of topics. [loose]

EXERCISE 8.3 ❯ *Varying sentence structures and beginnings*

Sample revision.

Landscaping serves more than an aesthetic function, even if few people realize it. Sheltering a building from summer heat and winter cold, small shrubs and bushes protect its foundation. Providing protection, especially in the winter, from strong winds that can affect interior temperatures and subsequently heating costs, large shrubs and small trees provide windbreaks for buildings. Keeping the sun's warming rays off the building's roof and consequently keeping the building cool, large trees shade a building during the summer. Landscaping does improve the looks of a building, often enhancing architectural details and softening harsh lines, but the surprise for many people is that landscaping can pay for itself in energy savings, which means it has practical as well as aesthetic benefits.

EXERCISE 8.4 ❯ Coordination

Sample revisions.

1. Many American cities are now concerned with maintaining their architectural characters, so building codes control the development of new buildings.

2. Codes often restrict the kinds and sizes of buildings that can be constructed, so architects must design structures that match the scale of existing buildings.

3. Many cities, such as Boston and San Francisco, need the vast commercial space provided by tall office buildings, yet these skyscrapers often cannot be built in some areas because of protective codes.

4. City dwellers do not want the severe shadows cast by tall buildings, and they do not want small, historical, and architecturally interesting buildings dwarfed by monolithic towers.

5. Citizens are now aware that poorly planned cities become unlivable. As a result, they have been supportive of new building codes. City development is now more challenging than it once was, for cities must now grow by controlled, aesthetically consistent patterns.

EXERCISE 8.5 ❯ Subordination

Sample revision.

Because some people never visit art museums or exhibitions, their only contact with art is through "public art," sculpture and other works that are displayed in public places. Monuments, one kind of common public sculpture, commemorate historical events or honor individuals or groups of people, such as veterans. People who often walk through plazas and courtyards near government buildings see sculpture that is frequently commissioned by the government displayed in these areas. Although most people are comfortable with traditional, realistic statuary of people, many people are less at ease with abstract sculpture because they say nonrepresentational sculpture doesn't "look like anything." In time, some grow more accepting after they learn to enjoy modern sculpture's use of form, texture, and material. Sculpture enriches public space because it provides visual and tactile stimulation, sometimes provides pleasure, and even supplies topics for conversation.

EXERCISE 8.6 ❯ *Coordination and subordination*

Although dermatologists continually warn people about the danger of ultraviolet rays, many people seem intent on getting dark suntans. During the summer, beaches and pools are crowded with people who want to "catch some rays." They smear on creams, lotions, and oils so that they can accelerate the sun's natural modification of skin pigments. Because they want to get deep tans, they lie on towels or stretch out on lounge chairs for hours, oblivious to doctors' stern advice. In most cities, tanning salons are quite popular because "California" tans are not always possible everywhere. For a fee, usually between three and ten dollars, people can lie down and subject themselves to artificial sunlight that is produced by ultraviolet bulbs. Many people think a tan looks healthy, but overly dark tans, in fact, cause serious skin damage that can last a lifetime.

 ## EXERCISE 9.1 ❯ *Active and passive sentences*

Sample revisions.

1. People who know their subjects well, either from personal contact or through study, often write biographies.

2. James Boswell, a personal friend of Johnson, wrote the *Life of Samuel Johnson,* a famous early biography.

3. In typical fashion, Boswell recorded facts, anecdotes, and quotations in his diary and then translated them into the biography.

4. When people like Benjamin Franklin choose to write their autobiographies, they often present experiences to create a positive impression.

5. Biographers once described the lives of famous people like Lincoln reverently.

6. Contemporary biographers frequently present balanced treatments of positive and negative qualities.

7. Joseph P. Lash presented a multifaceted view of the Roosevelts' relationship in *Eleanor and Franklin,* a combination biography.

8. Stassinopoulos-Huffington presents a fairly negative portrait of Pablo Picasso, the twentieth-century artist.

9. Well-known people with the help of professional writers usually write contemporary autobiographies.

10. Lee Iacocca and a cowriter wrote *Iacocca,* a typical recent autobiography, chronicling Iacocca's rise in the automobile industry.

EXERCISE 9.2 〉 *Concision*

Sample revisions.

1. Scientists know that four trillion gallons of precipitation falls on the United States daily. [13 fewer words]

2. Heavy rains and snows fill our waterways, as well as replenish supplies in our reservoirs. [10 fewer words]

3. Some areas of the United States receive annually fewer than five inches of rain. [9 fewer words]

4. Other parts of the United States benefit from more than twenty inches of rain each year. [6 fewer words]

5. Rain, snow, sleet, and drizzle are crucial to the well-being of the United States. [4 fewer words]

6. Most people know that water satisfies the needs of people, plants, and animals; however, they often fail to consider that water is also used in industries. [16 fewer words]

7. Water distribution should be managed by an independent national agency. [10 fewer words]

8. Until we have a national policy for water management, we can expect imbalances in the water supplies. [12 fewer words]

EXERCISE 9.3 ❯ *Concision*

Sample revision.

To understand the development and use of paper, we must return hundreds of years to China. By most estimates, the Chinese invented paper in 105 B.C., but it remained a state secret for hundreds of years. As far as we know, most transcriptions were done on bamboo sheets. The Moors discovered the invention in A.D. 750 when they were at war with the Chinese. The Moors established the link to Europe and in 1100 established a paper mill in Toledo, Spain. Gradually, the use of paper spread across Europe. When paper reached Rome in approximately 1200, the Catholic Church felt threatened by the invention and opposed the introduction of something so unfamiliar. According to the church, documents written on paper were not legally binding because it did not consider paper permanent. Still, people began to use paper instead of parchment, treated animal skin, because they were fascinated by the new medium, which was cheaper and more convenient than parchment. The use of paper reached England by 1400 and America by 1690. Soon, there was no other universally accepted writing surface. Today, we take paper for granted and use it daily. We do not even acknowledge that it was once revolutionary.

EXERCISE 10.1 ❯ *Parallelism*

Sample revisions.

1. "As Ye Plant, So Shall Ye Reap" is a moving and somewhat controversial essay about the plight of migrant workers.

2. Over the years, César Chávez has used his political power to draw attention to the harsh treatment of these workers, to garner support from politicians, and to orchestrate boycotts of selected produce.

3. Migrant workers are exploited not only in the Southwest but also in other parts of the Sunbelt.

4. The work of these laborers, which is extremely tedious and which needs to be controlled by labor laws, is traditionally undervalued.

5. To supply better wages and to provide better working conditions should be our goal.

EXERCISE 10.2 ❯ *Parallelism*

Americans like to play it safe, so it is not surprising that they want the places where they play to be safe. Not so very long ago, however, amusement parks were poorly supervised, dirty, and tasteless. On hot summer Saturdays, American families would head to places with names like Chain-of-Rocks Park to have a good time. Once there, they found that the parking facilities were not only randomly planned but also unguarded. The parks themselves were poorly maintained, with trash littering the sidewalks, with oil running on the sidewalks, and with food spoiling on the tables. The attendants appeared to be unmotivated and unkempt. They seemed to be alternately indifferent, callous, or threatening. Probably because of these unappealing qualities and other safety concerns, the amusement parks of an earlier time have been replaced by today's well-maintained, clean, and attractive parks like Six Flags, King's Island, and Disney parks. Yesterday's grimy and chaotic amusement parks have been replaced by today's safe, sanitized theme parks.

EXERCISE 11.1 ❯ *Pronoun reference*

1. In the opening act, the witches tempt Macbeth and Banquo with promises of greatness. The **witches** certainly are strange.

2. Teachers have long felt that *Macbeth* is a Shakespearean tragedy that appeals to students. **These educators** find *Macbeth* a valuable introduction to Shakespeare's other, more complicated works.

3. Although *Macbeth* has violence at its core, Nedah, Louis, and **I** found the Polanski film version bloodier and more perverse than necessary.

4. The elements of Japanese kabuki theater merge well with the symbolic dimensions of *Macbeth*. **These elements** make kabuki productions of *Macbeth* very appealing.

5. The last act of *Macbeth* implies that conditions in Scotland will return to normal. [words omitted]

EXERCISE 12.1 ❯ *Positioning modifiers*

1. No matter whether they affect adults, adolescents, or even children, the problems of alcoholism need to be honestly addressed.

2. Though acceptable within most groups in American culture, drinking is socially, physically, and economically costly.

3. Families and coworkers often fail to assess honestly the drinking habits of alcoholics and, as a result, fail to encourage alcoholics to seek professional help immediately.

4. Often, people who drink have liver trouble, among other medical and social problems.

5. Family members endure the emotional and physical abuse of alcoholics when they are inebriated.

6. Often, alcoholics must admit that their drinking problems are severe before they can get help.

EXERCISE 12.2 ❯ *Positioning modifiers*

Sample revision.

   Helping my uncle with his one-acre garden taught me that victories in the garden are won the hard way. Each morning before it got too hot, my uncle and I would do maintenance work. We would pull by hand small infestations of weeds and then spray larger growths of weeds with a post-emergent herbicide. Then we would mulch the plants whose foliage did not protect the soil from the sun's drying rays. Using straw and sometimes black plastic sheets, we would encircle the stalks of the plants, trying not to damage low leaves. We would sometimes have to spray with a pyrethrin mixture plants that were covered with parasitical bugs. Once we got started, we often worked without talking. A few comments on the growth of the asparagus or the tomatoes seemed to be enough. Once, however, when he felt talkative, Uncle Charles told me I was a conscientious worker. As the days passed, because of my own hard work, I began to realize how much effort goes into gardening. I must say that I now appreciate my fruits and vegetables more than I used to because they are grown with so much care.

EXERCISE 13.1 > Formal and informal diction

1. Many readers are **shocked** when Bigger Thomas **crushes** the rat in the opening scene of the novel.

2. The Daltons, a **very wealthy** family, had made a **great deal** of money by **exploiting** poor tenants in slum housing.

3. Their daughter Mary and her **liberal** friends **enjoyed spending time** in restaurants in black neighborhoods.

4. Bigger **fled** after he accidentally **killed** Mary.

5. Once the **police apprehended** Bigger, he was put on trial and **sent to prison.**

EXERCISE 13.2 > Connotations

1. Airport security has become restrictive in the last few years, as **people** who travel **frequently** have discovered.

2. At every concourse in major airports, people **stand** in lines, waiting to have their carry-on luggage inspected.

3. At these security checkpoints, people sometimes get **annoyed** about passing their **belongings** through scanning devices, but **periodically** someone is **surprised** when his or her luggage sets off the alarm.

4. The security guards **question** people whose luggage sets off the alarm to see if they have a reasonable **explanation,** and then the checking continues.

5. Although these security checks are an **inconvenience,** they help to keep air travel **safe.**

EXERCISE 13.3 ❯ Specific words

Sample revisions.

1. Running for a seat in the House or the Senate can cost thousands, even millions of dollars.

2. Over sixty thousand people attended the Democratic Convention in Dallas.

3. The children and spouses of American presidents have difficulty adjusting to invasions of their privacy.

4. Truman won the election of 1948, even though the press expected Dewey to win.

5. As the Kennedy-Nixon debates demonstrated, a politician's effectiveness in front of video cameras can affect the outcome of an election.

EXERCISE 13.4 ❯ Idioms

1. The National Geographic Society, founded in 1888, is a (type of a/<u>type of</u>) organization with diverse interests and goals.

2. On the one hand, the NGS often goes (<u>in search of</u>/in search for) exotic flora and fauna to describe in articles and broadcasts.

3. On the other hand, NGS also (tries and/<u>tries to</u>) make Americans aware of simple but subtle differences between peoples of different cultures.

4. Although the format for NGS television programs does not (differ with/<u>differ from</u>) that of other nature documentaries, they are nonetheless fascinating.

5. With over 10.5 million members, NGS will be (<u>sure to</u>/sure and) flourish into the twenty-first century.

EXERCISE 13.5   ❯   *Slang and regionalisms*

Example

rip-off (noun)
The insurance plan to supplement Medicare was a *rip-off*.
The insurance plan to supplement Medicare was a *fraud*.

Students should find this kind of translation entertaining but challenging. Emphasize particularly that slang and regionalisms are often inexact and are consequently difficult to translate. That is why they are poor word choices.

EXERCISE 13.6   ❯   *Euphemisms*

1. Weddings are often **expensive** displays by people and for people who fail to consider their **artificial** behavior.

2. Elaborate and expensive, many weddings must be financed through **credit.**

3. Even **pregnant** brides often wear traditional white bridal gowns.

4. Many **dishonest** people who do not attend worship services regularly insist on being married in **churches.**

5. Ironically, many of these marriages — begun with such elaborate display — end in **divorces.**

EXERCISE 14.1   ❯   *Clichés and trite expressions*

1. Some monuments **appeal to** the American people and can remind **us** of the value of public memorials.

2. The *Statue of Liberty* is an inspiring national monument, symbolizing how America **welcomed** European emigrants.

3. The simplicity of the Tomb of the Unknown Soldier and the **solemn** military display **affect** many visitors.

4. One **unusual** monument, St. Louis's Gateway Arch, reaches **upward** in a sweeping curve of shiny stainless steel.

5. With its **smooth marble,** the Vietnam Memorial is an **austere** monument honoring thousands of soldiers who **died** for their country.

EXERCISE 14.2 ❯ *Pretentious language*

Sample revision.

When **my friends and I graduated, we were filled with mixed emotions. We felt relieved** because **our** time in high school **was ending. Nevertheless, we felt** uncertain about what **lay** ahead. Some **of us would get jobs** immediately, others **would get married,** and yet others **would go to college.** For **all of us, graduation** symbolized an uncertain **change** in **our** lives.

EXERCISE 14.3 ❯ *Pretentious diction and jargon*

Sample translations.

1. **Too many** Americans **live foolishly,** ignoring **daily** dangers to health.

2. The **large numbers of car wrecks demonstrate** that **Americans** are oblivious to **rules for safe driving.**

3. The number of persons who **drink too much alcohol** is also a **depressing** statistic.

4. **Smoking,** although **banned** in many **businesses,** continues to **harm both men and women.**

5. **Guns** account for **thousands of** accidental **deaths** each **year.**

EXERCISE 14.4 **❯** *Figures of speech*

Sample revisions.

1. Like good soldiers, athletes get down to the regimented work that training sessions require. ["Getting down" and "rising to" create conflicting images. The second can be eliminated without a loss of meaning.]

2. Swimmers struggle through lap after lap during practices, building the tireless endurance necessary in races. ["Flying" and swimming do not create a consistent impression.]

3. With bursts of energy, basketball players jump for balls and then throw them down the court, hoping to hone skills to use in games. [Direct description works better than the mixed images of kangaroos and guns.]

4. With catlike speed, sprinters spring from starting blocks over and over again, trying to perfect an opening move that will put them beyond the rest. [A uniform impression, emphasizing catlike qualities is more effective.]

5. With intensity and fixed purpose, football linesmen practice rushing and tackling, leaving other players in their paths. [The image of trains, with their fixed tracks, does not work, nor does the water image.]

!   *EXERCISE 14.5* **❯** *Sexist language*

The blight which threatens theoretical culture has only begun to frighten modern **people,** and **they are** groping uneasily for remedies out of the storehouse of **their experiences,** without having any real conviction that these remedies will avail against disaster. In the meantime, there have arisen certain **people** of genius who, with admirable circumspection and consequence, have used the arsenal of science to demonstrate the limitations of science and of the cognitive faculty itself. They have authoritatively rejected science's claim to universal validity and to the attainment of universal goals and exploded for the first time the belief that

people may plumb the universe by means of the law of causation. — Friedrich Nietzsche, *The Birth of Tragedy*

EXERCISE 14.6 ❯ *Neologisms and archaic words*

1. **I think** that romance novels deserve more attention from serious readers than they have often received.

2. **Between** the covers of romance novels as varied as *Wuthering Heights* and *The Lady and the Highwayman,* readers will find quickly paced stories of intrigue and love.

3. The heroines and heroes of these novels are **often** innocent, sincere, and trusting people whose lives are threatened by **seeming** friends who are really enemies.

4. With their inherent reliance on historical context, these **entertaining but informative** novels provide readers with knowledge of past societies, as well as reading pleasure.

5. Although the reading of romance novels does not require much intellectual **involvement** from readers, these books provide innocent pleasure and distraction.

EXERCISE 15.1 ❯ *Fragments*

Sample revision.

The National Board of Teaching Standards has been formed recently to address matters of teacher training and certification because of inconsistencies that exist among states. Some states require prospective teachers to take a pre-professional skills test to establish the reading, writing, and mathematical skills of future teachers, but not others. All states require expertise in content areas that approximates that of traditional majors in each subject area, and some states require additional work in educational theory and practice, usually fifteen to twenty semester hours of work. These pedagogical courses emphasize general principles of teaching and general patterns of learning. No matter how theoretically sound these courses may be, inconsistencies exist since states establish their requirements individually. As a result, teachers moving from one state to the other may not be fully prepared to meet requirements. With prospects of taking the National Teacher's Exam, future teachers need the coordinated efforts of state departments of education to develop uniform educational programs.

 EXERCISE 15.2 〉 *Fragments*

New York. St. Louis. Knoxville. New Orleans. Los Angeles. These cities have all hosted those pretentious, glorious, overly expensive, and enjoyable activities known as world's fairs. Filled with exhibits, amusements, and restaurants, world's fairs offer people a chance to learn about the world while enjoying themselves. At these large fairs, nations from around the world build pavilions to showcase their national achievements, often sending examples of their best technology, art, and historical treasures and sending dancers, singers, and musicians. Visitors enjoy seeing native costumes and folk dances that illustrate the diversity of the world's cultures. Sometimes, even specialties of individual fairs have become common later on. In St. Louis, for example, the ice-cream cone was invented, and it has since become a favorite treat worldwide. World's fairs were originally planned to "bring the world closer together," but do they continue to serve this original purpose? Not really. Because people now travel by airplane and can see the countries of the world, they see much more than can be seen in national exhibits at world's fairs. [The opening fragments create emphasis, and the one near the end answers a question. The others are suitably revised.]

EXERCISE 16.1 〉 *Comma splices and fused sentences*

Sample revisions.

1. *Rock 'n' roll* is a generic term used to describe a wide variety of musical styles; nonetheless, each musical style remains distinct.

2. The term *pop music* was coined in the 1950s. It describes music that cuts across socio-ethnic lines and appeals to a wide audience.

3. *Acid rock* describes the amplified, electronic music of the mid-1960s. Artists in this subgenre of rock music were often part of the counterculture of drugs.

4. *Disco*'s emphasis on highly synthesized electronic music with an insistent rhythm made it popular dance music; nevertheless, its popularity faded in only a few years.

5. Black American music, sometimes called *soul music* and sometimes *rhythm and blues,* developed from gospel music. Its acceptance in conservative white culture attests to the power of music to break down barriers.

6. With its emphasis on shock value, *punk rock* created a brief sensation in the world of music, but people soon grew tired of being shocked by performers who often lacked musical skill.

!   *EXERCISE 16.2* ❯   *Comma splices and fused sentences*

Sample revision.

Book censorship in American high schools has become a standard practice these days, **as** individuals and groups have applied pressure to school boards everywhere. The books that have been censored range widely in subject **and** in literary quality as well. No book seems to be beyond the reach of book censors. Books treating sexual situations, like *A Farewell to Arms,* have been banned; books that contain questionable language, like *The Catcher in the Rye,* have been banned, too. *The Grapes of Wrath* has been censored in some communities because of its presentation of socialist ideology, **and** *Lord of the Flies* has been removed from libraries because of its violence. Even a book like *Huckleberry Finn* is now being brought into question **because** it has racially unflattering dialect. The American Library Association has come to the defense of these books; however, that has not kept them on bookshelves and reading lists in many American high schools.

EXERCISE 17.1 ❯ Subject-verb agreement

1. Archaeologists (studies/<u>study</u>) the buildings, tools, and other artifacts of ancient cultures.

2. Every archaeologist, especially field researchers, (know/<u>knows</u>) of a historic site ruthlessly desecrated by treasure-seekers.

3. Despite international agreements, unscrupulous museums or a wealthy private collector (compete/<u>competes</u>) for every major artistic discovery, stolen or not.

4. But laws and international policing (<u>reduce</u>/reduces) yearly the number of destroyed sites and stolen artifacts.

5. Excavations — better controlled than ever by teams of university archaeologists, students, local workers, and national representatives — (<u>proceed</u>/proceeds) slowly these days, avoiding the damage inflicted by yesterday's "grave robbers."

6. <u>Digs</u> (is/are) the current jargon used to describe an excavation site.

7. Recent decades (has seen/<u>have seen</u>) few finds of the historical significance of the discovery of Tutankhamen's tomb in 1922, but research in various locales (continue/<u>continues</u>).

8. For archaeologists, five or ten years (seem/<u>seems</u>) a reasonable time to work at a single site, so new finds will be made — but made more slowly than in the past.

EXERCISE 17.2 ❯ Subject-verb agreement

There **are** more and more adults attending college at a later age. Their motives, either to change careers or to get the education they missed, **vary.** Anyone walking on a college campus **sees** students in their thirties, forties, fifties, and even sixties carrying books and talking with friends. Almost every class and laboratory now **includes** at least one of these "nontraditional" students. Because their home and job situations and their preparedness **differ** from those of eighteen- and twenty-one-year-olds, these students face problems that **surprise** a younger student. Some of these adults **organize** their schooling around full-time jobs. Others care for families, as well as **attend** class. Nobody going to college and getting a degree **finds** it easy, but an adult student with adult responsibilities **has** extra problems to cope with. As this situation becomes more common, everyone **adjusts,** however, a process that already **has** begun. Even the media recognize this trend in American education. With humor and sympathy, *Kate and Allie* **provides** insights into the problems adults face when attending college. Who knows? Given a chance today, maybe even Lucy Ricardo or John Walton might enroll in a class or two.

EXERCISE 17.3 ❯ *Pronoun-antecedent agreement*

1. Greeks, Romans, Egyptians, Indians, and virtually every other civilized group had one or more methods of keeping **their** dwellings cool in summer months.

2. For example, all of these peoples hung water-soaked mats in **their** doorways to develop cooling moisture.

3. Leonardo da Vinci, with **his** usual inventiveness, created the first mechanical fan in about 1500, **its** power provided by running water.

4. The 1838 British House of Commons was first to enjoy systematic control of **their** ventilation and humidity during **their** sessions.

5. Neither Alfred Wolff (in 1902) nor Willis Carrier (in 1911) realized the impact **his** work would have on later generations.

6. After 1931, a passenger riding on the Baltimore & Ohio railroad could travel to **his or her** destination in air-conditioned comfort.

7. When Stuart Cramer first used the phrase *air conditioning* in 1906, **he** almost certainly didn't know that **his** newly coined term would be in universal use today.

8. Few people who live in temperate climates or who work in high-rise buildings would want to give up **their** air conditioning in the summer.

EXERCISE 17.4 ❯ *Pronoun-antecedent agreement*

Everyone who works in the United States must pay **his or her** income taxes on or before April 15. An employee of a traditional business has **his or her** taxes withdrawn in each pay period and at the end of the year receives **his or her** yearly statement, the W2 form. Neither employees nor the employer can decide how **his or her** tax accounts will be handled, but employees determine what percentage of taxes will be taken from **their** wages. For a self-employed taxpayer, the procedure for determining **his or her** taxes is not so clear. Artists, writers, free-lance contractors, and others whose incomes fluctuate must estimate **their** incomes for the year and pay **their** taxes in installments. Anyone who has ever tried to estimate how productive **he or she** will be in the next year can appreciate the difficulty a self-employed person has in estimating how much **he or she** will owe at the end of the year. In the past, the self-employed were granted some leniency in paying **their** taxes. However, in 1987, in spite of objections from some of **its** constituents, Congress voted to penalize people whose estimated tax payments were less than 90 percent of **their** taxes due.

 ## EXERCISE 18.1 ❯ *Pronoun case*

1. Hans Christian Andersen, the son of a shoemaker, began **his** adult life as an actor.

2. **He** failed on the stage, but because the king granted **him** a scholarship, Andersen was able to begin **his** writing career.

3. **His** writing of novels, plays, and long poems is almost completely forgotten, but almost everyone knows a few of **his** best fairy tales.

4. Ironically, Andersen did not set out to write fairy tales, but **he** wrote **his** first four to make money quickly.

5. Those stories succeeded beyond **his** expectations, and subsequently European nobility and royalty honored **him** for **his** work.

6. Although Andersen's tales may not be as well known as those of the brothers Grimm, **his** use of irony and humor, rather than violence, makes **his** work very appealing.

7. "The Emperor's New Clothes," one of **his** most ironic tales, alienated **him** from some of **his** noble patrons.

8. Contemporary readers, however, can enjoy the irony without insult and take delight in what was, for **him,** a troublesome piece.

9. The best children's writers — and **he** is among them — delight us as children and intrigue us as adults, providing in simple tales some lessons on life.

10. If you think about Andersen as a failed actor who became a world-famous writer of fairy tales, you'll discover why "The Ugly Duckling" was one of **his** favorites; in a professional sense, at least, it was **his** story.

EXERCISE 18.2 ❯ *Pronoun case*

1. The Better Business Bureau, a nonprofit organization, was founded to help people **who** are victims of questionable business methods and deceptive advertising.

2. Consumers should first address complaints to **whoever** has acted in an unbusinesslike manner.

3. The Better Business Bureau is a group to **whom** consumers can turn if they still are not satisfied.

4. The Better Business Bureau will answer questions and suggest strategies to **whoever** calls, but it will not take legal action against suspected businesses.

5. Since the Better Business Bureau refers cases to government agencies, however, it helps ensure that businesspeople **who** are unethical do not continue to exploit consumers.

EXERCISE 18.3 ❯ *Pronoun case*

When *I* [subjective] came out of prison, — for some one interfered, and paid that tax, — *I* [subjective] did not perceive that great changes had taken place on the common, such as *he* [subjective] observed *who* [subjective] went in a youth and emerged a tottering and grey-headed man; and yet a change had to *my* [possessive] eyes come over the scene, — the town, and State, and country, — greater than any that mere time could effect. *I* [subjective] saw yet more distinctly the State in which *I* [subjective] lived. *I* [subjective] saw to what extent the people among *whom* [objective] *I* [subjective] lived could be trusted as good neighbors and friends; that *their* [possessive] friendship was for summer weather only; that *they* [subjective] did not greatly propose to do right; that *they* [subjective] were a distinct race from *me* [objective] by *their* [possessive] prejudices and superstitions, as the Chinamen and Malays are; that in *their* [possessive] sacrifices to humanity *they* [subjective] ran no risks, not even to *their* [possessive] property; that after all *they* [subjective] were not so noble but *they* [subjective] treated the thief as *he* [subjective] had treated *them* [objective], and hoped, by a certain outward observance and a few prayers, and by walking in a particular straight though useless path from time to time, to save *their* [possessive] souls. This may be to judge *my* [possessive] neighbors harshly; for *I* [subjective] believe that many of *them* [objective] are not aware that *they* [subjective] have such an institution as the jail in *their* [possessive] village. — Henry David Thoreau, "Civil Disobedience"

EXERCISE 19.1 > *Tenses*

1. The design team for the theater production **met** to review the script for the play.

2. They **talked** about specific concerns and **mentioned** special needs they should consider.

3. The discussion **turned** to potential problems in lighting the production, as it always does, because the theater — a renovated movie house — is modified less than is needed.

4. The lighting designer **said,** once again, that the theater **would** need major electrical work before a computerized lighting system **could be** installed.

5. Completing the discussion of lighting, the team **turned** its attention to the set for the play.

6. The play chosen — *Who's Afraid of Virginia Woolf?* — **required** a single set, one room in a history professor's house.

7. The designers **described** productions they **had seen.**

8. The costumer **described** a production that was done in Baltimore.

9. The lighting designer **remembered** a collegiate production she saw in Iowa.

10. The director **said** he **wanted** this set to be more realistic in its details than others he **had seen.**

11. As **was** usually the case, the team **left** after the first meeting, having made only a few key decisions.

EXERCISE 19.2 > *Tenses*

Are owls wise? The Greeks (1) *thought* [past] so, identifying them with Athena, goddess of wisdom. In medieval illustrations, owls (2) *accompany* [present] Merlin and share in his sorcery. In fairytales they rival the fox for cunning. Children's picture books (3) *show* [present] them wearing spectacles, mortarboard, and scholar's gown. Soups and other confections made from owls (4) *have been credited* [present perfect] with curing whooping cough, drunkenness, epilepsy, famine, and insomnia. The Cherokee Indians used to bathe their children's eyes with a broth of owl feathers to keep the kids awake at night. Recipes using owl eggs (5) *are reputed* [present] to bestow keen eyesight and wisdom. Yet these birds are no smarter, ornithologists (6) *assure* [present] us, than most others. A museum guide in Boston once (7) *displayed* [past] a drowsy-looking barn owl on his gloved wrist, (8) *explaining* [present progressive] to those of us assembled there how small the bird's brain actually was. "You (9) [*will*] *notice* [future] the head of this live specimen appears to be about the size of a grapefruit," he said, "but it's mostly feathers." Lifting his other hand, he (10) *added* [past], "The skull, you (11) *see* [present], is the size of a lemon. There's only room enough inside for a bird-brain, not enough for Einstein!" We all laughed politely. But I was not convinced. Sure, the skull (12) *was* [past] small. The lower half was devoted to jaw and most of the upper half to beak and eye-holes. Yet enough neurons could be fitted into the remaining space to enable the barn owl to catch mice in total darkness. They can even snatch bats on the wing, these princes of night-time stealth. We have to invent sonar for locating submarines, radar for locating airplanes; neither (13) *is* [present] much use with mice or bats. Barn owls can also see dead — and therefore silent — prey in light one-hundredth as bright as we would need. Like the ability to saw a board square or judge the consistency of bread dough, that might not amount to scholarship, but it (14) *is* [present] certainly a wisdom of the body. It (15) *has worked* [present perfect] for some sixty million years. — Scott Sanders, "Listening to Owls"

EXERCISE 19.3 ❯ Mood

1. Increasingly, working parents in the United States are asking that every employer **acknowledge** the childcare problem.

2. A single parent especially often wishes a company-operated childcare facility **were** available at or near his or her place of work.

3. Lateness would probably decline if a parent **were** able to make one trip to a single location, instead of a trip to a childcare facility and then a separate trip to work.

4. If Congress **were** to partially subsidize childcare facilities, many companies might help their employees by providing on-site childcare.

5. But even if a company **were** to provide on-site childcare, problems in assuring sufficient daycare facilities would still exist.

EXERCISE 20.1 ❭ Adjective and adverb forms

1. Current methods of building construction will make homes (affordable/more affordable/most affordable) than they were in the past, without sacrificing quality.

2. Although prefabricated homes have always been (easily/more easily/most easily) constructed than conventionally built homes, they were not always built (good/well).

3. Now, however, factory construction of major structural elements is (increasing/increasingly) impressive.

4. Many home units — like kitchens and bathrooms — are being constructed with their plumbing and wiring embedded in wall units; then these "core construction blocks" are fitted together (quick/quickly/more quickly) in various ways.

5. Because installing plumbing and wiring is (costly/more costly/most costly) than other phases of construction, these "core blocks" keep on-site construction costs (low/lower/lowest).

6. With the money saved from structural costs, a homeowner can concentrate on architectural trim and interior design work that can make his or her home (unique/more unique/most unique).

EXERCISE 20.2 ❭ Adjectives and adverbs

Tapestries, fabrics with pictures woven into them, were used in medieval churches and palaces **often** as decorations but sometimes as insulation in the chilly buildings. **Unique** tapestries were produced in Arras, France, where the art of weaving pictures reached its **perfect** form in the

1400s. The tapestry makers of Arras worked so **well** that the word *arras* was soon used as a synonym for *tapestry.* The tapestries that have survived from the 1400s and 1500s are in various states of repair. Some, like the set of tapestries called *The Hunt of the Unicorn,* are in **really** sound condition. Their colors are still vibrant. The **most famous** panel of the set shows a unicorn sitting within a circular fence, surrounded by flowers and foliage of **bright** colors. Unfortunately, other tapestries have been treated **badly** over the centuries, and their colors are faded or their yarns damaged. Weaving tapestries is a **complex** craft that has been sporadically and **simplistically** revived in the last hundred years, but we will probably never approximate the **intricate** and reverential nature of tapestries done in the late Middle Ages.

!   **EXERCISE 21.1 ❯ End punctuation**

Harry Truman, the thirty-third president, was a spirited leader with a penchant for candor. He assumed the presidency in 1945, after Franklin Roosevelt's death, and repeatedly until he left office in 1953 challenged assumptions about how presidents ought to behave. His presidency was marked by controversy. Truman made the decision to drop nuclear bombs on Hiroshima and Nagasaki; he supported the Marshall Plan to help Europe recover from the devastation of World War II; he sent American troops to Korea, a sign of his unquestioning acceptance of his responsibility for key decisions. One of his favorite slogans became nationally known: "The buck stops here." Another of his favorites was "If you can't stand the heat, get out of the kitchen!" Supporters, using Truman's own flavorful language, often shouted this refrain: "Give 'em hell, Harry!" Truman made many difficult decisions and never attempted to avoid the controversy that resulted or to blame others for his decisions. Was he a great president? That is a judgment best left to history, but he certainly was an honest and an interesting one.

EXERCISE 22.1 ❯ Commas

1. Computers are now commonplace equipment in homes, schools, and businesses.

2. It is amazing how quickly, completely, and smoothly most people have become acclimated to the new technology.

3. Computerized cash registers are now common in grocery stores, at movie houses, in discount stores, and even at gas stations.

4. Computers in public and private libraries have made it possible for people to search for books, print lists of available materials, and complete research quickly.

5. Today, our mail comes with computer labels, our bank statements arrive with spread-sheet accounts of transactions, and even our grocery store receipts have computer lists of products we've bought.

EXERCISE 22.2 ❯ Commas

Sample revisions.

1. *Buffalo*, the name usually used to refer to American bison, is commonly used worldwide to describe several hundred kinds of large wild oxen.

2. Water buffalo in India have been domesticated for centuries, but South African buffalo and small buffalo on Pacific islands have resisted domestication and run wild.

3. Although in North America, especially on the Great Plains, huge herds of buffalo once roamed, by 1900, the bison population of approximately 20 million was reduced to fewer than six hundred.

4. Because he felt their extinction would be shameful, William Hornaday, an American zoologist, worked to protect the remaining bison and encouraged the National Forest Service to build fenced areas for small herds.

5. Although they cannot be trained or domesticated, bison are kept in captivity today because they are of zoological rather than practical interest.

EXERCISE 22.3 ❯ Commas

1. Built during the third and fourth centuries, the catacombs of Rome are the most famous in the world.

2. Intended for use as burial sites, the passages and rooms were used for other purposes too.

3. According to legend, early Christians kept the bodies of Saint Peter and Saint Paul hidden for a time in the catacombs.

4. In addition, Christians often took refuge in the catacombs because the catacombs were protected by Roman law.

5. Curiously, use of the Roman catacombs ceased in A.D. 400.

EXERCISE 22.4 ❯ Commas

1. *Beowulf,* which is one of the earliest examples of Anglo-Saxon literature, still appeals to those who like adventure stories, not only to scholars.

2. The character Beowulf, with a combination of heroic and religious qualities, goes to the aid of Hrothgar, the leader of a noble tribe.

3. The most famous episode of *Beowulf,* the battle between Beowulf and the monster Grendel, is a marvelous mix of supernatural and traditional Christian elements.

4. *Beowulf* is a historical-literary milestone; it is, however, a popular classic as well.

5. The plot elements of *Beowulf* — fights with supernatural beasts and tests of moral strength, for example — remain standard elements in today's science fiction films, perhaps explaining why *Beowulf* remains so popular.

EXERCISE 22.5 ❯ *Commas*

A.   Although zoos provide opportunities to see many exotic animals up close, the facilities for the animals do not always allow them to pursue, or visitors to observe, natural habits. Rhesus monkeys, very small primates, do not seem cramped in small places; they do not appear to suffer or experience any ill effects from their confinement. Chimpanzees, however, seem noticeably depressed in areas that do not allow them to move about freely. Orangutans, highly intelligent primates, also seem despondent. However, the jungle cats, tigers and leopards, seem to suffer most. They pace in their cages or lie inactive and inattentive. These large primates and big cats, which are usually among a zoo's main attractions, require more space and some distance from the crowds of eager spectators. In recent years, zoo keepers who have the animals' best interests in mind have begun building habitats for these larger animals. Most zoos have paid for these building projects, which can be quite elaborate, from general funds. Other zoos have launched major advertising campaigns, hoping for individual donations. Still others, stressing commitment to the community, have appealed to major corporations. These large building projects should continue, for they provide improved living conditions for large wild animals. As we maintain zoos that entertain and educate people, we must also remember that the animals that live there should not suffer for our benefit.

B.   Alaska, the forty-ninth state, joined the Union on January 3, 1959. The largest state geographically, covering 586,412 square miles, Alaska is also the least populated, with only 479,000 people. In fact, the entire state has fewer people than many American cities of moderate size, let alone Chicago, Los Angeles, or New York. Yes, the contrast in physical size and population presents an anomaly, but Alaska's history is full of such anomalies. Juneau, its capital city, has approximately twenty thousand people, making it roughly the same size as Texarkana, Arkansas; Augusta, Maine; and Winchester, Nevada. Alaska has fewer schools than many other states but has the highest teachers' salaries in the nation. Contradictions such as these have always been present. In 1867, when William H. Seward, secretary of state, arranged the purchase of Alaska for $7,200,000, most people thought the purchase a foolish one. But "Seward's Folly," as the acquisition was called, turned out to be not at all foolish. Rich deposits of minerals, oil, and natural gas have made Alaska one of America's greatest assets. (For more information on Alaska, write to the Alaskan Chamber of Commerce, 310 Second Street, Juneau, Alaska 99801.)

 EXERCISE 23.1 ❯ *Unnecessary commas*

Brackets indicate which commas are unnecessary.

1. Primary colors like[,] red, blue, and yellow are the most often used colors in national flags.

2. Interestingly enough, Libya's bright[,] green[,] flag is the only solid colored flag[,] in current use.

3. The small[,] Arab republic[,] Qatar[,] has a simple, black[,] and white flag.

4. Many countries — such as[,] Bahrain, Canada, Denmark, Indonesia, Japan, Monaco, Singapore, and Tunisia — use only red[,] and white[,] in their flags.

5. Most national flags use three[,] or four[,] bold colors[,] and use simple geometric shapes in their designs.

6. However, the ornate flag[,] of Sri Lanka[,] uses four colors[,] and black, and an elaborate design.

7. Only a few national flags[,] vary from the traditional, rectangular shape, including those of[,] Nepal and Switzerland.

8. The most frequently used colors[,] for flags[,] are red, white, and blue.

9. The U.S. flag[,] contains fifty[,] small[,] white stars on a blue field[,] and thirteen[,] alternating stripes of red and white.

10. As symbols of nations, flags serve[,] ideological[,] and political purposes — uniting citizens in times of peace, as well as in times of war.

EXERCISE 23.2   ❯   *Unnecessary commas*

Brackets indicate which commas are unnecessary.

We went fishing[,] the first morning. I felt the same[,] damp[,] moss covering the worms[,] in the bait can[,] and saw the dragonfly alight on the tip of my rod[,] as it hovered a few inches from the surface of the water. It was the arrival of this fly[,] that convinced me[,] beyond any doubt[,] that everything was as it always had been, that the years were a mirage, and there had been no years. The small[,] waves were the same, chucking the rowboat under the chin as we fished at anchor, and the boat was the same, the same color green[,] and the ribs broken in the same places, and under the floor-boards the same fresh-water leavings and débris — the dead helgramite, the wisps of moss, the rusty discarded fishhook, the dried blood from yesterday's catch. We stared[,] silently at the tips of our rods[,] at the dragonflies that came and went. I lowered the tip of mine into the water, tentatively, pensively dislodging the fly, which darted two feet away, poised, darted two[,] feet back, and came to rest again a little farther up the rod. There had been no years[,] between the ducking of this dragonfly and the other one — the one that was part of memory. I looked at the boy, who was silently watching his fly, and it was my hands that held his rod, my eyes watching. I felt dizzy[,] and didn't know which rod[,] I was at the end of. — E. B. White, "Once More to the Lake"

EXERCISE 24.1   ❯   *Semicolons and colons*

1. The Mediterranean Sea is bordered to the south by Egypt, Libya, Tunisia, Algeria, and Morocco.

2. The major ports on the Mediterranean Sea are Barcelona, Spain; Marseille, France; Naples, Italy; Beirut, Lebanon; Alexandria, Egypt; and Tripoli, Libya.

3. Because the Bering Sea borders both the Soviet Union and the United States, it is often patrolled by military ships from each country.

4. In the Western Hemisphere, gulfs are more common than seas; however, several seas are located off the northernmost coasts of North America.

5. Four seas are named for colors: the Yellow Sea, the Red Sea, the White Sea, and the Black Sea.

 EXERCISE 24.2 ❭ *Semicolons and colons*

Sample revision.

Ninety-six percent of Americans have eaten at one of the McDonald's restaurants in the last year. Slightly more than half of the U.S. population lives within three minutes of a McDonald's. McDonald's has served more than 55 billion hamburgers. McDonald's commands 17% of all restaurant visits in the U.S. and gets 7.3% of all dollars Americans spent eating out; McDonald's sells 32% of all hamburgers and 26% of french fries. McDonald's is the country's largest beef buyer, and it purchases 7.5% of the U.S. potato crop. McDonald's has employed about 8 million workers — which amounts to approximately 7% of the entire U.S. work force, and McDonald's has replaced the U.S. Army as America's largest job training organization. — John Love, *McDonald's: Behind the Arches*

EXERCISE 25.1 ❭ *Apostrophes*

Brackets indicate which apostrophes are not needed.

1. Even before people kept record[']s or conceived of science as a field of study, chemistry exerted its influence on their lives.

2. Early civilizations' understanding of elements was primitive — the Greeks['] and Romans' four elements were air, earth, fire, and water — but their applications of chemical principles were sophisticated.

3. Today, perhaps, it's difficult to understand how much the development of the alloy bronze revolutionized humans' lives.

4. During the Middle Ages, alchemists discovered how many chemical compounds work, even though trying to turn metals to gold was a chief preoccupation of their['ls.

5. By the seventeenth century, scientists' studies were more methodical and practical, as was illustrated by Robert Boyle's studies['] of gases, for example.

6. Even before the development of sophisticated microscopes, John Dalton's theories of atomic elements explained chemicals' reactions.

7. Dmitri Mendeleev, Russia's foremost early chemist, explained the relationships among elements and devised the periodic tables that still appear on students' tests in classes in introductory chemistry.

8. Marie Curie['s] and Pierre Curie's discovery of radium in 1898 further expanded scientists' understanding of chemistry.

9. Alfred B. Nobel's bequest of $9 million made possible awards in science and literature; one of the first five prizes in 1901 was an award for achievement in chemistry.

10. Chemists' work today is aided by sophisticated technology, but their search for knowledge has been shared by scientists['] of generation['ls past.

EXERCISE 26.1 ❯ Dashes

Sample revisions.

1. The Distinguished Service Cross, the Navy Cross, the Silver Star, the Distinguished Flying Cross, the Bronze Star, and the Air Medal — these awards are given to members of the armed forces to recognize heroism.

2. Soldiers — recognized for heroic behavior several times — do not receive additional medals but instead receive small emblems to pin on the first medal's ribbon.

3. Since 1932, the Purple Heart — gold and purple, heart-shaped, and embossed with George Washington's image — has been awarded to members of the armed forces who were wounded in combat.

4. The Badge of Military Merit — established by General George Washington in 1782 — wasn't given between 1800 and 1932.

5. The Congressional Medal of Honor — our nation's highest military award — was authorized in 1861 for the navy and 1862 for the army.

! EXERCISE 26.2 ❯ Hyphens

Brackets indicate which hyphens are not needed.

1. In the United States, senators are elected to six-year terms, presidents (and their vice-presidents) to four-year terms, and members of Congress to two-year terms.

2. Although these electoral guidelines are un[-]changed, little else about modern-day elections has remained the way our national founders conceived them.

3. In pre[-]computer elections, hand-tabulated ballots were the norm, and results often were not certain for days.

4. Today, with computer-aided counting, officials post fully three-fourths of election returns by mid[-]night of election day.

5. Television[-]networks quickly project the results of today's elections, usually on the basis of less than one-fiftieth of the ballots cast.

6. Consequently, presidents-elect now make victory speeches before mid[-]night on election day, rather than at mid[-]morning the following day. Times have clearly changed.

EXERCISE 26.3 ❯ *Parentheses, brackets, and ellipsis points*

1. To install a cable converter, simply follow these directions: (1) remove the converter from the box; (2) attach the blue adapter wires to your television set; (3) plug the converter into an electrical outlet; (4) select a channel and test the equipment by turning it on.

2. "The benefits to those who subscribe to cable services are amazingly varied, from more programs to better programs," explained Ms. Abigail Fitzgerald, a cable network spokesperson.

3. Most cable subscribers would agree that they are offered more, . . . but is it better?

4. Professor Martínez, media specialist at Arizona State University, commented: "Much of what's offered is junk. . . . When *Mr. Ed, Car 54,* and *The Munsters* make it to national rebroadcast, we have to question the uses to which cable is put. Of course, that's the long-standing issue in television broadcasting."

5. Then again, the American people have always enjoyed some unchallenging entertainment to relieve the tension and frustration of the day.

 EXERCISE 26.4 ❯ *Punctuation review*

The Postal Reorganization Act (P.R.A.), signed into law by President Nixon on August 12, 1970, created a government-owned postal service operated under the executive branch of the government. The new U.S. Postal Service is run by an eleven-member board, with members appointed by the president of the Senate for nine-year terms. The Postmaster General, who is no longer part of the president's cabinet, is selected by the members of the board. Since 1971, when the system began operating, four men have served as Postmaster General: Winton M. Blount, E. T. Klassen, Benjamin F. Bailar, and William F. Bolger. But has the postal system changed substantially since the P.R.A. went into effect on July 1, 1971? No, not to any great extent. First-class, second-class, third-class, and fourth-class — these still represent the most commonly used mailing rates. However, some services have been added. For instance, Express

Mail, which tries to rival Federal Express, Purolator, and other one-day delivery services, guarantees that packages will arrive at their destinations by 3:00 the day after mailing; the prices are steep as one might expect. In addition, the Postal Service has instituted nine-digit zip codes in some areas. For all practical purposes, however, the business at 29,990 post offices throughout the U.S. continues in much the same way it did before the P.R.A.

EXERCISE 27.1 ❯ Capitalization

1. Art 426 (or English 426) is an interdisciplinary course that offers a survey of important artists and writers.

2. The course is team-taught by Dr. Nicholas Bradford of the English Department and Ms. Marlene Jacobs of the Art Department.

3. During the fall of last year, I took the course to fulfill a humanities requirement.

4. We read a portion of Dante's *Divine Comedy* — but not in Italian — and saw slides of Michelangelo's frescoes in the Sistine Chapel, both presenting perspectives on Italian religious views.

5. We saw numerous paintings depicting the Nativity, the Crucifixion, and the Ascension and read several religious poems.

6. Turning our attention from Europe, we saw *Habuko Landscape* by Sesshu, a sixteenth-century Japanese painter, and read samples of haiku poetry to learn of the spare but elegant images both create.

7. Italian and Flemish artists dominated the months of October and November.

8. We learned, however, that by the 1800s, neo-classicism had emerged and artistic dominance had shifted to France, where it remained for over a century; we read Corneille's *Phaedre* and saw representative paintings by David and Ingres.

9. Over Thanksgiving break, I took a field trip with Ms. Jacobs and several other students; we went to the Art Institute of Chicago, her alma mater, to view their collection.

10. By the time we studied abstract art, national and artistic boundaries had been broken and painters like Picasso and poets like T. S. Eliot could be said to draw upon the same aesthetic traditions.

11. When Ms. Jacobs first said, "The fine arts are symbiotic, each reciprocally influencing the other," I wasn't sure I understood what she meant. Now I think I know.

! EXERCISE 28.1 ❯ Italics

1. E. D. Hirsch's *Cultural Literacy: What Every American Needs to Know* — especially its appended list — has created a fascinating controversy since its publication.

2. For instance, Herman Melville's name is on the list, but his famous novel *Moby Dick* is not.

3. The statues *David* and the *Pietà* in St. Peter's Church in Vatican City are listed, but their creator Michelangelo does not appear.

4. Many of the foreign phrases — including *ancien regime, bête noire, coup d'état, déjà vu, faux pas, fin de siècle,* and *tête-à-tête* — are French, although a large number are Latin.

5. The *Niña, Pinta,* and *Santa Maria* do not appear, but the unfortunate *Lusitania* and *Titanic* do.

6. The maudlin poem *Hiawatha* and its author Henry Wadsworth Longfellow both appear, but *Paradise Lost,* the brilliant epic poem, appears without its author John Milton.

7. *Birth of a Nation* is the only film on the list not produced first as a book or play with the same name.

8. The absence of *I Love Lucy, The Dick Van Dyke Show, The Mary Tyler Moore Show, All in the Family,* and *M*A*S*H* makes it clear that popular television culture does not concern Hirsch.

9. Oddly enough, the ampersand (*&*) appears on the list.

10. Including the novel *Tobacco Road* on the list but not the play *Who's Afraid of Virginia Woolf?* seems arguable, but the enjoyment in lists is in disagreeing with them.

> **!** **EXERCISE 29.1 ❭ Quotation marks**

1. "Running on Empty?" an article in *National Wildlife,* stresses that water management should be a universal concern.

2. The opening chapter of *The Grapes of Wrath* contains this central image: "The rain-heads [thunderclouds] dropped a little spattering and hurried on to some other country. Behind them the sky was pale again and the sun flared. In the dust there were drop craters where the rain had fallen, and there were clean splashes on the corn, and that was all."

3. "Dry as Dust," a local documentary on the plight of the Depression farmers, had special meaning in 1988, when water shortages occurred throughout the midwestern states.

4. The very real fear of drought was softened during the Depression by ironic songs like "What We Gonna Do When theWell Runs Dry?"

5. Nadene Benchley's dissertation, "Deluge or Drought: The Crisis in Water Management," ought to be published, for it contains information many people need to know.

EXERCISE 30.1 ❭ Numbers and abbreviations

1. Doctor Ruth Waller, an **economics professor** at UCLA, has written **twenty-six** articles and **two** books about Asian-American trade relations.

2. **One** of her books and **fourteen** of her articles are on reserve at the **Idaho State University** library — to be read by students in **Economics 236.**

3. Statistics in one article show that Japan's labor force is well diversified, with **11** percent in agriculture, **34** percent in manufacturing, and **48** percent in services.

4. Statistics also show that the **American** labor force is not as well diversified: we have **70** percent in services, with close to **one-third** of those in **information** management.

5. By **Friday, December 12,** each of us in the class must prepare a report on **an American company** that is affected by Asian-American trade.

EXERCISE 30.2 ❯ *Numbers and abbreviations*

Walter E. Disney, better known as Walt, was born **December 5,** 1901, in Chicago. After early work at the Chicago Academy of **Fine Arts** and at a commercial art firm in **Missouri,** he moved to Hollywood in **1923.** It was there that he revolutionized **U.S.** entertainment. **In 1928,** he produced "Steamboat Willie," a short cartoon that introduced Mickey Mouse as well as the use of soundtracks with cartoons. **Ten** years later, his studio produced the **first** feature-length animated cartoon, *Snow White and the Seven Dwarfs,* and **two** years later, *Pinocchio.* The success of Disney's films stemmed from their innovations, **that is**, their use of animated forms, color, music, voices, and story. After more than **twelve** successful films, Disney began work in television in 1950. In **1955,** Disneyland opened outside **Los Angeles,** and Disney's theme parks created a new standard for amusement parks. Few would have suspected, in **1926,** that the man whose first cartoon creation was Oswald the Rabbit would change entertainment in the **United States.**

EXERCISE 32.1 ❯ *General subjects*

Students' first attempts to select subjects probably will produce subjects that are very general. This is not a problem because students will have a chance to narrow their subjects; it is more important that students select subjects with promise — the promise of available source materials, potential controversy, or original presentation.

EXERCISE 32.2   〉   *Specific topics*

By using time, place, or special circumstances, students should be able to narrow their subjects to specific topics — topics with clear parameters that will make them researchable.

Encourage students to do preliminary reading — say in an encyclopedia — if they have trouble with this activity. General reading may show them the context for their topics and help them complete this exercise.

EXERCISE 32.3   〉   *Working thesis statements*

Stress that this work will produce thesis statements to guide their early research — not the thesis statements that *must* appear in their final papers. Students should complete this stage carefully but should be aware that their thesis statements will probably require modification later.

EXERCISE 32.4   〉   *Preliminary list of sources*

Assuming that your library has a reasonable collection, students should have little difficulty with this activity if they have chosen a topic well.

If students are unable to find this minimal number and kind of sources, they would be wise to change topics now, not in later stages of research.

EXERCISE 32.5   〉   *Evaluating a source*

If students follow the guidelines provided in the discussion, they should be able to evaluate their sources. Suggest that students move beyond the general criteria of the discussion to more particular criteria that apply to their topic. Most students — but especially those with little experience in writing researched papers — will have some difficulty determining whether a source will be useful during their later work. Encourage them to focus on matters of content and style if they are having trouble.

EXERCISE 32.6   〉   *Taking notes*

First of all, check notes for consistency of format and completeness of information. Mention that writers often develop their own special ways o arrange information on their note cards but stress that they must be followed in *all* their notes; also mention that writers record complete information about the location of information in sources, no matter where they place the information on note cards.

EXERCISE 32.7 〉 *Common knowledge about your topic*

This exercise, though difficult, is very useful. In part it is difficult because categorizing common knowledge is based on personal judgment and some categories overlap. Exactly how information is categorized is not as important as the students' efforts to interpret information and make distinctions that they might not otherwise make.

EXERCISE 32.8 〉 *Practice in note taking*

This exercise, with three alternative sets of paragraphs, gives students a chance to practice every kind of note taking. Each set of paragraphs includes information to be summarized, passages worthy of quoting, and ideas that can be usefully paraphrased.

This exercise works well in class when you can supervise this early work on note taking. It also promotes useful discussion. Ask students what they chose to summarize from McLoughlin, for instance. Ask what they quoted from Fleming — and why. Students will "test" their choices and strategies against those of other students and will get a clear sense of how note taking works.

Review matters of note taking format and check for completeness of information. Stress that summaries must represent the original source accurately and briefly, in outlined and abbreviated forms when possible; emphasize that quotations should be reserved for distinctive passages only and that they should be recorded precisely; advise students to paraphrase information that is useful but that can be expressed effectively in their own words.

Look for balance in the kinds of notes students take. Also check for instances of unintentional plagiarism; now is the time to draw students' attention to the mistakes in note taking that can lead to plagiarism.

EXERCISE 33.1 ❯ *Compiling a works cited page*

Works Cited

Addeo, Edmond, and Robert Burger. *Inside Divorce: Is It What You Really Want?* Radnor, PA: Chilton, 1975.

Bohannan, Paul. "Some Thought on Divorce Reform." *Current Issues in Marriage and the Family*. Ed. J. Gipson Wells. 2nd ed. New York: Macmillan, 1979. 249–63.

Calier, Auguste. *Marriage in the United States*. 3rd ed. 1867. New York: Arno, 1972.

"Data Shows Marriages Up, Divorces Down." *Washington Post* 16 Mar. 1983: A3.

"Divorce and Separation." *Facts on File*. 1984 ed.

Greene, Roberta. *'Til Divorce Do You Part*. Pittsburgh: KNOW, 1972.

Kramer vs. Kramer. Dir. Robert Benton. With Dustin Hoffman and Meryl Streep. Columbia, 1979.

Mead, Margaret. "Double Talk About Divorce," *Redbook* May 1968: 47–48.

Stahl, Rebecca. Personal interview. 19 Feb. 1988.

Westman, Jack C., and David W. Cline. "Divorce Is a Family Affair." *Family Law Quarterly* 5.1 (1971): 1–10.

34g ❯ *A sample research paper*

Although Michele's research paper on intelligence testing is a model of student work, not an exercise, it can be used in class discussion.

Read the paper and discuss the annotations, pointing out specific strategies, features, and formats. The annotations comment on rhetorical strategies and writing and documenting techniques when they first appear. After students become aware of particular patterns for writing and documenting a research paper, have them identify other examples of forms, techniques, and formats in the rest of the paper.

CORRECTION SYMBOLS

Symbol	Ref	Description	Symbol	Ref	Description
	30b	Abbreviation	lc	27	Lower case
t	9a	Active voice	ms	**Appendix A**	Manuscript form
j	6d, 20	Adjective	mod	12	Modifier
v	6e, 20	Adverb	md	19e	Mood
r	17	Agreement	n	30a	Numbers
	25	Apostrophe	¶	4	Paragraph
k		Awkward	//	10	Parallelism
	26d	Brackets	( )	26c	Parentheses
p	27	Capitals	pas	9a	Passive voice
	18	Case	.	21a	Period
h	4b	Coherence	pred	6c, 19	Predication
	24d–f	Colon	p	21–26	Punctuation
	22, 23	Comma	?	21b	Question mark
	16	Comma splice	" "	29	Quotation marks
	6d, 6e, 20c	Comparison	red	9b	Redundant
mp	1, 2, 3, 4	Composition	ref	11	Reference
n	9b	Concision	res	32–34	Research
	12b	Dangling modifier	;	24a–c	Semicolon
	26a	Dash	ss	7	Sentence sense
		Delete	su	7	Sentence unity
	13, 14	Diction	sp	31	Spelling
c	33, 34 **Appendix B**	Documentation	sub	7a–b, 8d	Subordination
			t	6c, 19	Tense
	26e	Ellipsis points	trans	4b	Transition
ph	9	Emphasis	∿		Transpose
	21c	Exclamation point	u	4a	Unity
g	15	Fragment	⊙	22	Unnecessary comma
	16	Fused sentence	us	**Glossary of Usage**	Usage
	6, 7	Grammar			
	26b	Hyphens	var	8	Variety
	13d	Idiom	vb	6c, 19	Verb form
		Insert	wc	13, 14	Word choice
l	28	Italics	w	9b	Wordiness
g	5	Logic	ww	13b, 13d	Wrong word